Embodied Communities

DANCE AND PERFORMANCE STUDIES

General Editors:

Helena Wulff, *Stockholm University* and **Jonathan Skinner**, *Queen's University Belfast*

Advisory Board:

Alexandra Carter, Marion Kant, Tim Scholl

In all cultures, and across time, people have danced. Mesmerizing performers and spectators alike, dance creates spaces for meaningful expressions that are held back in daily life. Grounded in ethnography, this series explores dance and bodily movement in cultural contexts at the juncture of history, ritual and performance, including musical, in an interconnected world.

Embodied Communities

Dance Traditions and Change in Java

Felicia Hughes-Freeland

Berghahn Books
New York • Oxford

First published in 2008 by
Berghahn Books

www.berghahnbooks.com

©2008, 2011 Felicia Hughes-Freeland
First paperback edition published in 2011

Library of Congress Cataloging-in-Publication Data

Hughes-Freeland, Felicia, 1954–
   Embodied communities : dance traditions and change in Java / Felicia Hughes-
   Freeland.
     p. cm. -- (Dance and performance studies ; v. 2)
   Includes bibliographical references and index.
   ISBN 978-1-84545-521-7 -- ISBN 978-1-84545-238-4
1. Dance--Indonesia--Java. 2. Court dances--Indonesia--Java. 3. Social change--
Indonesia--Java. 4. Java (Indonesia)--Social life and customs. I. Title.

   GV1703.I532J3836 2008
   793.3'195982--dc22

                        2008026236

British Library Cataloguing in Publication Data

A catalogue record for this book is available from the British Library
Printed in the United States on acid-free paper.

ISBN: 978-1-84545-521-7 (hardback)
ISBN: 978-1-84545-238-4 (paperback)

I dedicate this book to my parents, and to the memory of Dylan Francis (1955–92)

Contents

List of Figures and Tables

List of Tables

Preface and Acknowledgements

This book is aimed at readers who are interested in anthropology, dance, Java and Indonesia, performance, and cultural history. My approach to dance is holistic. I discuss movement, political symbolism, religion, acting, art, tourism and commoditization. Each of these areas has a complex literature, but I have sacrificed some of the background debates to reach a multidisciplinary audience, and to provide an account of dance from a number of different perspectives. My argument is that dance has social importance, and that it helps us to understand other areas of social life, including aesthetics and community.

I first became attracted to Javanese dancing when I was an English teacher with Voluntary Services Overseas in East Java in the 1970s. As a young, inexperienced, isolated Englishwoman, gangly and physically inept amidst the compact and confident Indonesians, I learnt Balinese dance and found a new way of being in my body. To a certain extent this interest in dance was motivated by its difference from what I was used to, and differed from the interest of local Indonesians. Performance attracted them as performers or as audiences because it distracted them from the fears and insecurities in which they lived. Trips in East Java up mountains or to coastal teak woods evoked memories of hungry, fugitive months during the 1940s during the Japanese occupation and the struggle to secure independence from the Dutch. On the road from Malang to Surabaya, friends who had lived through the crisis of 1965–6 could still see heads on the hooks at roadside stalls where coconuts and durians were now hanging. In our very different ways we found solace in performance. It distracted us from matters over which we had no control, reaffirmed our command over our sense of being, as well as giving the pleasure which I hope will come across in the account that follows.

I am grateful to the many institutions that have supported my research. The Department of Sociology and Anthropology at the School of Oriental and African Studies, London University helped me find the intellectual means to complete my Ph.D. The Social Science Research Council, the Leverhulme Trust, the Advisory Committee of Cambridge University Evans Trust, and the South-East Asia Committee of the British Academy provided funding at different stages of the research. The Indonesian Institute of Science and Education (Lembaga Ilmu Pengetahuan Indonesia) gave me research permission in Indonesia. The Faculty of

Philosophy and the Centre for Research into Culture (Pusat Penelitian Kebudayaan), both at Gadjah Mada University, kindly acted as sponsors in Yogyakarta, from 1982 to 1984, and during 1989 respectively. Funding from the Arts and Humanities Research Council's Research Leave Scheme in 2005 made the completion of this book possible.

As this book has evolved over so many years, space does not allow me to thank everyone who has influenced it. In Indonesia many individuals, institutions and families provided friendship, help and hospitality, some over a period of nearly thirty years. Sri Sultan Hamĕngkubuwana IX (†) and G.B.P.H. Yudhaningrat (B.R.M. Sulaksmana) graciously allowed me access to court offices and archives. K.R.T. Widyakoesoema (†) and his staff at K.H.P. Widyabudaya, the court Library and Cultural Office, gave a new meaning to archival research. Prof. Dr Endang Daruni Asdi (†) and Dra Siti Sundari Maharto-Tjitrosubono patiently taught me Javanese language and politeness. R.W. Sasmintamardawa (†), B.R.Ay. Kuswardhani-Yudhanĕgara (†) and B.R.Ay. Sri Kadaryati trained me in movement, manners, meanings, smiles and silences. G.B.P.H. Suryobrongto (†) and R. Susena (†) shared their memories of colonial practices and their contemporary insights into dance as a spiritual art. Drs N. Supardjan B.A., director of the Secondary School of Performing Arts (SMKI), and R.M. Dinusatama B.A., head of Yayasan Siswa Among Bĕksa, illuminated dance and Javanese culture, as did the staff of the Departments of Education and Culture, and Tourism. Drs Ben Suharto(†), Prof. Dr R.M. Soedarsono, and Prof. Dr I Made Bandem gave me access to the Academy of Dance (ASTI), which became part of the Indonesian Institute of Arts (ISI). Didik Hadiprayitno has been an important source and friend throughout the research. Dra Dyah Kustiyanti, Mas Sri Harjanto Sahid, Pak Didiek Teha, Mbak Prabarini and R.M. Jarot Wisnubroto were stoical, patient, diligent, adventurous and generous research assistants. I owe a special debt of gratitude to the many dancers who embodied the subject of this book and endured my endless questions, especially Tuti, Maya, Anggara, Tyas and Ning.

My intellectual interests in Java cannot be separated from the personal affection I have for the families of G.B.P.H. Suryobrongto, R. Susena, Drs N. Supardjan, Prof. Dr Endang Daruni Asdi, Mas Sri Hardjanto Sahid, Ny. Rinanto Roesman, Dr Gloria and Dr Soepomo Poedjosoedarmo, Mas A.G. Sardjono and Mbak Sri, Drs Siti Sundari Maharto, Mas Sugihartono, and Mbak Sunarti Soewandi. Debra Hoven, Olivia de Haulleville, Gordon and Nanies Bishop and Carol Block were resident 'outsiders' who provided priceless friendship and moral support during fieldwork in Indonesia.

In the later stages, Margaret Kenna, Marlene Heins, Theresa Buckland, Ruth Finnegan, John Morby and Garrett Kam provided feedback on chapter drafts, as did Nin Bakdisoemanto while translating the book into Indonesian. Felicity Breet kept me on schedule, Julia Ackerman's transatlantic phone calls kept me on course, Ro Jackson's emails kept me entertained, and my parents and other friends kept me going. I would also like to thank the many others who have also contributed in different ways to this book but who cannot be named here. Any mistakes, of course, are entirely mine.

Finally, I am grateful for permission to use revised versions of previously published materials. In chapter 4, I draw on 'Dance, dissimulation, and identity in Indonesia' (pp 145–162) in (eds) J. Hendry and C.W. Watson, *An Anthropology of Indirect Communication* (ASA monographs 37), London: Routledge, 2001.

In chapter 5, I draw on 'Constructing a classical tradition: women's dance in Java' (pp 52–74) in (ed.) T.J. Buckland, *Dancing from Past to Present: Nation, Culture, Identities.* Studies in Dance History, Series of the Society for Dance History Scholars. Wisconsin: University of Wisconsin, 2006 and 'Tradition and the individual talent: T.S. Eliot for anthropologists' (pp 207–222) in (eds) E. Hallam and T. Ingold, *Creativity and Cultural Improvisation* (ASA monographs 44). Oxford: Berg, 2007.

A Note on Spelling and Other Matters

Indonesian and Javanese spellings were rationalized in 1972 and 1973 respectively. Readers unfamiliar with the languages of the region might note that in old spelling 'oe' /u/ is used for the modern 'u', 'dj' is now 'j'/j/, and 'j' is now 'y'/y/. There are three 'e' sounds in Javanese; I follow Javanese orthographic convention which does not distinguish between é and è, but simply indicate the *pĕpĕt* (ĕ) (sounded like 'e' in 'the', and sometimes spelt as 'a'. In Javanese, but not Indonesian, true 'a' is often pronounced as 'o' as in 'yoyo'; thus the word *bĕdhaya* is pronounced '*bĕdoiyo*'. All foreign words are Javanese, unless otherwise indicated: Ar. = Arabic; D. = Dutch; I. = Indonesian; k. = *krama*, polite Javanese language code; ng.= *ngoko*, familiar Javanese language code; OJ = Old Javanese; MJ = Middle Javanese; Skt = Sanskrit.

All dates refer to AD unless otherwise indicated.

The average exchange rate of the Indonesian Rupiah (Rp) to the Pound Sterling at different periods was as follows: 1982–84: Rp1,000–1,500; 1989: Rp2,700–3,000; 1994: Rp3,500; 1999: Rp10,000.

It is conventional in anthropological monographs to anonymize sources for ethical reasons. When I asked well-known performers how I should refer to them, most expressed a wish to be named, often by their familiar name or nickname, so I have followed their wishes. Personal names vary considerably in their mix of old and new spelling. I have followed individual preferences and have tried to spell each person's name in a consistent way, even when it varies for their different publications.

Abbreviations

A.S.T.I.	Akademi Seni Tari Indonesia (The Indonesian Dance Academy)
B.K.I.	Bijdragen tot de Taal-, Land- en Volkenkunde
B.R.Ay.	Bĕndara Raden Ayu (title for high born married woman)
B.R.M.	Bĕndara Raden Mas (title for high born male)
Depdikbud	Departemen Pendidikan dan Kebudayaan (Ministry of Education and Culture
D.I.Y.	Daerah Istimewa Yogyakarta (Special Region of Yogyakarta)
G.B.P.H.	Gusti Bĕndara Pangeran Harya (senior princely title)
G.P.H.	Gusti Pangeran Harya (princely title)
I.K.I.P.	Institut Keguruan dan Ilmu Pendidikan (Institute of Teacher Training and Education)
I.S.I.	Institut Seni Indonesia (Indonesian Institute of Arts, incorporating ASTI and other arts universities)
K.B.W.	Kridha Bĕksa Wirama (first Yogyakartan court dance school outside the court)
K.G.P.(A.)A.	Kangjĕng Gusti Pangeran (Adipati) Arya (princely title)
K.G.P.H.	Kangjĕng Gusti Pangeran Harya (princely title)
K.H.P.	Kawĕdanan Hagĕng Punakawan (prefix for administrative sections in the Kasultanan)
K.P.A.	Kangjĕng Pangeran Arya (princely title)
K.R.T.	Kangjĕng Raden Tumĕnggung (senior court title)
M.B.	Mardawa Budaya (dance association)
P.B.N.	Pamulangan Bĕksa Ngayugyakarta (dance association)
P.D.K.	Pendidikan dan Kebudayaan (Ministry of Education and Culture)
S.A.B.	Siswa Among Bĕksa (dance association)
S.M.K.I	Sekolah Menengah Kesenian Indonesia (Secondary School of Indonesian Arts)
V.O.C.	Verenigde Oost-Indische Compagnie (Dutch East Indies Company)

Chapter 1

Introduction: Dance, Culture and Embodiment

This book is about dance in modern, postcolonial Indonesia. It is grounded in a long-term case study conducted between 1982 and 1999 into the dance traditions of the Sultan's court in Yogyakarta, in south central Java.

Dance matters because local and national communities use it to represent themselves to themselves and to others. It is part of a politics of representation, but in contrast to other material symbols, it is embodied. It has a special power because of this, and is both part of a system of representation and a form of action. My interest in dance is in how it helps us understand how people construct their worlds, both in everyday life and in staged performances. Dance can help us understand what social and cultural values are, and how people embody them and use them. It plays a symbolic role and an instrumental role in the construction and continuation of local and national communities. This double nature of dance means that it is understood as a form of social production and not simply an adornment to social life.

I approach dance from two perspectives: as movement that relates to the performance of everyday actions; and as formal choreographic conventions associated with power centres. I explore these two aspects of dance in relation to social and cultural change in the Indonesian nation state, and in the lives of individual Javanese-Indonesian citizens as they attempt to maintain a sense of coherence over a period of rapid change and development.

Yogyakarta (Yogya) refers to both a city and a province, known as 'The Special Region of Yogyakarta', after its Sultan became Governor when Indonesian independence was ratified in 1949. Most of the people I quote in my story were born when Yogyakarta was a colonial principality within the Dutch East Indies. They have been actively involved in changing court dance from a practice developed under colonial conditions into a resource which has relevance for developing and representing both regional and national characteristics. They will help us to understand in what sense court dance is both a political symbol and a form of social action, how it has endured, and what it reveals about the construction of a particular Javanese world. Concepts used to make sense of the world that I encountered in Java included the embodied self, the importance of self-control in social interaction, the moral evaluation of self-control as a spiritual discipline, and the importance of adjusting behaviour and practices to circumstance as appropriate. These ideas were presented by practitioners and connoisseurs as central to understanding court dance, and will be set within an analytical framework which addresses dance politics and the cultural significance of movement in a manner appropriate to the world-views encountered during research.

Dance at First Sight: The Sultan's Court, 24 October 1982

A guide led me from the tranquil inner compound through a dark arch where a watchman sat cross-legged next to a hollow log which he struck in emergencies. We continued through another courtyard to the Bangsal Kĕsatriyan (Hall of the Knights) in the bachelors' quarters, where the dancing would take place. The surrounding buildings, whitewashed with dark green paintwork, housed the court Arts Section office and archives, and museums of photographs and paintings. Ornamental palms, flowering shrubs and shady trees waved in the gentle breeze. The dance pĕndhapa (pavilion) was open on two sides, with a highly polished raised floor and green pillars supporting a timbered roof which was painted cream and rose to a carved central peak. Local and overseas tourists pressed around and on the dance floor.

Through the crowds came men and women wearing fitted jackets and long skirts of wrapped *bathik* (*kĕbaya* and *jarit*). They removed their shoes, raised their joined hands in a *sĕmbah* (gesture of respect), and stepped up into the building. The male teachers and dancers sat to the north beneath a modern clock. The female dancers waited in an adjacent building, in keeping with Javanese conventions of feminine modesty. To the south were the *gamĕlan* orchestra, singers, and a visiting American ethnomusicologist. Next to them was a rattan mat (*tikar*) fenced off by low red wooden panels, the space reserved for aristocratic women who gave up their Sunday mornings to teach dance in the court precincts. Eventually I would sit here, leaving my shoes to be trampled by visitors who, unaware of court etiquette, would stand over us to see better.

Sporadic wooden 'thuds' made by tourists sampling the court alarm system were interrupted by three strokes on a small gong to open the dance session. Four young women wearing red *kĕbaya* and brown and white *jarit* with daggers tucked into pink dance sashes tied round their waists, advanced to the west of the dance floor in a crouching walk, and took up their position facing the male teachers. When the music started, they advanced in a stately march. Once at the centre of the building, they sat down, as a man chanted in a stylized, accented manner. This was the *kandha*, the announcement of the story and the event for which the dance was being performed.

The dancers then performed identical movements in a series of symmetrical formations which altered by running swiftly on tiptoes in circles, or with measured sideways diagonal steps, their feet leaving the ground reluctantly, treading as if to test it. The gestures were tentative but uninterrupted. The dancers' hands pushed away and drew back something invisible to everyone but themselves. When they held the dance sash, or flicked it over to cover the hand, their gaze did not focus on it, but looked beyond, into the mid-distance. The dancers paused as a woman sang to the murmur of a rippling accompaniment. The full orchestra resumed, but the singing soon stopped. The drumming changed to a more syncopated rhythm, and the four dancers started to fight in pairs wielding small leather daggers. After a number of passes, two of the dancers knelt down while the others danced around them. Then the drumming eased to its previous rhythm, the singing resumed, and the dancers became introspective, their weapons tucked back at their waists. They crossed from one side of the stage to the other in pairs, in the mirroring pattern characteristic of this choreography. Then they knelt on one knee, as a man sang a closing song accompanied by strings and wooden xylophone, which tailed off until someone tapped a wooden box (*kěprak*). We had just seen the celebrated *srimpi* dance. Indonesian tourists said that it represented a story from the *Menak* legends about the Prophet Muhammad's uncle, but no one could say what this particular dance was about.

Later I found out that this had been Pon Sunday, a celebration of the Sultan's Javanese birthday which fell every thirty-five days on Lěgi Friday, so the session was conducted with more formality than usual. Normally the training followed a different procedure. A number of women would come onto the floor and advance to the centre in a crouching walk. The sound of the *gamělan* would gradually ripple out, then the women would rise and walk extremely slowly in a square, taking five or ten minutes to reach their starting place and sit down. After rising again, with their centre of gravity low, they would begin to move slowly but incessantly, shifting their weight from side to side as their necks and hands turned, manipulating the dance scarves they were all wearing around their waists, while making small but emphatic stamps of one foot behind the other. The female dance teachers would join them, and watch individuals in turn, and adjust their posture by gently restraining a wrist, a chin, or hipbones. After about twenty-five minutes, the dancers would sit down, raise their joined palms with thumbs by the nose in a *sěmbah* towards the men, and then leave in a slow squatting walk.

I became familiar with this training dance, *Saritunggal*, as I attended these Sunday sessions between October 1982 and February 1984. On my first visit I also saw *Tayungan*, the male training dance. Three men performed a slow and elaborate march to heavily accented music, back and forth under the guidance of the male dance teachers. Different dancers walked in different styles, with variations in their neck and arm movements. I later learned these were movement modes to fit the physiques of the dancers, and also associated with different character types in the court dance theatre. In contrast to the women, the boys and men frequently raised their feet off the floor, and the older ones spent much time standing on one leg, a distinctive feature of Yogyakartan court style. The programme continued with a dance fight for two women in choreography similar to the *srimpi* dance, a solo female *golek* dance, and a male duet danced in the strong style, culminating in an energetic club fight and much shouting and leaping. At about one o'clock, three strokes of the gong brought the session to a close. Leaving the cool of the Bangsal Kěsatriyan, we walked out through the dusty courtyards into the intense heat of a lazy Yogyakarta afternoon.

Fieldwork: Methods and Setting

This book draws on intensive participant observation in the field over a period of nearly twenty years (1982–99), including my Ph.D. research (1982–84) and a longitudinal study (1989–99).

I first became interested in dance when I was teaching English in East Java and Yogya with Voluntary Services Overseas (VSO) from January 1977 to September 1979. During this time I was struck by how much staged dancing there was. I 'converted' to anthropology at SOAS (School of Oriental and African Studies) in London and returned to Yogya in 1982 to research into court dance for a doctorate.

As a teacher I had had a recognized status in the communities where I worked. As an anthropological fieldworker it was a shock to find myself a social anomaly. I had to learn a new role, and to reestablish my credentials with different circles from the ones I had known before at the university. I lived in Kětanggungan, to the west of the *beteng* (court fortifications). This *kampung* (off-street community) of some 785 households was inhabited by students, court retainers and their families, including well-known musicians and choreographers, and also Sunarti Suwandi, singer, movie star, and former wife of the poet and dramatist W.S. Rendra, who I had first met in 1979 when Rendra was in prison for his political views. She arranged for me to live in this community which reflected Yogya's special mix of tradition and modernity.

The people in my research circles were highly educated, sometimes informally, and the court itself was a centre of patronage of all that was deemed civilized. To know something in Java, as anywhere, it is necessary to have been granted access to the world of that knowledge. As people said, 'you can only understand if you already know'. For the outsider the problem is how to get in the know in the first place; extensive library research does not necessarily give one the knowledge one needs to be entrusted with more. Although some never granted me access, most people willingly shared their knowledge with me in the (vain) hope that it would make me 'more Javanese': more temperate, more pliable and less materialistic. The obstacle to gaining access was more a matter of age than gender, as knowledge itself is a function of age. As one grows older, embodied knowledge changes from 'knowing *how*' (physical, technical) to 'knowing *what*' (metaphysical, interpretative). Over the years I became someone who was supposed to know *what*. I could no longer ask naïve questions, and conversations with people I already knew rested on shared knowledge and assumptions.

I invested extensive time and effort in learning how to dance, in order to fit into the social scene and to understand dance movement through my whole body, not just my eyes and ears. It is normal now, mandatory even, for an anthropologist to participate in the artistic activity being researched, but it was considered quite peculiar then. In London I had investigated the possibility of learning a dance notation system such as Benesh, Laban or Eshkol-Wachman, but I was discouraged by a leading notation teacher. She recognized that my object was to contextualize dance movement in relation to society, and reckoned that the effort would be disproportionate for the benefits to my analysis. Notations are seen as 'second hand scores', and can be read only by experts (Kersenboom 1995: 202). Participating in dance training and memorizing dance movement and choreographies was my 'first hand score'. As Javanese dance movement is gendered, I learnt the feminine mode. This allowed me to experience the sequences and rhythms of movement, and also how and *if* meaning was attributed to those sequences. Time spent in dance training gave me a role, credentials, and the right to ask questions. In some cases it gave rise to close friendships with my teachers. Without the physical experiences of learning dance, and the conversations that took place during dance training and watching performances, I would not have been able to write this book.

My research was on a human scale. Friends jokingly called my approach '*mubĕng-mubĕng*' ('going round and round'). This was a method of sorts, and I circulated the city on my motorcycle, mostly around the old centre of Yogya, building up a network and experiencing things as they happened. Through a combination of contingency, circumstance and serendipity, I gradually acquired information and understanding through what people said and did. As any researcher discovers, it never pays to expect much (if anything). In Java 'yes' can mean 'no' or 'maybe'. In a local almanac, Tuesday was 'the day when things don't happen', though others had their own preferred day to account for greater inertia than usual.

During this time I established a flexible routine. Mornings were spent talking to dance practitioners or administrators in schools and government offices, and reading in archives and libraries in the court, museum and dance academies. Afternoons were taken up with dance or Javanese language classes. In the evening I often joined Pak Pardjan, then head of the Secondary School of Indonesian Arts (SMKI), and his companions at the south square where they chatted as the sun went down – a motley group of court musicians and writers who jokingly called themselves 'Talking under the Tree' (*Kandha Waru*). They sometimes invited me along on their jaunts to villages to enjoy delicacies such as *pĕcĕl lele* (catfish and vegetables in peanut sauce) or *the teko*, tea poured over 'rock sugar'. My nights were spent watching rehearsals and performances, or writing up field notes. I attended every court ritual event that I could, and took photographs when appropriate. I hung out with whoever had time for me. In this way I totally immersed myself in Yogya's performance practices and practitioners. I also visited Jakarta to sort out bureaucratic matters concerning my research visa (which it had taken me two years to obtain, partly because of the presidential elections in 1982), and for archival research in the National Museum. And I went to Surakarta to see important rehearsals and performances at the Kasunanan court.

I returned to Yogya for a few months in 1987 to make a film about women's court dance. I then returned for a year in 1989, just before the accession of Sultan Hamĕngkubuwana X, to trace developments in the patronage of dance. I lived in a rented room in a friend's street-side house next to one of my dance teachers, and then moved to the home of a friend's mother (a well-known aristocratic *bathik* artist) and her young servant in a *kampung* to the southeast of the court. I also extended my research beyond the court and the city and surveyed the patronage of women's village dances across the whole Province, visiting remote areas to speak to patrons and performers and to observe performances and community events. I made further visits to the courts in Surakarta. I regularly visited Sragen and its surroundings in Central Java, the birthplace of my research assistant, the actor and writer Sri Hardjanto Sahid, where I observed and documented urban and rural performance practices for purposes of comparison.

Between 1990 and 1992 I visited Yogya regularly during a research project in Bali. I continued the longitudinal study in visits lasting six to eight weeks during the summers of 1994 and 1999. In 1994 I lived with my research assistant and his family in the fort area, and we revisited many people and places from 1989. I also made a video about a dance event in a highland village, and returned five years later to show the completed video to the community and the dancers and give them a copy. In 1999 I stayed north of the university campus with the family of my Javanese teacher from VSO days. The political and economic situation was unstable, making it unsafe to travel on public transport or to go out at night, so I made lengthy taxi rides across the much-expanded city to the south to catch up with old friends. These trips produced a new kind of informant, the dancer-cum-taxi driver, which tempered my frustration at being too cowardly to brave the polluted and crowded streets on a motorcycle and the recent increase of pickpockets working the city buses.

This book concentrates on my urban findings, mostly in the court area. The city (*kodya*) and four other districts (*kabupaten*) form the Special Region of Yogyakarta (Daerah Istimewa Yogyakarta, or D.I.Y.), a province of the Indonesian Republic, located in southern central Java (see Figures 1.1a and 1.1b. Its population in 1998 was 3,251,457 people, and that of the city itself 483,760, in 95,908 households.[1]

In 1983 the metropolitan area already sprawled across thirty-two square kilometres. By 1999 it had expanded in all directions and was encompassed by a dual carriage 'ring road'. In 1982 the city's roads had been leisurely spaces filled with bicycles, *becaks*, ox carts, horse-drawn carriages, 70cc motorcycles, and vans providing transport to the northern campuses. By 1999 they were choked with city buses belching out black fumes, cars and taxis, as well as the ubiquitous motor cycles.

The court area is one of municipal Yogyakarta's fourteen subdistricts (*kĕcamatan*). It includes the court itself (*kraton*) and the fort (*beteng*): four square kilometres of *kampungs* enclosed by stout white walls, and a reminder of Yogya's military origins. The court has political and cultural significance. Situated between the volcano Mĕrapi to the north and the Indian Ocean to the south, its physical geography also has a magical and metaphysical significance, in keeping with cosmological patterns in this volcanic archipelago. Most older people in Yogya know that the court, its sultan and its dances represent the universe in miniature, and they express this metaphorical relationship through a range of pre-Islamic and Islamic religious and philosophical identifications.

The court is approached from the north by a long straight road lined with shops, government offices and the main market. In front is a very wide expanse of grass, the *alun-alun lor*, used for court ceremonies, sporting activities, festivals and fairs such as Sĕkaten, held at the celebrations of the Prophet Muhammad's birth (Mauludan). To the south is the central court complex, consisting of a series of courtyards and

---

1. *Statistik Penduduk DIY 1998*: 14. Indonesia's population in 1997 was 198,675,836, with 116,513,412 living on the island of Java; by 1998 it was over 202 million (*Statistik Kesejahteraan Rakyat 1998*: 52–3; *Indonesia 1999*: 122).

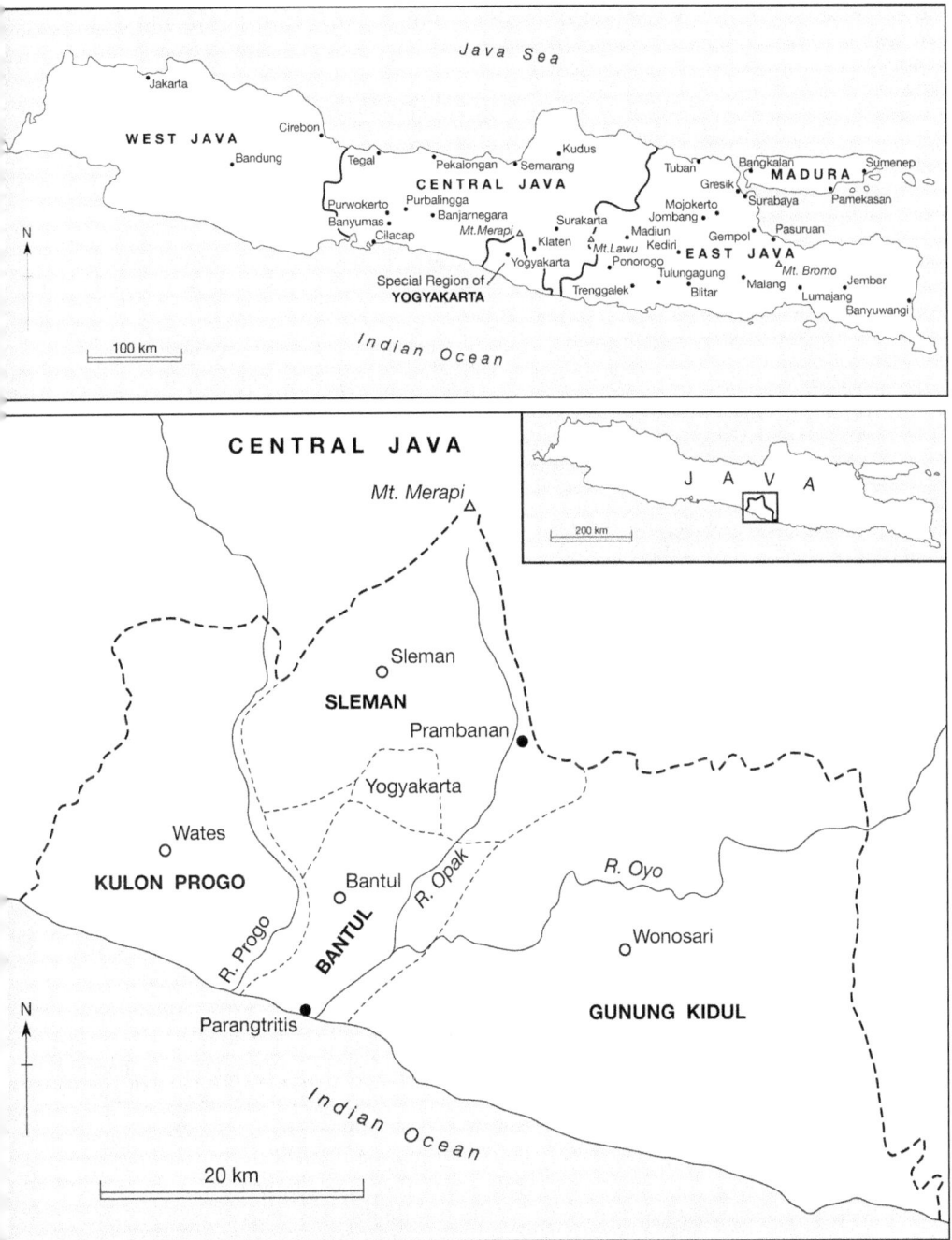

Figure 1.1 Maps of (a) Java and (b) The Province of Yogyakarta , (drawn by SOTEAS Cartographers, Swansea University)

compounds with whitewashed buildings and open-sided pavilions. First is the Pagĕlaran, a very large ceremonial hall used for large-scale performances and cultural events, and the Sitihinggil ('raised ground'), used for the accession ceremony of a new sultan. The current Sultan and his family live in the 'west court'; there are also offices, libraries, archives, ceremonial halls, and a number of small museums. Their elegantly pitched roofs are supported on rows of slender columns adorned with carvings painted in the palace colours: red for courage, green for peace and safety, yellow and white for clarity. Inside the court are two small mosques. The 'Great Mosque' and Islamic community are west of the north square. To the south of the court buildings is a smaller grassy square, and beyond is Nirbaya (or Gading), the southernmost of the fort's nine gateways.

In the fort around the inner court concourse are a number of *kampungs* and princely residences (*dalĕm*), several of which run dance associations. Non-Javanese people are forbidden to live here, but in practice students from all over Indonesia do, and so did I in 1994. In this area is the sultan's (then) derelict 'Water Castle' (Tamansari), and Ngasĕm, with its daily food and bird markets, food stalls (*warung*), small shops, primary and secondary schools, and film academy. Outside the fort walls are the *kampungs* of land and houses allocated to the colonial court regiments, and named after them – Kĕtanggungan, Wirabrajan, and so forth. *Kampungs* inside and outside the fort are inhabited by court retainers (*abdidalĕm*), close and distant court kin and students. Postcolonial Yogyakarta has also developed as an educational centre. Gadjah Mada, Indonesia's first university, was built to the north of the city, an area associated with change and progress, in contrast to the more stable and traditional southern parts. It is between these two orientations that its inhabitants live their lives and try to make sense of them.

In rural Java neighbourhood and memory, rather than kinship and blood ties, ground social relationships that differ for every individual.[2] To a certain extent the same is true of urban Yogya, which is often described as a collection of villages. Permanent residents identify themselves as Indonesian but consider themselves first and foremost as from 'Yogya' and more specifically from the *kampung* where they live. *Kampung* communities provided a sense of belonging: children performing here for independence celebrations were confident because they felt they were in their own family, not performing for 'other people' (*orang lain* I.). Scholars have distinguished the traditionally oriented working-class *kampungs* from the modern middle class street-sides, but in practice the boundary between the two is permeable.

These urban administrative units were established during the Japanese occupation (1942–45) and maintained by the nationalist government as Rukun Kampung (RK). Renamed Rukun Warga in the mid-1980s, they are further subdivided into neighbourhoods (Rukun Tetangga). *Rukun* (I.) means 'social harmony', but is an expression of hope rather than a description of actual social relations. These localities may function as autonomous units of social control,[3] and national identity cards (Kartu Tanda Penduduk) refer to one's local place of residence.

2.   Koentjaraningrat (1985: 148).
3.   Sullivan (1980); Guinness (1986); Watson (1987).

Community is a site of control as well as belonging. In a face-to-face community everyone has obligations. When I first moved into a rented house in a village just outside the city as a VSO in 1979, I had to host a community meeting and food distribution (*sělamatan*). Anonymity is not an option in a *kampung*. Residential space is intensely organized, with face-to-face community meetings and different kinds of surveillance, including an unpaid night watch (*ronda*) in which local men are obliged to participate.

During Suharto's politically repressive presidency the internal regulation of the *kampung* was breached by covert surveillance by informers and 'security' operations. In 1983 I experienced 'the knock on the door' in the middle of the night, and opened the door to an armed man in full riot gear. Young tattooed men suspected of gang membership were being shot in cold blood as part of a purge of 'criminal' elements. Java's rivers became blocked with corpses as they had in the 1966 purges of 'communists' after Suharto seized power. Many middle-class Indonesian citizens in Yogyakarta and elsewhere turned a blind eye to these horrors, explaining that Suharto's leadership had ensured that they had enough to eat for the first time that they could remember. They recalled their sufferings during the Japanese occupation and war against the Dutch in the 1940s, memories which had been revived during the terror of violent reprisals following the 30 September 1965 movement that followed the violent murder of six generals.[4]

Politics was a taboo subject for most of my fieldwork. Even before going to Indonesia, during my VSO training in Britain, my passing remark about Pancasila, the state 'philosophy', prompted a warning from a visiting speaker: 'You won't last long in Indonesia if you say things like that.' Indonesians had acquired the habit of wariness. It was well nigh impossible to discuss political matters directly, even with close friends. Censorship was used to control plays and poetry readings which might stir up normally contained emotions about injustice. In one celebrated case in the late 1970s, the poet and dramatist W.S. Rendra was imprisoned for his outspoken criticisms of the government. Letters of authorization from the local police and security sectors were required for all performances. In 1983, friends planning a street theatre performance using *jathilan* (horse dancing) were denied permits because their script hinted at protest. Censorship and criticism varied according to location and venue. Newer theatres thrived in delimited communities, such as a highly satirical dance theatre (*wayang wong*) performance at Gadjah Mada University's Dies Natalis celebrations in 1982. When the Jeprik theatre group performed in Yogya in 1989, it was more damning in its satire than it had dared to be in Jakarta. Friends who saw both performances said that this was because of the distance from the capital – a revealing example of local perceptions about the limits of state surveillance, rather

---

4. These events were immediately subject to revision and manipulation. The 'coup' was blamed on the Communist Party, up to a million people were murdered, mostly in Java and Bali, and 100,000 were imprisoned (Wieringa 2002). Only after Suharto's 'resignation' in May 1998 did the generation who grew up with feelings of absolute certainty about events such as these start to become aware that the truths they were told were partial at best.

than a response to recent policies of 'openness' (*keterbukaan* I.). In 1994 a performance of music and poetry by the charismatic social commentator and poet Emha Ainun Nadjib and the Kyai Kanjĕng Music group was 'aborted' in Yogya because some poems criticized the President. In a highly regulated society such as Indonesia where surveillance and censorship are part of the fabric of everyday life, performers and artists have had to find the means to situate themselves alongside, if not outside, the agenda of the state. It was also easier to obtain permits for dance-based performances than language-based ones, which is one reason for the profusion of dance in New Order Indonesia.

Surveillance and intense community membership were countered by flexibility of religion and lifestyle, within the legal requirement to identify a religion on one's identity card. Those interested in court performance were predominantly from the *abangan* (commoner) and *priyayi* (nobility, upper class) groups, many of whom were relatives (*sĕntana dalĕm*) of the sultan. Although *abangan* and *priyayi* have been distinguished from *santri*, self-consciously observant Muslims, *priyayi* is a professional identification. [5] Many *priyayi* are also *santri*, keeping their hereditary daggers next to the prayer room. Court retainers, dancers and musicians tended not to be *santri*. They joked about what they considered excessive displays of Islam (such as praying), and declared themselves to be 'statistical Muslims', observing Islam only during rites of passage. Traditionally the court and the sultan have been above specific religious orientations, and have used different religious practices in parallel. The *pĕmutihan* ('white ones') are responsible for prayers to Allah before dance performances, but court practices also include 'washing' heirlooms and making of offerings for well-being with 'incense and flowers'. Orthodox Muslims consider these practices to be Javanese but not Islamic, even when they occur in the context of Islamic rites.

From the outset, then, we should not think of court dances as non-Islamic. But although mystical Islam comes into dance interpretations, the dances are not Islamic either. It was unknown for people who dressed in Muslim style to participate in court dance. Women who chose to wear the *jilbab* (head covering) did not belong to the associations that taught court dance, but participated in Muslim drama groups, and attended poetry and music concerts by Emha Ainun Nadjib and others. Religious identity and its physical presentation vary over time. In 1979 I knew a young *priyayi* woman who was a keen court dancer. Twenty years later, looking at photos of her in a tight-fitting *golek* costume, she explained that she got fed up when dance rehearsals dragged on later than they were meant to, and then went to university. She became a lecturer at an Islamic university and then went to Canada to do a masters degree. There, she and her companions adopted full Islamic dress (*busana muslimin*), a presentation that she maintained after she returned to Yogya. This is a good example of how individuals can change the way they practise their religion and make it part of their social identity. [6] Conversely, not everyone born into a court or *santri* family

---

5. See Geertz (1960), Bachtiar (1973) and Nakamura (1983).
6. In 2006 one of my dance teachers wore a 'traditional' hair-do and *kĕbaya* to help dress a dancer for a court performance. The next morning she wore a head covering, long blouse and trousers to visit the graves of her in-laws.

retains that lifestyle. One of my landladies had been raised in the Kauman, the '*santrī* *kampung* behind Yogya's Great Mosque. Her father had been a low-ranking court retainer, and her grandmother used to prepare food for important court ceremonies. After she inherited land from her uncle, a soldier in the court's *Kĕtanggung* corps, she converted to Catholicism (to gain access to Catholic funds and networks, said local gossips) and set up various enterprises, including the student house where I lived. When I asked her about local traditions she replied, in Indonesian, that, 'In town there are activities, not rituals' – a remark indicative of her rejection of the practices and values of her youth.

As children are taught Indonesian in school, Javanese language and social values are being challenged. Larger-scale disembodied abstractions are being incorporated into a sense of national identity which is not imagined but part of everyday life and local community activity. Modernization also impels people to reaffirm their social identity in terms of traditional status systems and to join descent group organizations (*trah*) (Sairin 1982). Individuals may choose to assert a more personal validation of royal descent by requesting 'buttoning' certificates (*sĕrat kĕkancingan*) for themselves and their children from the court's 'Blood Office' (Tĕpas Darah). For instance, the head of Yogya's secondary school of arts obtained his certificate – 'Number 1591!' – confirming him to be at the 'eighth degree' (*dĕrajat*) from Prince Mangkudiningrat, the second Sultan's first son by his second senior wife. He did this before his daughter's graduation and subsequent marriage to formalize her title as Raden Rara. In 1991 he became a court retainer, further affirming his affiliation with the court in anticipation of his retirement from arts education in the Indonesian civil service. He has since transferred his energies to court performance and culture and by 1999 reached the upper echelons of the court hierarchy. Thousands of people can claim royal descent due to the large number of children sired by sultans by numerous wives, but not everyone chooses to activate these blood ties. Another *priyayi* and senior academic told me that she was 'fifth degree' from the Surakartan Prince Mangkunagara I. Her two brothers had requested their 'letters' but she could not be bothered. Regardless of whether or not a person chooses to self-identify with descent status, the place of residence and work shapes one's everyday identity within a face-to-face community, as well as providing a locus for one's national identity as a citizen.

Dance in the Imagined Community

The importance of dance both as an embodied practice and as a representational system is now recognized, socially, culturally and politically. Dance became more respectable as an object of serious scholarly investigation during the 1980s as a result of systematic scholarship by early groups in Europe such as the Study Group on Ethnochoreology that grew out of folk researches. The dominance of Western theatre art dance was challenged, and broader approaches were developed by pioneering dance anthropologists in the United States and Britain.[7]

---

7. Kurath (1960); Blacking (1977); Kaeppler (1978); Felföldi (1999); and see Buckland's succinct overviews (1999a, 1999b).

Most anthropological approaches to dance now include an account of movement and its social context. Hanna (1979) argued for an 'open' or extrinsic approach to dance using a contextual analysis, while Kaeppler asked that dance be treated not as a universal category but as the 'movement dimension of separate activities' (1978: 47). These contextual approaches were possible in cases where dance had not yet become objectified or commoditized – or analysed as such. It could be argued that dance became a legitimate object of study when globally it was being removed from its socially embedded conditions of practice. Exceptions were Mitchell's (1956) study of the *Kalela* dance and its function in the construction of ethnic identities among migrants moving to the city in Zambia's Copper Belt, and Ranger's (1975) account of the *Beni-Ngoma*, which satirized those in authority.[8] In both these cases, the dance had a symbolic function, representing the political construction of marginal groups, and treated performance as both personal agency and group dynamic. A contrasting 'intrinsic' approach analysed movement as sign systems. For instance, Williams's 'semiasology' (1991) became the foundation for 'human movement studies' (Farnell 1995), with an interest in embodiment which has become an important theme in the anthropology of dance and dance studies. This has restored debates about materiality to the analysis of dance that had previously been influenced by interpretive social analysis (Geertz 1973). These theoretical developments have also produced a blurring between the anthropology of dance, dance studies in Britain and the USA,[9] and the sociology of dance in Britain.[10]

The discussion in this book contributes to two recent themes in dance anthropology: dance politics and the cultural interpretation of movement. I consider first the political aspect. Dance communities and the roles and representations of dancers and dances have been implicated in changing discourses of colonialism and nationalism, particularly in the construction of history and 'authenticity', which in turn produce changes and innovations in particular dance cultures (Carter 1998; Buckland 2006). As such, dance plays an important role in the construction of social identity and community.

Dance is now recognized as playing an important role in politics at both national and regional levels (Reed 1998; Henry, MacGowan, and Murray 2000). Political symbolism and the power of emotional response are central for understanding political processes, from identity construction to the acquisition of power (Kertzer

8. Much British social anthropological dance analysis derived from colonial and postcolonial African ethnography (Spencer 1985; James 2003: 75–78).
9. Of particular interest are Novack (1990), Foster (1996). Morris (1996), Desmond (1997), and Bull (1997).
10. Thomas (1995) saw this as leading to renewed interest in British anthropological models. She initially had reservations about dance anthropology's continued emphasis on small-scale 'exotic' societies as a model for a sociological analysis of dance in Western industrial societies (1995: 23), but she has since given dance anthropology its due, and acknowledges dance analyses at home and in complex urban societies in different societies, including Ness's (1992) study of *sinulog* in Cebu City in the Philippines (Thomas 2003: 84–88).

1988). Power cannot, however, be reduced to its symbols; while being enhanced by 'colour, music, dancing and the human body [they are] *not fully accounted for by them*' (Cohen 1977: 121, my emphasis). In the political domain performance is symbolic *and* instrumental. It is caught up in the contradictions between the two dimensions of social interaction: the unintentional and moral nature of cultural action, and the amoral self-interest of political action (Cohen 1993: 8).[11] Any symbol can be articulated politically, but Cohen stops short of asking why *dance* is used, rather than, for instance, an emblem such as a flag.

The answer to this question will involve us in an examination of the wider relevance of analysing dance as an embodied practice, and an explanation of how political symbolism is constructed: the operations of power, and the uses to which dance is put within the processes of political reconfiguration. I will be suggesting that dance is *not* of the same emblematic and iconic orders as flags and anthems, to which Anderson compares 'folk dance' in his analysis of the nation as imagined community. Anderson argues that languages, and not bodies, produce 'imagined communities building in effect *particular solidarities*' (1983: 122). This popular notion of 'imagined community' has resulted in a lack of attention to smaller-scale day-to-day experiences of belonging. Anthropologists have responded to Anderson by proposing that community has a dual nature; it is experienced as personal, thick and entire, and as collective, symbolic and imagined. Contingent, changing and partial, community is one among many competing attachments.[12]

Dance in Java and Indonesia

Embodied performances in Asia have long formed part of religious and secular expressions of community. Ceremonial dances and dance theatres have also been associated with power centres and political ritual. Javanese court dance has been part of a community which is both embodied and imagined. It provides evidence for how dance traditions and practices become involved in social interactions, and generate a sense of identity in local face-to-face communities which are also part of the nation state. Court dance has undergone a process of debate, positioning and emergence in national cultural politics. Caught up in state rhetoric proclaiming Indonesian unity, it has been used to create the semblance of a glorious past for a territory contingent on colonial boundaries. This search for origins has been explained as a symptom of the 'logic of loss' during Indonesia's New Order (1966–98) (Pemberton 1994: 141–43). It is true that scholars often write about court dance as Indonesian culture by emphasizing its antecedents in the Hindu-Javanese period (*c.* 400–1300), but this approach is also found in Dutch scholarship on dance and theatre in the late colonial

---

11. Tambiah's work on ritual symbolism in Thailand (1985) uses the concept of indexicality to demonstrate how ritual can engage both with the political and the imaginative and cosmological dimensions.

12. See Amit (2002: 18–19): 'Community arises out of an interaction between the imagination of solidarity and its realization through social relations and is invested both with powerful affect as well as contingency, and therefore with both consciousness and choice … Community matters, but it is never everything.'

period.[13] After Indonesian independence, Marcel Mauss's student, dance anthropologist Jeanne Cuisinier (1951) transferred the religious aspects of dances she had researched in Buddhist societies in mainland Southeast Asia to Indonesia, and emphasized the sacrality of its dances. The next important study of dance formed part of Holt's seminal work on Indonesian art (1967). This drew on her field research from the 1930s and current dance scholarship to reveal a more complex context based on both continuity and change. During the 1970s and 1980s dance research by Indonesian and overseas scholars intensified. Historical and cultural analysis was dominant.[14] Interestingly, the gendering of court dance was rarely discussed, with the exception of Morrison (1977) and Choy (1984), and instead gender relations were explored in analyses of popular theatre (Peacock 1968; Hatley 1995).

My argument is that Javanese court dances are not 'natural' continuations of a previous tradition. They have been reconstructed in a self-conscious 'modern' way, and should be understood as set of embodied practices which has both worked on and been worked on by the interests defined by the idea of the political community.

This reconstruction has happened twice. The first time was after the founding of the court, Karaton Ngayogyakarta Hadiningrat or the Kasultanan, in 1756 by Sultan Haměngkubuwana I. This marked the conclusion of the Wars of Succession against his nephew, Sunan Pakubuwana III, and resulted in the division of a kingdom previously based in the court which had relocated to the city of Surakarta, situated sixty kilometres northeast of Yogya, founded in 1746. Before the concept of 'invented tradition' had been devised (Hobsbawm and Ranger 1983), the relationship between authenticity and tradition had been explored by the well-known historian of Java, Merle Ricklefs (1974). His intricate analysis of the foundation of the Principality of Yogyakarta in the eighteenth century showed that Javanese traditions arise from a process of political contingency and are strategically constructed, demonstrating that tradition is a process, not a thing. In this way the court's traditions acquired many associations which predate its chronological origins. In addition, the continuity of court culture has been dynamic. Transmitted through a process of *mutrani*, each work

---

13. To give a few examples: Groneman documented Yogya court dance (1888, 1899) and the *garĕbĕg* ceremonies (1895) with wonderful photographs by Cephas. Helsdingen-Schoevers gave a somewhat romanticized account of female dances in Surakarta (1912) with art deco-influenced drawings by Tyra de Kleen. Juynboll (1906, 1915) gave a general overview. After 1919 the Java Institute was founded and held its first congress in Surakarta, numerous articles and papers were published linking Javanese culture to Hinduism, including an important article about the prototypical *Bĕdhaya Kĕtawang* (Hadiwidjojo 1921). Lelyveld's (1931) text for the Colonial exhibition treated Javanese court dance as a modern version of Sanskritic performance. Pigeaud's (1938) encyclopaedic survey of performance also developed this theme but noted other influential factors as well.

14. Key sources in English and Indonesian include Choy (1984); Brakel-Papenhuijzen (1992), Hughes-Freeland (1988, 1991c, 1993a, 1997a, 1997b, 2001a, 2001b, 2006, 2007a), Kam (1986, 1987), Lindsay (1985), Soedarsono (1984, 1989, 1989/90), Suryobrongto (1970, 1976, 1978, 1981a, 1981b), Surjodiningrat (1970), Hadi (1988) and Wibowo (1981). I refer to other sources, including those for other kinds of performance (especially the shadow-play), when appropriate.

is considered 'the child' of the previous one: alike, but not identical. The replication of tradition is evident in the further proliferation of courts in central Java. The 'junior' court in Surakarta, the Mangkunagaran, was founded in 1757 by the Sultan of Yogya's nephew and former ally, Mas Said. Later Yogya's junior court, the Pakualaman, was founded in 1813 by the disgraced second Sultan's brother with the help of the British, who controlled Java briefly during the Napoleonic wars.

The second reconfiguration of court dance occurred when the Principality of Yogya became a province of the Indonesian Republic. The resulting political transformation of the relationship between the court's performance traditions and national cultural politics is an important theme in this book. The Japanese invaded Java in 1942 and Indonesian independence was declared following their defeat after the bombing of Hiroshima and Nagasaki in August 1945. The following year the Sultan invited the newly formed Indonesian government to base itself in Yogya. He also supported the subsequent guerrilla warfare against the Dutch who then attempted to regain their colony. His nationalist zeal was rewarded by his dynastic kingdom being changed into the Special Region of Yogyakarta, a province in the new republic. The other principality at Surakarta was absorbed into the Province of Central Java.

The formerly elitist activities of the colonial court became part of an identity-building agenda for the creation of a new nation of independent Indonesians, through different forms of education, and its dances became the foundation of provincial culture in the new Republic. The exclusive control of court dance had been breached when the seventh Sultan gave permission to two of his sons in 1918 to establish a school to train court dance. This opened up the repertoire to the children of the emerging middle-class nationalists, and contributed to dance's role in developing a sense of national identity after Indonesian independence in 1945. The reign of the last colonial sultan, Hamĕngkubuwana VIII (1921–39) had seen the consolidation of the court dance repertoire, and was the reference point for memories of former dancers and court retainers, which fed into the rationales and constructions of court dance and which allowed it to survive the end of colonialism.

Both court dance and its cultural classification have changed since Indonesian independence. The Javanese language did not distinguish dance from theatre. The court *wayang wong* used the panoply of theatrical elements – drama, dance, song, music – and is better described as 'dance theatre'. There is no general Javanese word for performance or dance. The Indonesian language, however, does have a 'dance' concept: *tari/an* (dance), *menari* (dancing, to dance) and *penari* (dancer). Today most Javanese people speak both languages, but these are not simply interchangeable. For instance, during fieldwork, if I told someone in Indonesian that I was studying Javanese dance (*tari Jawa*), they thought that I meant modern 'new creations'. When I said in Javanese that I was studying *bĕksa* (court dance movement), there was no confusion. For purposes of simplicity here I will use the word 'dance', and qualify it when relevant, but it is important to understand that 'dance' itself is a postcolonial and emergent concept.

After independence, court performance gradually spread from the house of the ruler and the princely residences to educational institutions, to heritage sites, hotels and theatres. Its aesthetic identity was distinguished by a contrast between inside and outside the court. This contrast was ideological. In practice the boundary was porous, and the court has always incorporated people and practices from outside. As an emergent category, 'court dance' (*tari kraton*) retained its distinctiveness from other kinds of performances classed as ' folk' and 'popular' which had been promoted by the left-wing cultural association, LEKRA. These categories were viewed with suspicion after 1965, the result of an anti-left-wing backlash after the so-called '30 September movement' blamed on the Indonesian Communist Party. This event provided the momentum for the overthrow of President Soekarno, Indonesia's first president, and the establishment of the 'New Order' under President Suharto (1966–98). By the mid-1970s court dance was being recast as 'classical Yogya-style dance'. Its contemporary and future roles were debated by interested parties which included educational professionals, aristocratic amateurs and government bureaucrats. By 1980, the performance repertoires of the Sultan's court of Yogyakarta had been confirmed as Indonesian 'classical dance' (*tari klasik*) that could be separated from their original context, and developed accordingly. This process constituted court dance as art and high culture, and separated it from popular and foreign culture.

The court's physical location continued to give material and spatial definition to national cultural ideologies, although the overlap between court, regional and state interests in the provincial administration was complex, and produced cross-cutting ties of allegiance. Officially, Indonesian culture is made up of a plurality of cultures, governed by Pancasila, the state philosophy that stipulates five principles: belief in God; Indonesian nationalism; humanitarianism; democracy through consensus; and social justice. Despite the rhetoric of promoting diversity through Pancasila, it is the unifying powers of this ideology which are given priority, and indeed, one of the more undisguised forms of education to develop modern Indonesian attitudes were the 'P4' Pancasila training programmes which ran during the 1980s to produce Indonesian citizens. The modern Indonesian word for culture, '*kebudayaan*', is itself an ideological concept (Bruner and Becker 1979: 307). When an Indonesian bureaucrat talks about culture, s/he is participating in the process of transforming previous practices into different historical and social frameworks.

As we will discover, there is a difference between the development rhetoric of the state and what happens in regional government. Yogya-style dances have a martial ideology and emphasis on the self-discipline of the dancer that has fitted state rhetoric about personal and national development. The court ethos retained the fire of early Soekarnoist nationalism, and presented an intriguing contrast with the repressive culturalization of politics during the regime of President Suharto, but the dances also became metaphors for a struggle for self-perfection, which was also represented as being at odds with post-revolutionary normalization and complacency.

Despite these political changes, the court origins of what became 'Yogya style classical dance' produced an acknowledged relationship between dance movement, manners and the person, understood as having a two-fold character, social and metaphysical. Dance has provided an education in the valuable technique and skills for the practice of everyday life, as I learnt when I trained in the feminine dance mode. Dance is now an art form, but it has not completely lost its relationship with religious or spiritual practices. Court *bĕdhaya* dances especially have been central to Javanese court ceremonial. Their abstract movements and complex but seamless choreographic patterns generated different metaphors of sexual and spiritual, and self and society. These have fed back into the significance of the dance movement, giving it both aesthetic and political power. These traditional identifications persist in modernizing statements and attitudes to court dance in the Indonesian context. However, by the end of the 1980s, its status as high art was being challenged by the commercial world of tourism, and the producers of court dance were struggling to resolve the conflict between the values of high art and the market place. The gradual diversification in the patronage of court dance was also being matched by a diversification of objects of patronage within the court. Yet despite the increased opportunities for dancers to perform at concerts for tourists, professionalism has remained an ideal in the 'honour not cash' economic ideology of both the court and the state.

Dance in Indonesian and Indian Nationalism

To draw out the more general themes and implications of the Javano-Indonesian case it is helpful to make a brief comparison with *bharata natyam* in India.[15] Both cases involve the changing role and status of dancers, the role of outside influences (intellectual and otherwise), the socioeconomic conditions which produced the roles of 'artist' and dance professional, the means by which dance practices are transmitted and transformed, and changing gender relations and representations. Both cases give insight into the way in which dance becomes both implicated in, and is also constitutive of, the embodied and imagined community of the nation state,

Bharata natyam has an ambiguous status. The name, 'dance of India', was given in 1932 in reference to the *Nātyaśāstra* the classical Sanskrit dance text by Bharata-Muni. It was a dance style based on the dances of the *devadasis*, the so-called 'temple dancers' whose erotic performances produced auspiciousness. The practice of dedicating *devadasi* dancers to the service of the temple became illegal following Indian independence in 1947, after a long campaign. The first Brahmin woman and nonhereditary dancer to perform the dance in modern South Indian history, was Rukmini Devi (1904–86). She founded the Kalakshetra academy in 1936 and taught the dance, designed by male orchestra conductors who adapted the secular *sadir* (or *dasi-attam*) dances of the *devadasis*, to the daughters of Brahmins. However, before their dedication was banned, *devadasis* had already started to perform dance concerts in theatres. It was hereditary *devadasis* such as T. Balasaraswati who spread the dance outside India, and who also prescribed the concert order of dances for *devadasis*. Nowadays *bharata natyam* dancers are neither hereditary nor professional. The dance has become an educational tool for the upper and middle classes, and 'transcends the

---

15. This account draws mainly on Gaston's major long-term participant ethnography (1996), with additional perspectives from articles by Margin (1985), Meduri (1988), Allen (1997) and O'Shea (1998).

artistic, providing instead the medium for acquiring a cultural identity and projecting examples of female role models' (Gaston 1996: 65).

Like Javanese court dance, *bharata natyam* has been given an ancient history, and its themes are drawn from Hindu mythology. However, what people have come to think about the performances and their antecedents shows history not as a set of documented proven events but as a semi-mythological force which invests the present with greater legitimacy to define how things will be done in the future. The 'revival' of *bharata natyam* resulted in the disenfranchisement of Muslim musicians and dancers in the north and south, and their replacement with mainly Hindu Brahmins. A re-ritualization of the dance occurred when of an image of Siva Nataraja was placed on *bharata natyam* stages in the 1940s by Rukmini Devi, endorsing claims that this was an ur-style, and linking the dance to ideological narratives endorsing a pan-Indian nationalism. Kalakshetra taught the basic movement sequences (*adavu*) through regular rigorous exercises like ballet class, giving the training legitimacy, and hybridizing Western and Tamil practices. Kalakshetra's 'reconstructivist' approach' meant that 'the community's religious and artistic roles were eradicated and its history reimagined', and served to endorse the Indian urban elite's efforts 'to claim a unified and legitimising image of Indian culture' (O'Shea 1998: 55–56).

Also like Javanese court dance, *bharata natyam* is neither 'invented' nor 'authentic'. The relationship between the name *bharata natyam*, its foundation in a movement associated with *devadasi*, and a new choreographic tradition is a matter of debate and political positioning. Court dance changed from a colonial to a postcolonial practice, as the internal transformation of the form with the transformation of Javanese court movement styles into Indonesian classical dance, and gender politics in Indonesia, although the details and emphasis differ, particularly with regard to the ethnicity of the players in relation to the state, and the religious background. Like *bharata natyam*, it involves family-based practices being incorporated into colonial educational institutions that then play a role in defining nationalism. And, like *bharata natyam*, the story of Javanese court dance is not about a simple change from a ritual foundation, via the social or commercial, to becoming a political symbol for the state.

This linear process is not the whole story. It is because practices are given an *extra context* (which may *not* necessarily take over one or all of the previous ones) that makes 'customization' necessary and analysts *aware* of inventedness. Processes of retraditionalization and ritualization accompany technological and bureaucratic change as characteristics of modernity.[16] The diversification of the audience is also implicated in these customizations. It has been suggested that dance forms become a

---

16. Bell (1992). Evans (1998) has spoken of the creation of continuity by 'customizing' traditions to provide political symbols for the People's Republic of Laos, but did not include dance. Chakravorty (2004) has described *kathak* dance as social memory in relation to embodiment and cultural transmission and transformation. The elimination of the past with the invention of year 0 in 1975 in Cambodia has also given classical dance an important role, cognitive, corporeal, and emotional (Shapiro 1995; Hamera 2002: 65–66).

means to embodying memories of practices and identities which no longer exist in an everyday sense but become part of 'social memory' (Connerton 1989), a second level of imagined belonging and collectivity.[17] However, what is remembered is not necessarily authentic in the sense of unbroken repetition. Continuity and innovation intertwine. As I will explain, Javanese court dance has had a dynamic continuity in which creativity, customization, appropriation, transformation and reinterpretation have all played a role.

Developing some of the themes of political appropriation, customization and contestation encapsulated in this brief overview and comparison with *bharata natyam,* one of my objectives in this book is to answer the question why court dance has had the political significance it has in Indonesia, thereby raising more general issues about dance and politics. I now turn to my second general theme, which is that the embodied nature of dance movement makes it a powerful form of social and political action.

Dance and Embodiment

Dance is important because, unlike many other material symbols of belonging, it is *embodied* action. Dancing is powerful because it is a cultural practice situated in the self and revealed through the actions of the body. Dance ethnography builds on anthropological holism, but dance has also become an object of analysis in its own right. This produces a contradiction: dance is not a universal category, but we identify certain kinds of movement *as* dance. This contradiction has produced debates centred on the relationship of dance to the body which have become caught up in theoretical issues arising from the Cartesian conceptualization of the person as split between mind and body. However, as Schilder pointed out long ago, the body is at once lived (*Leib*) and objective (*Körper*) (1935, in Thomas 2003: 29). The body is about lived experience and being-in-the-world, but it is also representational: it is seen-in-the-world. This duality has shaped the sociological 'body' project, and many theorists have attempted to synthesize representational and phenomenological models, particularly those of Merleau-Ponty (1962). Indeed, his ideas about embodied perception have been central in arguments for the phenomenological approach to dance.[18]

One has to start somewhere, but there is always a risk of reification. Starting with the body contributes to the polarization of analyses of dance as 'being seen' or as 'being'. Sally Ann Ness (2004) has recently contrasted these symbolic and phenomenological

---

17. In these terms, dancing becomes an embodiment not simply of discursive figures, but of what Connerton calls 'habit-memory', to represent the performative aspect of memory which is evident in commemorative ceremonies and bodily practices (1989: 23, 36). The problem with Connerton's argument is that habit-memory is associated with an internalized and individual sense of 'belief' which is not culturally universal, and, secondly, his social memory privileges the determinism of Durkheimian collective representations and, like these, confuses the capacities of the human mind with its social contents also at the expense of the agency of personal memory.

18. Sheets Johnstone (1984). Relevant discussions which reevaluate Merleau-Ponty's corporeality are Lewis (1992), Csordas (1994), Crossley (1995: 133) and Varela (1995).

aspects, and has criticized participatory approaches derived from phenomenology being used in cultural analyses. In her ethnography of Filipino *sinulog* (Ness 1992) she uses Peircian semiotics to analyse dance movement as visible and thus observable. She suggests that phenomenology is a part of a larger epistemological project in progress (2004: 140), and that dance analysts should be more cautious about prejudging the outcome. Others take a different approach to the relationship of vision and the body in different kinds of dance. For example, Bull (1997) contrasts the primacy of seeing, touching and hearing respectively in performing ballet, contact improvisation and Ghanaian dance.[19] More recently, Desmond, who is well aware of the dangers of 'physical foundationalism', has argued that 'we give equal weight to the intransigence of physical evidence in systems of social differentiation and track these operations in public discourse' (1999: 266). The visible appearance of the body can be a useful starting point, but it is not the end of the matter.

A fundamental paradox of embodiment requires analysis to go beyond the visible material body. The body is significant not simply by virtue of its materiality, but because that material is energized and cognizant, generating meanings and sense. In Blacking's words, 'from the dance of language and thought we are moved into thinking … body and mind are one' (1977: 22–23). Dancing is not just movement: it is a producer of movement and context. It is embodied action, but it is also action which is referred to. It is a way of making a world because it extends beyond movement, beyond the body, through the responses of actor-dancers in relation to memory and expectations. Dancing produces and is produced by not only bodies but persons.

Anthropologists who have focused on dance (and on ritual) have happily managed this paradox for a long time. They have shown how persons in performance can change the world (Kapferer 1991; Schieffelin 1998), emphasizing the instrumental nature of embodied performance, instead of the purely representational aspects. Rather than locating performance in the body, they have taken the person as their starting point.[20] By attending to the material and other aspects of the person we can escape the vicious circle of the post-Cartesian mind-body opposition, though we might wish to resist the slippage back into a visualist, 'reading' model of analysing dance which comes into some arguments. Attention to the materiality of the person is also important for resisting any lurking logocentrism.[21] Communication itself is 'a multiple, relative and emergent process' (Finnegan 2002: 28), as much performance as text. Given this broader approach, it would be ironic if dance were to be flattened into a rational linear textual narrative, and become detached from its nature as both staged and social performance, in Goffman's sense (1956).

---

19. Bull's work on contact improvisation was published under the name Novack (1990), and is discussed later in this book.

20. Analytically, the body is sometimes confused with agency or conflated with 'practice'. In realist naturalism, the seat of agency is the person (Archer 1995: 280).

21. 'Contemporary writings in the discipline of dance studies have often been influenced by postmodern readings of "dance as texts" … We argue that this textual approach neglects the fact that embodied *performance* lies at the core of the aesthetic practice of dance (Shusterman 1992)' (Wainwright and Turner 2004: 98).

The biological foundation of the body may be common to all societies, but its understandings vary cross-culturally and historically, and produce different styles of behaviour, different world-views (in Weber's sense), and different ways of being in the world (in Merleau-Ponty's sense). Porter's magisterial account (2003) of changes in concepts of the person and body in eighteenth-century Europe makes it clear that previously existing dualisms were transformed, and the seat of the self changed from the spiritual 'soul' to the secularized 'mind', eventually producing a social ethos characterized as 'post-god' in a Nietzschean sense, afflicted with Weberian disenchantment. The immaterial energy and consciousness of the individual person in such cases is considered in terms of soul or spirit: the element displaced by the mind in the Enlightenment. This is where an anthropological approach to the body diverges from the sociological 'body project' (Thomas 2003; Thomas and Ahmed 2004). The Western preoccupation with the mind-body division becomes redundant when we consider the elaborate taxonomies and epistemologies of the body in particular non-Western societies.

The Javanese body is conceived as multiple. The person in Java has two bodies: a visible material part, the gross physical body (*lair*); and an invisible and energetic part, the spiritual, subtle body (*batin*). Perception is based in the senses which pervade both. This body is metaphorized as a social body through the image of the microcosm and the macrocosm, a Hindu-Buddhist idea in which the person is an image of the universe. The material visible body is only one aspect of the body. Writing about performance in India, Kapila Vatsyayan observed that 'the body [is] … an essential prerequisite for transcending the body' (1980: 8). The microcosmic being of the dancer realizes the macrocosm, the totality of all that there is. Although the material body is not necessarily the seat of carnal weakness, it is not necessarily the delimiter of human aspiration either. Zarrilli's analysis of embodiment in a martial arts and healing practice in South India (1998) has a social context which is neither disenchanted nor post-god; the body has three parts, and these underlie practices which cross religion, place and time. In Java the dual perspectives of *lair-batin* also prevent objectification in any stable sense, and lead to discussions of dance not just in terms of its visibility but beyond, to metaphors and abstractions. A full performance of court dance includes dance movement, the resonance of *gamĕlan* music – gongs, drums, strings, vocals – the scent of perfume, rose petals and in some cases incense, as well as the visual glamour of the costumes, with their rich dark velvets and lavish gold adornments and headdresses. Dance movement brings the event into focus for the audience, but the experience of attending such a performance cannot be reduced to a purely visual experience. But the sensate experience of participating in and witnessing such a performance can produce a paradoxical situation where embodied dance choreography can symbolize disembodiment, in a similar fashion to Indian dance.

Movement and Metaphor

The metaphorization of the body blurs the boundaries between putting on a show and 'real' action. It bridges the representational and instrumental dimensions of performance. The body needs to be considered in its physical plenitude and as a generator of metaphors, which themselves provide a grounding for mutuality, the precondition for communication to take place (Sperber and Wilson 1988). These metaphors culminate in categories such as 'dance' and 'art'. Such concepts are necessary for purposes of comparison, but are produced through historical circumstances, shaped by contingency and social configurations (Goodman 1978; Bourdieu 1984), rather than by biology. Nelson Goodman's philosophical constructivism provides a useful alternative to correspondence theories of reference and the problem of definitions. It informs my object of untangling local dance discourses and explaining the contexts in which they occur. As there is a continuity between performed dance movement and everyday movement, my analysis aims to avoid criticisms made by dance philosopher David Best of 'dance' being lost when it is absorbed into 'movement'. I follow Best's proposal that dance should be subsumed 'under a concept which is determined by a whole set of circumstances by which it occurs' (1978: 132–37).

In these terms, dancing extends beyond the moment of embodied movement: it is a producer of movement and context after the moment of performance. It is both embodied action, and action which is referred to. It is 'bodily reality' and 'corporeal play', 'a tangible and substantial category of cultural experience ... which is vital to cultural production and to theoretical formulations of cultural process' (Foster 1996: xi), and, secondly, as the effect of a series of framings following Goffman's presentational model of behaviour (Wulff 1998a).[22] It is both lived and representational, and has the potential both to embody directly, and to mediate.[23] It is no less real for being performance (Schieffelin 1998). So rather than thinking of dance as *reducible* to text or symbol, I present it as action which also produces sense in the discursive domain. In particular, witnesses of dance generate metaphors and interpretations, which accumulate around the form as identifications, thereby enhancing its power as a cultural resource, even if that resource means different things to different interested parties and individuals.

My approach aims to resist 'thick description' in favour of a meta-interpretation which synthesizes concepts used by particular individuals who themselves enact a relationship between what they say and the cultural references at their disposal. What individuals say can be understood as a particular act of identification against a

---

22. Goffman's analysis of roles and situations using theatrical metaphors such as front and back stage to explain different aspects of behavioural presentation and 'multiple versions of reality' (1956: 131) and his dramaturgical metaphors have been used to explain social action as a complex system of symbolic and meaningful behaviour which produces an ordered understanding of the world. His model was intended as a fifth analytical perspective to complement existing technical, political, structural and cultural ones (1956: 154).

23. 'Human movement does not symbolize reality: it is reality. The experiences it provides are unique; they are not merely vicarious reflections of our real-life experience, through the medium of our symbolism' (Best 1978: 137). It also has 'virtual power ... [and is] a semblance of self-expression' (Langer 1959: 175, 189). Grau (2005) has drawn on her data about Aboriginal dance to make a case for the body being the landscape, not a metaphor for it.

background which could be called a script or a text, though I prefer to think of it as set of references. In this I follow Goodman's minimalist aesthetic models. The notion of 'cultural style' can be used effectively if due caution is applied but it can produce cultural reductionism when it arises in a semiotic approach. For example, Lewis's (1992) excellent analysis of movement in Brazilian capoeira, martial arts (ritualized self-defence) combines the material and metaphorical body, and balances the 'being seen' and 'being' perspectives already mentioned. Capoeira developed from slaves being prohibited from carrying any weapons. The main techniques employ every part of the body as an effective form of self-defence. Lewis approves of Peirce's semiotics because they are grounded in 'a comprehensive phenomenology' (1992: 9). He is normally at pains to specify place and voice, but he does raise the sceptre of interpretive reductionism when he generalizes the difficult movement when the body is turned upside down as a sign of the capoeira dancers' desire to invert social hierarchy, making the whole dance into a game which represents 'anti-structure' (1992: 83). This moment is at odds with the rest of Lewis's study, in which the exploration of 'strategic ambiguities' in capoeira suggests surprising moments of comparison with Javanese court dance, as we shall discover. For these reasons, then, I do not use a general semiotic model but try to locate the terms of reference of my analysis here as precisely as I can.

Following Goodman, I ask not 'what' but 'when' is dance (Hughes-Freeland 1997a). Bourdieu (1984) sees art as being capital for cultural politics because art is about a struggle, not things, in the context of the developments in Western art. This anti-Kantian view approaches Nelson Goodman's more radical claim that it is not the beautiful and the true which are at issue, but the appropriate: 'Truth and its aesthetic counterpart amount to appropriateness under different names' (1976: 264). The power to define appropriateness must be struggled for. The account that follows is thus 'a comparative study of these versions and vision of their making ... a critique of worldmaking' (Goodman 1978: 93–94).[24] Dancing is way of making a world because it extends beyond movement, beyond the body, through the responses of actor-dancers in relation to memory and expectations. Dancing dance and inscribing dance, whether in talking, writing or visual forms, are both situated social practices. Dance is something which Javanese people *do*, and something Javanese people do things *with*.

So, my account begins with local discursive idioms, but points to their wider implications. One analytical theme however represents my interpretation of what people have said, because the political culture of Java made it impossible to articulate in local terms. This theme concerns the extent to which dancing controls the individual.

Regimentation and Room for Manoeuvre

The individual body is where nature and culture meet. The body is the most 'natural' part of the self, but is also where sociocultural patterns are most visible, revealed in forms of dress and movement. Following Foucault, dance has often been seen as a technology of control by creating the social body and defining its gender. In these

---

24. 'Worlds are made by making such versions within words, numerals, pictures, sounds, or other symbols of any kind in any medium.'

terms education and acculturation are reduced to an effect of power and control, and personal agency is limited to the transgressive. As Foucault was developing his arguably dark domain of agency, anthropologists such as Victor Turner were celebrating the return of the ludic or playful in social processes. Turner's (1969) study of ritual in African societies led to him developing his model of ritual process, a model based on a contrast between social rules and anti-structure. Dance became part of a human experience that happens as if outside of society, a liberating form of human expression that freed people, momentarily, from social constraint. He later extended ritual process to dance and theatre as performance (Turner 1982), and merged the analytical boundaries between initiation rituals, social events such as carnivals, and specific theatrical performances as lived experience.

For Turner these moments of 'communitas' were associated with a more innocent spirit of fun, and also what has also been called 'inversion', a carnavalesque turning of the world upside down, a lighter and public version of Foucault's darker and altogether uninnocent transgressive styles of resistance. These collectivized moments of harmonious integration express faith in a human nature that transcends the divisiveness of self-interest and politics. Indeed, it could be said that at such moments society could be conceived of *as a* dance, as a metaphor for the loss of structure and social control. Kaeppler (1978) advised caution in thinking of dance movement as a 'reflection' of society. Rather, dance movement could *refract* normal social practice, an idea consistent with rules to be broken on particular ritual occasions, in a spirit of carnival.

Turner's processual framework, unsurprisingly perhaps given its tripartite narrative structure of beginning-middle-end, has been very influential. It also rests on a longstanding opposition between order and liberation which in Western thought has been traced back to the contrast of classical antiquity between the wild and dangerous dance of the female followers of Dionysius and the measured order of Apollo (Nietzsche 1956). This contrast marks the birth of tragedy, a perennial artistic form in Western dramatic culture, but it is also evident in debates about *bharata natyam*, which, as noted, were influenced by Western theosophy, which itself had already been shaped by the East.

The opposition between order and disorder might appear universal, but there is a need for caution. Feminist critic Janet Wolff has questioned why dance has so often been thought of as liberating (1995: 69). This equation of freedom with dance dates from the start of modernism in the late nineteenth century, and it has tended to operate in relation to gender, to women's dance. Dance has now become a trope of liberation within the language of social analysis. Wolff warns against this metaphor, and also against assumptions that dance is necessarily an embodiment of liberation from social constraint and the essentialism and polarization that this entails. Indeed, analyses of dances such as tango (Savigliano 1995) and samba (Browning 1996) as forms of resistance in relation to histories of authority and subversion have been criticized as being overly formalist, at the expense of processual and anti-essentialist approaches (Desmond 1997).

We need to hold back from assuming that dance implies liberation and communitas, and instead attend to what is a paradoxical conjunction of liberation and constraint in dance.[25] Anthropologists have long been aware that dance may promote disharmony and bring out latent conflict (Evans-Pritchard 1928: 459–60). Dancing – the movements and the events in which such movements occur – does not simply *reflect* an ideal, imagined or otherwise. Dancing involves forms of action within society which need to be determined according to their particular contexts. As will become clear, even dancing as formal and physically regimented as that of the Javanese courts, in a culture which favours stylistic conformity, may be understood as empowering for those who perform it in a different way from dancing tango or samba.

Various theoretical mergers have been proposed to present an account of embodied action (including dance) that achieves a balance between Foucaultian discipline and Turnerian bacchanal. One aims to correct Foucault's neglect of human agency by combining him with Merleau-Ponty (Crossley 1996). Others reject Foucault's discursive representational model in favour of Bourdieu's concept of '*habitus*' for analysing the embodiment and transmission of dance techniques (Thomas 2003: 118). Bourdieu revived the concept of *habitus,* developed in Mauss's early paper on techniques of the body (1935), to theorize the interpolation of social norms on the physical body. He also elaborated the concept of 'body *hexis*' as the basis of 'imperceptible cues' to apprehend 'the habitus … more precisely the harmony of ethos and taste' (1977: 82–83). In terms of this framework, dancing ceases to be discipline, and instead becomes a form of embodied knowledge (Bourdieu 1977: 81). Bourdieu's theory of practice is presented as critique of objectification and Durkheimian positivism in social analysis, and he prioritizes tempo and rhythm in embodied behaviour to counteract rule-based analyses of social action. Despite this critique, he remained highly sceptical of both phenomenological subjectivism (1977: 3) and of Goffman's actor-centred dramaturgical approach to self-presentation (1984: 579). Bourdieu thus reveals himself to be less oriented to agency and individualism than to collectivist analytical frameworks.

Indeed, De Certeau has criticized Bourdieu's model of practices for being 'an interiorization of structures (through learning) and an exteriorization of achievements (… *habitus*) in practices', for working only if the structure remains stable during this process. Otherwise there is a lag, and practices resemble the structure at the preceding point. As he notes, structures can change, but '*achievements cannot* … Achievements are the place in which structures are inscribed' (1984: 57). So although Bourdieu's *habitus* restores embodiment and the rhythms of everyday life to social analysis, we end up with something looking very like a rule-defined objectified social fact, with limited space for manoeuvre and agency.

For these reasons I prefer De Certeau's concept of 'space as … practised place' (1984) to Bourdieu's *habitus.* De Certeau's model of resistance within the context of discipline in everyday life gives space to agency while avoiding analytical excess in terms of liberation or constraint. He allows room for manoeuvre through his contrast between strategy and tactics. Strategy is the model for political, economic and

---

25. Blacking (1985); Novack (1995 cited in Reed 1998: 521); Lewis (1992).

scientific rationality' (1984: xix). Strategy has a Foucaultian character; it is the 'triumph of place over time; a panoptic place; where the "power of knowledge"' transforms 'the uncertainties of histories into readable spaces', with 'a certain power' being a precondition for this (1984: 36). Tactics by contrast form 'a calculus which cannot count on a "proper" (spatial or institutional location), nor thus on a borderline distinguishing the other as visible totality', and describe a 'calculated action determined by the absence of a proper place': 'an art of the weak' (ibid.: xix, 37).

De Certeau has been used by anthropologist John Pemberton to frame a critical analysis of a collectivized and generalized view of Javanese culture produced by top-down processes of government control, and to answer a question: how to write about such a culture 'without reformulating the very recuperative powers that one would critique?' (1994: 19). De Certeau's notion of 'the everyday' reveals 'Javanese' culture as originating in the penetration of the colonial 'Javanese' court by Dutch concepts, a form of domestification which continued during the New Order, when the repression of fear secured the appearance of normal life (1994: 8). 'Java' has, as Pemberton has argued, been used as an ideological figure.

While recognizing the appeal of this analysis, I would argue that Pemberton's arguments are not particular to Java. It is indeed important not to overstate locality and 'otherness' in cultural concepts (Hughes-Freeland 1997a: 473–95). As in *bharata natyam*, imported ideas have been assimilated in dance discourses to separate court dance from the context which produced it, and send it out into the world as classical culture. Also, this critical perspective ignores the experiences of the actors whose embodied reality becomes constituted by ideas they inherit and develop about themselves, their family and their community.

An alternative theoretical means of recuperating 'Javanese culture' using De Certeau reveals a counter-process to the operations of colonial and state power. Although my subject is ostensibly prestigious performance which comes out of elite, upper-class practices, it is not simply homogenous, static or monolithically powerful and approved, nor is it liberating in any clearly contrastive way with the social procedures which produce the disciplined dancing body.

De Certeau's model is helpful for unthinking some of the truisms about power centres and prestige. Associated as they are with resistance, subalternity and social spaces which cannot be read nor controlled and regulated, tactics might seem inappropriate to what has been described as an 'exemplary centre' in a political and moral sense (Geertz 1980:11–18). Nor is court dance movement in any sense 'make-shift' (De Certeau 1984: xiv). Nonetheless, the interpretations of people I interacted with in Java demonstrate the importance of paradox in the relationship between social values or ideals and their articulation in everyday life. As such, these may be understood as a form of 'anti-discipline', the effect of 'inferior access', working against the retainer colonial and postcolonial political regimes.

De Certeau's paradoxical and deconstructive approach to the everyday life of the exemplary centre is also supported by recent arguments concerning the Southeast Asian state. This has recently been characterized as having 'unreadable' regions which produce cycles of dynamic transformation, and a fluidity and substance which cannot be contained by bureaucracy in a 'rational' way.[26] Even peculiarly Southeast modes of state coercion might not be as ubiquitous and determinative as has been claimed. Postcolonial states share similar rhetorics of cultural identity or solidarity, but these are do not necessarily impinge predictably on everyday life practice. Indonesian cultural policies have promoted 'local peaks' (*puncak daerah*) of culture in a pluralistic polity, although Java culture has been privileged, largely because of the Javanese domination of the Indonesian elite and also because development has tended to flow from Java to the outer islands, as have people, including the many who are resettled though the policy of transmigration. The dominance of the Javanese is often commented on, normally in negative terms, and even, as we will discover, by the Sultan of Yogyakarta himself. Conversely, Javanese people have felt their cultural identity to be in crisis (Slamet 1982), and have objected to the state's cultural definition of Javanese-ness and the homogenizing potential of the rhetoric of custom and tradition (*adat* and *tradisi*). Cultural engineering on the part of governments has been known to etiolate previously dynamic and compelling forms, as has been the case with Malaysian *zapin* (Nor 1993) and *bangsawan* (Tan 1993). As we shall see, state policy becomes real through the everyday running of Indonesian bureaucracy, but, as elsewhere, this bureaucracy is fragmented and heterogeneous and less homogenizing than is often claimed (Handler 1988).

I do however diverge from De Certeau's formulation of society and the body as text. He takes a Foucaultian view of the body as 'inscribed', written on by social laws, which reproduces and realizes a textual 'fiction' that entextualizes individual bodies into a body politic: 'a body is itself defined, delimited, and articulated by what writes it' (1984: 139–42). In his 'scriptural economy', the fleshly materiality of the body loses the possibility of resistance to the discursive determinisms of the state. I qualify his logocentric excesses, as befits the supple subtlety of the Javanese body which, even as it is regimented and written about, creates a rhythmic space for resistance, a node of agency, and the indeterminacy of orality.

Instead of accounting for court dance as culture as being imagined by states and represented in rhetoric, I approach it as sets of situated practices comprising processes, negotiations and forms of resistance, which include state discourses. Cultures are dynamic, contradictory, and are made by the tactical actions of individuals; however circumscribed, there must be scope for personal creativity and social constraint, however oblique. Javanese court dancing incorporates cultural knowledge as embodied practice. Dancers themselves distinguish dance from the other (visual) arts, explaining that, apart from costume, musical accompaniment and so forth, the only material a dancer has is his or her own body. The skill of dance movement therefore lies in self-presentation and both physical and emotional (self-) control. At the level of cultural politics, the embodied visibility of Javanese court dance has given it an important role in the process of culture building, as has been the case in Indonesia since the 1950s where culture is based on appearances. It represents a maximally

---

26. Scott (1998); Day (2004). 'Tactics' and also 'the everyday' are parallel in Scott's (1985) analysis of rural resistance.

public and formalized expression of embodied politeness and the significance of physical gesture and movement in social interaction. Contemporary cultural policies in Indonesia incorporate active bodies into performance and sports, and organize competitions to channel potentially disruptive energies. At the same time, it empowers individuals by giving them the means to manoeuvre tactically through the manifestations of state and bureaucratic strategies.

From one perspective, then, the court is a 'panoptic place', and becomes a key symbol or reference for imagining order and enacting display and spectacle. From 1966 to 1998, Indonesia's government fostered political conformity and hegemony, and, within that context, the highly formalized dance movement of the Javanese courts might appear to reproduce this social control. From another, it is a site of immanent subversion, marked by the prophetic millenarianism that has been a longstanding feature of Javanese political thinking (Florida 1995). The practitioners and commentators of Yogyakartan court dance, aristocrats and retainers, also implicate dance in this idea. Dance is more than it appears: it is a site of latent resistance and concealment, and a source of tactics which work against other institutional locations – the centralized power of colonial and, now, state institutions. The role of Yogyakarta in the struggle for Indonesian independence during the 1940s is mixed with the circumstances of its foundation in the mid-eighteenth century. The idiom of resistance and revolution continues to be used, both within nationalist discourses and in counterpoint with them. What is at times consensus at other times becomes criticism. I propose to think about dance as both historically generated and generative, but I see the drivers as social actors who, in their various social roles (including that of patron), are not just at the mercy of those who provide them with the means to earn a living. In my experience, within the political constraints discussed above, Yogyakartans still invoked the struggle to be unique, even though heroism had gone into hiding, becoming a metaphor for 'the struggle of life'.

This book, then, presents Javanese court dance in Yogyakarta as a significant embodied practice produced by fleshly material bodies with a metaphorical force which goes beyond the visual and material aspects of embodiment. Javanese interpretations tend to dematerialize substance and appearances, although these have everyday importance for denoting prestige and status. Starting from the body is an analytical perspective on Javanese court dance that reveals the processes of disembodiment in indigenous models. Metaphors of conflict and unification serve the symbolism of the state, but they also demonstrate how poetics replace open political debate. Ambiguous and oblique metaphors of resistance and transcendence used in discourses about court dance and Javanese practices themselves are tactics to evade incorporation.

The fine discriminations and interests of particular groups and individuals within the court and their memories of past practices have both contributed to a sense of continuity, through the transmission of embodied practices and the interpretive field of rationales and constructions of court dance. The moralizing and martial ethos of Yogyakarta-style court dance has been formulated by individuals who grew up in the court of the eighth Sultan of Yogyakarta. To understand the relationship between court dance and the Indonesian state, we have to go back to the colonial memories which have informed cultural politics since independence, collusively and critically. Having established the importance of this late colonial ethos, in Chapter 3 I trace the reconstruction of dance during the postcolonial period. Chapter 4 explores the physical experience of dance training, and what dance contributes to social skills. Chapter 5 investigates how a particular dance symbolizes political power in relation to aesthetics, metaphysics and gender representations. Chapter 6 examines the official philosophy of court dance. Chapter 7 explores the diversification of patronage of court dance, including tourism and increasing commoditization. And Chapter 8 draws some conclusions about the lessons of this ethnographic example for dance anthropology, and also points to developments in Indonesian cultural politics following the end of Suharto's New Order.

Chapter 2

Before the Nation: The Heyday of Court Dance

Court dance survived the end of colonialism because of processes which occurred in the last thirty years of colonial rule during the reign of Sultan Hamĕngkubuwana VIII (r.1921–39). This period also marked the start of the nationalist movement in Java. The eighth Sultan's reign made it possible for court dance to have a place in cultural politics after independence, and also consolidated the court repertoire.

Producing Memories, Making History

Javanese court dance is not an invented tradition, nor does it demonstrate an unbroken tradition stretching back to antiquity. The influence of the concept of 'invented tradition' (Hobsbawm and Ranger 1983) is evidence of how much ritual and political symbolism overlap. Nations and subgroups establish links with the past as they represent their present interests for the future. A brief historical overview will provide some background to the period regarded as the heyday of Yogyakartan court dance.[1]

Many attempts have been made to trace modern practice to the Hindu-Java period (AD *c.*400 to *c.*1400). God-kings (*dewa-raja*) sponsored ceremonial dances and spectacles for religious and political purposes. Different kinds of performances, including puppet theatre, mask plays, fighting dances and dance-dramas, are first mentioned on the inscribed copper plates of Jaha in AD 840, with actors coming from as far away as Sri Lanka and Southern India (Holt 1967: 281). The Javanese versions of the Mahābhārata and Rāmāyaṇa (henceforth spelled without diacritics in contemporary Indonesian contexts) and particular aesthetic principles have survived from this period (Zoetmulder 1974). The earliest written account of court dances in Java is found in the *Nāgarakṛtāgama,* a fourteenth-century chronicle from the reign of Hayam Wuruk of Majapahit (r.1350–89), but it provides no evidence for specific choreographic continuity.[2] The scant archaeological and textual sources explain little,

---

1. For a fuller discussion, see Hughes-Freeland (2006).
2. The Dutch scholar and colonial administrator, Pigeaud (1960–63) added extensive commentaries, including speculative and anachronistic glosses arguing for a structural correlation between past and present court practices which have inspired a number of Indonesian history-makers. A translation of another recension of the manuscript is more restrained (Robson 1995).

if anything, about the content of earlier performances, and have frustrated attempts to establish a factual historical account.

The Hindu-Javanese era closed with the kingdom of Majapahit's defeat by Java's first Islamic state, Demak (*c.*1478– *c.*1550), which was defeated by Pajang (1568–82), itself defeated by Mataram (1582–49). At this time, the *Kidung Sunda* (*c.*1550) described performances at royal funerary rites which included plays (*men-men*), beautiful dances (*igĕl*), martial dances (*babarisan*), dancing girls (*ronggeng*), shadow puppet plays (*pawayangan*), and mask plays (*patapĕlan*) (Holt 1967: 288–89). This period is particularly important in contemporary Indonesian history. The semi-historical Panĕmbahan Senapati Ingalaga (r. *c.*1568/1584–1601), and his grandson, Sultan Agung (r.1613–45), have been models of leadership for the Indonesian state. Sultan Agung consolidated the Islamic kingdom of Mataram in Central Java and formed a relationship with the Dutch East Indies Company (V.O.C.). He is credited with the creation of *bĕdhaya*, the court's most exclusive women's dance form which is practised to this day. Also associated with this period are the stylized Javanese shadow puppets (*wayang purwa*) and the masked dance theatre (*topeng*), allegedly invented by Sunan Kalijaga, one of the nine 'saints' responsible for bringing Islam to Java. For the next one hundred years Javanese politics was marked by political factionalism, rebellion, and the increasing involvement of the V.O.C. Finally, civil war resulted in the division of the Central Javanese dynasty into the Principalities of Yogyakarta and Surakarta.[3]

The core of the contemporary court repertoire of performance is regarded as an heirloom (*pusaka*) of Yogya's first sultan, Hamĕngkubuwana I (r.1749–92).[4] He founded the court and principality of Yogyakarta in 1755–6 after waging a war against his nephew, Sunan Pakubuwana III, head of the Central Javanese dynasty at Surakarta. Hamĕngkubuwana I initiated a gradual reworking of royal traditions to establish the legitimacy and distinctiveness of the court that could equal Surakarta as an *axis mundi* (Ricklefs 1974). Although legitimizing narratives also predate the forms back to the historical periods outlined above, this reign is a point of origin for Yogya-style court dance.[5] The reality of past practices has been less enduring and less fixed than certain historical texts might indicate. Instead there is a range of interpretations that combines archaeological and ideological interests to varying degrees. Javanese historiography conceals the contingency of events by writing them into a larger pattern of repeating cycles, eliciting precedents *after* the event. The first Sultan of Yogyakarta needed to establish stability and inscribe the foundation of the second principality in a structure of inevitability (Ricklefs 1974). Similar principles would be used later on a much larger scale when disparate colonized societies were unified into a nation state.

---

3. Ricklefs has written an engrossing history of this period, from 1677 to 1726 (1993), 1726 to 1749 (1998), and from the foundation of Yogya to the death of its first sultan (Ricklefs 1974).

4. See Appendix 1 for a list of the reigns of the sultans of Yogya.

5. One theory about what happened when the kingdom was divided is that Yogya received the 'old' forms, and Surakarta devised 'new' ones (Suharto 1981: 112), hence the older 'origins' of some dance forms.

The work of contingency in the production of the court repertoire is still concealed by narratives of origin, but much of the repertoire in the late twentieth century would not have been instantly recognizable a hundred years earlier, even though the repetition of established practice and precedent is valued over innovation or individual artistry. Performances act as references for other 'texts'; for instance, *wayang wong* dance-theatre is modelled on the shadow puppet theatre. Other dramatic genres are identified by the source of stories they draw on, the main ones being the Indian epics Mahābhārata and Rāmāyaṇa, the Southeast Asian Pañji tales, the Javanese Damarwulan folk tales, and the Malay-influenced *Sĕrat Menak* which recounts the adventures of the Prophet Muhammad's uncle. So each kind of performance event is built upon a set of references to existing texts and practices. However, although each event supposedly repeats a previous one, no two performances are ever identical. Even the oldest of the surviving conventional forms have been practised with different inflections over time, and each sultan made adjustments or additions to the repertoire. Not all of these have survived, including the mysterious *kĕmbang* and *ronggeng* dances involving flowers, shields and snakes, witnessed by Raffles when he was Lieutenant-General in Java during the Napoleonic wars (1811–16).[6]

A debate about the ritual significance of court dance developments in Hamĕngkubuwana's reign illustrates the Javanese approach to history. Prof. Dr Soedarsono, a leading dance historian and former head of the Academy of Performing Arts (ASTI), has argued that when Yogyakarta was founded, *wayang wong* replaced *bĕdhaya* as state ritual. He traces the form back to the tenth century '*wayang wwang*', in which Mahābhārata stories about the conflicts between the Pandhawas and their cousins, the Korawas, were performed without masks (1984: 36–38).[7] Other evidence suggests that *wayang wong* was established in the mid-nineteenth century during the reign of the fifth Sultan, but even then it was not clearly defined and did not become fixed in its present court form until after the 1920s (Lindsay 1985). This is a good example of how particular court forms are given deeper histories to increase their significance from ceremony to ritual, which in turn imbues regimes with legitimacy.

The Court Repertoire

What follows is an introduction to the repertoire. We will be returning to most of these forms and their transformations in greater detail later. The dance repertoire of the Kasultanan court of Yogyakarta (Table 2.1) was established by the start of

6. Raffles (1978 [1817]) also witnessed the Sultan's Nyutra soldiers performing fighting dances using bows and arrows, and *bĕdhaya* and *srimpi* dances. In the 1830s, in the Mangkunagaran court in Surakarta, Scottish broadsword dancing was popular (Carey 1992: 461). Carey has written about court culture from the British period (1811–16) (1974; 1992) up to the end of the Java War in 1830 (1981), and discusses the relationship of politics and *wayang wong* in the reign of the third Sultan (1993).

7. The court centres still squabble about who created or 'revived' *wayang wong*. Lombard wonders whether Chinese patronage contributed to its development in the late eighteenth century (1990, II: 227–28), a theory not commonly discussed in Yogya.

Haměngkubuwana IX's reign (1940–88) and passed on to his son. During the colonial period, court dances contributed to the event associated with specific ritual or ceremonial occasions. Court usage continues to identify each form by a name that also implies the context in which it figures. Although I use the word 'dance', Javanese language codes do not allow a general word for 'a dance'. In the 'familiar' language code (*ngoko*) the word '*joged* is used of dance in a general sense, but is not usually applied to court dance, which is distinguished from practices done outside the court. Javanese-speakers either refer to court dance according to specific named forms associated with particular rituals and ceremonies, or as *běksa*, which refers to a unit of movement. Performers are described either as 'the one who does dance movement' (*ingkang běksa*), or according to the name of the character being danced. Javanese language does not distinguish dance and drama as Western audiences usually would. Dance-theatre has plots (*lakon*) that are executed through dance movement (*běksa*). Characterization is expressed through a system of movement which I refer to as 'modes', to avoid confusion with dances as *forms*, and regional variations as *styles*.

Table 2.1 Court repertoire 1940–88

Name	Form	Participants[8]
Bědhaya	ceremonial abstract dance	nine women
Srimpi	fighting dance	four women
Lawung	fighting dance	sixteen men
Etheng	fighting dance	twelve men
Wayang wong	dance theatre	men and women
Golek Menak	dance theatre	men and women
Běksan (or *pěthilan*)	set fight from either dance theatre	men/women in pairs
Golek	adornment dance	one woman
Klana	adornment dance (sometimes masked)	one man

Dancing is not just a visual form, but involves the hierarchy of senses. Every Javanese court dance form uses some or all of the following elements: architectural space, dancers, dancer-actors, performers, singers, musicians, choreography, music, songs, costumes, make-up, spoken introductions (*kandha*), texts performed by a 'puppeteer' (*dhalang*), dialogues (*antawacana* and *pocapan*), offerings of flowers and incense, and an audience. Although each audience brings its own expectations, these vary according to the knowledge or interest each individual brings: an audience of family members with practical performance and cultural knowledge will experience the dance event quite differently from an audience of visitors from outside Yogyakarta who respond to the immediate sense data as best they can.

All Indonesian dances have been described as war dances (Onghokham 1983), but it is helpful to classify the court repertoire into women's dances, fighting dances, dance theatres, and solo dances.

---

8. In Table 2.1 the number and gender refer to normal practice, but these sometimes vary.

Group dances for women

There are two group dance forms for women, *bĕdhaya* and *srimpi*. *Bĕdhaya* is the longest and most complex dance choreography, and particular dances are named after the dominant musical theme.[9] Nowadays nine young women (usually) perform it for grand occasions, such as the sultan's birthday, foundation and accession anniversaries, royal marriages, and receptions for important visitors of state. A form for seven dancers used to be patronized outside the court in the residences of princes and regents. *Bĕdhaya* is still the most demanding form for women, due to the slowness and subtle differentiation of its movements and the duration of the dance. In the past it could last over two hours, but most court *bĕdhaya* dances nowadays last about one hour.

The dance has two main sections, framed by stately militaristic entrance and exit marches (*kapang-kapang majĕng* and *kapang-kapang mundhur*). The first section (*lajuran*) is abstract and embodies philosophical and moral meanings. The second is also abstract, but is accompanied by song from a narrative, most commonly the *Sĕrat Menak*, a text from the Malay epic *Hikayat Amir Hamzah* recounting the conquests of the Prophet Muhammad's uncle (Soedarsono et al. 1989), the Mahābhārata, or a story from a Javanese legend or chronicle (*babad*). Most dances have as the second part a dagger fight between the two leading dancers, though sometimes bows and arrows are used. This fight represents a conflict in the story, and is often an act of resistance before the submission of the female character to the ardour of her suitor. The conflict is also subject to interpretations that go far beyond the particulars of the original narrative. Any inherent drama is muted through the regular pacing, stylized gestures, and the impassive faces of the dancers.

Choreographers emphasized the martial elements in *bĕdhaya* as distinctively Yogyakartan in contrast to *bĕdhaya* dances at the Kasunanan court at Surakarta, although older choreographies do not have fights. Both courts trace the *bĕdhaya* form to Sultan Agung's reign (1613–46). According to legend, the dance was first performed by Agung's supernatural spouse, Ratu Kidul (Queen of the South). This is commemorated at the annual anniversary of the *susuhunan's* accession in Surakarta when the *Bĕdhaya Kĕtawang* is performed. Subject to extensive prohibitions and regulations it is as ritual expression of the legitimacy of the ruler. Yogyakarta no longer reserves a special dance for accession anniversaries, but *bĕdhaya* remains an important symbol of the sultan's power (see Chapter 5).

Srimpi dances are choreographies for four female dancers who duplicate one pair of rivals. A simplified form of *bĕdhaya* (Surjodiningrat 1970: 23), *srimpis* share sources and themes with *bĕdhaya*, and are either performed before them or at less grand occasions. Normally lasting less than an hour, these dances, like *bĕdhaya*, have entrance and exit marches followed by two sections. The first part is a protracted build-up (*enjeran*), as the rivals vie with each other to the accompaniment of a chorus.

---

9. See further Brakel-Papenhuijzen (1992). A ten-minute section of *Bĕdhaya Gandakusuma*, in rehearsal by Siswa Among Bĕksa is included in Hughes-Freeland (1988) and may be found at http://www.oraltraditions.org (Hughes-Freeland 2005).

After the story is sung, the music swings into the vigorous *ayak-ayakan* rhythm and the dancers draw their daggers and engage in battle. As the loser falls to one knee, the conventional pose for defeat in court dance, the music eases back to the *kĕtawang* rhythm. *Srimpi* fights are more elaborate and dramatic than those in *bĕdhaya*, but *srimpi* is nowadays considered a less prestigious form and certainly makes fewer demands on its dancers and audiences. An exception is *Srimpi Rĕnggawati*, performed by five dancers, which refers to the tale of how Princess Rĕnggawati rescued King Angling Dharma, who has been bewitched and turned into a white bird. This dance may have been inspired by or inspired a '*buksan*' (*bĕksan*) in a noble house. A British traveller attending a reception given by Tumĕnggung Mĕrtonĕgara in mid-nineteenth-century Yogyakarta witnessed a number of performances, including 'srimpis' and a 'buksan … a scenic performance' about Prabu Sindolo who turned into a bird, performed by six girls (d'Almeida 1864, II: 154–59). *Srimpi Rĕnggawati*, like *bĕdhaya* (for nine dancers) and *lawung* (below), is considered to be an heirloom of the first Sultan. Performances of these dances were restricted to the court, due to their difficulty (Suryobrongto 1981b: 32). Both *bĕdhaya* and *srimpi* use the feminine dance mode (*bĕksa putri*, literally 'princess or daughter dance'), which is also used for women's roles in *wayang wong*, whether performed by men or women.

Group dances for men

Male dance modes are more numerous, and are associated with different body types and characters, or with shadow puppet characters. The male dance modes form a continuum between dancing which is refined and restrained (*alus*), and robust and energetic (*gagah*). The Yogyakartan court is famous for its fighting forms for men and women, which represent its militaristic past. The male dances include dialogue and joking as the dancers make their bets on each fight, and evoke the lively macho ethos of the court barracks and the tournaments (*watangan*). In colonial times these tourneys took place on the court's north square to a *gamĕlan* accompaniment every Monday and Saturday (Surjodiningrat 1970). The most prestigious of these dances is *Bĕksan Lawung*, a series of lance (*lawung*) fights between champions on horseback (Suryobrongto 1976: 15). The 'great' (*agĕng*) form, also known as *Bĕksan Trunajaya*, commemorated the Trunajaya section of the Nyutra corps who originally performed it (Suryobrongto 1981b: 102). The *lawung* fights use forceful muscular movements accompanied by the powerfully accented *gangsaran* music and the distinctive 'thud' of the *bĕdug* drum, and still provide the best opportunity for male dancers to demonstrate the spirit of its 'creator', Yogyakarta's first Sultan (Suryobrongto 1981b: 31–33). It uses 'robust' male modes while the 'small' (*alit*) form, in which two dancers wear distinctive feathered headdresses (but do not represent cockerels as some suggest), is for 'restrained' and mixed male modes. Nowadays both forms are performed by up to sixteen dancers but in the late nineteenth century a 'Great Lawung' was performed by forty-two men (Groneman 1888: 51–52). In the late colonial period the privileges associated with these two forms represented the division of power between the sultan and his prime minister, who received his salary from the Dutch government and acted as its representative at the court. *Bĕksan Lawung Agĕng* was associated with royal marriages, and would be performed in the prime minister's residence (Kĕpatihan) to represent the sultan in his absence. The following day *Bĕksan Etheng*, another fighting and gambling dance, would also be performed here by twelve dancers.[10]

Nowadays both these dances, regarded as heirlooms of the first Sultan, retain their function as ceremonial entertainment. *Bĕksan Etheng* was performed in 1982 in the Pagĕlaran for the opening of the Sĕkaten market to celebrate the Prophet's birthday. Bĕksan Lawung remains more exclusive and is normally only performed for very grand occasions in the court, such as the sultan's birthday in 1989. On that occasion the 'Great' or 'Strong' version was performed by eight men, with two commanders, two attendants and four 'strong' combatants, performed by Yogyakarta's most senior cultural figures. Another commonly performed version is *Bĕksan Lawung Jajar*, in which the four combatants are lower-ranking, red-faced *jajar*s in the court hierarchy.

Dance theatres and extracted dances

Other forms in the repertoire are either dance dramas or excerpts (*fragmen* I.) from the larger forms, *wayang wong* and *golek Menak*. *Bĕksan* (or *pĕthilan*) are short dramatic fighting duets or quartets, based either on *wayang wong* or, from 1970, on *golek Menak,* and are more commonly performed than the plays from which they derive.

Wayang wong was conceived as a form of human shadow theatre, and has been given an ancient genealogy, as already explained. In the Yogyakarta court it enacts stories from the Mahābhārata or, less commonly, a hybridized combination with the other ubiquitous Indian epic, the Rāmāyaṇa. During the reign of the eighth Sultan these performances often lasted for three days. After his death, there were only three four-hour-long fragments, performed on prestigious occasions such as the Sultan's birthday or on dance associations' anniversaries. The performances include spectacular group choreographies, dramatic fighting scenes, and humorous comic interludes, but some argue that contemporary audiences find the long and formalized Javanese dialogues difficult to understand and boring to watch, and interest latterly has turned to *golek Menak* and choreographies from princely houses, outside the court repertoire.

Golek Menak is inspired by the *golek* (rod puppet) theatre, and enacts stories about the prophet Muhammad's uncle from the *Sĕrat Menak*, also a source for *bĕdhaya* and *srimpi*. *Golek Menak* was Hamĕngkubuwana IX's personal contribution to the court repertoire, and incorporated styles of music and dance from West and Central Java and West Sumatra. In *golek Menak*, dancers have to imitate the angular neck and shoulder motions and the straight wooden hands of the rod puppets. This produces a jerky motion which is very different from feminine and restrained male movement modes as performed in *bĕdhaya, srimpi,* and *wayang wong,* where movement has to be very fluid and graceful, with the feminine mode being characterized by a continuous turning of the wrists and neck. During the ninth Sultan's reign (1940–88), *golek Menak* was performed in the court mostly as female

---

10. Dewan Ahli Yayasan Siswa Among Bĕksa (1981: 36–7).

fights. It became popular for the novelty of women dancers fighting with lances and, on special occasions, battling princesses mounted on huge brightly coloured eagles, who off-stage would grumble about the suffocating heat of their enormous feathered costumes.[11]

Solo dances

Most court dances are group dances, which carry more prestige and social value. This is demonstrated by the fact that the two solo forms, *klana* and *golek,* were not included in the court repertoire until the 1930s.

Klana represents a man adorning himself to meet his beloved. Different dances portray different characters from the Pañji cycle, using the dance mode appropriate to each character. These dances are derived from masked dance-dramas (*topeng*) performed in villages. After being revived outside the court, they were performed unmasked inside the court from around 1937.[12] *Klana* was often promoted through local government-sponsored competitions in the 1980s, and is also performed masked or unmasked at weddings and concerts outside the court.

Golek is influenced by *klana.* After the dancer's entrance, a song (*sĕkar tĕngahan or alit*) describes her beauty, and she dances in place and in a circle making hand gestures to depict her toilette. *Golek* was first performed in the court in the 1930s by a male dancer in female dress.[13] The dance was sent to Holland for the marriage of Crown Princess Juliana and Prince Bernard in 1937 (Suryobrongto 30/3/83). Until independence, young men and boys performed female roles in the dance theatre and in some *bĕdhaya* and *srimpi* dances. *Golek* is distinguished by the clapping by male singers during the rhythmic drumming sections normally associated with the dancing of *ledhek,* women who dance with men for money at *tayuban* events which mostly happen in villages, and with the *gambyong* dance in Surakarta. *Golek* remains close to the boundary between court and outside, and is often disparaged for being too like the overt eroticism of *ledhek.* However, after 1973 women performed *golek* dances in the court and in court-sponsored concerts, and it became the most popular female court dance in Yogyakarta. In contrast to other female dances, it 'gives an impression of rapidness and cheerfulness' (Koentjaraningrat 1959: 10), and dancers also like its simplicity and (relative) shortness – it lasts around 10–15 minutes. Like *klana* it is frequently performed at wedding receptions and at *kampung* celebrations for Indonesian Independence Day.

11. The 1939 production of the *wayang wong* play, *Pragolamurti* included a number of costumes and a fight on birds later used in *golek Menak* (*Tekstboek* 1939).

12. One source claims that K.R.T. Purbaningrat produced 'gentle' and 'demonic' (*dĕnawa*) dances for thirty-one *klana* performers in the Bangsal Kĕncana (Proyek Penelitian dan Pencatatan Kebudayaan Daerah 1977: 106, 110), but it is unclear when this happened and whether they were masked or not.

13. Created by the seventh Sultan's brother to imitate the dance of a wooden rod puppet (*golek*) which closes the shadow play in Yogyakarta (and sometimes in Surakarta), *golek* was first used outside the court to end the dance operettas patronized by princes and prime ministers from the late nineteenth century (Lelyveld 1931: 64–65; Choy 1984: 56).

The Legacy of Hamĕngkubuwana VIII (r.1921–39)

The last reign under the colonial regime was regarded as the heyday of court performance. In 1983 court retainers (*abdidalĕm*) estimated that by 1939 there would have been about 8000 *abdidalĕm* and soldiers. With the exception of close relatives or spouses of the Sultan, all dancers belonged to his staff inside the court (*jĕro*), in contrast to staff working outside (*jaba*) for the prime minister (*patih*). They were organized into various groups. *Abdidalĕm punakawan bĕdhaya jaler* were ceremonial attendants who had the best access to the Sultan and, reputedly, the best looks. Some became the highly privileged male *bĕdhaya* dancers who dressed as women to perform *bĕdhaya, srimpi*, female roles in *wayang wong* and, later, the *golek* dance. *Abdidalĕm prajurit* were the soldiers who performed in fighting dances and dance theatres and marched in the impressive *garĕbĕg* ceremonies three times a year. *Abdidalĕm punakawan* were attendants of lower birth with responsibilities such as bringing chairs on stage for important roles in the dance theatres. *Kĕparak* were female retainers who were figures of authority in the women's quarters with special ritual and ceremonial responsibilities, such as leading the *bĕdhaya* dancers out to the performance. *Golongan kanca wiyoga* were the 300 musicians and singers who were divided into 'east' and 'west': singers of the west (*wiyoga kilen*) accompanied *bĕdhaya* and *srimpi* dances, and those of the east (*wiyoga wetan*) accompanied *wayang wong* (Suryobrongto 18/5/83).

Each *abdidalĕm* held a rank in a hierarchy. At the bottom were *magang*, unlettered and unsalaried apprentices who, after a period of service, would be promoted to *jajar*, and then, if successful, up the ranks of *bĕkĕl, lurah, wĕdana, riya* and *bupati*. Each promotion resulted in a new title and name, from Raden Bĕkĕl up to the prestigious Kangjĕng Raden Tumĕnggung (K.R.T.) with names ending in -nĕgara, or –ningrat. Names also described a person's work: Sasra for drinks, Rĕsa for tea, Nata for electrics, Mangun for chairs, Kawindra or Widya for the Widyabudaya Library, and Atma for *abdidalĕm bĕdhaya jaler* (Suryobrongto 18/5/83). The twin hierarchies of inside and outside the court and the three main groupings were discontinued after independence, but the hierarchical organization within the court has continued even since the tenth Sultan initiated a process of 'modernization' in the late 1990s.

The organization of dance training within the court was structured around *wayang wong, bĕdhaya* and *srimpi*. Despite its hierarchical structure, the court was responsive to talent. Dancers were recruited from all levels of society in rural and urban communities and incorporated into the court hierarchy. A leading dancer and musician, K.R.T. Wiradipradja (b. 1907) told me how he entered the court in the 1920s as a *magang* with the title '*abdidalĕm jajar punakawan bĕdhaya*'. His duties were to paint puppets and masks and do life drawing. When he showed an aptitude for performance, he was promoted to the higher rank of *abdidalĕm bĕdhaya*, and he danced 'apprentice' (*cantrik*) roles from the age of sixteen. Three years later he was performing the major *wayang wong* role of Gathotkaca (pers. comm.1983).

There were about forty court dance teachers at this time. Male dance teachers were responsible for the selection of performers from the trainees, and could earn between thirty and fifty gulldeis a month depending on rank, a decent wage by court standards (Suryobrongto 30/3/83). They were accountable to the Director of

Performance, a post held by Haměngkubuwana VIII when he was Crown Prince (1914–21). The Director had to have musical as well as choreographic skills, unlike many eminent dancers. Gusti Suryobrongto unashamedly admitted to having 'tin ears' and no sense of melody.

There were sixty *bědhaya–srimpi* dancers in the female quarters (*kěputren*), including the Sultan's wives and daughters, and daughters of court officials or nobles. According to a senior court dance teacher, K.R.T. Dipuradanarta, the most experienced dancers worked on *bědhaya*, the less experienced ones on *srimpi*, training on alternate days (pers. comm.1989). These trainees also had ceremonial duties which included acting as *manggung*, bearers of the royal regalia at *garěběg* and accession ceremonies. Talented dancers were rewarded with promotion, and might secure a royal spouse, including the Sultan himself. In 1938, one of the Sultan's secondary wives (*garwa*

Figure 2.1 B.R.Ay. Suryobrongto as a *bědhaya* dancer, 1938. Reproduced with permission from the Ywanjana-Suryobrongto family.

ampeyan) danced Endhel, a leading *bĕdhaya* role. Among the other dancers was B.R.Ay. Suryobrongto, who showed me her photograph of this group of dancers (Figure 2.1) and reminisced (5/4/83) about her own career. Granddaughter of the seventh Sultan and daughter of K.R.T. Duttadiprodjo, a high-ranking court official specializing in music and dance, she took up an apprenticeship in dance in the court when she was seven years old. She moved into the female quarters when she was fully trained, and was granted a new status and name, confirmed in a 'buttoning certificate' (*sĕrat kĕkancingan*). She made a grand marriage to G.B.P.H. Suryobrongto, son of the eighth Sultan, leading light in court performances, and a key source in this book. *Bĕdhaya–srimpi* dancers were not usually allowed to perform after marriage, but continued to teach dance if they wished.

Hamĕngkubuwana VIII is best remembered for his productions of *wayang wong*, and was the most enthusiastic patron since Hamĕngkubuwana V. After his accession, he advertised across the Principality for *wayang wong* trainees, and the best were appointed to his personal bodyguard, the Nyutra corps (Suryobrongto 20/4/83). Dance training took place daily, and it could take up to eighteen months of rehearsal before a *wayang wong* was ready for performance. During his reign there were eleven performances of which at least seven lasted for three days with up four hundred dancers. They were produced to celebrate events of state, such as the Sultan's sixty-fourth birthday, or a royal wedding in The Netherlands: a reminder that this court depended on colonial political and financial support. Dance audiences always included Dutch officials as special guests.[14] The plays were written under the Sultan's direction during the Islamic fasting month, confirming their status as 'sacred' heirlooms (Soedarsono 1984: 104). The play started at sunrise and ended at eleven or twelve at night. The enthroned Sultan sat at the centre of the Bangsal Kĕncana, the grandest court hall, with gleaming marble floors, and a hipped roof supported by rows of slender ornamented pillars. He faced east, a position symbolizing his identification with the Hindu god Wisnu (Holt 1967: 157; Suryobrongto 1981b). Behind him, in the green shadows, was the Prabayĕksa ('Great Aureole'), where the court heirlooms are kept. The performances took place on the long rectangular marble stage imitating the proportions of the shadow theatre screen, slightly below the raised floor of the Bangsal where honoured guests were seated. These

---

14. *Jayasĕmĕdhi* and *Sri Suwela* (3–6 September 1923); *Sambasabit* and *Ciptoning Mintaraga* (1925); *Parta Krama, Srikandhi Mĕguru Manah, Sĕmbadra Larung* (13–15 February 1928, for the marriage of two sisters and three daughters); *Jayapusaka* (14 July 1929, for the marriage of a brother, a sister and three daughters); *Sĕmbadra Larung* (26 February 1932); *Sĕmar Boyong, Rama Nitik, Rama Nitis* (22–24 July 1933); ibid. (18–20 August 1934 for the Sultan's sixty-fourth *tumbuk dalĕm*, most important of the eight-yearly *windu* birthdays); *Ciptoning Mintaraga* (16–17 January 1937 for the marriage of Crown Princess Juliana and Prince Bernard); *Mintaraga* (January 1938); *Prĕgiwa-Prĕgiwati, Ankawijaya Krama Angsal Siti Sundari, Pancawala Krama Angsal Prĕgiwati* (18–20 March 1939 for the fortieth day after the announcement of seven court marriages); *Pragalamurti* (19–20 August 1939, for the birth of the first child of Juliana and Bernard (Kats 1923; *Programma van de Wajang-Orang-Voorstelling* 1932–38; *Teksboek van de Wajang Wong Voorstelling* 1939; Suryobrongto 1981b: 46-7).

performances were social events. High-status guests were served frequent meals, and the court women played cards and gambled. There was also a large audience of distant kin, retainers, and their families. They were expected to bring their own mat, food and a coconut leaf to sweep the courtyard after the performance had ended for the night. After one three-day performance, over thirty thousand of these leaves were collected (Suryobrongto 30/3/83).

As mentioned, most of the current court repertoire gained its appearance and structure at this time. In *wayang wong* new costumes which looked more 'Indian' were designed to replace the simpler court dress of jacket and wrapped *bathik* (*sorjan* and *jarit*). These new costumes imitated the iconography of puppet characters in the shadow theatre (Soedarsono 1984: 236), as did the greater use of make-up, and the elaborated range of dance modes. Despite this increased semiotic imitation of the shadow play, *wayang wong*'s narrative balance shifted from dialogue and narration to more elaborate and technically demanding dance movement, distancing it from the shadow play's structural balance of movement and language Lindsay (1985: 87–96, 109–12, 142).[15] The Sultan's innovations for *bědhaya* were on a smaller scale. Older court officials explained that he introduced coloured ostrich feathers to be worn with gilded leather crowns by *bědhaya* and *srimpi* dancers because of his admiration for French can-can dancers, though they could not remember if he had ever seen it in performance. Previously only male *bědhaya* wore crowns; female dancers wore bridal hair-decorations and costume.[16]

Hamĕngkubuwana VIII's reign marks the end of dance as a purely oral tradition.[17] This period was formative for the players on the post-independence scene, and many who started out as court dancers, including some sons of the eighth Sultan, played a significant role in transferring court dance to national education. It also produced the memories and references that defined much of the discourse and values of the first fifty years of the postcolonial period. Dance had been transmitted through imitation and memorization, and a number were classed as heirlooms. Javanese people have valued objects and practices for having been passed down (*naluri*), but just as valuable inherited daggers only retain power if they are ritually sustained with annual cleansings or 'feedings' of arsenic, so dance will only be a significant inheritance if it is fed through memories, expressed not only as mental images and words but as embodied practice.

In my research I was struck by how many of the older people I spent time with brought to dance an inner life and passion, deriving energy from the memories dance embodied for them *personally* during this period. These experiences in turn produced

15. An employee of the Sanabudaya Museum suggested that more attention was paid to make-up because electricity replaced oil lamps in the court after 1925 (Pak Barsono 17/12/82).
16. Bird motifs are a feature in dance costumes across Southeast Asia (Garrett Kam 23/7/2006). It is unclear if the costume designers who introduced feathers for *bědhaya* were aware of this but they would certainly have known about the dance's association with heavenly nymphs and its use of flying movements.
17. Only one Yogyakarta manuscript (B/S 7), from Hamĕngkubuwana VII's reign, includes dance notation (Brakel-Papenhuijzen 1992: 280ff.); Lindsay et al. (1994: 37) suggest it is from Hamĕngkubuwana VI's reign.

ideas which were not shared unreflectively but discussed, sometimes heatedly. Over time these differences have been ironed out and have been processed into histories, becoming a political resource. Commemorative ceremonies and bodily practices carry 'social habit memory', in contrast to 'cognitive memory', which keeps 'the past in mind by habitual memory sedimented in the body' (Connerton 1989: 36, 102). However, this notion of a conventionalist and collectivized memory as 'unreflective traditional memory' (ibid.: 16) raises questions about who is doing the remembering – and the forgetting. Court dance might be explained as the embodiment of social memory, and the persistence of court dancing as an embodiment of memories of a version of Javanese identity that no longer exists, or maybe never did. But although dance can only be transmitted through the embodied practice of dancing and might seem to be a case of 'social memory', it is more than this. These practices are brought into cultural memory and then into history by the ways they are interpreted and rendered meaningful in what people say about them. So it is useful to approach social memory not simply as a collectivized and unified phenomenon, but as a processual and emergent level of production which also includes strategic forgetting. It will become clear that as court dance started to leave the court precincts, it also left behind its character as an oral tradition, and became the object of written codification.

The Ethos of Commonality and Militarism

Although the court constituted an elite which was highly differentiated by title and rank, members of the elite themselves regarded the ethos generated by *wayang wong* performances as egalitarian. Gusti Suryobrongto (1914–1985), son of the eighth Sultan, dancer of leading roles, and later personal secretary to his half-brother the ninth Sultan, argued vehemently that the ethos of these events was not hierarchical but one of comradeship and common endeavour. This was exemplified in the levelling effect of *bagongan*, the special court language which, unlike the other Javanese language codes, has one single generalizing word for 'you'.[18] He recalled sitting on the floor in a *wayang wong* performance while people of lower status in real life had higher status in the play and sat on chairs. This internal hierarchy also extended to the logistics of organizing the one thousand people or so – four hundred dancers, their helpers, the shifts of singers and musicians – who were responsible to their stage superior. In this way the play's internal rankings could subvert the ranking and elaborate status systems of court hierarchies. Gusti Suryobrongto had a life-long friend, R. Kawindra Susena, who I called Rama Sena out of respect. They were related through their maternal great-grandfather (a *tunggal mbah mindo* relationship, see Table 2.2), but as Rama Sena lacked a royal grandfather he was of a lower rank, unlike his half-brother who had the higher title of Raden Mas.[19] Together they revelled in memories of the generous allocation of baskets of food *per* role during performances regardless of real-life status, with the nostalgic pleasure of people remembering camping trips.

---

18. This is also the case in Japanese court language (J. Morby pers. comm. August 2006).

19. Rama Sena was also a sculptor, *bathik* painter, choreographer of martial arts, and father of twelve children who all became dancers or painters, he contributed to my understanding of dance and Yogya in many ways.

Gusti Suryobrongto was one of the leading voices for the relevance of court values at this time in the post-independence period. To some extent, the memories he chose to share were those which endorsed the relevance of the values of court dance to the Republic.[20] This emphasis was not on the court's ranking and elaborate status system but on its *commonality*, rather than egalitarianism proper, and is significant for later self-representations of the court circle in Yogya. It also raises questions about the theory of 'communitas' or 'anti-structure' (Turner 1969) that might be thought to be supported by these memories. The main roles in *wayang wong* were usually played by princes and high-ranking officials. There is no record of high-status people taking low-status roles as attendants. These performances reaffirmed the differentiation of role and responsibility within the court and the state, but they were also occasions for play and for bonding. A good dancer of lower birth and rank could be cast in a higher-status role, and was normally rewarded by promotion up the court hierarchy. Despite the ethos of communitas in large productions, court dance was social structure on legs, and also a means of climbing up the social ladder – both on and off stage. This was no undifferentiated festival, but a highly structured event with some elements of carnavalesque inversion which have given rise to a remembered ethos of equality, informed by later self-doubts among some of the court circle about the feudal dimensions of colonialism.

Table 2.2 The 'tunggal mbah mindo' *relationship between two key sources*[21]

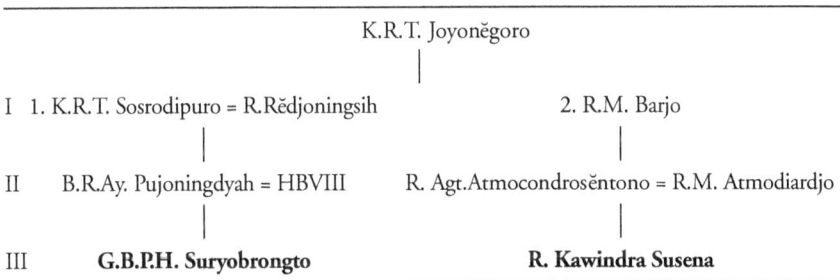

	K.R.T. Joyonĕgoro	
	|	
I 1. K.R.T. Sosrodipuro = R.Rĕdjoningsih		2. R.M. Barjo
	|	|
II B.R.Ay. Pujoningdyah = HBVIII	R. Agt.Atmocondrosĕntono = R.M. Atmodiardjo	
	|	|
III **G.B.P.H. Suryobrongto**	**R. Kawindra Susena**	

20. Similarly, the use of language in court dance is interpreted to accord with the Indonesian ideology of 'unity in diversity' to acknowledge the many ethnic and linguistic groups. *Bĕksan Etheng* uses court *bagongan*, Banyumasan dialect, Madurese, Buginese and Malay, a practical reflection of the different groups of soldiers who performed these early fighting dances (Djoharnurani 1991).

21. It is ethnographically relevant to mention that this kinship relation was not easy to establish. Rama Sena's wife had provided a version where R.M. Barjo was Joyonĕgoro's *grandson*, putting Rama Sena a generation below Gusti Suryo. When I asked Mbak Kadar again which version was right, she insisted that the other was correct, saying that the fact that cousins are allowed to marry in the court makes it 'more confusing'; she then changed her mind the last time I spoke to her (23/7/2006). Rama Sena's mother was indeed first married to R.M. Purwo, grandson of Hamĕngkubuwana VII through his daughter Juminah; the son of that marriage was R.M. Bagong Kussudiardjo, a well-known choreographer of 'new creations'. A *golek Menak* choreographer, K.R.T. Wiradipradja, also had the same great grandfather (through his father), but was not in the same circle.

Memories of this period also lead to the court being characterized by an ethos of heroic militarism. Gusti Suryobrongto and Rama Sena both emphasized the intimate relationship between dance and the martial arts in court performance over the centuries, reflected in the prevalence of fighting choreographies. Rama Sena himself ran a martial arts association using such a lethal technique that his students had been banned from participating in National Sports Week contests. During the 1980s he concentrated on developing fights for the plays produced by Gusti Suryobrongto's son and daughter-in-law's Suryakěncana dance association. His researches for this built on his previous knowledge of manuscripts while working as a 'polisher' of texts in the court library before independence. He remembered *Běksa Rangin*, a dance from Senapati's time based on self-defence which involved throwing daggers and lances in the air and catching them on the chest.[22] He maintained that martial arts had originally been taught by Chinese immigrants in Tuban, on the northeast coast of Java, home of Sunan Kalijaga, who had a Chinese father, and was one of the nine sages said to have brought Islam to Java from China. This military ethos was central to Gusti Suryobrongto's dance philosophy, as we will discover in Chapter 6.

For some in Yogya, the heroism of court performance was a sign of a resistance to contemporary power centres. They compared it to Haměngkubuwana I's dance patronage as resistance to the collusion of the house of Surakarta with the Dutch back in the early eighteenth century. I heard much about secret pacts between Yogya and Surakarta against the Dutch up to the time of the Java War (see further Carey 1981). One senior court dancer told me that the *lawung* dance was the result of the Dutch banning military training under the first Sultan (K.R.T. Dipuradanarta 18/7/83). Rama Sena had a similar theory that fighting dances had been a secret means to keep the court troops in peak condition after the Dutch had restricted military activities in the Principalities.[23] This nationalist oratory about 'the Dutch' was applied anachronistically to a time when there was no single enemy, and the Dutch were merely a trading company, struggling to feed their staff in Batavia. Such theories are historically unsubstantiated, but belong to a pervasive local oral tradition which is used to keep the heirlooms of the past alive in the present for the future.

Dance and Early Nationalism

The golden age of court performance was also a time when dance's future relevance through its educative role in the independent nation state was established. It is unlikely that dance would have gained its role as a form of producing a properly behaved Javanese person and a properly behaved Indonesian citizen had the eighth Sultan not used dance and drama to train appropriate codes of comportment, gesture and language.

---

22. Unfortunately he did not record his source, and our library searches in Yogya and Surakarta failed to track the manuscript down.

23. Lewis makes an identical point about Brazilian capoeira being martial arts concealed as dance (1992: 40). In both cases dance acts as a form of concealed action or indirection for those who perceive themselves as disempowered, as slaves or as colonial subjects.

Older dancers and retainers often spoke of the significance of all the royal children participating in dance training as part of their education. Hamĕngkubuwana VIII was an innovator and a modernist, and his sons were sent away from the court for a time to live with Dutch families before being instilled with court codes and values.[24] Despite this Western element to their education, eleven of the princes performed in *wayang wong*, including the future Hamĕngkubuwana IX who danced the hero Gathotkaca. The eighth Sultan is also remembered for his strictness (Suryobrongto 1981b: 101). Former *wayang wong* dancers spoke about the physical enactment of inner discipline, endurance and self-control while they were within the Sultan's gaze. They did not always remember or choose to mention that opium had sometimes helped them survive the lengthy performances (Suryobrongto 20/4/83).

Bĕdhaya and *srimpi* provided training in grace and decorum for all trainees, from princesses to male and female attendants. A dancer who mishandled her dagger in rehearsal would be reported to the Sultan and incur his wrath. Suryobrongto (30/3/83, 20/4/83) remembered his future wife being reprimanded for glancing sideways, instead of maintaining her gaze straight ahead and lowered to the floor as required by court convention. The Sultan also maintained strict discipline over women off stage, and the *kĕparak* checked that all male visitors had left the women's quarters at five o'clock each evening.

More importantly for long-term developments, Hamĕngkubuwana VIII took crucial steps to promote court dance as a form of education outside the court walls. In 1918, on his father's instructions when he was Crown Prince, he gave his brothers P.A. Surjodiningrat and P.A. Tedjokoesoemo a monthly subsidy to found Kridha Bĕksa Wirama for this purpose. Twelve other court performance experts were involved in setting up the new school (Suharti 1989: 6). This team became crucial for extending and modifying court practice. It also generated the conditions for an ongoing critique of dance practices inside the court, and was still producing argument and alignments within the community of court dance teachers and choreographers in the 1980s.

What were the reasons for extending court practices beyond the court's control? One theory is that court performance patronage had stultified following the untimely death of the first Crown Prince in 1913. This made his father fall into a depression, and he neglected *wayang wong*. Others said that Hamĕngkubuwana VII was generally stingy in his patronage of performance.

A more likely reason is the evolving nationalist movement. Both Central Javanese principalities were seats of proto-nationalist movements. The first nationalist association, Budi Utomo, had been founded by Dr Wahidin Soedirohoesodo, the court doctor, in 1908, and introduced Malay as its official language the following

---

24. His heir was sent aged four to live with a Dutch family in Sukabumi for a year. Here he learnt Dutch, etiquette, and gained his life-long passion for football. He then went to a Dutch boarding school and on to university at Leiden for nine years (1930–39) (Atmakusumah 1982: 26–31).

year. Meanwhile, the nationalist Islamic Union became Sarekat Islam in Surakarta in 1912.[25] This was followed in Yogyakarta by the modernist Islamic Muhammadiyah movement, founded by Ki Ahmad Dahlan in 1914. One view is that members of the newly formed student nationalist group, 'Jong Java', had approached the court with the suggestion it start a dance school (Suryobrongto 1981b: 108; Suharto 1981: 126–27); and subsequently two delegates worked with the school team. In 1926 Habirandha, a training school for puppeteers, was also established in the court (Wibowo 1981: 211).[26] By engaging with early nationalism in this way, the court unwittingly ensured that its performance culture would survive the radical political changes that lay ahead.

The Kridha Běksa Wirama dance school developed alongside Budi Utomo and the Tamansiswa schools ('Garden of Pupils'). Founded in 1922 by the educationalist Ki Hadjar Dewantara (1889–1959), a scion of the Pakualaman, Tamansiswa built on Budi Utomo's ideas. It played a crucial role in activating a modern Javanese identity by defining Javanese culture and providing a model of culture and character building as was later conceptualized in the newly-independent Indonesia. The Dutch had associated Islam with political unrest from the nineteenth century onwards (Kartodirdjo 1973: 69). Tamansiswa was syncretic, in contrast to the modernist Islam of Muhammadiyah, and shaped subsequent religious pluralism in Indonesian education (McVey 1967: 134). It expressed religious and political freedom within a Javanist cultural framework. It did not follow the colonial government's curriculum, nor did it receive a subsidy. It thus inspired self-reliance (*berdikari*) during Soekarno's presidency (Lombard 1990, I: 200). Tamansiswa's stance on education and citizenship was based on a multiple system of respect for God, parents, older siblings and teachers, and adumbrated the Javanese principle of 'leading from behind' (*tut wuri handayani*) for subtle but effective socialization.[27] It trained its pupils in Javanese

25. Kartodirdjo (1973: 145) discusses rumours about the Surakartan court involvements with Sarekat Islam (1973: 181–82), but does not examine the Yogyakartan court's nationalist activities. According to Rama Sena's stepfather, a court *wedana*, the seventh Sultan granted Dr Soedirohoesodo funds of 30,000 guilders and required all male *abdidalěm*s to join Budi Utomo, coordinated by Prince Surjodingrat; the other princes and women *abdidalěm*s did not join, but other royal children and grandchildren did (Sena pers.comm. 14/8/83).

26. Sears argues that these court puppeteer schools were founded to counter modernity by writing down and refining the plays to ensure their future and that of Javanese nationalism, as well as to control puppeteers (1996a: 151–2). The influence of theosophy in this enterprise is comparable to that on *bharata natyam* and Indian nationalism (Allen 1997).

27. The complete formula is 'setting an example from the front' and 'giving encouragement from the centre'. Kenji (1987: 215) shows how Ki Hadjar Dewantara's ideas of democracy and leadership influenced Soekarno's 'Guided Democracy' in the 1950s. The anthropologist Koentjaraningrat, who taught in Tamansiswa, thought that its Javanism held Indonesia back (1985: 75), a point reiterated by the tenth Sultan at Tamansiswa's Cultural Seminar II in 1999. Koentjaraningat's claim that Tamansiswa's ethos of suppressed heroism disappeared after independence was not vindicated by what I heard during research, including the comments about militarism.

music, dance and visual arts, combining custom and creativity to make a significant contribution to what became Indonesian art (Holt 1967: 195). Many of Yogyakarta's leading dance practitioners and administrators in the 1980s and 1990s were educated in the Tamansiswa system, and its influence remains strong in Yogyakarta and beyond.[28] As final evidence for the link between the nationalist movement and Kridha Běksa Wirama, its director, B.P.H. Surjodiningrat, set up the nationalist Pakěmpělan Kawula Ngayogyakarta in 1930. Nine years later its membership of 260,000 was already approaching that of Muhammadiyah; in 1951 it became a political party, the Indonesian People's Movement (Gerinda) (Ricklefs 1981: 178). Surjodiningrat remained in charge of Kridha Běksa Wirama until 1948, when R.R. Kusumobroto took over (1948–59), followed by B.P.H. Puruboyo (1959–1980s).

Kridha Běksa Wirama's Contribution to Dance Education

Patterns of cultural maintenance and transmission occur through particular social groups, whether defined by occupation, lineage, professional company, or family as is the case here. The first court dance school in Yogya and the nationalist Tamansiswa schools may be compared to the foundation of Kalakshetra shortly before Indian independence, and which produced a hybridized indigenous movement with training practices imported from ballet (O'Shea 1998). Court dancing had been family capital (Bourdieu 1984) until the founding of Kridha Běksa Wirama, which initiated its extension to the sphere of educational capital. Once this happened, a process of classicization began which would be carried forward by the modernizing nationalistic work with dance in the 1930s and 1940s and beyond. Bourdieu's theory of how practices change from the sphere of family capital to education capital in the context of national development and the imagined community provides a model for examining how particular group practices become part of broader national interests through the role of education, and can account for the broad similarities between the Indian and Indonesian examples discussed previously. At the same time, though, it is important to see what happens to those groups after the context has diversified. A transformation of capital does not necessarily mean that the previous sphere of value inherent in family capital becomes obsolete. Rather, these earlier values become associated with anti-commercial ones, and caught up in arguments about cultural value and the nature of art, as will become clear in Chapter 7.

Kridha Běksa Wirama and Tamansiswa are important institutions because they laid the foundation for contemporary dance education in terms of ideology, methods, and the gendering of roles. Kridha Běksa Wirama initiated the transformation of an essentially oral tradition to a written one. In dance training in the court the pupil began by being manipulated into the correct position by the teacher, and gradually

---

28. Kridha Běksa Wirama had the support of Mangkunagara VII, who invited its members to perform at his court in Surakarta and sent his eldest daughter to Yogyakarta to train with it (Suharti 1989: 8–9). Kridha Běksa Wirama was also patronized by the Java Institute, a cultural association established in 1919, which published the Javanese–Dutch periodical *Djawa* in Yogyakarta (Ricklefs 1981: 156ff.; Lombard 1990: 196–200).

progressed to imitating the teacher (*nyorekakěn*). Kridha Běksa Wirama staff developed a technique based on counting in cycles of eight to help the dancers keep time. They also standardized dance movement, nomenclature and choreography, and produced photographic records of 'correct' movements (Soerjadiningrat 1923, 1926; Suryobrongto 1981b: 108–9). They classified court dance movement into eight 'basic' dances (*joged pokok)* or modes on a continuum from restrained (*alus*) to rough (*kasar*) (see Chapters 4 and 6). They also formalized a practice of walking to music (*tayungan*), derived from the way court warriors used to walk in ceremonial processions (Carey 1992: 460–61), which trained male dancers in a sense of rhythm and the basic movement patterns for all the dance modes. By 1931 this formed the first stage of the curriculum that took four or five months to learn. Next came fighting (*enjer*) (levels 1 and 2), and then *klana* (gentle and strong dances). The *Saritunggal* training dance, created to teach the twenty-three feminine dance motifs (*běksa*), took ten to twelve months to learn.[29] Girls then learnt *Srimpi Pandhelori* and *Bědhaya Gandakusuma*.[30] Kridha Běksa Wirama published their formulations in *Djawa*, the periodical of the Java Institute, and in books of standard dance movement (*pathokan*).

These innovations fed back into court practice. Kridha Běksa Wirama instigated the convention of performing *wayang wong* in fragments lasting four hours instead of over three days, which became court practice during Haměngkubuwana IX's reign. *Tayungan* and *Saritunggal* both formed a standard part of the court training sessions established in 1973. It is also unlikely that *klana* dances would have become part of the court repertoire had they not been developed from the village masked tradition and standardized by Kridha Běksa Wirama (Resink-Wilkens 1924). By the 1980s all court dance associations used its counting and formal training dances, but there were still disagreements about the standard positions, and how to classify dance modes and transitional dance movements (*sěndhi*).

Most significantly for the future of court performance, Kridha Běksa Wirama initiated radical changes in the conventions regarding gender and its representations which would give court performance a more relevant contemporary significance for gender roles in early Indonesia. Previously, women could only perform *bědhaya* and *srimpi*. Female roles in *wayang wong* were danced by men. The reason women were not allowed to perform in the other forms was that they were deemed to be public and unsuitable for 'ladies', even though they took place inside the court. Women did not appear in a court production of *wayang wong* after independence until the early 1950s (Lindsay 1985: 88). These gradual changes are not well documented, and were related to me by the head of SMKI, Pak Pardjan (11/12/82). The first appearance of a woman performing in *wayang wong*, but not in a fighting dance, took place in Kridha Běksa Wirama in 1928. Women participated in dance fights using bows and arrows

---

29. This dance lasts for forty-six gong cycles; it has more transitions than the court version choreographed by Basuki and Kuswaraga, which has thirty-five gong cycles and lasts about thirty minutes (Tedjokoesoemo 1981).
30. Pringgobroto (1959); Tedjokusumo (1981). Sudharso Pringgobroto was responsible for developing Kridha Běksa Wirama's analytical dance instruction methods (Koentjaraningrat 1985: 308).

for the first time in 1935. After independence, in 1946, Kridha Běksa Wirama teachers helped to establish Irama Citra, the first national organization for what would become classical Javanese dance. In 1949 it staged the first-ever dagger fight between a man and a woman, bringing men and women closer together on stage than they had ever been. So Kridha Běksa Wirama initiated changes in gender conventions in court performance that had lasted for nearly two hundred years, and which produced the gendering of the repertoire as characterized above.

The Kridha Běksa Wirama teachers worked with existing court forms, but also introduced Western theatrical ideas based on mimesis. Inside the court, dance movement was considered to be above the animal domain and gesture was largely abstract, not mimetic; in *wayang wong*, monkeys were given human characteristics, and did not scratch. In the 1950s P.A. Tedjokoesoemo created *Langěn Tirta*, a dance based on the movements of animals (Wardhana 1981: 214). Kridha Běksa Wirama had also started to 'revive' masked dance, and performed complete masked plays, starting with stories from the Pañji cycles and then historical stories of the kingdoms of Singasari and Majapahit (thirteenth to fifteenth centuries). The Yogya court had not permitted the use of masks for humans, only for monkeys and demons, and masked performance had become associated with village performance, allegedly because the Surakarta court took on the development of masked dance theatre at the division of the kingdom in 1755 (Soedarsono 1984: 14).[31] There were still many masked dance troupes in villages during the 1930s but twenty years later Ki Hadjar Dewantara was already expressing his regret at their decline (Surjodiningrat 1970). Even at this early stage, then, Kridha Běksa Wirama was taking on a conscious role to preserve a disappearing heritage, an important theme in national cultural policy after the 1960s, and also innovating choreographies and producing students who would themselves expand and elaborate court movement styles and choreographies by incorporating movements and choreographies from outside.

Conclusion

The legacy of Haměngkubuwana VIII's reign was a dance ethos that would allow practices formalized under a colonial regime to become part of the culture of the Republic of Indonesia. The repertoire as practised in his reign, along with the innovations introduced by Kridha Běksa Wirama, was largely what was called 'court dance' in the reign of his son. The Sultan's educative and moralizing stance on dance as discipline, and the role of dance in early nationalist education, fortuitously gave it a function that would have relevance in the modern nation state. With hindsight it can be argued that his support of Kridha Běksa Wirama outside the court and the subsequent modernization of court practices were preconditions for 'dance' to emerge as a bounded form of action which was not confined to ritual and ceremonial

---

31. When Pigeaud writes that *topeng* was refined by the Yogya court (1938: 345–49), he must be referring to Kridha Běksa Wirama. According to Surjodiningrat, there was no *wayang topeng* in the Yogya court (1970: 39); masks were only used in *wayang wong* for demons, monkeys and *garudha* birds.

contexts. This also marked the start of an increased move from an oral to a written transmission of dance movement, as standards began to be written down and documented with systematic photographic sequences. Court dancing had been family capital (Bourdieu 1984) but the founding of Kridha Běksa Wirama marked the start of its development as educational capital. Once dancing was in this sphere, a process of classicization began, and was carried forward by the modernizing nationalistic work with dance in the 1930s and 1940s. This ultimately ensured its survival as a special category of performance. Kridha Běksa Wirama and Tamansiswa established court dance as part of an emergent and modern Javanese cultural identity that they would later describe as 'the art of Indonesian Javanese dance' (Surjodiningrat 1981: 138). They also established the terms of debates about culture and nationhood which would continue after independence.

Despite subsequent changes in court dance, Hamĕngkubuwana VIII's reign provided the most important point of reference for the many leading dance proponents whose careers started in the 1920s. His children and grandchildren formed the most enthusiastic and rigorous supporters of court performance, and also helped to transfer court dance as a tradition into independent Indonesia. Although the dance became educational capital, it also remained family capital, as will be clear when we turn to developments during the reign of Hamĕngkubuwana IX, the first sultan in the independent Indonesian Republic.

Chapter 3

From Colony to Nation: Dance in the Reign of Hamĕngkubuwana IX (1940–1988)

This chapter examines the changes that transformed the court repertoire into an Indonesian classical tradition. When a nation gains independence, its leaders and citizens try to represent the new political entity as a tangible reality. This often takes the form of expressive spectacles, including music and dance, which make the nation visible and audible. These undergo processes of ritualization even as they create new communities.[1] Despite these changes, family patronage and the ritual nature of Indonesian bureaucracy have been crucial for the survival of Javanese court dance in Indonesia, and for constituting embodied communities in the nation state. Rather than being transformed into Weberian rational bureaucracies, Southeast Asian states remain based on kinship networks, family ties and patron-client relations, with their rules contingent and their bureaucracies ritualized (Day 2004: 167–69).

It is central to my argument to emphasize that the Sultan's court in Yogyakarta is an Indonesian institution. Hamĕngkubuwana IX (1940–88) was both Sultan and Governor of Yogyakarta. Indonesian independence marked the end of the organization of performance inside the court as established by the previous Sultan. A gradual diversification in the patronage of court dance occurred as members of the court brought dancing into the domain of nationalist educational projects, and state and private dance training venues. Some scholars have described this period as the end of *wayang wong* in the court, or as a period of 'desacralization' and 'capitalization' of court dance.[2] Other commentators have characterized Yogya's court dances since its foundation as ceremonial rather than ritual (Moerdowo 1963: 37). As we shall see, the reign of the ninth Sultan witnessed the further transformation of the court, as the intertwining between ritual, bureaucracy, and everyday life imbued court dance with a mystique whose appeal was apparent to Javanese leaders in Indonesia.

---

1. Kertzer (1988). Bell defines ritualization as 'a way of acting that is designed and orchestrated to distinguish and privilege what is being done in comparison to other, usually more quotidian, activities' (1992: 74), a definition which, significantly, also applies to performance.
2. Soedarsono (1984: 33); Hadi (1988: 86, 88–93); Lombard (1990, I: 146–47).

The National Role of the Sultan

Haměngkubuwana IX became Sultan on 18 March 1940 following the death of his father on 22 October 1939. The Sultan and Prime Minister introduced governmental reforms during the Japanese occupation (Selosoemardjan 1962: 55–58) but events following the declaration of Indonesian independence in 1945 played a crucial role in shaping the Sultan's role as leader. In January 1946, the Sultan invited the revolutionary Indonesian government to move to Yogya from Jakarta, and he became Minister of State. Even at this early stage, nationalist fervour was tempered by Yogya's loyalty to its Sultan. When a West Javanese was appointed to lead this government, Selosoemardjan, the Sultan's secretary, noted that 'There was no demonstration of overt rejection, but neither was there any enthusiasm to co-operate' (1962: 80). This form of 'passive non-cooperation' (Scott 1985) was still evident during my research in Yogya. The government remained in Yogya while nationalists waged guerrilla warfare against the Dutch who were battling to retrieve their former colony. On 19 December 1948 they attacked Yogya and captured the Indonesian leaders. On 1 March 1949 a certain Lt. Col. Suharto liberated the city for six hours. The Sultan was involved in negotiations that resulted in the Dutch leaving by 30 June 1949.[3] Soekarno was installed as President in the court's Sitihinggil on 17 December 1949, and the Indonesian Republic became official at the Hague Round Table Conference on 19 December 1949.[4]

From this time, the Sultan's former Principality became a province with special autonomy, the Special Region of Yogyakarta (Daerah Istimewa Yogyakarta, D.I.Y.). He became governor, and the head of Yogya's junior court, K.G.A.A. Pakualam, became vice-governor. The Yogyakartan self-image based on rebellion was enhanced by the Sultan's effectiveness in securing a niche in the new nation state through revolutionary zeal and political savvy.[5] As Governor the Sultan combined the two colonial roles of sultan and prime minister, and he quickly set about dispersing the court's mystique. He opened it to visitors free of charge, and allowed Gadjah Mada University, Indonesia's first university, to use some court buildings for lecture rooms.[6] He continued to promote Yogya as a national centre for education, and students from all over Indonesia have attended its many secondary and tertiary institutions (Selosoemardjan 1962: 358–71). He also allowed the hitherto exclusive *Běksan Lawung* to be performed as part of Gadjah Mada university's Dies Natalis celebrations in 1953 (Surjodiningrat 1970). As his personal secretary wrote, 'instead of symbolically uniting himself with his people through the *garěběg* festivals three times a year, the Sultan began personally to

---

3.   Critchely, Australian representative, United Nations Commission for Indonesia (in Atmakasumah 1982: 162–65).

4.   Atmakusumah (1982: 284); Ricklefs (1981).

5.   His counterpart in Surakarta opted to have his territories subsumed into Central Java Province and became head of the court as a national cultural institution rather than taking up an overtly political role.

6   When I attended the court exhibition for Sěkaten with a friend, he became nostalgic, recalling classes he attended at the Social and Political Sciences Department in the Pagělaran as late as 1968 (Bambang D. 29/9/89).

unite himself with his people, six days a week' (Selosoemardjan 1962: 54). His political career subsequently included the roles of Vice-President and Minister of Sport. These political changes separated the Sultan's traditional magical energies (*sěkti*) from his political power and authority (*kekuasaan* I.) (Koentjaraningrat 1985), but the modernization of the Sultan's role within the republic did not completely expunge his supernatural powers. Many considered him to be the long-awaited millenarian 'Just King' (Ratu Adil), destined to lead the people in active struggle once the Dutch had left.[7] By the 1980s some were sceptical about his traditional role, observing that 'the Sultan's just a normal king, with no *sěkti*', but any reservations about his powers as sultan, exacerbated by his unpopular final marriage to a Sumatran divorcée, were forgotten after his death in 1988 when thousands of people lined the road along which his coffin was carried out to the royal mausoleum.

Changes in the Organization of Court Dance

Like his brothers and sisters, Haměngkubuwana IX had been educated in dance and theatre. He continued the tradition of royal patronage by creating *golek Menak* dance theatre and commissioning six new *bědhaya* and *srimpi* dances.[8] After the Japanese invasion of Java in February 1942 during the Second World War, performance was not a priority. Regular daily court practices were reduced to two a week (Hadi 1988: 81–82), and performance was limited to the Sultan's annual birthday, ceremonies and Pahing Saturday. Court retainers recalled with amusement how Japanese commanders asked the Sultan to arrange *bědhaya* performances for their entertainment, but on no less than five occasions they were politely and consistently fobbed off with performances of the much less prestigious *běksan*. Only three *wayang wong* plays were performed at this time, but in a much reduced form.[9]

After independence, Haměngkubuwana IX's national roles produced changes in the court performance. When his responsibilities required him to move to the new

---

7. Onghokham (1983: Ch. 3). A son of the fifth Sultan had led a messianic movement in 1918 (Kartodirjo 1973: 98 ff.). Geertz considered that in the 1950s the Sultan retained his magical power while acting as role model for the new Indonesian Javanese, particularly the middle classes (1960: 237).

8. These all have *kandha* and song texts in the Kridha Mardawa library: *Srimpi Rěngganis*, *Sapta Bědhaya*, about Sultan Agung's establishment of the boundaries of Sunda, first performed in the 1940s by seven dancers (Soedarsono et al. 1978); *Bědhaya Wiwaha Sangaskara*, a love dance performed by six dancers at some marriages of royal children; *Bědhaya Ranuměnggal*, *Srimpi Sri Raras*, and *Bědhaya Těmanten*, another wedding dance. The Sultan departed from established tradition, as two *bědhaya* dances were not for nine dancers.

9. There was a seven-hour dress rehearsal plays of 'Irawan's Wedding' (*Rabinipun Irawan Angsal Dewi Titisari*); a three-hour fragment, 'The Rout of the Kingdom of Dwarawati' (*Bědhahipun Nagari Dwarawati*) in the Sanabudaya Museum (Suryobrongto 1981b: 47), and a semi-dress rehearsal of *Prěgiwa-Prěgiwati* (Soedarsono 1984: 33). The first took place in 1940; before 1945 there were four performances held for Japanese guests, which *did* include *bědhaya* dances (Hadi cited in Soedarsono 1989: 14).

capital in Jakarta in 1950, he instructed his half-brother, G.B.P.H. Yudanĕgara, to set up a branch of the court Arts Section, Bĕbadan Among Bĕksa, in the Purwadiningratan, inside the fort near the western gate. Until 1973 all court dance was practised here, including concerts for the Sultan's birthdays, and other commemorations and receptions, including a *lawung* dance for his eldest daughter's marriage in 1969.[10] Only the *Uyon-Uyon Hadiluhung* music concerts broadcast by the local Radio Republic Indonesia station were performed inside the court. These developments may be seen as an attempt by the Sultan and his family to ensure cultural continuity, but the vacuum of patronage within the court resulted in a proliferation of cross-cutting networks with varying degrees of affiliation to the court. Kridha Bĕksa Wirama maintained close links with the new court dance training venue, Bĕbadan Among Bĕksa, which adopted its curriculum with minor adjustments. It used a different *srimpi* and added an extra male fight training dance, *wiraga tunggal*, to replace *klana* (Pringgobroto 1959: 21). It also used Kridha Bĕksa Wirama's criteria for standardized assessments and certificates, and often the same examiners (K.R.T. Mĕrtadipura 18/10/83).

These developments occurred against the background of a perceived need to create a national Indonesian culture and debates about what form this should take. Political rhetoric emphasized the role of culture in national development. The Ministry of Culture and Education built cultural policies on principles inherited from early nationalist groups. To foster the citizen's personal cultural identity (*kepribadian* I.) was a principle developed by Budi Utomo and applied in Tamansiswa's educational philosophy. In the 1950s, together with Tamansiswa's principle of 'standing on one's own feet' (*berdikari*), *kepribadian* became a key concept in national educational policy during Soekarno's presidency (Lombard 1990, I: 200). Education has been much more than vocational and academic training. Education imparts cultural values, as a former Indonesian cultural attaché to London noted (Moerdowo 1963: 21). Cultural and educational policies aimed to develop Indonesian nationhood by educating Indonesian citizens in the appropriate form of selfhood, expectations and aspirations to lead to development. The object of Indonesian dance education was not initially to produce professionals and artists, but to build a nation, 'to embody a stable identity ... and to make a happy citizen'.[11]

From early after independence, court dance served as a template for performances to celebrate and commemorate the revolution in private and national institutions of government and education. As in the case of a massive epic theatrical production by Sri Murtono in front of the Kasultanan in 1952 (Soemargono 1979: 102), the intention was not to revive feudalism, but to counter the influence of Western films and music. Court dance forms were also performed for national celebrations in

---

10. Hadi (1988: 91); Surjodiningrat (1970: 30). The exam paper for 1955 gives the organization's name as K.H.P. Kridha Mardawa Among Bĕksa. In 1952 the Sultan also set up Panguyuban Siswa Among Bĕksa from members of Bĕbadan Among Bĕksa Kraton, which took court dance overseas in the 1970s (Wibowo 1981: 226–27; Soedarsono 1984: 34).

11. The Indonesian is '*membentuk kepribadian jang stabil ... menjadikan warganegara jang bahagia'* (Wardhana 1958: 196) translated by the author).

surprising new ways. Kridha Bĕksa Wirama's Sudharso Pringgobroto and the former court dancer R. Mangkuharjuno choreographed new *bĕdhaya* dances, including 'The Foundation of Tamansiswa' to commemorate Tamansiswa's 1952 anniversary, the 'Revolution Bĕdhaya' in 1959, 'Pancasila [state philosophy] Bĕdhaya' and the 'Virgin Mary Bĕdhaya'.[12] They also established dance courses in primary schools in the Province. However, despite the early nationalists' use of Javanese court dance in education, it did not become part of the standard Indonesian national curriculum, but was learnt as a matter of personal choice.

During the 1960s court dance training was further incorporated into national education. The Secondary School of Indonesian Music (SMKI-KONRI) was founded in 1961 at the Tejokusuman under the directorship of R.R. Kusumobroto who had just stepped down as head of Kridha Bĕksa Wirama. The school rented accommodation adjoining the court's south square from members of the aristocracy. In 1976 it became part of the Secondary School of Indonesian Arts (Sekolah Menengah Kesenian Indonesia) and in 1983 it moved to a large campus just south of the city limits provided by the government. The Indonesian Dance Academy (ASTI) was founded in 1963 close to Gadjah Mada University in the north of the city. In the late 1980s it became part of the Indonesian Institute of Arts (ISI), and by 1994 had moved to a new campus some ten kilometres south of the city limits.[13] These institutions trained students in all court dance forms except for *wayang wong* and *golek Menak*, and other Indonesian regional styles, including Surakartan court dance, Balinese and Sundanese dance, and also contemporary dance (usually Graham Technique), choreography, music, and puppeteering. In 1982, a dance training course was also introduced in Yogya's leading Teachers' Training College (IKIP Karangmalang).

During the 1980s Tamansiswa's ideas were still influential, as demonstrated in a speech by the head of dance at Siswa Among Bĕksa's second anniversary:

> An arts education is a means to raise the interest or appreciation of arts and culture of the Indonesian people, which needs to be related to *Nation and Character Building* [English in the Indonesian original], in the name of National Security, so arts education needs to be continued, with the people joined together as a subject together represented in artistic activities.[14]

Cultural policy by now had three objectives: to build, to develop, and to perpetuate.[15] These were implemented in the spirit of the Indonesian state motto, 'Unity in Diversity', and followed Tamansiswa's ideal of establishing 'peaks of regional (cultural) excellence' (*puncak daerah* I.) rather than a single form of Indonesian culture. Despite

---

12. Wibowo (1981: 219); *Proyek Penelitian* (1977: 121–22).
13. The merger between the dance, music, and arts schools (ASTI, AMI, ASRI) had been mooted back in 1981 (*Tempo* no. 22 vol. XIV, 28/7/81).
14. Noeradyo (1983), translated from the Indonesian by the author.
15. '[M]*embina, mengembangkan melestarikan*' (staff at the Sub-Dinas office of the Department of Education and Culture, 19/4/89).

this cultural pluralism, leaders of state educational institutions had to deal with a tension between their regional and national allegiances. While the Javanese domination of Indonesia was putting other 'regional peaks' at risk, Javanese culture itself was not unified. In dance, the Surakartan style was more widely known because there had been a tradition of commercial popular *wayang wong* performance in the city. A conservatory had been established there in 1950, followed by a tertiary academy. Many people in Yogyakarta claimed that Indonesia's first president, Soekarno, had favoured the Surakartan Kasunanan court style, and President Suharto's wife was related to the Mangkunagaran court. The director of ASKI in Surakarta, Dr Hoemardani, was related to the court and also had access to the president through his brother, who was Suharto's personal spiritual adviser. These factors gave Yogyakartans the impression that the Surakartan dance was a strong contender for defining what Javanese-Indonesian dance should be, not without reason.[16]

By this stage state education was promoting vocational outcomes and influencing the transmission of court dance through specialization. At SMKI students specialized in a regional dance style or puppetry, for instance, but were also encouraged to gain a wider competence. All dance-focused students were required to learn some *gamělan*. When they went to ASTI, they specialized in music, dance, composition or drama, with the option to take minor courses in other fields. In terms of 'cross-competence' (Brinner 1995: 50), musicians usually know more about dance movement than dancers know about music, although dancers have knowledge of drumming patterns. Formal training of performance professionals in state academies reduces the specialization in specific roles (Suryobrongto 1981b: 81–82). My surveys in SMKI and ASTI in 1983 showed that girls tended to describe their dance preferences with reference to specific forms, such as *bědhaya*, while boys cited modes or roles – a reflection of the limited scope for girls in dance theatre. Despite increased specialization in choreography or music, there is a perceived need for a wider scope. Today's dance students, like music students (Brinner 1995: 163–64), learn a much wider repertoire and range of styles and modes than court performers. As the head of SMKI said, 'If you can only dance one role, you can't get a job!' (Pak Pardjan 23/3/83). These changes in the context and scope of dance training have produced variations in the transmission of performance and its objectives, and a new concern with producing specialized professionals and artists (see Chapter 7).

Court Dance Returns to the Court

In August 1973 the Sultan reinstated regular performance inside the court to increase the profile of Yogyakartan-style court dance, and in response to the New Order government's policy to develop national and international tourism. The first venture was dance shows during meals (*andrawina*), organized by the court and the government tourist agency, Nitour. The experimental package cost US$2 a head and included Sunday lunch, cooked by two of the Sultan's wives, K.R.Ay. Pintakapurnama and K.R.Ay. Hastungkara, and performances of fully costumed *srimpi*s and *wayang*

---

16. Claire Holt had noted this rivalry long before (1967: 152).

wong fragments from eleven o'clock in the morning through to the evening. The prince in charge of Kridha Mardawa later told me that they also ran *andrawina* between 1979 and 1982, but they stopped because of boredom (*bosan*) and being cheated by tour operators: 'They still owe us!'[17] Conversely, weekly music and dance practices held every Sunday morning in the Bangsal Kĕsatriyan from 1977 were very successful (Hadi 1988: 96–98). Instead of the hundreds of performers who had camped here during the *wayang wong* marathons of Hamĕngkubuwana VIII's reign, there were hundreds of tourists jostling for a better view, as described at the start of this book. These sessions were presided over by senior dance teachers, including some who had danced during the eighth Sultan's reign, and were accompanied by a *gamĕlan* orchestra and male and female singers. There was a set programme: the *Saritunggal* and *Tayungan* training dances; a *srimpi* (see Figure 3.1); a *klana* or male *bĕksan*; a *golek* or female *bĕksan*; and finally an energetic male *bĕksan*. *Bĕdhaya* and *wayang wong* fragments were not normally included because of the problem of getting the numbers to turn up for what some referred to as 'community obligations' (*gotong royong*). The Sunday sessions were also used as rehearsals for major court concerts, and would be ruthlessly extended through the heat of the day for five hours without a break or refreshments, often until as late as four o'clock in the afternoon, to general

Figure 3.1 Srimpi dance, Bangsal Kĕsatriyan, 1982

---

17. Information from Bu Putri (17/6/83), who had participated regularly, her father, K.R.T. Dipuradanarta (11/4/89), and B.R.M. Sulaksmana, later G.B.P.H. Yudaningrat (1983 and 25/8/89).

disgruntlement. Other concert rehearsals took place here at night, often until well after midnight. They were closed to the public, but researchers might gain access by writing begging letters in their best polite Javanese.

The Sunday sessions were not pure 'tourist art' (Graburn 1976). In the colonial period, Dutch guests were always invited to court performances, which often honoured Dutch royalty. The modern training sessions were also motivated by the ninth Sultan's enthusiasm to educate the citizens of the new nation. They were also more than tourist entertainment for another reason. The sessions embodied a direct link to court traditions, using techniques of imitation and physical adjustment and the pattern of dance training instituted by Haměngkubuwana VIII as a form of physical education. They also had a ceremonial life. To celebrate Haměngkubuwana IX's birthday every thirty five days, on Pon Sunday the sessions would be more formal than usual, marked by a fuller contingent of musicians, semi-dress rehearsal costume and make-up for the dancers who had to perform without the help of their teachers. These occasions provided an excellent opportunity to eavesdrop on the women teachers as they exchanged jokes and gossip and observed their pupils, making aesthetic judgements about this disastrous wrist action and that inappropriate facial expression. What these teachers did *not* do was exchange or sell handbags and sheets, a feature of one court dance association's rehearsals. Choreographic experiments, such as a *klana* for four dancers, would be premiered on Pon Sunday, and so was Bu Yuda's *Saritunggal* for six dancers (17 April 1983). Despite the presence of tourists wandering about, these events were like small concerts that brought together dancers and key players in the court dance scene, and maintained the networks and dance discourses as well as the dances themselves.

Major court concerts took place in the Pagělaran, the very large hall on the northernmost side of the court. In December 1982, the court exhibition held here for the annual Sěkaten fair as part of the celebrations for the Prophet's birthday (Mauludan) was opened by a concert featuring *Běksan Etheng, Srimpi Rěnggawati* and *Běksan Golek Menak*.[18] The court invited family and friends, who sat and watched the dancing as other visitors glanced over as they passed by on their way to the demonstration of dagger-making and exhibition of court objects, from typewriters to shadow puppets. By 1989 the court was selling tickets to tourists for this event. The concert for the Sultan's annual birthday (*wiyosan dalěm*) also took place here. In February 1983 this included *Bědhaya Genjong* and the *wayang wong* fragment 'The Birth of Gathotkaca' (described in Chapter 6). Otherwise the ninth Sultan entertained in his capacity as Governor at Jakarta or in the Provincial headquarters at the Kěpatihan, a bright and imposing public space for prestige state-sponsored court performances with its high-roofed *pěndhapa* decorated in glossy cream paint with touches of red and gold and hung with massive chandeliers, for performances such as the 1981 and 1989 projects (see below); or at the Pakualaman where, it was said, parking and security were better. The court also made the Pagělaran available for other events, such as the Festival of Regional Performing Arts, organized by the Ministry of

---

18. Sěkaten is aimed at locals and domestic tourists, as is Garěběg Mulud.

Culture and Education in 1983, but usually the Kĕpatihan pavilion was used for high-profile provincial government-sponsored events.[19]

The court ethos had also changed since the reign of the eighth Sultan. By 1983 there were approximately 1,370 *abdidalĕm* (compared to 8,000 in 1939), drawn mostly from the Sultan's brothers, sons, nephews and male affines, and also retired locals with practical skills and artistry or an interest in tradition and history.[20] They were assigned to one of thirteen offices which managed different court activities. Performance and ceremonial costumes were the responsibility of the court Arts Section, K.H.P. Kridha Mardawa, which had two hundred members, including around ninety musicians. Female singers for *bĕdhaya* had been transferred to the jurisdiction of the Women's Quarters. In 1982 the Tourist Office managed sixty-one guides, court kin and *abdidalĕm*, including one who worked as a waiter in a local restaurant and to this day sells tickets to overseas tourists. The court no longer had its own brigades of soldiers. After the *garĕbĕg* ceremonies were restored to something of their former glory from 1971 (Bonneff 1974), the soldiers were played by court retainers or volunteers from nearby *kampung*s.

The teachers and regular performers in the court were not full-time. Most had at least two other organizational affiliations and others were retired. I was aware of the low fees paid by the court, but even as a long-serving foreigner, I was unable to obtain details of the court's finances. Fortunately Sumandio Hadi, a dancer and lecturer at ASTI, researched dance in the reign of the ninth Sultan and made this information public in his masters' thesis. In 1987 a *wayang wong* fragment of Ramayana produced for the Sultan's birthday involved two hundred people. Each performer received Rp200 for a rehearsal (only three instead of the usual ten or fifteen) and Rp1,000 for the performance, a total honorarium of Rp1,600 (about £1). The production costs were Rp3,000,000 (about £2,000); tickets were sold for Rp1,000, and outside funding provided Rp250,000. Overall, the production ran at a deficit of Rp2.75 million (Hadi 1988: 114–15), despite claims that dance had become 'capitalized'. Practitioners constantly reminded me that court dance was not a commodity, and could only be transacted 'for honour, not cash' – hence the very small payments to performers, and the relatively low price of ticket. Participation in dance events inside the court has been motivated by the benefits of belonging to a well-connected community of interest as well as by passion, so there has always been a degree of carefully disguised social climbing. In the spirit of openness already discussed, talented students of dance associations and academies were welcomed regardless of birth, though the idioms of incorporation would vary.

---

19. The court did not sponsor any dance performances for Indonesian Independence Day. In 1983 there was an event in the Kĕpatihan (which I missed), but usually during the last fortnight in August there would be a surfeit of cultural activity in the princely residences and *kampung*s, including performances of *wayang wong*, *bĕdhaya*, shadow play, *golek* and other dances. In 1983 in my *kampung* in Wirobrajan, there was a carnival which included the 'red chilli pepper' Wirobrajan court soldiers, named after the shape of their headgear.

20. The Sultan's sister-in-law, Bu Yuda, told me she did not have a rank as an *abdidalĕm* (23/9/94).

Private Dance Associations

By the time that dance and drama returned to the court in 1973, there was a proliferation of venues, training and performance. However, of the thirteen 'classical dance' associations registered with Yogya's Education and Culture office in 1982, ten were Surakarta style, and only four claimed to specialize in Yogya style court dance; these data, however, were incomplete, and omitted the two leading associations discussed below. As well as competition between the senior courts at Yogya and Surakarta to establish court performance practice as national culture, members of privately-run associations set up between 1950 and 1979 who collaborated inside the court also competed *outside* to shape the standards and substance of court performance's place in Indonesian versions of high Javanese culture. Lines of fracture developed between royal siblings, and between royals and lower-ranking court retainers about how best to maintain the dances as 'things passed down'. When I started research in Yogyakarta in October 1982, Kridha Běksa Wirama's base, the Tejokusuman, had just been sold. Although not officially disbanded, it was 'unable to make things happen' (Suharti 1989: 10), but it did continue to influence competitive discourses about court dance standards. In the 1980s, the two main associations were Siswa Among Běksa, and Mardawa Budaya, which also ran a training section, Pamulangan Běksa Ngayugyakarta (henceforth PBN). Despite their common ground, the two associations practised court dancing differently.

Siswa Among Běksa saw itself as the heir of the defunct court branch, Běbadan Among Běksa, and was also based in the Purwadiningratan. In 1983 some still referred to the Monday-night training sessions as 'Běbadan Kraton' (Bu Putri 17/6/83). It was not formalized as a foundation until 20 July 1978, but had been part of the court's international tours in the 1970s (Wibowo 1981: 226–27). Close royal kinship links and royal patronage played an important role in the membership of this group (Table 3.1). It was run by R.M. Dinusatama, a grandson of Haměngkubuwana VIII, through his mother, G.R.Ay. Sindurěja, and son-in-law to Gusti Suryobrongto, the vociferous adherent of the eighth Sultan's moralist educative ethos, encountered in Chapter 2. Gusti Suryobrongto's daughter-in-law, Mbak

Table 3.1 Dance kinship connections: cousins and court dance associations

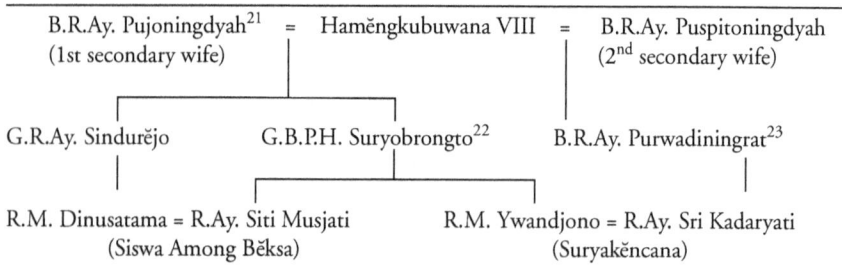

B.R.Ay. Pujoningdyah[21] (1st secondary wife)	=	Haměngkubuwana VIII	=	B.R.Ay. Puspitoningdyah (2nd secondary wife)
G.R.Ay. Sindurějo		G.B.P.H. Suryobrongto[22]		B.R.Ay. Purwadiningrat[23]
R.M. Dinusatama = R.Ay. Siti Musjati (Siswa Among Běksa)			R.M. Ywandjono = R.Ay. Sri Kadaryati (Suryakěncana)	

21. Older sister of K.R.T. Brongtodiningrat (see Chapter 5).
22. He married R. Ay. Suryobrongto, granddaughter of Haměngkubuwana VII.
23. She married K.R.T. Purwadiningrat, son of K.R.T. Wiroguna.

Kadar, a granddaughter of K.R.T. Wiroguna, the composer responsible for music at Kridha Bĕksa Wirama (Wibowo 1981: 210–14), taught here when not occupied with the Suryakĕncana dance association which she ran with her husband, R.M. Ywandjono. Other teachers included two of the ninth Sultan's sisters-in-law who also taught regularly at the court's Sunday sessions: B.R.Ay. Prabuningrat and Bu Yuda (as she preferred to be called), the leading female court choreographer and dance teacher. The dancers included royal grandchildren and other relatives who danced as a hobby, and talented enthusiastic dance students from the academies who wanted extra training and practice. Mbak Kadar described the association as being for the children of court kin (*kĕrabat kraton*) and retainers, and explained that outsiders would be incorporated by being classified as the 'children' of these 'members' (17/7/06). The nocturnal meetings were normally well attended. There was ample tea and gossip, and sometimes the female teachers sold items like sets of sheets and handbags. The atmosphere was relaxed and informal (by Javanese standards). There was a feeling of being at home (*krasan*), which many literally were, while others were relatives, friends and inhabitants from adjoining *kampung*s. Together they formed the core audience for concerts, along with other family members and friends of the performers.

In this way Siswa Among Bĕksa exemplified the cultural value of court dance as 'family capital' (Bourdieu 1984), and regarded itself as the keeper of court traditions. Its participants considered themselves to be custodians of the ethical and moral performance values that had enabled dance to survive in the postcolonial period. The fine distinctions of movement and attitude could be understood to form a code of class practice, but people also asserted *local* cultural identity and descent from the first Sultan. His militarism and revolutionary spirit was applied metaphorically to the goal of culture, as expressed in one of the organization's few publications:

> Yogya style classical dance was created in an atmosphere of rebellion to chase away the colonialists: it was born in the midst of blood, sweat, and tears. So this dance has the characteristics of a strong courageous fighter who never surrenders; it is loyal, simple, and sincere. It thus possesses a high sense of nationalism, a legacy of energy and value, such as the one which we now tend and cultivate.[24]

This rhetoric encapsulates the congruence between the foundational militaristic ethos of Yogya and of the republic, with its local national heroes, including the ninth Sultan himself.

Siswa Among Bĕksa drew on the entire court repertoire for its anniversary concerts. Its members aspired to maintain *bĕdhaya* and *srimpi* 'as of old' (*kina*). They conducted research into court manuscripts, and restored and revived forgotten court

---

24. R.M. Dinusatama, in Dewan Ahli Yayasan Siswa Among Bĕksa (1981: 7), author's translation from the Indonesian.

dances.[25] Despite this emphasis on 'pure' and 'authentic' (*asli* I.) practice, the association had also been very active in developing the full range of new movement modes for *golek Menak* dance drama.[26] Just as the colonial court had incorporated and refined outside forms, Siswa Among Běksa continued Kridha Běksa Wirama's work of extending the repertoire of *adiluhung* 'high' 'art' and 'classical Yogyakartan dance' with compositions from the colonial period developed outside the court in the residence of the crown prince, the prime minister, and other royal kin. For example, in 1977 they revived *Langěndriya*, and in 1982 *Golek Gambyong*, both 'by' Mangkubumi, a son of Haměngkubuwana VI.[27] Aware that things passed down are never simply repeated and retain power only insofar as they *are* renewed, the association was chary of innovations going beyond what was considered to be appropriate. This would lead to the decline and 'contamination' embodied in the 'new creations' by other family members, and also in the more subtle but subversive activities of their main rivals in Mardawa Budaya.

The competing association, Mardawa Budaya, was founded in 1962. It had princely patronage and commercial sponsorship from the international company, Caltext Oil (Wibowo 1981: 228–29).[28] It was established to provide training and, from 1971, performances of court dance for tourists. A further training section, Pamulangan Běksa Ngayugyakarta, was established in 1976 with assistance from the Ford Foundation in Jakarta. The public face of the associations was that of its general director, the charismatic R.W. Sasminta Mardawa (1929–96), known by his students as 'Rama Sas'. The association was based in the Pudjokusuman residence where he lived with his sister, wife of Prince Pudjakusuma, who had been a dancer and then head of the court Arts Section. Rama Sas had started his career as a court dancer specializing in women's dance, including *golek*, and had also trained at Kridha Běksa Wirama. By the 1980s he was involved in teaching, choreography and performance in court productions, and regularly appeared in *wayang wong* as the Bathara Guru (the Hindu god Śiva) (see Figure 6.1). He was also on the permanent staff at the Secondary School of Indonesian Arts (SMKI). Many pupils from this school also

---

25. For example, two fighting quartets from the reign of the first Sultan, Běksan Guntur Sěgara ('Thunder of the Sea') for clubs and shields, and Běksan Tuguwasesa for forked lances (Dewan Ahli Yayasan Siswa Among Běksa 1981: 26–34).

26. Dewan Ahli Yayasan Siswa Among Běksa (1981: 58ff.).

27. 'Pleasures of the Heart' was created by Prince Mangkubumi IV in 1878 using a distinctive squatting dance style with songs inspired by the Damarwulan stories performed in *macapat* songs and was also enacted in *klithik* (flat wooden) puppet plays until 1913. This is not to be confused with the Mangkunagaran court's *Langěndriyan*, an all-female dance drama. In *Golek Gambyong*, Golek's husband, Gambyong, is so lazy that she has to work as an itinerant *ledhek*. She performs a *golek* dance with Canthang Balung, a proud, rich, lustful soldier – 'he might be a Dutchman' – who ultimately fails to seduce Golek (R.M. Dinu 27/11/89).

28. Its patrons were sons of Haměngkubuwana VIII, including G.B.P.H. Puger, also court Arts Section head in the early 1980s, and K.G.P.H. Mangkubumil, later the tenth Sultan (Wibowo 1981: 228–31).

trained in PBN, as did other dance students and overseas researchers, including me (see next chapter). Indeed, I had been given the impression, wrongly, that Siswa Among Bĕksa did not accept foreign students, a rumour quite possibly disseminated by its rival.

Like Siswa Among Bĕksa, Mardawa Budaya aspired to maintain court standards. Its members pursued archival research, published texts about dance, and issued recordings of musical accompaniments to dances. It also 'revived' and maintained the dance opera, *Langĕn Mandrawanara* ('many monkeys'), created by Danurĕja VII before he became prime minister around 1890 (Sastrowiyono 1981) to present certain episodes from the Ramayana. Both associations produced dances that were classed as 'high and noble' (*adiluhung*), but whereas Siswa Among Bĕksa fostered an ethos of militaristic heroism and embodied nostalgia for the days of Hamĕngkubuwana VIII and represented family capital, Mardawa Budaya was interested in innovation, and represented artistic capital. Rama Sas was famous for his choreographies. He said: 'I personally like to make something new so that the dancers aren't bored. And in the court too – there are always dances being made' (12/12/82).

His dances looked like traditional forms, but he altered court standards for dance movement. In particular he increased the number of weight shifts and transitions within a single gong cycle, producing complicated footwork. He also created shorter *golek* and fighting dances for training purposes. For these reasons Rama Sas was an ambiguous and controversial figure in the court dance scene in the 1980s. His rivals respected his musical rigour, but some said he was 'too clever by half' (*kuminter*). Overtly individual creativity has never been part of the court tradition. New choreographies were attributed to the sultan of the day, and even innovative solutions to problems of reviving lapsed dances by choreographers such as Bu Yuda would be assimilated to the traditional collectivity. I annoyed Rama Sas when I asked him why his dances were labelled as 'court dance' and not 'new creations'. He responded rather curtly that the dances 'look classical and the audience don't know they aren't'. The association's work to make court dance forms more interesting and inventive was also motivated by making it accessible to the regular audiences of (mostly) overseas tourists. From 1982 to 1984 it was giving three concerts a week of court forms: male and female *bĕksan* from both *wayang wong* and *golek Menak, golek* and *srimpi* dances, and also a new form, *sendratari* (see below). Rama Sas's style of inventive classicism with its technical challenges worried purists but was hugely appealing to dancers and choreographers in higher education dance institutes, and recent generations of dancers have been greatly inspired and influenced by his work, including Bambang Pujasworo who, together with Mbak Siti Sutiyah, Rama Sas's wife, took over the association after his death in 1996.

The competitive rivalry between Siswa Among Bĕksa and Mardawa Budaya/PBN in the 1980s was a function of the changing conditions for performance, and brought personal differences into the open. The vaunted Javanese ideals of harmony and politeness were stretched to capacity, and tempers were running high. Some explained the vitriol as dating back to the early 1970s, when royal grandchildren were included on a prestigious overseas court dance tour, but not dancers like Rama Sas.[29] This gave the disputes a class dimension arising from the court kin's attempts to keep dance as family capital. Some accused others of putting their government interests before those of the court. Other upped the ante on personal credentials, arguing that to call oneself a senior dance teacher, one should have taught *in* the court before 1939 – a snipe at the Kridha Běksa Wirama faction. Others argued that to call oneself a 'court dancer' one should have performed in *at least one* full-scale *wayang wong* before 1939, and not simply in a fragment or a *golek* – a snipe at Rama Sas and the younger generation. Siswa Among Běksa accused Mardawa Budaya of representing the Kridha Běksa Wirama style, not the older court standard. Mardawa Budaya accused Siswa Among Běksa of being elitist and boring. Some elaborated on a polarization between Kridha Běksa Wirama and the court. Gusti Suryobrongto made a splenetic remark that during the Japanese occupation, when people had to register their profession, the 'court people' identified themselves as 'dance-makers' (*tukang tari* I.), whereas the 'Kridha Běksa Wirama people' registered themselves as 'artists'. This reveals the different evaluations of court dancing among the elite which were sustained through the competing approaches to dance by Siswa Among Běksa and Mardawa Budaya/PBN. Arguments about credentials were also arguments about the future role of dance and its practitioners, and how to maintain court values in the face of artistic, professional and commercial ones, a theme I examine in Chapter 7.

These arguments also show how people invoked the past to protect their status and family control of culture while forgetting the innovative activities of their own relatives who had been happy to work outside the court with Kridha Běksa Wirama, and also its role in making it possible for arguments about 'court standards' even to be happening in the postcolonial era. Despite their rivalrous rhetoric, both groups were committed to education, and endorsed the role of dance in education advocated by Tamansiswa in the 1920s and 1930s. They cooperated in court productions and in their teaching jobs at SMKI and ASTI. And although senior teachers remained loyal to one association, participation in the groups was not always mutually exclusive. I remember the very slight embarrassment of one young dancer whom I knew from my lessons at Pamulangan Běksa Ngayugyakarta when I met her later, teaching at Siswa Among Běksa. So these were arguments *within* a structure, although the structure itself was continually transformed by innovations which slowly became assimilated to the canon.

---

29. The tours were to the Netherlands and Hong Kong (1970) (Soedarsono 1984: 34); Holland, Belgium, England, Italy and West Germany (April–July 1971); Hong Kong Arts Festival and Japan March and July 1973 (SAB programme notes 1987). In 1975 the court's Art Section toured to raise money to restore Borobudur (Hadi 1988: 98).

The Court and the State

By the early 1980s the court no longer had a monopoly on its traditions. The patronage of the court dance had extended to dance associations and academies. Performance had come out of the court and been reintegrated into a modern classicism as part of national policies concerning cultural development and education. The production of Javanese culture in the Indonesian political system was in the hands of people affiliated to the court in different ways. Social relationships in Java have long been structured around patron–client relations, and although these have been hierarchical, they have also operated as a moral relationship (Scott 1975). The Sultan himself was in a patron–client relationship with both central government in Jakarta and its local offices, and provincial government offices (Koentjaraningrat 1985). Like the performers lower down the pyramid of prestige, he had different social roles, sometimes acting as a patron, sometimes as a client. These cross-cutting ties of patronage gave the court network a certain amount of clout in cultural politics, and made it difficult to untangle loyalties to the Sultan from loyalties to the state.

There has been a close relationship between the values and interests of the court and those of emerging modern Indonesia. Modern bureaucracies in the Special Region of Yogyakarta included many who had been socialized into the court system and had an interest in transferring its values and statuses to the institutions and values of emerging modern Indonesia. Many government officials working towards the goals of the New Order – security, order, peace, prosperity, development and preservation – were also members of the Sultan's family, especially uncles, aunts and cousins, or related to him through a more distant ancestor.[30] Others had served the sultan or the prime minister in the colonial period when the court received subsidies from the Dutch. In 1983, the regional branch of the Department of Education and Culture (Depdikbud) subsidized the court Arts Section. Hamĕngkubuwana IX's youngest brother, G.B.P.H. Drs Puger, was simultaneously patron *and* client in this transaction. This is just one instance of the difficulty of drawing too hard a line between court and government interests.

Cultural policies during Indonesia's New Order (1966–98) have been criticized for attempting to homogenize a national culture out of a diversity of local cultures and traditions which it appropriates and legislates for its own purposes.[31] Arguments that the state is homogenizing all regional performance into spectacle need qualification, as there is evidence of subtle forms of regional resistance to a homogenization. Such arguments credit the state with an

---

30. The court descent system downgrades rank at the fifth generation, but it can be upgraded by marriage to someone above five removes. The elite (*priyayi*, civil servants and nobles) is not homogenous but differentiated by internal status hierarchies.

31. The argument is that culture has been replaced by spectacle, '[A]t the level of display, not belief, performance, not enactment … Culture has become art throughout Indonesia, but for the most peripheral even that art has been prescribed by the state' (Acciaioli 1985: 161–62). See also Hough (1992) and Widodo (1995).

effectiveness it does not have.[32] They also privilege product over process, and deny the perspective of social actors. What happens and what endures is not only the result of options available to performers, but how they respond to those options. Over my years of research it has become clear that none of the nationally sponsored activities in urban centres or rural communities could take place without passion and commitment. In the remoter areas of the Province, such as the Wonosari district, there is a proliferation of art because it lacks electricity and has limited facilities. 'It's a region that needs entertainment', said an official of the PDK arts section; these activities arise from the people themselves, and are occasional, not for making a living (Pak Supardi Achmad, 19/4/89). I often found that local self-nominated 'cultural officers' (*penilik kebudayaan* I.) would act as a catalyst for creative activities at grass-roots levels.[33] The state may assist and direct, but without support and energy at provincial levels and below, their projects would come to nothing. So there are limits on the attempts of Indonesian governments since independence to create commensurability between the provincial units that make up the Republic.

There is also a contradiction between the promotion of national unity and the fragmentation of the bureaucratic apparatus.[34] In Indonesia, social relations combine with this bureaucratic fragmentation to make top-down policies less deterministic in practice than in principle. It is difficult to establish who controls the court 'brand', and where 'top down' ends and 'grass roots' (even in an elite context) begin. The government's administration of culture in Yogyakarta demonstrates how fragmentation in the organizational framework of cultural policy-making limits the effectiveness of its 'operationalization' in the field. Indonesian government administration has had a three-tier structure. Level 1 dealt with central administration in the capital with branch offices in the Provinces. Level 2 were offices in provincial capitals like Yogyakarta city. And level 3 operated in the districts (*kabupaten*) down. This means that in provincial capitals we find a parallel system: level 1 or central, offices known as Kanwil (Kantor Wilayah, 'Regional Office'); and level 2 provincial offices, or Dinas. All the Kanwil offices liaise with the third tier of offices (Kandep II) in Yogyakarta's five districts: City (Kodya), Bantul, Sleman, Kulon Progo and Gunung Kidul. Each district capital represents the lowest level of autonomy, and organizes

---

32. Yampolsky suggests that Acciaioli exaggerates the efficacy of government agencies in Indonesia, and argues for a rich artist life running parallel to 'official' culture (1995: 714, 719). Lindsay argues that government structure does not just mould change but is itself moulded by 'concepts of performance, audience, patronage, image. Cultural policy and procedure is part of performance culture itself' (1995: 670). Hellman (1999: 211) also concludes that the imagined community is only realized in specific local communities. Pemberton (1994) discusses the selectivity of official culture, and Florida (1995) the diversity of what it conceals. Bourchier (1997) shows how the clarification of Indonesian cultural identity has also inadvertently clarified criticisms of it.

33. Sutton (1991: 173) makes a similar point, and discusses the failure of state policy to promote Javanese regional musical traditions (Ibid.. 173–91).

34. Compare Handler's (1988) study of Canadian cultural politics.

what happens in the subdistricts (*kecamatan*), villages (*desa* I. *dusun* J.) and hamlets (*dukuh*).[35]

The administration of culture in the Special Region of Yogyakarta under the Ministry of Education and Culture (Depdikbud) was divided between Kanwil and Dinas (until 1998). Kanwil (the level 1 office, generally referred to as 'Depdikbud') handled policy making under Jakarta, and had particular responsibility for academic and vocational secondary education, and culture, including a local Arts Unit (Bidang Kesenian). Kanwil also liaised with the director general of Higher Education responsible for state universities and the Indonesian Arts Institute (ISI). Dinas (the level 2 office, generally referred to as 'PDK'), was under the control of the governor, and had executive responsibilities for primary schools and culture. At least, this was the division of labour 'in principle'.[36] In practice, Dinas PDK cooperated closely with Kanwil, especially the Arts Unit, the Dinas and Kanwil offices of Tourism, Post and Telecommunications (known as 'Parpostel'), the Dinas sub-office for tourism, the Council for the Coordination of Arts in Indonesia (BKKNI), and the Regional Development Planning Office (BAPPEDA).

We might take note of the 'fragmentation' involved in this list alone. Different local sources told me that committee members often hold regional government positions and block the necessary consensus by prioritizing their own departmental interests.[37] The regional 'double' structure also produced reduplication and competition between the national and provincial levels of administration, even when led by aristocratic dancers, as was the case with the Sub-Dinas and the Kanwil Arts Unit. When I visited what had been the Dinas office in 1999 to update my performance statistics, I tried to provoke cooperation from the head, R.R. Pangarsobroto, by mentioning other data from the Kanwil Arts Unit. 'Well' he said, pointing to huge piles of documents on the floor tied up in string, 'They get theirs from us!' The piles were the data for March 1998–99, but the figures for 1997–98 were available. Both he and the head of the 'culture section' supervised my note-taking and warned me not to take the statistics too literally, partly because of the negative impact of the 1997 economic crisis.[38] When I went to the Arts

---

35. This summary describes the situation before legislation to increase provincial autonomy was initiated in 1999. The policy did not work out; provinces were by-passed, and autonomy devolved to the districts (*kabupaten*).

36. Pak Pardjan (2/4/89), then head of SMKI. Further information was provided by Pak Supardi Achmad, head of the Sub-Dinas PDK arts section, and his staff, on 11/4/89 and 19/4/89; the other two Dinas sections were Schools and Libraries.

37. Pak Bakdi, head of the Yogyakarta Arts Council (1989). An artist and entrepreneur from Gunung Kidul district preferred to apply to Jakarta for funding: 'I got Rp250,000 ... if I did it locally, there wouldn't be much left by the time it got to me ... I've won a few prizes, so the sub-district head lets me make direct applications.' He said that the provincial Depdikbud 'closes' the arts: people siphon off funds and take credit for what others have done (Pak Prapto 7–8/11/89).

38. Longitudinal comparison was not helped by the 1994 categories 'classical' and 'folk' (*klasik* and *rakyat*) having been changed to 'traditional', 'composed' (*garapan*) and 'nontraditional'.

Unit, they offered me the 1996–7 tables to photocopy; apart from the shadow play, the 1997–98 data would not be ready until September. In this case, the local office was ahead of the national one.

Despite the baroque structures of local government organization, these departments succeeded in patronizing a wide range of cultural and artistic activities, such as the 'cultural programme' that formed part of the Sĕkaten fair, mentioned above. In 1983 this included 'arts and sports events for primary schools': *gamĕlan* and traditional songs; a 'new creation' dance (*Arjuna Wiwaha*); communal morning exercises; a hobbyhorse dance duet; regional and popular songs of Indonesia accompanied by the then-fashionable bamboo xylophones (Filipino *kolintang*); floor and rhythm exercises; and *slawatan*, a ritual Islamic musical performance. In 1989 Sĕkaten included children performing a broader range of recently 'revived' folk dances, and a popular, rather rowdy venue with a woman singer-dancer accompanied by a 'Malay Orchestra' (Orkes Melayu, or O.M.) playing Javanese hard-rock called *dangdut*. The sinuous and salacious gyrations of the singers attracted large and enthusiastic audiences from *becak* drivers to elite dance brokers, but were considered unsuitable for an ostensibly religious event such as Maulud, so the *dangdut* was closed down.

Events of this kind result from development projects initiated nationally or provincially. Competitions across the Province bring together winners in regular events, such as 'Sports and Arts Week', festivals, or one-off project-related competition events. In 1982, for example, the Dinas PDK held a *golek* and *klana* competition, while the Kanwil Arts Unit ran a number of projects for 'Folk Performing Arts', including *ketoprak, sendratari* (see below) drum bands, and sports. Many people in the various Education and Culture offices told me that organizing these competitions is time-consuming and exhausting. This is due to responsibilities being divided and then reduplicated in an overlapping system. The complex administrative structure also makes planning, funding and budgeting highly complex. For example, in 1989, the annual Arts Week (Pekan Kesenian) was funded by the Arts Council, which itself was funded by the regional government. It received another Rp20 million from BAPPEDA, but nothing from the Department of Tourism, Post and Telecommunications.

An example of a successful local government project is the annual Sendratari Festival. This met with such enthusiasm from the public that it was posing a challenge to court-derived classicism by the end of Hamĕngkubuwana IX's reign.

Sendratari: A Competing Classicism

Many of those working in tertiary state dance education were the grandchildren, nieces and nephews of the princes who founded Kridha Bĕksa Wirama. They looked away from the formal ethos of the court – while being of it – and played major roles in attempts to find specifically Indonesian forms of expression, developing dance and theatre in the curricula of dance academies. Some challenges came from those working within court performance conventions, others from those experimenting with different styles and idioms, collectively called 'new creations' (*kreasi baru*).[39] Among these new forms was *sendratari*.

Sendratari is a compression of 'SEni DRAma Tari', 'the Art of Drama and Dance', but it is more appropriately classed as ballet than dance theatre because it emphasizes dance movement and narrative (Lim 1995: 110). Kridha Bĕksa Wirama had already produced a number of dance dramas in the 1950s (Surjodiningrat 1970: 44), and dance conservatories in the two cities (KOKAR, SMKI-KONRI), court artists, and inspired individuals such as Sri Pakualam and Sardono W. Kusuma, who also combined their efforts in experiments to develop a new Indonesian form.[40] The result was the well-known *sendratari*, the 'Ramayana Ballet', performed for the first time in 1961 on an open stage in front of the moonlit (and later floodlit) Lara Jonggrang temple at Prambanan. Organized by members of the junior Pakualaman court through its Lara Jonggrang Association, it combined Surakartan and Yogyakartan dance styles, and became a major tourist attraction. For overseas tourists there used to be a language barrier in *sendratari* (Surjodiningrat 1970), but it could be appreciated with the help of a plots outline on a sheet of paper without a prior knowledge of characterization, history and philosophy.[41] For uninformed domestic tourists and local audiences, its flexible length, numbers of dancers, dance style, and increasing emphasis on movement made it more accessible than *wayang wong* or *golek Menak*.

Sendratari has been sponsored by the state as part of national development for local consumption as well as being associated with tourist entertainment. The dance-ballet had been developed in the 1960s in ASTI in Yogya, and also STSI in Bali (deBoer 1989). Apart from tourist-oriented Ramayana stories, festival *sendratari* are stories from folk tales or semi-legendary heroic lives. Despite sometimes being described as 'folk dance', *sendratari* has become part of the classical repertoire, and is a significant competitor to *wayang wong* and *golek Menak* for investment of Depdikbud time and money.

By the 1980s *sendratari* was growing in popularity, and was being taught in secondary and tertiary dance schools and in the Mardawa Budaya dance association. The festival had become a prestigious 'Culture and Arts Development Project' of the

---

39. The best-known examples are former Kridha Bĕksa Wirama graduates R.M. Bagong Kussudiardjo, whose large-scale choreographies, such as the 'ASEAN Dance' in 1983, were commissioned for state events, and Dr R.M. Wisnu Wardhana, whose dancing ranged from mimes inspired by Marcel Marceau to *wayang wong* heroes, and who choreographed new dances in the court style, such as *Tari Ruwatan* (1983) which alluded to exorcism rituals traditionally conducted using the *Murwakala* shadow play.

40. Marlene Heins (November 2005), drawing on her conversations with Pak Ngaliman and Pak Pardjan. Gusti Suryobrongto regarded Ramayana Ballet as 'politics, not art' (30/3/83). Lombard (1990, I: 202) attributes the idea of having a Ramayana at Prambanan to Dr Prijono Winduwinoto, Indonesian Minister of Culture and Education from 1957 to 1966.

41. In Bali, when the Arts Festival started in 1979, the role of the narrator (*dhalang*) assumed a greater importance, and the non-Balinese-speaking audiences declined (Bandem and deBoer 1995: 137).

Dinas PDK, patronized by the 'big five' for arts and culture in the Province,[42] with an invitation 'signed' by the head of Kanwil Depdikbud. For two days performances by the finalists from each district were held in the prestigious Kĕpatihan pavilion in the provincial headquarters in the city centre. My field notes give something of the atmosphere:

> The festival is very well attended. Saw Kulon Progo's offering, with comic end when dying character's moustache came off, to the hilarity of the audience. Kodya (City) offered more polish but less fun – I'm tired of the endless tragic deaths and the white sheet that now seems to be de rigeur as a polyvalent symbol. A little girl sitting next to me said Bantul had a red sheet – they should have won for originality. Everyone was there, including various ex-pats and foreign researchers. R.M. Dinu and Pak Pardjan were on the jury. While they deliberated, we had clowns (lawak) who'd played at the Yogya Arts Festival: their sketch was a parody of wayang orang/sendratari in high Javanese (krama inggil) … Field notes 21/10/89).

The winner that year was Yogya city. It won again in 1993 with Sang Prawara, a life of Hamĕngkubuwana IX, which opened with a football dance, in 'traditional' dress (Kompas 27/10/93), in memory of the ninth Sultan's great love of the sport.

Despite the grand venue and my own rather jaded response, the atmosphere at these festivals had a lively quality (ramé) lacking in court dance theatre apart from its clown scenes. Its power to attract audiences has been seen as a challenge to the court-originated dance theatre as the public face of Javanese-Indonesian culture. The head of ASTI, Prof. Dr. R.M. Soedarsono (whose grandfather and great-uncle founded Kridha Bĕksa Wirama), had returned to Yogya in the 1980s after completing his doctoral thesis on wayang wong in the America. He criticized wayang wong for representing irrelevant outdated 'feudal' values, and for failing 'to communicate' to contemporary audiences, suggesting that it should instead follow the example of folk dance and sendratari. Indeed, sendratari has been an important factor in transforming the internal dynamic of court dance as classical Indonesian art, and has furthered a breakdown in the balance between narrative and dance movement in wayang wong which it has influenced (Lindsay 1995: 150–51).

The Diversification of Court Dance Patronage: Golek Menak

Developments in court dance during the reign of Sultan Hamĕngkubuwana IX can be summed up with reference to an event on 17 March 1989, ten days after his son succeeded him as Hamĕngkubuwana X. This was a performance of golek Menak, 'The Marriage of Kĕlaswara' (Kĕlaswara Partakrama). Golek Menak had been 'created' by Hamĕngkubuwana IX, and was the newest form in the court repertoire. It drew its movement styles, characters and stories from the wooden golek puppet

---

42. 1. Local government (Pemda tingkat 2) (Dinas PDK); 2. District (Pemda tingkat 3); 3 Kanwil Depdikbud; 4. the Arts Council; 5. BKKNI (glosses as above).

theatre.[43] Hosted by the head of the provincial sub-office of Arts and Culture, before an invited audience of around one thousand people, this first 'perfect' *golek Menak* consolidated the patronage of court performance by the nation state as classical Indonesian performance (Figure 3.2.). Delayed so as to become part of celebrations following Hamĕngkubuwana X's accession, it served to incorporate his son into a cultural strategy initiated by his father, but not fulfilled during his lifetime. The 'perfection' process involved coordination between the Sultan, government and private cultural institutions and associations in Yogyakarta and Jakarta (Soedarsono et al. 1989: 37–62). The sixty-three performers (twenty-five singers and musicians, and thirty eight dancers) were drawn from Kridha Mardawa (the court Arts Section), Kanwil and Dinas Education and Culture offices, ISI (the Institute of Indonesian Arts), the Secondary School of Indonesian Arts (SMKI),

Figure 3.2 *Golek Menak* dance theatre, Court Festival, 1994

43. Although the influence of West Javanese *wayang golek* is usually mentioned, this form enacts Mahābhārata and Ramayana stories. It is *wayang golek* from Cirebon, coastal Central Java, and the Yogya region that dramatizes stories from Sĕrat Menak about the Prophet's uncle, Amir Hamzah (Garrett Kam, pers. comm. May 2007). Movements were patterned along the same lines as that of *wayang wong* (Soedarsono et al. 1989: 54, 58–62). It is possible that older court choreographers remembered a 'human' *wayang golek*, devised in 1879 by prime minister-in-waiting Danurĕja VI with stories from *Sĕrat Menak*, dialogue like *wayang wong*, and movements like masked dancing (Prijono 1982: 69–70).

and four dance associations: Bagong Kussudiardjo's Padepokan dance studio, Siswa Among Běksa, Mardawa Budaya, and Suryakěncana.[44]

In 1981, the 'Three Generations *Wayang Wong*' play, *Bhisma Mahawira*, had celebrated Yogya's classical tradition in the style of Haměngkubuwana VIII. Like this performance, the 1989 *golek Menak* revealed the broad range of institutions involved in the patronage of court dance.[45] Both productions were Arts Development Projects of the Department of Education and Culture, and both were performed in the Kěpatihan pavilion in the provincial government's headquarters. Both productions represented the performances and ideas of three generations, from colonial dancers to graduates of the Indonesian Institute of Arts (ISI), including the two brother-sister teams (Ben Suharto and Theresia Suharti, and Bambang Pujasworo and Dyah Kustiyanti) who played leading roles in each production, evidence of how court performance has moved from the domain of amateurs to professional academic specialists. Both projects were inscribed in texts celebrating the essential connection between the personal patronage of the Sultan and the two dance-theatre events as court performance *qua* government project. The first was a collection of writings by court experts, *Getting to Know Classical Yogya Dance*, edited by Fred Wibowo (1981) and published by the Arts Council of the Special Region of Yogyakarta.[46] The second was about the life of the Sultan and story of *golek Menak*, *Sultan Haměngkubuwana IX: the Flowering and Renewing of Yogyakartan Style Dance*, edited by a team lead by Soedarsono (1989) and published by the Local Government of the Special Region of Yogyakarta. These texts are the modern equivalent of the colonial court's *Sěrat Kandha*, texts which list the proclamations for performances during a particular sultan's reign. The second one firmly identified Haměngkubuwana IX as the creator of *golek Menak*. Before the performance, the heads of the provincial and central offices of Education and Culture presented ten 'Appreciation of Artistic Contribution' awards. Haměngkubuwana X accepted one on behalf of his father for creating *golek Menak*. By affirming continuity and reframing court dance as 'Classical Yogya Dance', this cultural gala inscribed the life of Yogyakarta's first postcolonial cultural Sultan as history – a history which his successor was helping to produce, as well as producing official culture, as his father had done before him.

There is still evidence that the court maintains its power to integrate the dissent which characterized the long process of *golek Menak*'s development. Normally factionalism and competitiveness make it difficult to coordinate the different groups that make up the court dance network. Only a court command could unify so many

---

44. Between June and August 1988 each group performed a fragment which was video-taped so the Sultan could evaluate them and select which aspects should be developed further (Soedarsono et al. 1989: 58–62).

45. For Lindsay, *Bhisma Mahawira* had also revealed the triumph of kitsch over classicism in the court traditions, a decline that started in the 1920s and 1930s when the balance between visual and verbal imagery was lost and the story was condensed so much that it became unintelligible (1985: 159ff.); see also Kam (1987).

46. Wibowo was production manager at the Catholic Media and Culture Centre (PUSKAT), and later head of the Yogya Arts Council.

diverse and disharmonious elements to produce effective cooperation. Despite the apparent state control of the event, the long hours of participation in its projects brought little financial reward, and performers were flattered to be invited to dance in the court, in the tradition of service to an institution still perceived to be alive with the spirit of its founding Sultan. Nonetheless, after the completion of the project, there were mixed feelings about the performance. For some, the production was not yet 'perfection', but 'only the first stage'. Others were dubious about the combination of Sundanese drumming, movements from Minangkabau martial arts, and the foundation in the jerky movements of rod puppets. 'Where has it come from, this dance?' asked a senior dance teacher, 'Certainly not from the court'. Although the performance was represented as an expression of cultural consensus, this was not the whole story. Nor was it a happy unification of court and local government. A senior male dance teacher said that no one from Kridha Mardawa had been invited to the show, even though they had designed the costumes.[47] Bu Yuda later told me that she had not been invited to the premiere, nor had the many other court kin (*sĕntana dalĕm*) who were not civil servants. Senior court dance personnel had been sidelined in favour of state bureaucrats.

A significant feature of the *golek Menak* project was the Jakarta connection. Siswa Among Bĕksa and Mardawa Budaya had performed *golek Menak* fragments in 1974 and 1980 respectively at Taman Ismail Marzuki at the invitation of the Jakarta Arts Centre, and Siswa Among Bĕksa again in 1984 at the invitation of the Directorate of Arts in the Ministry of Education and Culture. In May 1987 Hamĕngkubuwana IX viewed *golek Menak* fragments by Siswa Among Bĕksa and ISI, and suggested some improvements. This took place at Taman Mini Indah Indonesia's Yogya pavilion, as did a performance of *Kĕlaswara Partakrama*, by a team of eighty people at the end of August 1989. Taman Mini was founded by Mrs Tien Suharto in 1975 to represent the culture of each Indonesian Province.[48] The Guntur Madu Foundation (Anjungan Mataram), run by General (retd) Widodo and managed by Dra Murywati Darmokusumo, one of Hamĕngkubuwana IX's daughters, promotes Yogyakartan dance and organizes performances here. This is one example of the martial Yogya style performance being patronized by court kin with military careers. Another culturally active former military man was General (retd) Nick Lany, a member of the Pakualaman, born in Yogya, who had served as military attaché to Washington, and

---

47. K.R.T. Dipuradanarta (19/3/89); he then launched into a critical evaluation of the movements. A female dance teacher said that it lacked dynamism (*grĕgĕt*), that the build-up for the women's fight was 'flat' (*kĕmbo*), but praised the clowns. A prince who will remain nameless said it was 'like popular theatre – chaos' ('*seperti ketoprak – tidak karuan*') (25/8/89).

48. Taman Mini epitomizes New Order cultural policy (Pemberton 1994: 152–61), but is also a recent version of miniaturization as a longstanding feature of Southeast Asian political and religious symbolization. Each Province supports its own pavilion. A Yogya Depdikbud official said (11/4/89) that his office gave Rp7.5 million to the Mataram pavilion at Taman Mini for operational elements (but not building maintenance), and the DIY Finance Office gave Rp6 million; a total of about £4,500.

as Director General of Immigration in Jakarta. He became the main patron of *Langĕn Mandrawanara*, developed by Mardawa Budaya (above), and also performed at Taman Mini.

The Jakarta connection was no doubt catalyzed by the appointment of the ninth Sultans's youngest brother, Drs G.B.P.H. Puger, as Director General of Culture in 1983. During the 1980s patronage expanded outside Yogya in Jakarta, as many aristocrats established businesses and households in the capital. The success of court dance at Jakarta varied according to venues. At a *Langĕn Mandrawanara* performance at Taman Ismail Marzuki in 1985, the audience figures were disastrously low: 27, 15 and 7 over three nights. Yet all the court networks in Jakarta attended concerts performed by Yayasan Guntur Madu, ISI or SMKI at Taman Mini. This is an indication of the court's continued kudos during the ninth Sultan's reign. As a Dinas Depdikbud official put it, 'the charisma draws them' (19/4/89).[49]

On the face of it, *golek Menak* marked the culmination of the classicization of court dance in an Indonesian arts and culture policy which had been developing during the ninth Sultan's reign. However, as my account makes clear, it is difficult to separate loyalties to the Sultan from loyalties to the state. Textual inscriptions of 'classical Yogyakartan dance' may allow contradiction to coexist, but they do not eliminate the forms of fragmentation which shape the processes of cultural production. Family ties and the interests of the court network both inside and outside Yogyakarta have impeded the development of a homogenized court dance as national culture, and what was produced as 'classical' emerged from ongoing internal dynamics and dissent.

Conclusion

What became of nationalist visions from the 1930s for the role of court dance in the creation of national identity in the first four decades of the postcolonial state? There were three changes. In terms of repertoire, there was the introduction of the *golek Menak* movement style, which was used only for danced fights in the court during the ninth Sultan's reign. Secondly, there was increased participation by women, in *wayang wong*, *golek Menak* and set fighting dances. This has had major significance, and has their widened women's access to dance education and education in general. Thirdly, and most significantly, patronage of court forms extended outside the court, through state dance schools and privately run dance associations.

In short, the context of court dance had changed. A repertoire which had been associated with particular ceremonies and events in the colonial court had by the end of the century been reclassified as a 'local cultural peak' and an Indonesian classical tradition. This change was first brought about by the court, and then by the influence

---

49. In late March 1989 K.R.T. Dipuradanarta went to Jakarta for a Yayasan Guntur Madu concert of Javanese dance at Taman Mini to celebrate the tenth Sultan's accession for the 'big family' of Javanese in Jakarta. He later told me that he went as adviser for four days. Tickets cost Rp25,000 and they sold 2,000 = which brought in Rp50 million, on top of the Rp13.5 million in subsidies (2/4/89).

of networks of royal kin and court officials and their descendents, which mostly retained their territorial affiliation to Yogyakarta, but in some cases extended beyond the Province.

In 1945 court dance was largely an oral tradition apart from several court manuscripts itemizing dance sequences, and Kridha Bĕksa Wirama's codifications. The dances were kept alive in the memories and bodies of court members from Hamĕngkubuwana VIII's time, and they transmitted it to their children and students in a considerably expanded range of training institutions. However, as an heirloom, court culture only survives through being fed, and many who had done this were dying. Whereas in the 1920s and 1930s the court traditions seemed strong enough to be subjected to radical development, by the 1980s they were less robust. Other cultural resources were competing for the time and attention of younger people who before would have gladly become dancers, and questions were being asked about the future of the traditions. The labelling of activities as *adiluhung*, high and noble, indicated a new self-consciousness that things passed down would not survive without intensified support. Traditions were at risk of being swamped by competing cultural resources from both inside and outside Indonesia. There was competition within the elite to determine how the past would shape the future, and questions also arose about whether *all* the things handed down would survive.

Since the 1960s educational institutes and government offices have produced all manner of records and images of dancing. Academic texts, such as ASTI's dictionary of dance and music terminology (Soedarsono et al. 1978), contributed to codification. During the 1980s there were a number of seminars taking place, including one to consider the standardization and codification of court dance gesture, at the instigation of Siswa Among Bĕksa, with the encouragement of the Ministry for Education and Culture. Systems like Laban Notation may help to document dance movement, but they do not replace the human embodied means of transmission. It will be for future scholars to consider the extent to which the development of dance notation in the academies will fix the movement in ways that transmissions from teacher to pupil do not. Educational institutions have been assiduous in preserving existing traditions as films and photographs, but dance is always oral in the sense that it needs a live teacher to pass it on, even if the means of transmission becomes a video tape. It is significant that during the 1980s ASTI/ISI invited Bu Yuda to teach *bĕdhaya*, *srimpi*, *Saritunggal*, and *Golek Lambangsari Wĕtah* according to court standards, and Mbak Theresia Suharti continues the tradition at ISI.

Cultural forms change to meet the needs of their audiences. By the end of Hamĕngkubuwana IX's reign, court dance was both for locals and domestic and overseas tourists. Practitioners were balancing the desire to preserve traditional values with that of attracting audiences. Audiences for court dance had tended to be practitioners and their families. They attended to support the family and the group, and were not well known for their attentiveness – a characteristic of Javanese audiences in general: a shadow play audience is often absent or asleep. Court dance has always been one element in a multifaceted event, and audiences have also been participants, engaged in activities other than simply watching. Audiences are now more diverse, and include groups who are prepared to pay for performance as entertainment (see Chapter 7). Local styles of attention have changed. Between 1977 and 1989 audiences' concentration at performances increased, possibly because people had learnt to pay attention in the classroom, or simply because many performances were shorter – to the irritation of traditionalists, and the pride of modernists. However, Javanese audiences have not yet become 'consumers', and there is still a sense that entertainment should be free as part of a larger event. When people do buy tickets for a performance, they are not passive spectators, but interact with each other, even in the cinema. Participation remains part of being in an audience, a process of reiterating shared identifications or becoming more familiar with them. In the early 1980s, students were always interested in novelty, and experimental events on campus which combined cabaret and rock would be packed out, but innovation was mostly regarded with suspicion. Bagong Kussudiardjo's 'new creation' (*kreasi baru*) dances, which formed part of the early New Order plan to create 'Indonesian culture' resulted in disappointment and scepticism. As a female musician said, 'No one knows what standards to judge them by; now he's taking dances from Kalimantan, so nobody knows if they are good or what.' Audiences in Yogya tended to prefer to know what they were being shown, so that they could engage aesthetically with the performance, expressing approval at the time and sharper critical views afterwards. This conservative sense of knowing the standards has diminished and during the 1990s there was more openness to innovation.

In this way court dance survived the transition from colony to nation state and transformed into classical Yogya style dance. Although it has been said that independence, education and inflation 'undermined' the court's 'central role in Yogya's social structure and culture' (Selosoemardjan 1978: 236), the court's involvement with education during the reigns of the eighth and ninth Sultans ensured that court values adapted to the demands of the nation and the times. Paradoxically modernization under Hamĕngkubuwana IX stimulated the regeneration of the traditional references, including performance traditions, for the assertion of a distinctive Yogyakartan identity. Despite the diversification of training and performance venues, the court was still regarded by many as the exemplary centre of excellence and the most prestigious arena for performance in Yogya. Even experienced dancers described participating in the court's Sunday training sessions as 'awesome', and members of the court Arts Section considered it as the best conservatory for 'ripening' performers in court dance.

Having outlined the changes in the context of court dance, I now turn to a more detailed consideration of its social significance. I begin with a discussion of how the early nationalist concepts were used in republican policies for culture and education, and how dance served to embody Javanese values that continued to be used as forms of socialization for Javanese-Indonesian citizens.

Chapter 4

Embodying Culture: Dance as Education

This chapter explains Javanese values, their embodiment in court dance and their contribution to the production of citizens in the Indonesian Republic. Javanese court dance has become a resource within the domain of cultural politics as a performance event, but learning to dance has also provided individuals with useful resources in the domain of social interaction. Javanese socialization processes have been extended and transformed to shape an Indonesian model of identity. The principle developed in the Tamansiswa educational system that dance reflects the character of the person has resulted in a restricted set of physical practices and performance contexts becoming associated with an education in embodied self-control, which many Javanese Indonesians consider to be central to their identity.

The extent of the interest in court performance never ceased to surprise me. In 1983 when I had to renew my research visa, I discovered that a document which I should have obtained from the police twelve months earlier was missing. My anxieties about this were confirmed when I went to the relevant police station to be met with menacing questions about my 'activities' in Yogya from the burly man at the window. To my surprise, as I uttered the magic words, 'court dance', he became all smiles, and started to tell me about the roles he had played in *wayang wong*; my bureaucratic crisis became an incidental trifle. As substitute documents were signed and handed over, I discovered that the fitness programme for police trainees in Yogyakarta at that time offered a choice between volleyball, the martial arts and dancing.

This anecdote is important for understanding the relationship of Javanese court dance in Indonesia to identity, to belonging, and to power. Dance in Java does not suffer the marginalization of dance, for instance, in Britain and the United States (Ncss 1992: 2–3). The diversification of venues for court dance training in the past fifty years has made it mainstream. Unlike classical Western ballet, for example, where ageing normally ends a dancer's career (Wainwright and Turner 2004), people of all ages participate in Javanese court dance and dance theatre. They do it for fun, as an elegant form of physical education, as part of formal education, from kindergarten through to professional development programmes. They learn in state schools, private schools, dance associations, or from teachers (*mĕguru*). Many organizations and institutions, such as banks and schools, run their own *gamĕlan* and dance groups, in which they encourage their employees and students to participate.

People had different ideas about how dance fits into an individual's personal development. It is not necessary to begin dance training very early. Before Indonesian independence, children as young as seven already trained in the court, but Kridha Bĕksa Wirama stipulated a minimum age of eleven so as not to interfere with the child's general education. When I joined the beginners' class for girls at Pamulangan Bĕksa Ngayugyakarta (henceforth PBN), most of the other students were aged about fifteen years old, and had already learnt dancing in associations for juniors. Some thought that dancing belonged to childhood, with shadow-puppetry and music being more suitable for older people. Others reckoned that male dancers started by focusing on technical brilliance, and only reached their peak in their late thirties and forties, when they developed the inner aspects of dancing. The visual effect of the wide range of age groups participating in court dance is striking. In court performances of *wayang wong* in the 1980s, the massed ranks of the gods were performed by older influential men who worked as government officials and educationalists. They were hardly recognizable in their make-up, chests bared, and bellies strapped in, wrapped round with yards of stiff fabric. Once their physiques were beyond even these material supports, older men with an interest in the performing arts would either teach or play *gamĕlan* music, and perhaps sing. For women, marriage or motherhood used to mark the end of a performing career at the court but they could continue as dance teachers instead. In the 1980s and 1990s older men and women alike performed regularly in the court training sessions on Sundays. For instance, Bu Putri appeared in *wayang wong* fragments, together with her teenaged daughter Ning, who trained and performed at Siswa Among Bĕksa, and her two sons, who had been trained in the court by their maternal grandfather, K.R.T. Dipuradanarta. Dance dynasties such as this are not uncommon in Javanese traditional arts, and demonstrate the ongoing importance of kinship ties in the transmission of court dance.

Learning dances from the court repertoire is no longer limited to a particular status group, though royal children and grandchildren run most court dance associations. Learning to dance has produced communities of interest, and dance has also represented the widest national community, both to itself and to the outside world. As this chapter will show, people who have learnt court dance have been neither isolated nor marginalized. This is because dance has been associated with social status, but also with early nationalist ideas of personal development.

Dancing Is an Education in *Rasa*

'Dancing is as an education in *rasa*' (ng. and I; *raos* k.). This central pedagogic principle in Tamansiswa was often referred to by Gusti Suryobrongto and other dance educationalists and aristocrats. Tamansiswa's policy was to develop personal and social identity through educating an individual's *rasa*.

Rasa carries a heavy freight of significance in Javanese philosophical, religious and ethical discourses, and has been translated as 'taste, feeling, inner experience, deepest meaning, essence'.[1] Although it has been associated with *priyayi* religion, *rasa* extends from the distinguishing taste of *priyayi* as an occupational class, to a spiritual capacity which is not limited to elite sensitivities.[2] It invites a range of local interpretations, as illustrated in this metaphor of embodiment by a court musician:

> three of the five [*gamělan*] tones (*barang, gulu, dhadha*) ... together comprise a symbolic imagery of the human body. The tone *lima* [five] suggests love, i.e. love for all sorts of beauty – springing from the five senses, and the tone *ěněm* [six] suggests feeling (*rasa*) which penetrates the whole body and soul. (Sastrapustaka 1984: 316)

Rasa is used in a number of philosophical systems and in a general way, giving a Javanese stamp to phenomenological explanations about being in the world. In this book it takes on the meaning of embodied consciousness or perception. However, rather than being a clue to some essential Javanese 'otherness', *rasa* belongs to the class of concepts which are culturally useful precisely *because of* their vagueness, blocking off questions, short-circuiting philosophical elaborations, and promoting belonging through mutual collusion.[3] Words of this kind are found in any society in how people speak of collective rhythmic dispositions and personal tactical negotiations of daily life.

In the Javanese context, *rasa* is important in an ethnographically grounded approach to the body for understanding embodied practice. Although dance might appear to contribute to education as an embodied skill, *rasa* can be thought of as consciousness because Javanese ideas about the person do not use the body and mind dualism which resulted from Western Enlightenment thinkers' attempts to eliminate the soul (Porter 2003). The embodied self is a starting point for understanding dance, but as embodiment includes more than the biological physical self, it is important to consider local understandings of the body, the self, and the relation between them.

---

1. Uhlenbeck (1978). I provide some semantic glosses in the notes because Indonesian-Javanese commentaries about dance do this to extend the significance of its techniques and evaluations, including a long history through etymological derivations from Sanskrit (Skt) via Old Javanese (OJ).

2. Geertz has emphasized 'feeling' and 'meaning', noting that *rasa* combines two senses (taste and touch) with emotions 'within the heart'; the combination of feeling and meaning gives 'a complete picture of the phenomenological analysis of experience upon which the *prijajis* base their world-view', and he quotes an informant: 'Whatever lives has *rasa*, and whatever has *rasa* lives' (1960: 238–39). Gonda says (1952: 158) 'hidden meaning' and blending of an ultimate hidden meaning and tactile sensation are from two different Sanskrit roots, *rahsya* and *rasa*, but in Modern Javanese *rasa* combines the two. There is a wide range of cognates of *rasa*, including (in *krama*): *pangraos* (feeling); *rumaos* (to sense, with instinct – in contrast to *ngěrtos*, 'to know with the intellect'); *ngraosi* (gossip, in a bad sense); *raos-pangraos* (more inner feeling, deeper and intense); *raos/rumaosing manah* 'less deep' (although 'in the heart'); *suraos* (meaning, content).

3. As Paul Stange has rightly observed, *rasa* is like a 'repetition of formulae within ordinary social discourse as *a way of avoiding "meaning"*' (1984: 134, my emphasis).

Javanese people refer to the person as both visible and invisible, with senses, faculties and consciousness (*rasa*), all of which are embodied. A person is explained as having two aspects, *lair* (*lahir* I.) and *batin*, often said to refer to 'outside/form' and 'inside/essence'.[4] *Lair* is the physical body and the exoteric conditions arising from one's birth, such as rules imposed by others, including status, physical desires and so forth. *Batin* is the esoteric questing inner self. This contrast is different from the 'mind-body' dichotomy in Western thought because it conceptualizes the person as constituted by visible and invisible processes which are made manifest in the body.

The relation of the body to the self in Java may be compared to other Asian philosophical systems. The Tibetan Mahayana *prasangika* teaches that, 'There is no innate conception of a person - coarse or subtle - in which the person is conceived to be a different entity from mind and body' (Hopkins 1977: 182). A Muslim martial arts teacher in southern India explains that there are three bodies: fluid, muscular and subtle (Zarrilli 1998: 84). Here 'self', 'agency', 'power', 'body' and 'behaviour' are put in quotation marks, 'to suggest the problems with Western essentialization and reification, and in order to emphasize that all five should be considered provisionally ... [as] dynamically "crafted" in the constantly unfolding creation of the self in particular contexts of experience' (ibid.: 7).[5] In Java too, embodiment is always more than the visible and material *lair* body, though the *batin* is normally contained by the visible body. The embodied Javanese self is best understood not as a single entity but as a heterogeneous field of forces and potentials, some of which are more bounded than others.[6]

Oral and written discourses on the Javanese person have absorbed ideas from Hinduism, Buddhism, Islam and Christianity. When a philosophically minded aristocrat said, 'Dance is the shadow of the moving of your mind; the gods are in your own body, in your *rasa*' (Pak Yu 27/4/83), the second part of the sentence shows that he meant *batin*, not 'mind'. In conversations of this kind, people would often cite Ki Hadjar Dewantara's educational philosophy for Tamansiswa. Here the *batin* is formulated as the triad of creative thought, sense and will (*cipta-rasa-kĕrsa*), derived from the fourfold scheme of body (*raga*), *cipta,* spirit (*jiwa*), and *rasa* in *Sĕrat Wĕdhatama*, an influential nineteenth-century philosophical poem. These concepts have been equated with the fourfold path of Sufism, with *rasa* corresponding to gnosis

---

4. These words derive from the Arabic *ẓahir* and *batin* (Gonda 1952: 161) in the nonorthodox radical monism of Ibn al-'Arabi found in Javanese *suluk*, religious works in verse (Zoetmulder 1995: 253).
5. Zarrilli borrows Kondo's concept of 'bodymind' from a study of Japanese martial arts to describe the experiencing 'self' (1998: 18) so as to facilitate cross-cultural comparison.
6. The dialectical fluidity between *lair* and *batin* is beautifully represented as a double spiral illustrating the subtle geometry of the self in *Sĕrat Wirid Hidayat Jati,* by the nineteenth-century Surakartan court poet, Ranggawarsita (1954: 63). Geertz's model of the person based on a circle with a dot in the middle (1960: 255) fails to represent these qualities. There are many words in Javanese for the self and body, including *angga, awak, awak dhewe, dhewe(ke), salīra* or *sarīra* (both *krama Inggil* from Glu 'body'), while *dĕdĕg* and *wadhag* mean 'physique'.

(*ma'rifat*) (Robson 1990: 38–47). In *Sĕrat Centhini,* another nineteenth-century text, *rasa* does not mean feeling or sentiment, but refers to a third level of being in a relation with God (Magnis Suseno and Reksosusilo 1983: 136). The shadow puppet theatre also structures local interpretations of the self. The eldest Pandhawa brother, Puntadewa, stands for soul (*atma*), the second brother, Janaka, for creative thought (*cipta*), and the third brother, Wĕrkudara (or Bima) for character (*budi*) (Rama Sena pers. comm.1983). Other bodily aspects, such as liver (*ati*), spirit (*jiwa*) and soul (*suksma; atma*) are also used synonymously for aspects of *batin* in the various philosophical systems.

Despite the importance of nineteenth-century court mysticism in what Geertz (1960) calls the '*prijaji* world view' and what Pemberton (1994) calls 'the subject of Java', there are many everyday recognitions of the close interrelation between *lair-batin*. This is expressed in the Javanese proverb 'a brick in its casting mould' (*satu munggĕn rimbagan*). And at the end of Ramadan, the Islamic fasting month, it is common to clean one's social slate and apologize 'inside and out' to one's relatives, friends, neighbours and colleagues by saying '*Ma'af lahir batin*'. As a lecturer in a Teacher Training College in East Java I had to attend a formal annual *halal bihalal* reception, which involved shaking hands with colleagues and uttering this statement. Nowadays people also send this message in greeting cards, emails and texts. In Indonesian Java, this twofold notion of the person is general, not arcane.

An education in *rasa* is based on values associated with early nationalism which then shaped ideas of education within Indonesia. This education began as a form of socialization into *cara jawi*, literally 'the Javanese way'.[7] *Cara jawi* also means 'Javanese language', but Javanese people often used it during my fieldwork to refer to Javanese culture or identity. They usually implied a contrast with Indonesian-ness, often associated with the negative aspects of modernity. *Cara jawi* encapsulates the idea of tacit knowledge and practical know-how, derived from experience and developed through practice.

The Javanese person is understood as the result of the civilizing effects of education, and is not a *natural* given as Lelyveld (1931) and many others have thought. Children under the age of five, a foreigner, or an insane person, are all considered 'not yet' Javanese (*dhurung Jawa*). My Javanese language teacher explained this as 'not being able to think yet', adding that '*ora jawa* means someone who doesn't know order'.[8] In the words of poet and dramatist W.S. Rendra,

---

7. Pemberton (1994: 66–69) considers that *cara jawi* as the reification of a style resulting from the 'ritual process' that was the 'logic of domestication' *cara Walandi* (Dutch practices) into court procedures in the early part of the nineteenth century. I find it more helpful to think of it as a generative, open-ended and emergent discourse rather than a Foucaultian one. 'It must constantly manipulate events in order to turn them into "opportunities"', producing 'the forms not of a discourse, but of the decision itself, the act and manner in which the opportunity is seized' (De Certeau 1984: xix). In another explanatory framework, *cara jawi* may be understood as a context that defines mutuality (Sperber and Wilson 1988: 119).

8. Geertz (1961: 105). On differing patterns of socialization in Central Javanese urban and rural contexts, see also Koentjaraningrat (1985: 233–42), and Keeler (1987: 51–84).

Apparently Javanese culture [*kebudayaan*] has consciously balanced the violent character of its masses. Their *kawruh* [general knowledge, not *science* [*sic*]], spirituality [k*ebatinan*], language and arts ... are the final form of the elaborations of experienced controlled sensibilities.[9]

'Controlled sensibilities' is my translation of Rendra's phrase, '*perasaan halus*'. 'Controlled sensibilities' are the *opposite* of the natural and untutored (*kasar*) inclinations which are often freely displayed in public spaces: the street, the bus, the cinema, the campus. For instance, when a young foreign woman was spotted, there were inevitably shouts (in English) of 'Hello mister, where you go? You wan' free sek?' Locals in Yogya blamed this uncouth behaviour on students from outside, although my informal 'street survey' of where such people came from did not endorse this claim. One person explained that the conflict in the Mahābhārata between the five virtuous Pandhawas and their one hundred uncontrolled Korawa cousins represents the disproportion of disruptiveness and virtue in the individual, and is proof that without education and training, Javanese-ness will never be acquired (Pak Yu pers.comm.1983). Being Javanese is thus daunting. Young Javanese told me that they did not *feel* properly Javanese because they lacked competence in *naluri*, the intuitions and 'things handed down' you need to possess and know to be Javanese. Many young people felt that *naluri* are too difficult to learn. Older friends explained that this has *always* been the case, and did not see this as a reason for the Javanese 'inheritance' being under threat.

Despite the frequent lack of 'controlled sensibilities', it is impossible to spend any time in Java as a Western foreigner without being told that Javanese people are *alus*, well-mannered, refined and restrained – unlike you, the foreigner. *Alus* has aesthetic and moral resonances but is a term of approval as ubiquitous in Java as 'nice' is in England; and its generalized opposite, *kasar*, resembles the English word 'nasty'.[10] Sensitivity, refinement, and self-control are strategic adjectives which recur in local discourses as well as the generalizations of outsiders, and play their part in defining and shaping national programmes of identity production. Like *rasa*, *alus* encapsulates a way of being in the world, and can only be understood if it is already understood, entailing a collusiveness that comes from belonging.

The cultural interpretation of movement always runs the risk of settling on a single metaphor or concept which reduces all cultural attributes to itself.[11] This has

---

9. Rendra (1983: 11), translated from the Indonesian by the author. The writer and performer Emha Ainun Nadjib described the polarities of Javanese culture to me as '*adiluhung*' (high and noble) and '*sadis*' (cruel) (9/10/89).
10. In the *priyayi* world-view *alus* means 'pure, refined, polished, polite, exquisite, ethereal, subtle, civilized, smooth', and *kasar*, 'impolite, rough, uncivilized' (Geertz 1960: 232).
11. This problem arises in Ness's otherwise excellent study of Filipino movement. She identifies three versions of *sinulog* dance – candle-sellers', troupe and parade – but these versions are not distinguished by locals (1992: 221). She claimed that 'the grasp of the *tinderas* thus symbolized a widespread strategy for handling social process: the *tinderas* literally had a hold on social life as they performed' (1992:126), but this is an interpretation which is rather detached from what people told her about movement and its social value.

been the case with *alus* in much Javanese ethnography. *Alus* does come into what people say about court dance, but rather than taking it at face value, I have tried to situate it in relation to other cultural concepts. For this reason I avoid giving a general gloss for *alus*, and instead discuss it in relation to other ideas about embodied knowledge, including the correct adjustment of behaviour – language, tempo and rhythm – to the particulars of place and person. These ideas form the basis of a two-way flow between dance and everyday life, which has resulted in dance aesthetics providing metaphors for social ethics.

Alus has also been implicated in discussions of gender ideologies in Java. The truism that gender relations in Southeast Asia are 'complementary' – equal but different – is now routinely examined rather than presumed, producing evidence of changes in gender relations and many examples of men having greater prestige than women.[12] It has been suggested that Javanese women are inferior because their practical power over household finances in the *kasar* material world and their inability to control their emotions precludes them from achieving the *alus* potency and spiritual authority of men (Keeler 1987). This argument generalizes a masculine Javanese ideology at the expense of other perspectives. Women have power in the home and in the marketplace *because* they have more self-control than men, who cannot control their sexual desires or be relied on to bring home the profits from the market (Brenner 1998). Court culture in Java has esteemed women for their ready ability to learn and embody *alus* qualities (Hughes-Freeland 1995). Court dance values the feminine mode based on subtly and flexibility over and above the brute strength and brawn of the robust modes. The feminine mode was performed by men in the past, and the most subtly powerful male characters dance in modes which are very similar to the feminine mode, so it is important not to overemphasize an essential relationship of *alus* and femaleness either. The qualities of the feminine and restrained male dance modes are associated with approved manners and social know-how for both men and women in polite social interactions. Participation in dance training also socializes young women by enabling them to establish contact with men outside their family and neighbourhood, including the teacher. Formerly a male teacher would use a pencil or ruler to correct a female trainee's posture, although I did not observe this during my research. Dance training in many associations is an opportunity for physical and verbal flirtation. However, in most dance associations, as in the court, men may watch women during their training, but the women usually retire when it is the turn of the men. These conventions were explained as the Javanese way of doing things, motivated by modesty.

Javanese culture (*kebudayaan Jawa* I.) itself was explained to me as 'the results of character [*budi*] given form in various media'; it is always 'education in disguise'.[13]

---

12. Gender inequalities in Indonesia have been explained as arising due to different factors, including urban military and bureaucratic domains and ideologies since 1966, or poverty (Sears 1996b).

13. Pak Pardjan, head of SMKI (16/6/83, 2/9/83), citing Tamansiswa's ideas. Culture (*kebudayaan* I.) has a complex etymology from *kabudayan*, which is from *budaya* (OJ) 'talented, intellectual, culture, civilisation' (Gonda 1952: 319).

Dance is one such 'medium' which continues to be valued for its power both to instil 'controlled instincts', and to reveal the person as he or she is. Gusti Suryobrongto (30/3/83) said, 'Dance reflects the character of the person.' Bu Yuda (20/10/83) said, 'When a person dances, their character [*watak*] appears – you can see the person', adding that 'Even if someone's speech is not very clever, if they sit well, that's good.' She laughed when I told her about clever Western professors with bad posture. I heard numerous anecdotes about unruly individuals or groups who had been transformed into 'proper' Javanese people through dance, such as Javanese children being raised in Jakarta (the Indonesian capital) whose parents and teachers were at their wits' end until the children learnt Javanese dance and became controlled, quieter and compliant. A senior courtier spoke of this positive transformation in visual terms: 'I didn't recognize her. Could this be the same person?' So such changes are manifestly visible in physical comportment. It is also significant that the child in question was in an environment where exposure to Javanese culture did not automatically form part of her socialization, but had to be actively chosen. As training in rhythms and measures appropriate for behaviour in polite Javanese society, court dance provides the means to manoeuvre in social circles where such behaviour is still valued. It both empowers and transforms the *lair-batin* person.

Learning to Dance

I now turn to my experience of learning the feminine mode (*běksa putri*) in court dance. Dance movement (*běksa*) refers to a mode, a form (such as *bědhaya*), a named sequence of movements, and particular elements of movement called *patrap* (position).[14] *Patrap* means 'walk, behaviour, order, arrangement' and is cognate with *atrap*, 'to arrange', as in *atrap sumping*, 'to arrange one's ear ornaments'.[15] These positions become dance movement within the parameters set by *pathokan*, fixed conventions or standards. So *běksa* is 'dance movement', or *patrap*-in-motion, performed according to particular standards. According to Suryobrongto (1976: 28), these standards apply to: (1) the gaze; (2) the neck; (3) the stance; (4) movements of the pelvic girdle; (5) turned-out thighs; (6) turned-up toes; (7) downwards bend. The turn of a wrist (*ukěl*) is *běksa*: as the wrist turns, the fingers should be held in *ngithing*, with the thumb and centre finger forming a circle. *Ngithing* is a *patrap*, but the action of turning the wrist and moving the hand is *běksa*. The word *běksa* is sometimes

14. I borrow the word 'mode' from Mauss (1973: 79) to avoid confusion with regional 'styles'. *Běksa* derives from *baksa* (OJ), 'to display one's skill', 'to dance' (Zoetmulder 1982: 1927). Other related terms are *banyol(an)*, a joking act; and *tandhak*, formerly synonymous with *běksa* but today meaning 'capering, cutting a figure'. Lelyveld (1922) refers to dance movement sequences as 'flowers' (*kěmbang*), a usage not current in Yogyakarta. In Surakarta dancers describe dance sequences as '*sěkaran*' or '*kěmbangan*' (flowers), and in Bali dance figures are also called '*sekar*'.

15. *Patrap* derives from '*patra*' (Skt): drinking vessel, bowl cup; any receptacle; capable or competent person, anyone worthy or fit for or abounding in; actor's part or character in a play; in OJ it came to mean 'able way of moving, especially the dance like movements when eager and challenging to a fight' (Zoetmulder 1982: 1326).

applied to named dance movement sequences such as *ngĕndherek* (see below), which includes as many *patrap* as are needed. As will become clear, not all *patrap* are given names, nor do *patrap* sit neatly in a classification as a sub-element of *bĕksa*.

The self may be an intertwining of *lair-batin*, but young Javanese dancers often told me that they were ignorant of the *rasa* or philosophy of dance, and just interested in technique. This account will start with technical matters, but will move to consider a more advanced stage in dance training by discussing the perspectives provided by teachers on aesthetics and where *alus* fits in. These aesthetics vary, so I will first introduce my three dance teachers.

Three dance teachers

In 1982–83, I participated in classes taught by Rama Sas at Pamulangan Bĕksa Ngayugyakarta (PBN). This charismatic and controversial teacher was well-known for challenging the choreographic standards of court dance while maintaining their traditional appearance, and has already been introduced in the previous chapter. A detailed account of his classes follows below.

After a year's study with Rama Sas, I took private lessons with B.R.Ay. Yudanĕgara (1931–2004) and learnt *Saritunggal,* the court foundation dance for female dance. Bu Yuda, who asked me not to address her by her title 'Gusti' or 'Ndara', was the daughter of K.R.T. Wiranĕgara, a well-known dancer and composer, and later head of the Bĕbadan Among Bĕksa dance association, established in 1952 by G.B.P.H. Yudanĕgara, whom Bu Yuda married when she was thirty years old. A leading court dance teacher and choreographer of *bĕdhaya* and other female dance forms, she taught at Siswa Among Bĕksa, at the court's training sessions on Sundays, and at the Indonesian Arts Institute (ISI) from the late 1980s till 1991. In 1994 she also taught at IKIP two or three times a week, training trainee dance teachers in *Bĕdhaya Sinom* for their exam. Bu Yuda always wore traditional dress and usually spoke to me in Javanese. She lived in a large but unostentatious traditional house in a *kampung*, and taught me in her simply furnished living room behind which was concealed the *pĕndhapa* where she taught *bĕdhaya* to more advanced pupils. Despite her rank she was unassumingly self-effacing with a dry sense of humour. Unfailingly kind, friendly and straightforward, she treated me like a rather unpredictable daughter. She admitted that the slow pace and the subtle differentiation of *Saritunggal*'s movement sequences that make it so resistant to memorization and difficult to learn had taken her six years to perfect when she was young. A patient teacher, she understood my determination to reproduce the subtle and elusive patterns of movement, to understand, not to perform, them. She also allowed me to photograph her demonstrations of the positions.

My third teacher was B.R.Ay. Sri Kadaryati (b.1944), who I address as Mbak ('older sister') Kadar. She gave me extra help when I was having difficulties with my classes at PBN and has remained a close friend. Her mother was B.R.Ay. Purwadiningrat, nineteenth daughter of the eighth Sultan. She trained at Kridha Bĕksa Wirama for two years to *srimpi* level, and then in 1953, aged nine, started again from the foundation with Siswa Among Bĕksa, because 'the court is the source of classical dance'. She later continued to teach and choreograph there (2/11/82). She said she liked teaching everywhere, but observed that on no account would Siswa Among Běksa teachers teach at PBN. She went on the European tour in 1970, which she says included participants from *all* the different training venues. She and her husband R.M. Ywanjono, a royal grandson through his father Gusti Suryobrongto, were civil servants working for the provincial government Arts and Culture office. They also ran Suryakěncana, a *ketoprak* and court dance organization. Mbak Kadar was vivacious and extrovert. She normally wore Western dress, and admitted that the reason she did not attend the court's Sunday dance sessions was because of the bother of having to wear traditional dress. In 1994 she was finally persuaded by her cousin, Sultan Haměngkubuwana X, to become an *abdidalěm*, and told me she would have to go to offer flowers to the heirlooms in the Prabayěksa every thirty-five days on Wage Fridays (25/9/94). Mbak Kadar had a range of entrepreneurial interests and skills in the commercial as well as cultural domain; in 1999 she worked as an 'Avon lady' selling beauty products. She and her family taught me much of what I know about Javanese behaviour, custom and also loss. It was always with Mbak Kadar that I would visit the graves of Gusti Suryobrongto from 1989, and B.R.Ay. Suryobrongto from 1991 in the royal cemetery at Kota Gedhe.

Learning the basics of feminine dance at Pamulangan Běksa Ngayugyakarta

My participation in Rama Sas's classes for beginners at PBN taught me how culture becomes embodied. The classes took place in the open-sided pavilion (*pěndhapa*) and veranda (*paringgitan)* of the residence of Rama Sas's late brother-in-law, Prince Pudjakusuma. Three times a week in the heat of mid-afternoon, I would drive my 70cc Honda *bebek* ('duck') motorcycle along the noisy Jalan Brigden Katamso, which runs parallel to the eastern wall of the court *beteng,* turn eastwards down a dirt track past a shabby row of stalls selling snacks and watered-down petrol to a large *běringin* tree, and then north through the gates into the dusty courtyard of the Pudjokusuman. Arriving at this haven of calm after the hot journey always lifted my spirits. The elegant whitewashed buildings, and the well-maintained *pěndhapa,* with its highly polished floor and carved wooden pillars, provided a fantasy setting for research, but the ensuing class was very real, and required nerve and stamina to cope with the demanding physical challenges.

At PBN the other twenty or thirty level-one students were mostly senior high school girls in their mid-to-late teens who were already proficient in dance. Some were specializing in dance, while for others it was a hobby. One girl told me that her father had danced in *wayang wong,* classical dance used to bore her, but by dint of watching she gradually became interested (Lies 14/12/82). We learnt four dances: the elements of feminine (*putri*) dance movement; *Rěngga Mataya,* the fighting foundation dance; *Běksan Srikhandi-Suradewati,* a fighting duet with dialogue; and *Golek Kěnya Tinembe,* a solo dance. I also observed level-two classes in *běksan* and *golek* dances, and level-three classes in *golek Menak* and *sendratari,* the classical form developed outside the court.

Learning to dance may be an education of the *rasa,* as already mentioned, but one first has to learn physical techniques. Before starting anthropological research I had worked in Indonesia and had learnt Balinese dance, so I was used to sitting cross-legged on the floor, an important aspect of court dance. Merely assuming this position, and rising from it back into a standing position requires a particular physical control not easily acquired by Europeans, who are mostly not comfortable sitting on the floor. Despite this previous experience, I found Javanese dance movement extremely difficult to learn.

In my field notes I recorded Rama Sas's general tips on some basic principles:

> body straight, movement from the pelvic girdle, no swaying from the waist or shoulders, no looping heads; elbows firmly in place when making the hand movements, which should not go out to the side, nor should elbows cramp in or stick out; the shoulder blades should pull together but the shoulders themselves should be natural (hard to do); legs should be turned out, feet with toes tensed when needed. The head should not bend down or come forward (hilarious tortoise-like impression of bad students) but the gaze should. (Field notes 2/12/82)

Learning each *position* involves controlling and harmonizing eyes, neck, body angle, arms, hands, hips and pelvic girdle (*cĕthik*), thighs, knees, feet and toes. The knees have to be turned out, and the hips kept in a line with one's spine, not tilted to the side as in Balinese dance. In the upper body /armpit (*kelek*), upper side (*lĕmpĕng*), lower side (*lambung*) and waist (*punggung*), the elbows should be held so that the armpit is not too tight or wide, and should not flap about. The female armpit is eroticized in Java. In Yogya it was considered important to conceal it as a sign of decency, in contrast to the exposed armpits and uncontrolled arms of the Surakartan style, and the upper arms of Balinese dance, which are usually extended in a line from the shoulder. These contrasts are misleading not least because a number of Yogya arm movements *do* reveal the armpit, but show how movement is imbued with moral significance, in this case in reference to ideas of femininity. Managing the correct gaze is also difficult, especially for a beginner trying to copy the teacher or, in my case as I was normally in the back row, the nearest student. The dancer's gaze should always fall on the floor at a distance of about twice her height in the court, or three times her height outside it (a practice introduced at Kridha Bĕksa Wirama), except when hitting and pursuing an opponent in fighting sequences. I later discovered that looking up or glancing sideways is considered coquettish (*kĕnes*) or vulgar (*rongeh*), as bad as showing one's armpits. The lowered gaze is crucial to the effect of the dance and the distinctiveness of feminine court performance, and is a particular point of contrast with the allegedly provocative eroticism of women in folk performance.

Feminine dance requires constant attention to detail in the position of the hands. There are only four basic single-hand positions (*patrap*) to learn: *nyĕmpurit, ngruji, ngithing, ngĕpel* (Figures 4.1–4.3). Detailed hands are a feature common to court and temple dance across Southeast Asia and a reminder of the impact of the cultural influence from India *c.*AD 400–1000. There are similarities to classical

Figure 4.1 Nyĕmpurit, ngruji

Figure 4.2 Ngithing

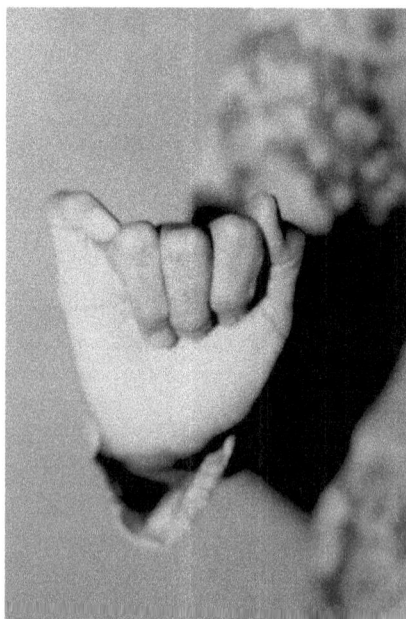

Figure 4.3 Ngĕpel

Indian hand positions, but in Java these are never *mudras* and never represent elements in a narrative, so Lelyveld is misleading when he describes them as single-hand gestures (*asaṁyuta-hasta*) (1931: 77). Unlike classical Indian *abhinaya*, where the face and hands communicate the meaning of the words and moods, as they do in sections of *bharata natyam*, feminine dance movement does not enact the words of the song expressively. In Yogyakarta court dance, as in Bali, there is no 'core meaning' in the dance hands; they are strictly conventional, 'for beauty'.[16] The rules are simple: when the left hand is in *ngruji*, the right should be in *nyĕmpurit*, whether the arms are bent or straight. They become dance *movement* through actions of the wrist, in a full or half turn (*ukĕl asta wĕtah* or *jugag*) or as part of an arm gesture in a movement sequence.[17] This can be demonstrated in the opening sequence. All women's dances begin in a sitting position (*sila panggung*), hands folded in the lap, left under right, the left thumb resting between right thumb and first finger (a hand position which is unnamed). The usual sequence is as follows. First you make a greeting (*sĕmbah*) in which you bring your hands together, thumbs level with the nostrils. Next you shift into the half-kneeling position (*jengkeng*), with the left hand in *ngithing* at right angles to the wrist resting on the raised right knee, right hand at the waist in *ngĕpel*. As you stand up, *ngadĕg*, you straighten both elbows and make the hands into *ngithing* at the sides. Next you draw up the hands in the *panggĕl* movement, taking hold of the dance sash (*udhĕt, sondher, sampur*), which is tied round the waist and hangs to the floor in two lengths, and shift the body weight to the left, the left hand in *ngruji* with the sash over the wrist, and the right hand in *nyĕmpurit*, sometimes holding the sash.

Balance and tension

After attempting to put one's body together according to basic dance principles, the second challenge was learning to lower the body's centre of gravity (*mĕndhak*), turning out thighs and knees, and moving one's weight into the right or left leg (*ngleyek* and *ngoyog*). The expressive power of *all* court dance movement rests on a sustained control over any desire to take off, in complete contrast to the pattern of sweeping climax, release and dying fall of the élancé, presentational style of classical ballet. Javanese dance is about keeping in contact with the ground, and keeping

---

16. Hughes-Freeland (1991a, 1991b). It is interesting to note that there are many (and confusing) regional variations on hand position names. Surakarta: *ngruyung (ngrayung)*; *ngĕpel, mangĕnjali*; Sunda: *meuber, ngeupel,* [no equivalent]; Bali: *ngruji, megemelan, panyembrana* (Supartha and Supardjan 1980: Ch 4). Surakarta also has *ambaya mangap* and *purnama sidi* which combine in *sangga nampa* (Soedarsono et al. 1978).

17. *Nyĕmpurit* is called *driji wanara* ('monkey fingers') in the shadow play (Soedarsono 1984: 223–24). Rassers cites the seventeenth-century *Sĕrat Cabolek* which compares the heretic Seh Lĕmah Bang to a *gambuh* actor who plants a stake and asks 'Who would know my name if I did not mention it myself?' and then cites a similar episode where a *gambuh* actor playing Pañji asks virtually the same question, 'with his left hand on his hip and the other hand holding *the sign of the monkey*' (Rassers 1922: 107–8, cited in Drewes 1978: 70). This riddle warrants further research.

within the limits of one's body, while extending it to the maximum.[18] There was general agreement in Yogyakarta that the dance is 'always on one leg'. This is easily seen in the very muscular 'strong' male modes, in which a dancer regularly has to raise his knee, extend his leg at a right angle to the torso, hold it, and return it to a right angle with the thigh, the foot level with the other knee, the height of the leg and the angle to the body varying according to the robustness of the mode. This one-legged technique is less visible in feminine and *alus* masculine dance but equally central to the dynamic, as I soon discovered.

Balance depends on considerable muscular control due to the pace of the movement, which must be slow and sustained. A filmed sequence of feminine dance movement played back without sound looks as if it is in slow motion. Moving the body weight downwards (*mĕndhak*) through the centre of gravity to the pelvic girdle requires extensive practice, as the weight should remain centred, and move into the turned-out knees away from the pelvis. One of hardest (and most painful) techniques was learning to control the pelvic girdle by concentrating on one's hip bones to move one's body weight laterally from left to right (*ngleyek* and *ngoyog*).[19] When I tackled the more protracted figures of the *Saritunggal* dance with Bu Yuda, I had to learn to shift my weight extremely slowly from one side of the body without allowing the hips to break away from the line of the torso for a count of eight beats – breaking the line is unacceptable in Javanese dance, in contrast to Balinese. The aim was to perform the subtle shifts of weight from one foot to the other smoothly, and empty a foot completely of weight without wobbling or falling over, before drawing it forward with toes flexed, to catch the front pleats of the *jarit* (wrapped *bathik* cloth worn by women in dance training), and then drawing it back to complete with a light tap of the ball of the foot behind the supporting leg – a complex movement known as *gĕdrug* (Figures 4.4 and 4.5). Moving the weight swiftly upwards (*ĕncot*) was also a test of balance and of grace. Learning to perform these smooth shifts of weight in a steady, elegant manner produced the hard thigh muscles of an experienced skier.

The proper aesthetic effect, so obvious when right and so difficult to achieve, requires constant attention to the body's centre. *Ngĕncĕng* (to concentrate, to discipline), is a central concept in Yogyakartan-style dance, and also the name of the feminine dance sequence. Kridha Bĕksa Wirama's name for the feminine mode was '*bĕksa ngĕncĕng ĕncot*'. The dancer has to balance concentration with ease, and strength with grace. The dance is grounded in the feet, which are tensed by the toes being turned up (*nylĕkĕnthĕng*) (Figure 4.6). By concentrating on these tensed toes, I found

---

18. Javanese court dance shares this with contact improvisation, 'experiencing movement from the inside … orientation or focus inwards … secondary attention to shaping the body in space', using 360° space, and 'going with the momentum, emphasizing weight and flow' (Novack 1990: 119–21); these similarities can be explained by aikido being part of contact improvisation's 'movement environment', as martial arts are in Javanese court dance.

19. Susindahati, a secondary school dance student who won first prize for her dancing at Siswa Among Bĕksa in 1987 demonstrates these difficulties in the film, *The Dancer and the Dance* (Hughes-Freeland 1988). This movement was also said to strengthen the muscles needed for childbirth.

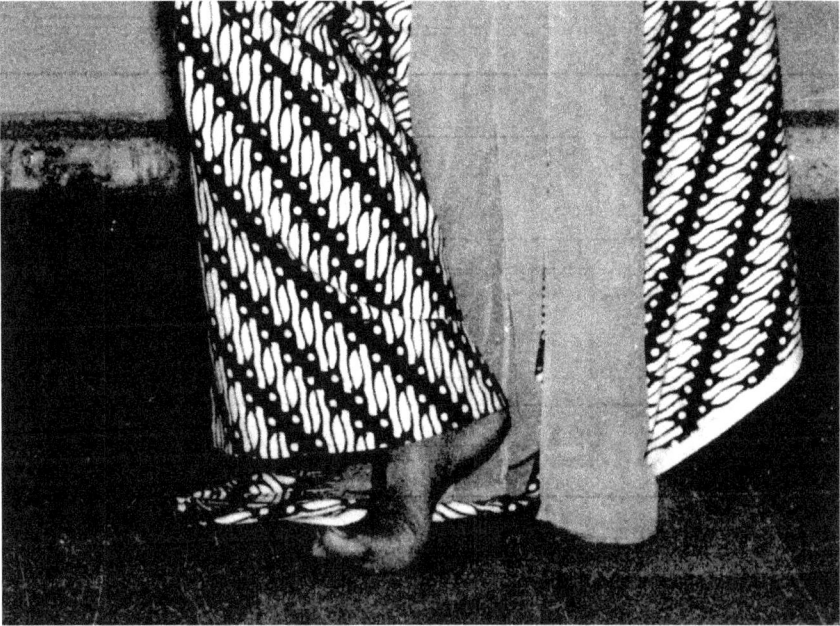

Figure 4.4 Gёdrug, start

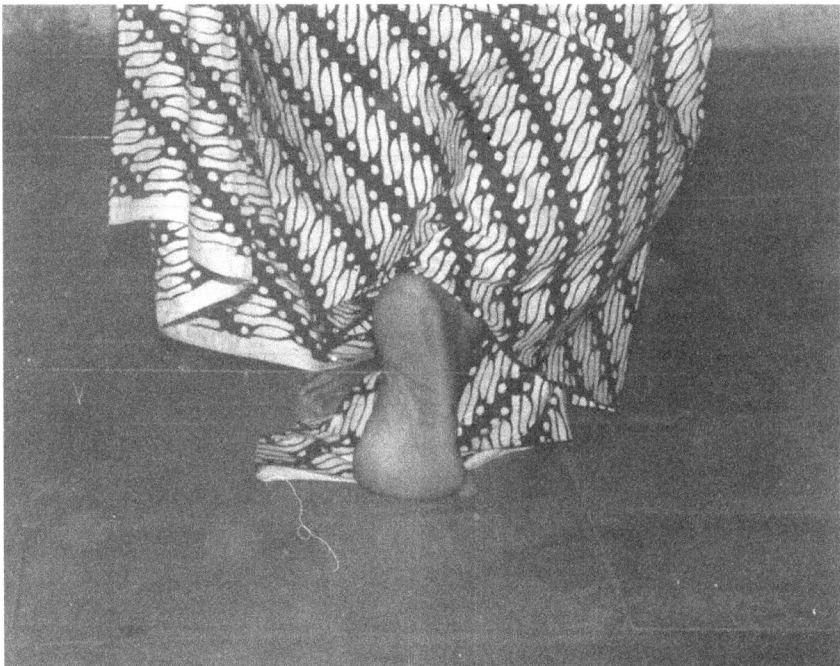

Figure 4.5 Gёdrug, finish

Figure 4.6 Nylëkënthëng toes in *kicat nyangkol* movement

it easier to hold the position of the trunk. The tension of the dance and the effort to keep balanced must be concealed. A dancer should *look* as if s/he has no bones, only muscles (Rama Sena 21/6/83). This aesthetic contrasts starkly with the visible dramatic tension of Balinese dances, and is frequently noted (Soedarsono 1974). Yogya experts also contrast the discipline of their court style with the more curvilinear patterning of the main Surakartan court style, and emphasize the Yogya style's strict convention in the control of the arms and elbows which are held in a square shape (Soedarsono 1984). This requires sustained muscular effort in the upper and lower arms, but with a fluid and supple wrist and precise control over the fingers, which must be neither tense not relaxed, so that there is a contrast between tension and fluidity.[20] When I studied with Mbak Kadar, she started me off with her usual exercises of raising the arms, twisting the hands in and then outwards and upwards to as close to a right angle to the wrist that one could manage, keeping the fingers straight, to make the wrists supple and the arms strong. When I studied with Bu Yuda, she emphasized that Javanese hand positions themselves require *ngĕncĕng*. Despite their resemblance to Indian hand positions, *ngithing* and *nyĕmpurit* should balance grace and tension, unlike Indian or Balinese hands. 'Javanese hands are more pleasing [*luwĕs*] than Indian hands', she said, patiently trying to train my hands 'to look like orchids'. As anyone who has attempted Javanese feminine dance knows, turning a hand in *nyĕmpurit* inevitably makes the little finger stick up rigidly – precisely the kind of minute mistake that can ruin the desired aesthetic. Some young dancers had started to flutter their fingers in *ngruji*, a practice Bu Yuda strongly disapproved of for breaching the approved plain (*lugu*) quality of the Yogya style. So tension is in the turned-out thighs and knees, the turned-up toes, the centred pelvic girdle, and the pulled in stomach. Fluidity is in the wrists, ankles, neck and the sides of the body, all of which should be as supple as possible.

At the very simple level of detailed physical skill and control, then, court dancing is already a challenging practice. Watching the other Western students in advanced classes, I could see that longer legs also caused problems. The men's dancing especially seemed to be too *pointed*, refined and inflected in a presentational way reminiscent of ballet, instead of allowing the weight to be carried through on the muscle to create a sense of tautness and limitation.[21] Even pointing the toe in the male leg extension movement should *come from* the hip, rather than *going out to* the foot. It was impossible to determine whether the other Javanese students with previous dance experience were finding it as difficult. Not only did they learn faster than me, but they also *looked* right when they were dancing, whereas I just *felt* all wrong. When I resumed my dance lessons with Bu Yuda in 1989, she remarked that my dancing had improved since I had been practising the Alexander Technique to work on my

---

20. This may be compared to other contrasting dynamics in dance energy, such as the Balinese contrast between *keras* (strong) and *manis* (sweet) (I Made Bandem, in Barba and Savese 1991).

21. Novack (1990) provides a very helpful discussion of the 'presentational' quality of ballet in contrast to the inward focus of contact improvisation which also characterizes Javanese court dance.

physical 'directions'. So learning the sensibilities of Javanese bodily techniques can be assisted by those from other cultures.

I gradually realized that learning Yogyakartan-style dance is to learn how to assert presence by restraining movements within the limits of one's own body space. The exception to this boundary is when one or both sides of the dance sash are thrown out and back from the waist. Just as maintaining control of the elbows and flexibility of the wrists does not come easily, the difficulty of handling the dance sash with any degree of success, let alone grace, is yet another surprising (and disagreeable) experience for beginners, and may take non-Javanese students a very long time to learn. By August 1989 I had been learning *Saritunggal* for three months over a period of six years. Bu Yuda charitably observed that if one could learn the sequence in six months it would be fair going. It was only in October that year that she started to teach me details such as the turn of the wrist, the timing in bringing the arm up from the side in *ngithing* to the front, and how to deal elegantly with that sash. Bu Yuda explained (20/10/83) that the male influence on female dance was evident in PBN's technique of running one's hand round the whole sash from the knot before letting it go to hold the edge in *jimpit*. Her technique was to take the sash half-way down, making it much easier to manipulate.

Although standards apply to the look, the neck, the stance, movements of the pelvic girdle, turned-out thighs, turned-up toes, and low centre of gravity, there are variations in how those standards are embodied and performed. I was able to recognize these variations by learning with three teachers. Bu Yuda and Mbak Kadar taught a fluid, softer stance, with the shoulder blades held apart. PBN and SMKI taught a more angular stance, with the shoulder blades pulled together, reflecting Rama Sas's male physique and maybe the influence of *golek Menak* dance movement. In the sideways shuffling movement 'shifting sands' (*wĕdi kengser*), the court tradition requires dancers to keep their feet apart, whereas the dancers in Kridha Bĕksa Wirama bring them closer together. In 'stepping on a hot surface' (*kicat*), the court requires a flick of the foot as it is placed on the floor, omitted in Kridha Bĕksa Wirama. In the elegant 'waves of water' (*ombak banyu*), in which the dancer stands, arms out at not more than forty-five degrees from the body (Figure 4.7), and moves her weight from side to side, PBN dancers keep the feet on the floor, but in the court they lift them on and off the spot, with the feet far enough apart not to overbalance, but not so far that the dancer looks as if she is 'urinating' (Bu Yuda 4/10/83).[22] Finally, in the elegant arm movement 'elephant rolling its trunk' (*gajah ngoling*) the Kridha Bĕksa Wirama style is to stretch the arms for a slight moment right out in front, which Gusti Suryobrongto (1/6/83) compared to arm movements in the dance mode for demonic roles (*bapang*). These variations were used to support the claims about authenticity in court style among practitioners already discussed.

---

22. Feminist readers might be interested to know that Simone de Beauvoir's famous discussion in *The Second Sex* about women not being able to urinate standing up has not been an issue for Javanese women when they wear traditional dress (a *bathik* cloth wrapped round the lower body) which leaves them unencumbered.

Figure 4.7 *Ombak banyu, upright centered position*

Interaction and orientation

So far I have concentrated on balance in relation to learning to dance in my own body. Competence in dance is a matter of balance which arises because of the slow pace of the movement when it is performed in place. But it is also about interaction with other dancers, and moving through space. Traditionally dance is orientated to all four sides of the *pĕndhapa*, and movements are repeated in different directions. This open-sided pavilion has a roof supported by at least twelve pillars around the edge and four in the centre. It is difficult to avoid bumping into one of these when you are learning how to walk and run with twenty other people, your gaze lowered to the floor. Choreography requires dancers to go backwards (*mundur*), forwards (*majĕng*), laterally and diagonally. Bu Yuda described this set of moves as *iguh*,[23] an important means of achieving the desired effect of being in place (*mapan*) in an assured and settled way (*mantĕp*). As most dances are for groups of two, four, nine or more, dancing is not only about personal physical disposition, but relations with others in space.

The risk of disorientation and ensuing collision soon became evident when we started to learn fighting duets. In our classes with Rama Sas, once we had improved the balance, fluidity and control in our own dance, we started the *Rĕngga Mataya* dance. This included dagger fights, but for reasons of safety we had to grasp our dance sashes in our wrists instead of using the equally harmless leather dance daggers. It was difficult enough learning to parry and thrust (Figure 4.8) with someone often six inches shorter than me (I am 5'6"), but the hardest part was having to run in little circles on tiptoe (*srisig/trisik*) to end up facing my partner. Fighting choreographies are dizzying in their rapid turns and changes of direction. In *srimpi* dances the choreography is duplicated by two pairs of dancers who mirror each other's movements, producing powerful moments of interchange, reflection and deflection. The male fighting dances *Bĕksan Lawung* and *Bĕksan Etheng* also use chiasmus, a crisscrossing of forms and alignments, as two rows face each other, one turns north, the other south, and then both switch sides. In our fighting dance classes we all experienced a loss of directional control, but it took me longer to orientate myself than my Javanese classmates.

Learning these fighting routines helped me to understand that although feminine dance movement is slow, changes in floor patterns are not. This is most evident in *bĕdhaya* dances when nine dancers all change places at high speed to move into a different asymmetrical floor patterns (see Chapter 5). These patterns are oblique and elliptical, and the transformations between them are hard to discern; the formations alter as if by magic. A graceful performance of these rapid transitions requires astute coordination and bodily instincts as the nine dancers move swiftly around the pillars on tiptoes to regroup without interrupting the sustained rhythm of the dance. Even very experienced dancers can lose their bearings.[24] I never aspired to the standard for

23. This means 'moving in an acceptable way', 'a way of acting' (Poerwadarminta 1939). Bu Yuda thought that the complete expression, *iguh pratikele* might derive from the Dutch, an instance of the colonial notions of order being incorporated into Javanese behaviour and manners.

24. During a rehearsal of the duel in *Bĕdhaya Gandakusuma* at Siswa Among Bĕksa, one of the dancers broke into a smile because she had circled in the wrong direction, a moment I was gratified to have captured on film (Hughes-Freeland 1988).

bĕdhaya but had I not discovered the difficulty of ending up facing my partner in a simple fighting duet, I would never have appreciated the logistical skills demanded by *bĕdhaya* choreographies. This most esteemed form is also the one in which the chances of collision are the greatest, and it is probably also for this reason that *bĕdhaya* is reserved for more experienced dancers. It is not only the matter of balance and control of one's own movements but the interaction with others which is part of *bĕdhaya*'s particular beauty.

Figure 4.8 Dagger thrust (*nyudhuk*)

The Aesthetics of Flowing Water: Toya Mili

After a year of learning to embody dance and talking about it, I understood the physical objectives of dance movement. My discussions with Bu Yuda and Gusti Suryobrongto in particular extended beyond technique and physical expression and helped me understand the terms of approval for dance movement and its aesthetics.

As already explained, approval in Javanese is often expressed by the generalizing word 'alus'. For outsiders, be they Sumatran students or British colonial officers, alus means slowness, as becomes clear from an historic comment by Crawfurd (1820, I: 122):

> To the gravity and solemnity which belong to the inhabitants of a warm climate, any display of agility would appear indecorous, as their stately and sluggish minuet dancing appears insupportably tiresome to our more volatile and lively tempers.

Students in Yogya's Secondary School of Indonesian Arts (SMKI) used alus as a general term to contrast the Yogyakarta style with the Surakarta style, which they described as 'lively' (lincah). In Yogya this adjective is applied to golek dances, and expresses an ethical and aesthetic ambivalence about a form dangerously close to the boundary of much more formal court decorum. This shows that alus defines a shifting boundary which includes 'us' and excludes 'them'.

In aesthetic discourses about dance in both Yogyakarta and Surakarta, the desired effect of dance movement is described not as alus, but as 'flowing water' (toya mili ng. or banyu mili k.). Flowing water describes the effective balance between the measures of music, movements and direction, defined also as 'movement, density/concentration, and direction' (gerak, pekak, jarak I.), or as timing, pleasure and expression (wirama, wiraga, wirasa).[25] The Indonesian word 'ragam' was used by Rama Sas and other teachers to describe some of the units designated by dance movement (bĕksa), but it

---

25. From Skt virama, 'pause, end of, caesura within a verse, or at the end of a sentence'; ma-wirama means 'singing in time (to the accompaniment) … in Javanese irama means "measure" (in music; also wirama) and "acquired habit"' (Gonda 1952: 109). According to Gonda, wiraga (MJ from Skt viraga, cognate with raga) has become a term for 'studied or over-carefully elegant (of one's motions or movements)... it should be inquired into whether this word was first used in connection with dancers who had to impersonate supramundane beings etc. – it actually applies to Javanese dancing – and afterwards interpreted in a more or less depreciating way … [but according to Kern] wiraga represents OJ piraga "pleasure, affection"… [from] Skt raga- "loveliness, pleasure"; there may have been a blending with Skt viraga' (1952: 367–69). I discuss wirasa in relation to characterization in Chapter 6. The Surakartan 'Hasta Suwanda' ('Eight Characteristics') system emphasizes pacak (style), pancat (matching of person to role), lulut (harmonious), wilĕt (rhythmical), luwĕs (graceful), ulat (the proper facial expression), irama (response to the musical measure), gĕndhing (knowledge of the melody) (Pudjasworo 1982: 65ff., translations by the author).

does not 'mean' *běksa*.[26] On one occasion Gusti Suryobrongto explained the dance sequence as a musical sentence: 'The music is like punctuation in a sentence; the *kěnong, kěmpul,* and *kěthuk* are commas, the big gong a full stop; one musical sentence is then filled in with two or three motifs [*ragam* I.]' (pers. comm. 1983).

This analogy may be helpful to introduce the relationship of dance movement to music, but it is an oversimplification. Using grammatical analogies or analyses produces a reductive account (Best 1978), and leads to a different understanding of movement from one that is based on Javanese terms which themselves are subject to variation and disagreement. For instance, Woodward's (1976) search for the grammatical structure in *golek* uses categories inferred from her experience of dance training at PBN, but they do not correspond to the ones used by Javanese choreographers. When I attempted to classify dance poses and movements, practitioners did not use *běksa, patrap* (position) and *sěndhi* (transitions) in a fixed and categorical manner.[27] In the court, *gědrug* (foot tap), *panggěl* (the first movements once the dancer stands up), *tancěp* (standing during dialogues) and *ngancap* (collecting oneself before changing direction) were classed as transitions. 'Flying' (*nyamber*) was a *běksa* in the court, but a transition at PBN. *Gědrug* (foot tap) outside the court was variously classed as *patrap, běksa* and *sěndhi*. These inconsistencies within the Yogyakarta traditions are partly due to dance being an embodied 'oral' tradition rather than a textually determined one.[28] They also represent a form of competition within court groups for control over the dance as it will come to be remembered. However, the capacity of movement to elude categorization and break boundaries is precisely what makes dance powerful, a theme I return to in the next chapter.

The grammatical analogy is particularly inappropriate because of the impact of 'flowing water' on timing or measure (*wirama*). 'Flowing water' is achieved by sustaining dance movement across the musical beats. In Bu Yuda's words: 'The "flowing water" is in the counting, the count of eight. The count of eight is full of movement. From the first count there is always movement. Counting 1, 2, 3, 4, 5, 6, 7, 8, all those counts must be filled.'[29] The movement is more often than not in counterpoint to the music, but it runs parallel, with a personal inflection and responsiveness, grace (*luwěs*) and rhythm (*irama*). A less experienced dancer will interpret literally the counting in *ngěndherek*, one of the simplest movement sequences from the *Saritunggal* dance, and make the mistake of rushing the shift of body weight at '4' and then either execute the kick too soon or be left with a

---

26. *Ragam*'s meanings include 'melody', 'manner', 'caprice', 'style', and 'register' (Echols and Shadily 1990: 445).

27. *Sěndhi* is from *sandhya* Skt, 'comma, link, concealment' (Supardjan 1975: 11) and is used in different linguistic contexts to identify connections, relations and correlations.

28. There are other confusing differences between classifications in Yogyakartan and Surakartan (Brakel-Papenhuijzen 1992).

29. Bu Yuda's words describe images of dance movement in Hughes-Freeland (1988). Although a Balinese-like tension is not desirable in Javanese dance, unceaselessness in Yogya movement and Balinese tension may both be compared to *wiri* in Maori dance, part of a range of important shaking and quivering movements (Shennan 1991).

hesitation between '5' and '6' (see Appendix 2). This physical precision requires an anticipation which only comes with experience, as does the ability to exploit rhythmical spaces between the layers of musical texture, between the percussive gongs and the tapping of the wooden *kĕprak* which is used to signal a major change of position, such as standing up (Soedarsono 1984: 169–81). The experienced dancer moves with a fluency which is at once continuous, sustained and measured, not rigidly set against the musical structure, but in a flexibly responsive way. The relationship between movement accents and musical accents should be what Gusti Suryobrongto (23/3/83) called *nggampuh* 'to be late but not late'. Indeed, I later traced a reference to *toya mili* in Gusti Suryobrongto's lecture on classical Yogya dance, discussed in relation reference to the music used for the for *impur* dance: this should be '*toya-mili* or *vloeiend*' (Dutch 'flowing'), with the rhythm not 'beating time [*nuthuk*]' but slightly 'off beat [*nangguh*]' (Suryobrongto 1976: 19). So when Bu Yuda spoke of *toya mili*, she extended this idea to feminine dance movement, making it her central aesthetic. The main criterion for dance movement to be *alus* is for the movement to relate in a supple way to the rhythm. Simply to follow the beat would be *kasar* or crude.[30]

According to Bu Yuda, in the feminine mode the dancer's neck is 'the key' to embodying the aesthetic of 'flowing water': 'If the neck is alright, the other little mistakes don't matter.' It should move smoothly 'like a snake', tracing a figure of eight (*tolehan*) (Figure 4. 9). By turning the neck correctly, the dancer ensures that the sides of the upper body will move with the desired suppleness, and the movement will flow unceasingly: 'The movements of the body are like – what? In Javanese we say *kadal* [lizard] … There is much turning. The sides of the body move the way a lizard moves.'

Flowing water means that the dancer's movement should never cease. She is always turning a hand or letting her chin lead her neck in a graceful turn after the transfer of body weight has been completed, sustaining movement which centres on an incessant shifting of weight from one leg to the other. The effect of 'flowing water' is especially noticeable in the patterning of the neck movement in relation to the stresses of the *kĕnong*, on the eighth beat when the neck is turning but should continue to turn through to the next beat, thus ending its movement after the beat. Dance students also spoke about the problem of timing the neck movement in the context of changing direction in entrance marches; as the dancer sinks down and turns ninety degrees, the chin is supposed to lead this particular movement; what often happens is that inexperienced dancers turn their chins too far ahead of moving their weight into the advancing leg, and stop moving the neck and head before the rest of the body has followed.[31] Bu Yuda explained that at the maximal point in the turn you should be able to see the round of your shoulder – something not even the best ASTI dancers always do (9/3/83). A problem for Western dance students learning the *tolehan* was that they tended not to swivel the neck far enough round to follow through the body; the length of their necks also caused problems with the accentuated lateral neck movements

---

30. This resonates with the Filipino notion of 'resilience' In movement (Ness 1992: 222–23)
31. This error is demonstrated by Susindahati in Hughes-Freeland (1988).

Figure 4.9 The neck movement, *tolehan*

(*coklekan*) from *golek*, which Rama Sas had used in other dances using the feminine mode although in the court it should never be used for *bĕdhaya* and *srimpi* dances.[32] Court choreographers like Bu Yuda had problems with the accents of this kind of movement, as they did with the new *golek Menak* movement style, with its jerky neck and shoulder movements that are supposed to imitate wooden puppets, in an aesthetic which seems to be the opposite of flowing water.

In court practices, very small differences are very expressive. While formal contrast provides the basis for variation, the performer's skill and the audience's pleasure are in the *minutiae* of contrast which are often so small as to be indiscernible to the untrained or unfamiliar sensibilities. Memorizing the basic sequences of feminine court dance is extremely difficult because of the small and subtle variations

---

32. The four standard neck movements in court dance are *pacak gulu*, *tolehan* (normal and *nglĕnggot*), *coklekan* (for the *golek* dance, monkeys and apprentices only), and *gĕdheg* (for strong modes) (Suryobrongto 1976: 28).

between them. For example, the *ngĕndherek* sequence which uses the sash and moves sideways is followed by *imbal*, which does not use the sash, and it moves forwards. From an observer's point of view, the dance sash also contributes to the effect of flow and provides accents. The sash normally provides an accent every eight and sixteen beats. In movement sequences where this does not occur, a tiny absence creates a powerful effect by going against the grain of the audience's unconscious expectation of rhythmic repetition. The point here is that absence of movement, a tiny hiatus in a system of flow, can be as expressive as overtly energetic movement, if not more so. The expressive power of omission is subtle, and lies in restraint. Such variation is typical of classical Javanese choreographic principles: the movement sequences must contrast and provide variation, subtle and invisible to the untrained eye, albeit within the limits set by conventions. These subtle minutiae and the precision of timing contribute much to the pleasing effects of dance movement.

We now know something of the work and aesthetics involved in the feminine mode in Yogyakartan style court dance. The proper control of the balance between fluidity and tension, the relationship between wrists and ankles, elbows and knees, performed with the sense of timing that comes from judgements gained from experience, together create the aesthetic of 'flowing water'. The dancer's interpretation should produce an effect which is evaluated not as *alus*, but as graceful (*luwĕs*), correct (*patut*, *srĕg*), clear and precise (*bersih dan cermat* I.) (Suryobrongto 1976: 11; 1981b: 60–67). The challenges are often in the minute details of movement and timing, which produce a bad effect when they fail to follow the correct pattern and rhythm. Although I have warned against generalizing particular phrases or concepts, '*toya mili*' or 'flowing water' was also used to express approval in other situations, from the steady supply of tea and snacks at a tea party, to a properly played wooden xylophone (*gambang*), and even to the metaphysical philosophy of 'whence and whither' (*sangkan paraning dumadi*), discussed below.

The emphasis on timing is important because it is evidence of dances as being more than written on the body by society. The inflected and supple movement performed as *toya mili* are what may be described as *alus*. In group dances it is noticeable that the performers are not 'following the beat' but finding their own accommodation to it. Similarly, keeping the physical movements in the desired balance between tension and fluidity also requires maximum concentration for beginners. The dancer is not driven by the music in a regimented and mechanical way; this would be considered crudely obvious, or *kasar*. Instead the dancer is expected to develop her/his own response to the music, using the skills of the body to achieve a supple dialogue with the music. The dancer becomes the writer, responding to a script, but realizing it through her own movements. Although the standards (*pathokan*) discussed above cannot be abandoned, they are shaped by the interpretation and taste of the dancer, which is nonstandard but conforms to an aesthetic code. Dance sequences (*ragam tari*) can change, which means that the dance is still developing. (Suryobrongto 1976: 28; 1981b: 94–109).

So we can say that the standards for movements of the body are more defined than the movement patterns and choreography, but they are not rigidly fixed. In the context of the feminine dance mode, *alus* is achieved by an active, discriminating and responsive embodied judgement. It is this sense of timing and judgement which help to explain the relevance of this elaborate dance technique as an 'education' of the *rasa*. Court dance movement trains the person so that s/he can operate more effectively in social interactions, and some of my teachers and discussants were keen to demonstrate in what way dance has had an educational role in daily interactions.

Dance and Everyday Life

The principle of dance being 'an education of the *rasa*' developed against the background of court dancing in the colonial period being understood as a means of teaching *tata-krama*, manners or etiquette (Tedjokoesoemo 1981: 124). Gusti Suryobrongto had been responsible for court protocol in the postcolonial court after he stopped performing as a dancer. He explained the relationship between dance and *tata-krama*, which he glossed as ethics (*etika* I.):

> There are four kinds of *tata-krama*, ethics. The first is *trapsila* [comportment],[33] meaning every movement is ordered ... Everything is in dance movement: how to stoop so as not to be taller than someone you are passing in front of; how to do *lampah pocong* [the squatting walk used to by servants and by dancers coming on and off the dance floor]; how to sit, maybe for hours, as in *wayang wong*, in *sila marikĕlu* ['broken rice-stalk', the masculine position of respect to the sultan, cross-legged with the knees close to the ground, with the hands folded in one's lap], without fidgeting and shifting around; how to hold the front pleat of one's *bathik* with the left hand so that the fold does not flap open in the wind in a sloppy way (*ngĕlomprot*); how to kneel down holding a tray so that the glasses don't spill [to offer drinks to revered guests]; how to hold one's arm so that your armpit does not show indecently. Second is *subasita*, being polite, having a friendly attitude, and being modest, not arrogant, respectful and considerate of others. In Yogya the princes express this by using *krama* [polite language] to people ... Third is *unggah-ungguh*, proper language use. Fourth is *udhanĕgara*, politeness in general ... if you say 'yes' you should mean 'yes'. *Ethok-ethok* ['to pretend'] is not in keeping with *udhanĕgara*, which means 'a king is as good as his word'. If you control these four [elements], you are well-educated; without them, your rhythm (*irama*) isn't right ... .These four kinds of *tata-krama* all come into dance ...' (Suryobrongto 30/3/83)

In terms of comportment, some dance positions are the same as embodied postures of respect used in everyday court interactions with superiors. These include kneeling, the 'squatting walk', and the *sĕmbah*, the respectful salutation of joined palms, thumbs just below the nostrils. Dancers make this salutation before they stand up. As a gesture of respect – to God, the sultan, the audience – it is communicative,

---

33. *Trapsila* is abbreviated from *patraping kasusilaan*, literally 'deportment of decency'.

but some described it as formal and decorative rather than a sign, as an embodied exemplification of grace and good manners. These forms of behaviour are still used inside and outside the court, despite attempts to 'modernize' manners.

Apart from dance movement replicating court codes of physical behaviour, dance training produces practical skills and insights relevant for appropriate behaviour and behavioural tactics in broader contexts. Politeness and language use are closely related. Proper language use, *unggah-ungguh*, has often been the focus of cultural interpretations which emphasize social hierarchy. The nine 'levels' are used according to whether an interaction is formal (*krama*), semi-formal (*madya*), or basic (*ngoko*) (Koentjaraningrat 1985: 234). Javanese language is performative as well as informative, and relies as much upon the gestural as the verbal, as much on the body as the word. *Krama* is melodious, measured, 'muted gesturally' (Errington 1988: 245), and used for first-impression management, distance-preservation, and for keeping on the safe side. When speaking Javanese it is better to be polite than sorry.

The intertwined relationship of being Javanese, speaking Javanese, and Javanese manners was nicely expressed by a court musician, who explained that however perfect one's linguistic skills, an utterance is only complete (*jangkěp*) when accompanied by the appropriate gestures. He demonstrated 'complete *krama*' by accompanying a sentence with a gentle forward inclination of the shoulders, which someone else compared to *gamělan* accompaniment. Another *krama* gesture is to hold the right hand in a loose fist, thumb on top, allowing it to rise and fall with the speech cadences, an action frequently used in *wayang wong* dialogues. Not all theatrical hand gestures are appropriate in everyday interaction, and it is usually more polite not to fidget or gesticulate, and to keep the hands still. By contrast, the informal and semi-polite codes, as used in *ngoko* and lower *madya*, often have a bickering insolent tone and a ragged, fraying timbre. *Ngoko* is rich in word play and its pungently derisive or ironic effects are often exploited in comic performances of all kinds. *Ngoko* expresses a hint of contempt or hostility, a proximity to open physical violence which tends to be overlooked if one concentrates on polite areas of speech behaviour. The difference, in short, is that where *ngoko* has a screeching nasal laugh, in *krama* a smile is quite enough. The rhythms of *krama* are the rhythms of dance measures as they are practised in the court; these do not exclude the possibility of violence but it is kept on a strict rein.

Javanese language practices are determined by the ideas of balance and appropriate placing of politeness in a very extreme way. *Unggah-ungguh* refers to communicative practices which do not simply (or necessarily) impart information: dance shares in an aesthetic of politeness, and instils unconscious actions which are expressed through the body, and which socialize a person into the group. It also teaches more conscious social 'tactics'. The concept of *ěmpan-papan* refers to the practical, self-aware use of physical and verbal behavioural codes which make social and personal interactions smooth. Language levels may appear to be deterministically hierarchical, but it is more accurate to understand them transactionally, and to translate *ěmpan-papan* as 'impression management' in Goffman's sense. The linguistic options can be understood as 'styles' in a 'matrix of face-saving practices' (Goffman

1967, in Errington 1988: 238).[34] Language codes are more than speech acts. They are tactical styles of behaviour which are used to manipulate relative social statuses. Dewey (1978) argued that deferential language levels conceal the user's intentions, giving him or her power over the person who is being offered such codes. Taking an 'an instrumental speaker's point of view' (1988: 246–56), Errington similarly demonstrates 'the relative values of language' and shows how a person's speech and comportment are purposefully adapted relative to the status of the addressee as a means to social ends 'extrinsic to norms of etiquette' (ibid.: 228).[35] The Javanese are well aware of this instrumental power, as demonstrated when Gadjah Mada University tried (unsuccessfully) to enforce the use of Indonesian instead of Javanese on campus, because a Javanese lecturer would be more likely to grant a student's request made in polite Javanese language using full honorifics than a request made in Indonesian. Politeness can be used forcefully, and speakers become agents instead of being constrained by codes.

Ěmpan-papan requires a person to know the styles of behaviour appropriate to time, place and other persons – knowledge which is summed up as *cara jawi*, the Javanese way, discussed earlier. Being on one's best behaviour depends on where one is and with whom. For example, just as the *pěndhapa* is the public part of a traditional house, so *pěndhapa* behaviour is 'front stage' public behaviour. Here of all places, it is most misconceived to assume that a 'natural' manner is in any way desirable. The codes of conduct appropriate to the court stand in an exemplary relationship to practices in other places, in particular the behaviour appropriate to the formal interactions which take place in the front sections of houses, the *pěndhapa*, also the traditional social space of court dance. Dance movement developed as a specific enactment of *ěmpan-papan*, in its assured and graceful taking up of positions or stands according to the requisite conventions of the practice, and also as an aspect of *ěmpan-papan* appropriate to the court. It has been an art and an exemplar of good manners. Dance movement is thus doubly appropriate, and stands in a relation of synecdoche to codes of politeness in the court. It is, as it were, the politeness of the politeness.

The principle of *ěmpan-papan* also reveals a common ground of know-how that allows a space for freedom if freedom is understood as room for manoeuvre. For instance, a Javanese speaker can use indirection to subvert the rules governing a situation by directing the speech *away* from the addressee to him/herself by using the familiar code, *ngoko*. This 'as-if' internalization frees the utterance from constraints and gives it licence to be daring, blunt, shocking and funny. The comedian Pak Guna explained different kinds of indirection to me. Soliloquizing (*ngunandika*) was the most general comic discourse, and analysing one's own feelings aloud (*ngudhar rasa*)

---

34. Errington (1988) concentrates on changing style and semiotics in the use of speech styles among aristocrats in Surakarta, but the theoretical approach is applicable to Yogyakarta as well.

35. Errington's concept of 'pragmatic salience' in this discussion (1988: 233–37) is similar to Sperber and Wilson's 'mutuality' (1988), already mentioned in relation to *cara jawi*.

is the deepest, the most 'in'. An intermediary comic style is publicly analysing your own thoughts (*ngudhar gagasan*) (Wolff and Poedjoseodarmo 1982: 70–79). Comedy can deal with political matters which can only be articulated by virtue of indirection and humorous framing and can articulate things which the normal rules of Javanese discourse and real-life Indonesian politics have made it otherwise impossible to say.

Dancing differs from soliloquy, but despite being so directly visible, court dance can also be understood as a form of indirection, a kind of turning in, an 'as-if' display, rather than direct expression. To acquire the ability to dance is to become empowered. Empowerment always occurs within a system, and a system always builds in constraints. The disciplined patterning of the body in Javanese court dance paradoxically produces the power to be Javanese, thereby gaining access to the resources which the knowledge on which that being rests makes available. The self-conscious forms of behaviour produced by Javanese socialization and the detailed patterning of dance movement sometimes strike outsiders as inhibiting and restrictive, but the codes of behaviour presented here which embody the principle of *ĕmpan-papan* create a space for freedom. This is given clear boundaries provided by codes of behaviour, expressed in language and movement.

As well as balancing deference with one's own status, appropriate language use also includes the dissimulation of fact and feeling, a practice known as *ethok-ethok*. Hiding information and emotion is a form of self-protection and avoidance of conflict. Although Javanese ethics often emphasize the interests of the group over those of the individual, as expressed in the sharing of food at most important events, celebrations or commemorations, the 'I' is both social and also unique.[36] The 'controlled sensibilities' produced by an education of the *rasa* provide a fragile safeguard against social disaster and personal pain in a wider set of social contexts beyond formal and public ones. Javanese people are polite in situations where it is strategically expedient to be so, but may equally prefer to maintain distance by minimizing interaction with certain people. Young urban Javanese children are trained to feel respect (*hormat*) for their elders and to feel fear (*ajrih*) and awkwardness (*sungkan*) with strangers: '[E]ach time that he faces an unfamiliar *alter ego*, a Javanese individual will either evade the situation and run away, or remain inactive and wait to see how the situation develops'(Koentjaraningrat 1985: 250). Incompetently handled codes cause offence, and create bad *rasa* (sensibilities) in others and oneself. The way to avoid this is evasion; as Rama Sena put it: 'I don't want to hurt him so I conceal my *rasa*; if I hurt him, I hurt myself.' Logically, the next step would be, 'Therefore, I conceal my *rasa* to protect myself' (*aku*).[37] Enforced sociability in Java's crowded urban communities tests everyone's patience, and much value is placed on nonreactiveness and emotional self-control (*sabar*). In ongoing situations in everyday

---

36. A well-known Javanese proverb expresses this communal sharing with the saying: 'To eat or not to eat (is not the question), as long as we can be together' (translation from Marlene Heins).

37. In some cases the 'me' or 'I' has the sense of 'ego', but in some philosophical contexts it stands for the collectivity of the Absolute (God), oneself, one's friends, relations and spouse (Magnis Suseno and Reksosusilo 1983: 142).

social interaction, avoidance and not-speaking are equivalent to not bumping into other dancers or pillars, and also to the prolonged build-up to danced conflicts. In a household I often visited, avoidance was the only means for fifteen siblings to co-habit.[38]

When impression management breaks down and anger is shown, Javanese manners and 'culture' rapidly disintegrate. Accusations of hypocrisy (*munafik*) are often heard, and there are degrees of acceptability about kinds of lies: presenting a false reality, disguise, deceit, trickery and gossip. There is a difference between saying something patently (and verifiably) false intentionally to deceive and make mischief, and not saying what you think or feel because of controlling your feelings by not reacting to provocation, and concealing your hand or negative views and emotions. Once people break this polite distance, the interaction is no longer in the idealized 'Javanese way' - though the withdrawal after intimacy and confidence sharing is done in a very distinctive manner, and often disseminated through true and false rumours by gossip, itself a generalized form of indirection.

Evasive politeness is one style, but it is not the only style. Nor is everyone convinced that *ethok-ethok* is a desirable social value. For Gusti Suryobrongto, the fourth kind of *tata-krama* is to speak the truth. He explained the absence of masked dance forms from the Yogyakartan palace as the result of an ethos of openness. The dancer's eyes carry the role, and a mask would conceal the truth of that gaze. This opinion contrasts nicely with the association of Javanese politeness with deceit (Geertz 1960: 246), a view symptomatic of more general assertions about 'Eastern' cultural tendencies to value manners above morals (Hughes-Freeland 2001a: 145–46). Gusti Suryo's views also reflect different value systems, which have shaped the colonial Javanese court, including Dutch ones, and which undermine simplistic East-West oppositions. For instance, we might say that in Anglo-American culture it is a compliment to call someone's behaviour 'natural', whereas in Java this would tend to be a criticism. But even this simple contrast becomes questionable if we think of everyday life as a performance, organized in contexts classified as 'front stage' and 'back stage' to which styles of behaviour are adapted with varying degrees of formality. If politeness conceals 'the dirty work' of social interaction, *ethok-ethok* becomes the Javanese version of Goffman's 'false fronts', 'tact' and 'manipulation' (1956: 28, 38, 146, 162). This theoretical comparison is appropriate because Javanese-Indonesian statements about behaviour also break down the boundary between performance as a formal event and the performative dimension of everyday social interaction, as Gusti Suryobrongto's formulation on *tata-krama* above demonstrates. There is a continuum between public and intimate, demonstrated in the shifts of familiarity and respect in speech levels. The 'natural' elements in human behaviour are understood to be 'uncontrollable' unless they are mediated and tempered by the attuned *rasa*.

Court dance in the feminine mode is an exemplar of politeness and social grace, both of which are displayed in staged performances. It also embodies and enacts

---

38. The ethnography of Java is peppered with memorable examples of everyday Javanese avoidance, as in Jay (1969: 204), Geertz (1961: 136), and Sullivan (1980: 22–23).

certain principles which characterize desirable styles of social interaction in everyday life. *Effective* competence and performance of *ĕmpan-papan* includes judging the time and the place as appropriate for formal and informal behaviour. This approved behaviour is classed as *alus*, but it cannot be forced. Nor should a dancer *try* to be *alus*. Instead, she should strive for a physical balance between tension and fluidity, attending to the rhythmic interaction of dance and music, and the subtlety of movements being late-but-not-late in relation to the beat. The goal of physical dance is to keep moving, in an unceasing shifting which cannot be represented as a pose. *Alus* in everyday life is, as in dance, a question of timing and orientation, and also a sign of the appropriate response to time and place. Misplaced or excessive manners (*njawani*) are not *alus* at all; they are mannered, badly performed, *kasar*, and are the subject of much gossip and judgement among court (and academic) circles in Yogyakarta. People should appear to feel at home (*krasan*) (in all senses), and their behaviour should *appear* natural, unconstrained and graceful, however controlled it is. *Alus* cannot be forced in everyday interactions, but is an indirect and unintended consequence of behaving appropriately to circumstances.

Conclusion

Dance is a refraction of social life, not simply a reflection. Dancing trains an individual to construct social space, and is a practice which expresses Javanese ideals about behaviour, both for individuals' sense of self and for their interrelations with others. It thus represents fundamental orders of practised behaviour appropriate to person and place that form part of the practical knowledge about being Javanese (*cara jawi*), and may also become a metaphor for principles of harmony.

Although dancing is a form of disciplined physical practice, it also provides an individual with resources to manoeuvre in the social world. While it instils Javanese values and a sense of rhythm and measure as learnt from the court, a 'practiced place' of control and strategy (De Certeau 1984), the performance of dance movement also creates a tactical space which evades codes and control. Tactics such as indirection permit the subversion of the order of hierarchical language codes. We should not forget that dance-as-play never simply mirrors social practices, but is able to reverse them. An education in dance provides a means to undermine social rules and norms as well as embodying them. The metaphorical extension of ideas about action with respect to place enables connections to be made between dance and action which is socially approved. Freedom is never free of the knowledge of operations within codes which come with knowledge, and with that knowledge, subtleties about the constitution of knowledge, and its abstractions from material grounds.

As a manifestation of an 'education of the *rasa*', court dance's continuation into the Indonesian republic contrasts with another revolutionary situation, one in which the royal body was rejected. In eighteenth-century France, state powers were inscribed on the body in a Foucaultian manner (Melzer and Norberg 1998: 4–5). Dancing to 'stiff regimented French music' regimented the courtiers themselves, as they struggled to emulate the king's own embodied self-control and grace, a dancing body which also *was* the state. Music was one among what Foucault has called 'technologies of the body … one of the means by which people learn about their bodies – how to move, how to feel, how (finally) to *be*' (McClary 1998: 87). However, in this case it did not work. Instead of encouraging obedience, 'the technologies of the body' produced resistance (Melzer and Norberg 1998: 4–5). Even before the revolution, the Baroque opera ballets of the court with their gestures based on social status were being challenged by Marie Sallé's egalitarian narrative ballets, which drew on Enlightenment philosophies of the subject and the citizen and which were danced by 'mimetic bodies' (Foster 1998: 173). Although there are some contextual parallels here with Java, there is a major difference. In Java, the royal body was used in the republic as a model for citizenship. Learning court dance in Java is not Foucaultian regimentation but cultivates important skills to manoeuvre through polite (and less polite) society in a tactical manner. The dancer works in relation to the music, rather than being driven by it. Dancing is a form of socialization and social control exercised through the body of the dancer, but it is more than this. There is room for agency.

I have concentrated on the technical aspect of dance education but it has not been possible to speak only of the body. The Javanese concept of *rasa* integrates the self in such a way that the *lair-batin* relationship has to be seen as a duality, not as two opposite forces. It will become clear later that, in practice, technique, *rasa* and characterization cannot be separated in the way that I have separated them here for purposes of explanation. What moves is not simply the manifest body (*lair*), but the total person, animated by all the energies and sensibilities at his or her command. Embodiment in this sense creates an overlay between aesthetic and ethical judgements which, as I have been emphasizing in this chapter, refer back to court ideas of politeness. *ěmpan-papan*, *mapan* and *tata-krama* establish the connection between movement, manners and identity.[39] These concepts describe an orderly world with moral and spiritual dimensions. As the Javanese-Indonesian philosophers Magnis Suseno and Reksosusilo have written:

> [T]he category of right place has the greatest significance for the Javanese. Well-being depends on whether s/he finds the place or whether s/he is in place there. The right place is the one where he does not collide with anyone or anything. For the Javanese, to attempt to achieve the right place is of priority and vital; in the right place s/he will most certainly be in a state of well-being.[40]

Here *tata-krama* is more than the show of manners implied by the word 'etiquette'. It refers to the prior knowledge and sense of appropriateness necessary to know when and how to put on such a show, and when to play it down. In the broader context of the potential chaos of Javanese everyday life, *alus* could be seen as a kind of rationality or morality for Dutch-educated Javanese *priyayi*: for Gusti

---

39. As we shall see, *mapan* is also used to refer to how a dancer 'sits' in a role (Chapter 6).
40. Magnis Suseno and Reksosusilo (1983: 94, translation by the author from the Indonesian). Well-being (*slamět*) is highly valued in Java as has often been noted; see Koentjaraningrat (1985) and Keeler (1987).

Suryobrongto, its absence would produce barbarism. Like others to whom I spoke about these ideas, he was well aware that their context of relevance is no longer founded on linguistic know-how. Many people in Yogyakarta cannot manage polite Javanese now, and some can't even speak *ngoko*. Some rely entirely on Indonesian, others use it as a code to avoid imputing relative statuses. The ability to manoeuvre by means of and through Javanese language codes is no longer something that educated Javanese people have in common. This has paralleled the transformation of Javanese dance movement (*běksa*) into Indonesian dance (*tari* I.). Even since the conversations used in this chapter took place, the connection between dance movement and manners in the court as a movement context has been reduced. Since 1989 the current Sultan, Haměngkubuwana X, has been trying to replace the *sěmbah* with the handshake to modernize gestural court etiquette. The future of the educative power of dance, emphasized since the 1920s and sustained by aristocrats and educationalists who wish to preserve Javanese values, is in the process of negotiation.

However, despite these changes a complex and living body of knowledge and tradition continues to provide a resource for the present. I now turn from dance movement as politeness and social power to the relation of dance movement embodied in staged performances of women's *bědhaya* dances to the power of the sultan and his court within the Indonesian-Javanese political universe.

Chapter 5

Performance and Symbolism:
Bĕdhaya and the Poetics of Power

Court dance movement is valued for itself, and for its instrumental power to produce effects in the social world. This chapter examines the relationship between dance movement and political symbolism with reference to court *bĕdhaya* dances, using both oral and written accounts from the court circle. Court *bĕdhaya* dances have long been the prerogative of the sultan (*lĕlangĕn dalĕm*). Since 1945 they have normally been performed by women, and have high status as Indonesian culture. As such they are strongly associated with power and prestige.

Bĕdhaya is a dance form where the court's highly valued system of allusiveness is most evident. At performances of *bĕdhaya* dances, the ethereal quality of their music and songs, the abstract fluidity of their dance movements and formations, and the formal surroundings of a great court hall inspire in audiences feelings of witnessing something which is archaic and out of time. They provide an excellent example of the intricate metaphorical relationship of the body, cosmology and power. In their abstract movement sequences and floor patterns, dancers are identified with parts of the body, and more generally, *bĕdhaya* as a genre generates metaphors of embodiment which evoke the sultan's cosmological and spiritual significance within a mystical philosophical framework. The Javanese court has a metaphorical relation to the universe. It is the universe in miniature, the microcosmic embodiment of the macrocosmic whole. This symbolism can be seen as a classical instance of how politics draws on religion, concealing the ground of its own contingency as it participates in a transcendental cosmology. The symbolic profusion of *bĕdhaya* dances befits their connection to the power of their owner, the sultan, and by extension to a philosophy of human experience. As such, *bĕdhaya* can be said to be a dance about the meaning of life. Its power lies in the quality of the dance movement, and the way in which sense is made of it, by a metaphorical conjunction of the embodied *lair* and *batin* perspectives on action and experience.

This ethnographic case also supports the argument that the study of human movement should include an account of how movement generates metaphors.[1] I explore the relationship of movement to metaphor in the authoritative twentieth-century account of the philosophy of Yogyakartan court *bĕdhaya* which interprets the dance as a spiritual struggle, using concepts from both pre-Islamic religions and Sufism. But, as we will discover, this account ignores *bĕdhaya*'s mythological associations with the sultan's supernatural spouse, Ratu Kidul, the Queen of the South. There is ambivalence about this association in Yogyakarta, which is the result of the relationship between power, genre and gender in court practice. Ambiguities in the ways that *bĕdhaya* has been interpreted have significant implications for the relationship of court dance to national Indonesian ideologies about gender identities.

Ethnographic Interlude 1: The 'Accession *Bĕdhaya*'

It is 1 July 1989. In the Purwadiningrat residence in Yogyakarta, a large, low pavilion open to the night on three sides is adorned with red and white bunting, the colours of the Indonesian flag. At the centre nine young women dressed as traditional Javanese brides are dancing. They are dance students or the children of dance enthusiasts from the aristocracy and court staff. Their movements flow smoothly and effortlessly. Behind them are the large *gamĕlan* orchestra and choir. As the large gong sounds, wrists and heads start to turn, and dance sashes flick back. The audience of around three hundred people includes the two surviving wives of Hamĕngkubuwana IX, royal kin, local dignitaries, families and friends of the performers, literary luminaries, a smattering of researchers, and thirty or so few bemused overseas tourists. They attend to the dance, and to Sultan Hamĕngkubuwana X seated on a velvet chair. The programme, which includes advertisements for the sponsors of the event, Djarum cigarettes and Coca Cola, informs us that the dance, *Bĕdhaya Jumĕnĕngan* ('Accession Bĕdhaya') or 'The Marriage of Hĕrjuna' (*Bĕdhaya Hĕrjuna Wiwaha*) has been composed and performed for the 37th anniversary of the Siswa Among Bĕksa dance foundation in honour of the tenth Sultan's accession ceremony in March 1989.[2]

Hamĕngkubuwana X is a businessman and a politician but his traditional role is spiritual and above any one religion. His regalia (*upacara*) are golden objects representing the eight attributes of kingship (*astabrata*) or meditatory images: the goose of purity; the deer of quickness; the cock of bravery; the peacock of dignity; the king dragon of might; the handkerchief of cleanliness; the powder box of

---

1. Metaphors enable us to 'see aspects of reality that the metaphor's production helps to constitute' (Black 1979: 39), but we should not forget that it is people in power who 'get to impose their metaphors' (Lakoff and Johnson 1980: 157).
2. The dance was choreographed by Bu Yuda, and its name evokes the eleventh-century poem 'The Marriage of Arjuna'. The music is partly taken from the 'old' melody from *Bĕdhaya Durma,* possibly performed at Hamĕngkubuwana III's accession in 1812 (Bu Yuda 12/7/89). In *Sĕrat Kandha Bĕdhaya Srimpi* (1854) *Bĕdhaya Pusaka Sumrĕg* seems to have been performed at the accessions of the third and fourth Sultans, a view expressed by Mbak Kadar (17/7/2006), although there is no evidence In accounts from that time (Carey 1992, 1993).

benevolence; and the lamp of illumination (Brongtodiningrat 1975: 18–19). His emblem is the wing of the *garudha* bird, usually seen as the mount of the Hindu deity Wisnu (Vishnu), and yet he also represents Allah as caliph.[3] The Sultan of Yogya bears a heavy burden of religio-cosmological attributes. His titles themselves stand as a metaphor of Java's metaphysical palimpsest, consisting of animism, Hinduism, Buddhism, and the last religious arrivals to the region, Islam and Christianity. The titles are 'Sampeyan Dalĕm Ingkang Sinuwun Kangjĕng Sultan Hamĕngkubuwana, Senapati Ingalaga, Abdurrahman Sayidin Panatagama, Kalifatullah Ingkang Jumĕnĕng Kaping X'. Hamĕngkubuwana means 'He who holds the world in his lap'; he is also 'Commander-in-chief, servant of the Lord, ruler of the religion, representative of Allah and (currently) tenth in line'.

This religious complexity contributes to the complexity and allusiveness of the court culture epitomized by *bĕdhaya* dances and their local interpretations. In the colonial period, *bĕdhaya* choreographies for nine dancers were long and abstract, and the story was only mentioned in the spoken introduction (*kandha*) and parts of the song lyrics. No formations (*rakit*) depicted or simulated events, and the story was simply expressed by Batak and Endhel, the lead dancers, going in and out of the 'line' formation (*lajuran*). The story has been more important since the 1950s, but even so it is not performed through readily accessible gestures. When the choir sings of the Sultan's titles to the melody '*Endhel*', Bu Yuda's choreography depicts the events of the actual accession ceremony in March 1989. Readings from the Qur'an and the proclamation by the religious leader are expressed in a gesture called *ngilo*, 'looking in a mirror', where the end of the dance sash is held in both hands. The moment after the Sultan has acceded it is represented by Endhel, one of the leading dancers, standing at the front of the three-by-three formation (*rakit tiga*) (Figure 5.1). The second part of the dance is a duet that describes the joy of the Sultan and his wife, Kangjĕng Ratu Hemas, and formations representing the banquet and the departure of the guests, described in songs: 'The Sultan has been seated in *siniwaka* on the golden throne … the guests are being served refreshments …'. The singing is textural rather than textual: the audience hears the sound but not the words. There is no sign as to which of the identically dressed dancers 'is' the Sultan, the religious leader, or the queen, nor is there any obvious mimetic connection between gesture, formation and the events being referred to in the song. The only clear signal is the sounding of the *Monggang* melody when the 'Sultan' was installed, recognizable to audience members familiar with its association with the Sultan's presence. The dancers themselves are less interested in the dance's 'meanings' than in dancing as well as they can, and surviving the hour-long performance without mishap – losing part of their costume, their balance, or their consciousness. Further anxieties for the leading dancers arise from the swiftly changing pattern of orientations in their duet, while for the remaining dancers it is holding the half-kneeling position, and enduring the excruciating ache in the big toe which begins

---

3. Sultan Agung secured the right for himself and his dynasty to hold the Islamic title of 'Sultan' after 1641 (Ricklefs 1974: 15–16), but did not remove any previous religious associations of royal power.

after several minutes. This is why *bĕdhaya* is said to be abstract. Its 'meaning' is detached from textual and gestural semiotics, and produced by various interpretations.

There had been no *bĕdhaya* dance at the tenth Sultan's accession (Hughes-Freeland 1991a), but the present performance reaffirms his traditional ownership of court *bĕdhaya* dances, in a new Indonesian-Javanese style. The dances are introduced by a mistress of ceremonies, in Indonesian, then in English. After the dance, microphones are arranged, and the Sultan comes in to the dance space, dressed in trousers, an orange and green floral silk jacket, and a white open-necked shirt. He stands facing R.M. Dinu(satama), the head of the dance association and his cousin, and Bu Yuda, the choreographer and his aunt, both of whom wear formal Javanese dress, and the dancers stand behind them. R.M. Dinu makes a short speech in Javanese explaining that the association wishes to make a presentation to the Sultan, and the main dancer who performed the Sultan comes forward with a tray covered in yellow velvet, which R.M. Dinu takes from her and gives to the Sultan. This is the dance text and a video tape of the dress rehearsal recorded the previous Thursday.[4] The dance is now 'by royal prerogative' (*lĕlangĕn dalĕm*) and can only be performed with the Sultan's permission (Bu Yuda 4/7/89). The Sultan makes a four-minute speech of thanks and encouragement in Indonesian, not Javanese. He praises the association's initiative and creativity in making this new *bĕdhaya,* and expresses his enthusiasm to perpetuate and

Figure 5.1 'Accession *Bĕdhaya*': the Sultan accedes, 1989

4. R.M. Dinu gave me a video copy later, in exchange for the video I gave him of the film I made with the association's help (Hughes-Freeland 1988), and whose 'star', Susindahati, obtained her award of first prize for 1987 on this occasion.

develop Yogyakartan culture further. He asserts his modern Indonesian identity by shaking hands with R.M. Dinu, Bu Yuda, and each of the dancers. This iconoclastic gesture has been a source of considerable embarrassment since his accession. The recipient intends to make the *sĕmbah*, the traditional gesture of respect bringing hands with palms together to the nose, then shakes hands Javanese-style, with both palms, then makes a final attempt to retrieve the situation and slips a *sĕmbah* in after the handshake. Tradition runs deep, and a performance of awed respect of the sultan has been central to Yogyakartan manners in and out of the court.

The anniversary concert lasted over four hours. We also saw *Sari-Sari* (a new welcoming dance) and, after the speeches and a prize-giving ceremony, a *wayang wong* fragment, *Prĕgiwa-Prĕgiwati*. The Javanese audience had witnessed a performance intended to generate in them the same mood as that of the dancers, a mood which elicits a sense of belonging and a feeling of pride in their past and also in their present local identity.

A Brief History of Women's Court Dance

In South and Southeast Asia there has been a long tradition of female dance endorsing royal, and normally male, power. In Java as elsewhere, influences from India from about AD 400 turned courts into images of the houses of the Hindu gods, as local rulers sought to consolidate their authority by drawing on Hindu concepts of cosmic power and the god-king (*dewa-raja*).[5] Theatrical performances contributed to the paraphernalia of power and the principle of royal patronage. Abstract choreographies performed by female dancers said to represent heavenly nymphs formed part of this court symbolism, from *Nang Keo* in Laos to *lakhōn phūying* in Thailand. Women have also carried the king's regalia, the symbols of his authority, from thirteenth-century Cambodia (Cœdès 1944: 278) to the twentieth-century colonial Javanese court, where bearers (*manggung*) were selected from female *bĕdhaya* dancers. And women have also borne the king's heirs and followers, with rulers and powerful men having many wives before and after Islam was introduced to Java in the fourteenth century.[6]

Regional patterns might lead us to expect to find a Hindu-Buddhist proto-*bĕdhaya* in Java. Oral traditions from the Surakarta courts in particular give the court *Bĕdhaya Kĕtawang* a Hindu origin in *Lĕnggotbawa*, a dance created by Śiva in AD 167 as a symbol of the *Śiva-liṅga*, and brought to earth by seven heavenly nymphs (Hadiwidjojo 1981). The Mangkunagaran court's *Bĕdhaya Anglir Mĕndhung* for seven dancers also 'originates' in the dance of seven heavenly nymphs (Lelyveld 1922: 3). A semi-mythical Surakartan history also attributes the creation of both *bĕdhaya* and *srimpi* to the queen of Jĕnggala in AD 1341.[7]

---

5. See Heine-Geldern (1942), Berg (1965), Moertono (1968), Selosoemardjan (1978), Carey (1984), Wisseman Christie (1986).

6. The seventh Sultan of Yogyakarta (r.1877–1921) had seventy-eight children by three primary wives (*garwadalĕm padma*), fifteen secondary wives (*garwa ampeyan),* and two unofficial wives (*pĕlara-lara dalĕm*).

7. Warsadiningrat (1987: 124), citing Prince Kusumadilaga's *Sastra Miruda.*

There is remarkably little decisive evidence for the existence of ceremonial women's group dancing in any of the Javanese courts before the seventeenth century. The oldest descriptive performance data in Java comes from a chronicle of the fourteenth-century pre-Islamic Majapahit court when its ruler, Hayam Wuruk, favoured Tantric Buddhism (Pigeaud 1960–63; Robson 1995). The existing text gives no evidence for any specifically religious or group dances, but describes three performances by women: the ritualistic dance of the solitary Queen, watched by her marvelling ladies-in-waiting on the seventh day of final obsequies for the king's maternal grandmother in 1362 (Robson 1995: 73); humorous bawdy performances by the female Juru i Angin and an ambiguous figure called *buyut*, 'great-grandmother'; and a '*rakĕt*' play in which the king himself jokes, sings and dances with eight *tĕkĕs*, noble female performers. These historical records describe female performances less like postcolonial court performances than the erotic humorous performances at *tayuban* still held today in remote Javanese villages to celebrate harvests and rites of passage, in which men take it in turns to pay for dances with two or three singer-dancers (*ledhek*) (Hughes-Freeland 1993a).

The 'creation' of Asian women's ceremonial dances has often been associated with moments of political expansion and acts of legitimization. It is therefore not surprising that the weight of the Indian heritage has been an important legitimizing theme in Javanese cultural self-images and identity.[8] Histories written in the twentieth century have used images of the present to create an account of the past which in turn endorses present practice. In Indonesian history making, the citation of previous sources parallels how names gain weight, much as the accumulation of previous references gives 'authority' in the field of scholarship and knowledge building (De Certeau 1984). When I asked Gusti Suryobrongto about his allusion (1970) to Lelyveld's (1931) theory of Indian diffusion in his discussion of Yogyakartan court dance, he said he had done so, not because he agreed with the ideas, but simply because ' Lelyveld had mentioned them' (15/6/83).

In Indonesia, the number of dancers has been used as crucial evidence of historical continuity (Hughes-Freeland 2006). Oral and written myths of origin suggest that Sultan Agung (r.1613–46), while preserving Hindu-Javanese practices and consolidating his authority using Islam and the Dutch East Indies (Reid 1993: 78), extended an existing dance representing the seven heavenly nymphs of Hinduism to nine, a number with sacral connotations for both Hindu-Buddhism and for Islam, including the number of Islamic saints (Pudjasworo 1982: 40–50). Warsadiningrat (1987) recounts how one of these saints, Sunan Kalijaga, gave Agung his blessing to compose the *Kĕtawang* melody. To this day it remains taboo and extremely dangerous due to its associations with the royal supernatural spouse, Ratu Kidul (Queen of the South). Agung selected daughters from each of his eight *bupati nayaka* (high-ranking nobles) and another from the family of his *patih dalĕm* (chief minister), 'to encourage

---

8   *Nang Keo* was 'created' by Fa Ngum after he established his kingdom at Luang Prabang in 1352 (Stuart-Fox 1986). *Lakhŏn-phuying* was 'revived' after the fall of Ayudhya in 1767 by King Taksin when he established Thonburi (Rutnin 1993: 47).

unity among the leaders of the kingdom'. He allowed highly ranked close male agnates and cousins, his minister, *bupati nayaka*, and *bĕkĕl* to compose melodies for the old dance for seven (ibid.: 80–82; 92). This story explains how the mythical dance of seven nymphs became the model for *all* successive court *bĕdhayas* for nine dancers.[9]

Contemporary sources suggest that during the later Kartasura period the numbers seven and nine were not fixed. In 1724 Sultan Amangkurat IV (r.1719–26) gave his son costumes for seven *bĕdhaya* dancers (Ricklefs 1993: 213), but not long after Pakubuwana II's succession (r.1726– 49) Pieter Gijsberg Noodt, the Dutch East Indies Company commander at Semarang, saw fourteen groups of seven dancers, followed by nine dancers of the king, and then another group of seven *royal* dancers (Ricklefs 1993: 392; 1998: 6–7). In 1727 twelve courtiers' troupes of seven performed, then to five canon salutes, Pakubuwana II's nine, then four other troupes of seven, then to five canon shots, nine of Pakubuwana II's unofficial wives (*sĕlir*), and then Prince Buminata's troupe of seven: 'Thus, 137 women danced between 5.30 pm and 2.00 am' (ibid.: 7). In 1733, 1737 and 1740, troupes of seven followed by the king's troupe, and 'all the princes and other courtiers who were present turned their backs so as not to look upon the royal *bĕdhaya*'. By 1740 this was customary, 'out of awe'. Like other royal regalia, *bĕdhaya* was 'too sacred to be watched by any Javanese but the king himself' (ibid.: 8), but it is not clear *which* dance was taboo, as it is not named by the sources. Evidence suggests that although a strong taboo was attached to the royal *bĕdhaya*, nine and seven dancers had not become standardized as status markers. As late as 1755 the Bupati (Regent) of Ponorogo reputedly had seven groups of *nine bĕdhaya* (Soerjadiningrat n.d.; Suharti 1972). During British rule in Java (1811–1816), Raffles describes *eight bĕdhaya* dancers who are 'in some respect to the nobles what the *s'rimpi* [sic] are to the sovereign', the concubines of nobles, but for reasons of economy boys, not women, were used instead (1978: 342). On his travels to West Java in the 1860s, the Regent of Kudus recorded that:

> … the *bupati* of Sumedang has the rank of *pangeran*. That evening he put on a *bĕdhaya* performance for me, danced by eight of his concubines, their costumes ablaze with gold and gems. In Sunda this dance has reached incomparable heights. (Bonneff 1986: 103–4)

So as late as the mid-nineteenth century, dances referred to as *bĕdhaya* were not necessarily what were understood by *bĕdhaya* one hundred years later.

Whatever the specifics of its historical background, women's court dance in Java defined a boundary between the power and status of the sultan and his court and the outside world. By the late nineteenth century court *bĕdhaya* was among the most prestigious court performance genres, and *bĕdhaya* for nine dancers was exclusive to

---

9. Female dancers are generally called '*badhaya*' in Cirebon (Arjo 1989: 169). This is a possible origin for the dance name, as Sultan Agung's chief wife, Ratu Kulon, and one of his religious advisers were from Cirebon, and Agung also imitated Cirebon's architecture (Pigeaud and De Graaf 1976: 46, 54).

the Kasultanan and Kasunanan courts (Groneman 1888; Mayer 1897). Other dignitaries were allowed to develop *bědhaya* dances for seven dancers only, and were active in sponsoring other kinds of dance. From 1918 in Yogyakarta, *bědhaya* for nine dancers was taught and performed outside the court at Kridha Běksa Wirama with the Sultan's permission. When the Prime Minister, who acted as the Sultan's representative in dealings with the colonial authorities, wanted a *bědhaya* performance in the Kěpatihan for the August celebrations of the Dutch Queen's birthday, he had to ask the Sultan for permission to borrow nine court *bědhaya* dancers (*Platen-Album* 28: Pls 1–10). After independence *bědhaya* as a form became even more democratized, but some dances, such as the Accession Bědhaya, are still considered the property of the Sultan, and are a sign of his prestige.

It is important to emphasize here that, in contrast to Western understandings of performance as fictional, illusory and deceptive, performance can also be understood to create reality (Schieffelin 1998). As such, performance needs to be recognized as what Nelson Goodman has called a 'way of world making' (1978). The instrumentality of Javanese court dance performances in constructing worlds has been controversial. Anthony Reid (1988) has argued that since Islamicization in the seventeenth-century, women's court dances have been ceremonial with no religious function, apart from the royal cult of glory, compared to women's ceremonial temple dances (*rejang*) in Bali. Conversely Merle Ricklefs (1998) has demonstrated that *bědhaya* dances still retained powerful associations with the supernatural in the Kasunanan court in Surakarta in the early eighteenth century. Ritual itself has been theorized has being central to bureaucracies in the Southeast Asian state, which cannot be explained in terms of Weberian ratio-legal insitutions (Day 2004). Not surprisingly scholars like Ricklefs and Day who prioritize local world-views and writings are much more likely to recognize the instrumental power of symbolism to construct worlds.[10] In explaining how performance creates worlds, we have to recognize the role of the imagination. In Javanese court dance, reality is constituted by inner perspective as well as outer constraints. Making sense of reality is understood to come from consciousness and sensibilities (*rasa*), not just intellectual cognition. This produces what could be described as a poetic response to the world. It plays an important part in producing metaphors. These in turn produce an instrumentality which is more than representational symbolism. *Bědhaya* is an example of indexicality, a concept used by Tambiah (1985) in his work on ritual symbolism in Thailand to demonstrate how ritual engages with both the political and the imaginative, cosmological dimensions in a performative manner. In this way political symbolism contributes to political

---

10. These arguments have centred on Geertz's analysis of the theatre state in nineteenth-century Bali: 'The dramas of the theatre state, mimetic of themselves, were, in the end, neither illusions nor lies, neither sleight of hand nor make believe. They were what there was' (Geertz 1980: 136). Ricklefs has reservations about the early particularism of Geertz's formulation but approves of his later approach where 'the easy distinction between the trappings of rule and its substance becomes less sharp, even less real; what counts is the manner in which, a bit like mass and energy, they are transformed into each other' (Geertz 1983: 124, cited in Ricklefs 1998: 345–46).

legitimation in a process by which culture becomes naturalized and acquires a sense of inevitability and normality. By the end of the twentieth century the instrumentality of Javanese court performance had long been in question, and the court could no longer be characterized as a political and moral 'exemplary centre' (Geertz 1980: 11–18). But even so, for many in Yogya and elsewhere in Java, the Sultan of Yogya and his court in Yogya still embodied a particular kind of energy or supernatural power (*sěkti*), even in the modern version of celebrity (Hughes-Freeland 2007b). Indeed, court culture still provided metaphors for social values and world-views which fed back into the physical dance and imbued it with further instrumentality.

So, despite recent changes in court etiquette, the *bědhaya* dance could simply be understood as a symbol of a highly elaborated *sěmbah* to the Sultan, but of all the central Javanese court dance traditions, it has the greatest capacity to generate myths and interpretations. Although it is no longer restricted to court ceremonial, it remains the dance form most redolent of royal power, and exemplifies court performance both as service and devotion to the sultan and to the dance, and as an important element of the highly valued 'high and noble' (*adiluhung*) culture with its roots in a communal and glorious past. As such, *bědhaya* has had a particularly important place in Indonesia's New Order myth making, and has been subject to the construction of origins which is *always* part of the political process. As we will see, the dance has gained historical and political weight, and has generated a wide range of meanings. It has been able to do this because of the abstract nature of its dance movement.

Bědhaya Dance Movement and Meaning Making

Patterns in Indonesian dancing have often been described as having codified denotative meanings, but the names of Javanese court dance movements are 'merely descriptive', as Claire Holt, the influential scholar of Indonesian culture, astutely observed (1937: 846). It has been suggested that Islam had eroded the meaning of dance movement (Soebardi 1975: 87–89), but there is convincing evidence against this argument. In un-Islamicized Bali, there is no alphabet of gestures either. Dance hand positions are 'flowers', for beauty, and *mudras* are used by priests in prayer (Kleen and Kat Angelino 1923). In Thailand, Buddhism sporadically *curbed* traditions of dance and theatre, and hand gestures are simplified *mudras*, but are not meaningful (Rutnin 1993). Finally, in contemporary Indian theatres, stylized gesticulation patterns, especially of the hands, are mostly absent (Vatsyayan 1980: 13, 62). For instance, *bharata natyam* dance uses denotational gesture in some sequences, but distinguishes between single and combined hand gestures (*asaṁyuta-hasta* and *saṁyuta-hasta*) used for dramatic purposes and 'dance hands' (*nrtta hasta*).[11]

It is more helpful to understand what Collingwood described as 'obsolete meanings' (1979: 7–8) as a feature of artistic interpretation than a sign of actual loss. Movement in *bědhaya* is abstract. The dance sequences (*běksa*) have names but these names do not describe gestural meaning. They help a dancer to memorize the order

---

11. For critical discussions of the Java-India connection, see Brakel (1976) and Hughes-Freeland (1991b, 1991c).

of sequences and the order of movements within the sequence, and act as a notational system for writing down choreography. There are four kinds of Javanese dance sequence names in *bĕdhaya* and the feminine dance mode (*bĕksa putri*): self-referential, fighting actions, self-adorning actions, and natural phenomena. There is no consistent and unified scheme for making movements and giving them names. Each group of names presents specific problems for interpretation.

Self-referential names have a practical technical significance, but do not convey the 'meaning' of the movement in a mimetic sense. For instance, *nglayang*, 'gliding' (Figure 5.2) is performed in the kneeling position as a close to the second section of *bĕdhaya*. This beautiful stretching movement is performed in the half-kneeling position, as the

Figure 5.2 Nglayang, Court Festival, 1994

dancer leans back diagonally while extending both arms forward, completing the phrase with turns of the neck and wrists before returning the hands back to *ngithing* and *nyĕmpurit* in the same position which opened the dance. A salutation is then made before the dancers sit in *sila panggung*, arrange their sashes, and make a final salutation. Some people spoke of *nglayang* as 'the nymphs returning to heaven', alluding to Hindu identifications of the dance, but *nglayang* presages the end of the second section of *bĕdhaya*; afterwards the dancers will stand and leave in the exit march.[12] *Nglayang* differs from *nyamber* ('flying'), a movement through space, running on tiptoe (*srisig*) holding up the sash, and which represents either flight from danger in fighting sequences, or is simply a transition to a different floor pattern. An exception to this general rule is 'circling with *rimong* (the sash over the shoulder)' which expresses sadness or difficulty, found in *Srimpi Rĕnggawati* (Bu Yuda 23/10/ 89).

The fighting and self-adorning categories might be expected to mime the gestures to which they refer. Fighting actions include low sideways thrust (*sudukan, nyuduk*); both sides fend (*ecen*); one fends (*ĕndho*); straight stabs (*jĕblosan, nyĕblos*). Self-adorning movements include fixing one's hair (*atrap rikma*), forehead hair (*atrap sinom*), earrings (*atrap sumping*), crown (*atrap cundhuk*), or belt (*atrap slepe* or *cathok*); powdering the face (*tasikan*); and looking in a mirror (*ngilo*). However, fighting and self-adorning sequences were explained specifically according to the form in which they occurred, and not given a general meaning. *Bĕdhaya* fights are not understood as dramatic representations of physical conflict but are '*simbolik I.*'. They are simpler than *srimpi* fights, and in old *bĕdhaya* dances would not be represented in physical movements at all (Bu Yuda 12/7/89). The significance of *bĕdhaya* fights is not semiotic, and is apparent only to those who are aware of the metaphorical significance, as explained below.

Bĕdhaya (and also *srimpi* and *bĕksan*) self-adorning sequences do not usually have a mimetic significance, and are appraised for their fulfilment of aesthetic fittingness (*patut*), such as the flexibility of hand and wrist when 'earrings are put on', 'faces powdered', or 'hair tidied'. Aesthetics require that sequences using detailed hand movements, frequently performed on the spot, should alternate with movements such as *ngĕndherek*, a self-referential 'walking' sequence, that are characterized by movement across space and/or the use of the dance sash (Pudjasworo 1982) (see Appendix 2). These apparently mimetic movements may be used to represent something else they resemble. Bu Yuda said (12/7/89) that in the 'Accession Bĕdhaya' she choreographed 'looking in a mirror' (*ngilo*) to represent the moment in the ceremony when the Muslim officiant read out the ruling for the accession because *ngilo* 'looks like someone reading something'. It is unlikely that the audience will be interested in identifying such sequences or seek mimetic references in *bĕdhaya* (or *srimpi*) which are usually described as 'abstract', nor does their appreciation depend on recognizing such references should the choreographer have made them. Self-adorning movements are

---

12. This can be compared to the folded sleeve (*shiu hsiu*) gesture for happiness in nineteenth-century *Ching Hsi* opera in a song which did not denote the feeling but signalled the imminent end of the song (Strauss 1975: 37).

self-exemplifying, and described by Javanese as 'abstract' or 'for beauty'. When they do have a mimetic quality in *klana* and *golek*, they will also be interpreted metaphorically.

The allusive power of dance movement is most evident in the Javanese movement names which refer to natural phenomena: areca palm in the wind (*pucang-kanginan*); waves of water (*ombak banyu*); sand bank (*wĕdi kengser*); elephant rolling its trunk (*gajah ngoling*); picking a flower (*ngunduh sĕkar*). Let us consider 'elephant rolling its trunk'. This sequence has a very beautiful stretching movement of the hands and arms away from the face (Figure 5.3). The elephant is an important hieratic symbol of power in Asia, and elephant salutations occur in various Southeast Asian performance traditions.[13] In Yogya people explained the movement with reference to the colonial practice of sultans keeping elephants in the south square for ceremonies when the elephant would kneel to the sultan and roll his trunk in a mighty salutation. The movement is not designed to refer to elephants in a narrative or iconographic manner. The dancer's arms in *gajah ngoling look like* the movement of an elephant's trunk, which itself is a product of training, a cultural artefact. The plait of jasmine buds hanging down from a bride's hair is also called '*gajah ngoling*', but the gesture was never said to represent these flowers; if anything, the flowers are so named because

Figure 5.3 Gajah ngoling

Figure 5.4 Pucang-kangingan

13. The Lao women's dance of Luang Prabang, *Nang Keo*, includes such a sequence. In the Malaysian *mak yong* theatre, 'elephant raising its trunk' occurs in the opening sequence and is a sign of the hero's encounter with a god and has a subsequent association with fertility (Danaan 1986: 115).

they look like an elephant's trunk 'rolling'. Similarly, 'areca palm in the wind' *looks like* the movement of a tree bending gracefully in the breeze, as the dancer shifts her body weight slowly, first to one side, then to the other, leaning out slightly over an extended sash while the other sash is stretched around a bent elbow (Figure 5.4).

So Holt's account of dance movement names as 'merely descriptive' needs qualification. The descriptive name does not refer to external objects, but describes movements which evoke feelings about qualities of movement referred to in that name. Ultimately, the movements exemplify themselves. Dance movements are named for a *quality of movement* identified with a specific kind of tree, flower, animal or feature in the physical world. They are not identified with *the thing itself*, but for the *feelings* evoked by the movement of a natural object. This principle can be compared to Indian performance traditions in which 'waves of the sea' describes the effect of the natural object, but do not represent it in a denotational manner (Vatsyayan 1980: 71). In Tongan *lakalaka* performances, also characterized by graceful sinuous arm movements, movements in the story section allude not to things but to their actions which inspire feelings (Kaeppler 1985: 107–8). Dance movement does not imitate the specifics of the natural world, but it partakes of its rhythms. My dance teacher, Mbak Kadar, distinguished dance movement from other kinds of movement by describing it as being imbued with the vitality of the natural world (*sari alam*), an extra quality lacking in everyday movement. This is quite different from dance being 'a stylization of everyday movement' (Suryobrongto 1970). Dance *is* nature, but recreated through the process of artistry.[14] Dance movements do not denote realities in a material world; they generate new kinds of subtle feelings and forms, and elicit ones that already exist.

Interpretation and Instrumentality

The 'higher' the form, the less self-evident its meaning. In Javanese 'high and noble' *adiluhung* culture, allusiveness is a characteristic of 'high' art. *Bĕdhaya* dance movement and lyrics *conceal*. Dance movement is not a text in itself, to be deciphered. Its *social* significance is communicated semiotically or iconically at a physical level through the quality of movements represented in the different modes (see further Chapter 6). However, its aesthetic appreciation is elaborately mediated through training, habit and practice. When experts write that the meaning of dance gestures will become clear when one knows them, they do not mean that a lexicon will be revealed, but that grounds for appreciation will be developed through the sensitization of *rasa* or embodied consciousness. Western semiotics distinguishes between science and nonscience on the basis of the way in which symbols and signs behave; in science, symbols have a solid base constituted by theoretical formulations of proof and evidence (Goodman: 1976). A Javanese science of reality (*ngelmu*) operates on principles which include intuition, energy, and the capacity to elicit persuasion. In these terms, high Javanese culture can be said to be a matter of rhetoric and self-citation (De Certeau

---

14. This is similar to the aesthetic of aikido, in which art does not imitate but *is* nature, incorporated into contact improvisation dance in the USA (Novack 1990: 185).

1984), and one which always returns to the body. This process will become evident in the way in which *bĕdhaya* is interpreted.

There is an inverse relationship between communicability and power in performance: performance produced by power centres is the least accessible because it is the most allusive and convoluted (Barber 1991). Court cultures in general place a high value on allusiveness over direct communication, and the Javanese courts are no exception. In fact, it is arguably the abstraction of the movement which makes possible the capacity of the dance to carry many meanings. This does not prevent dance movement from being subject to meaning-making strategies:

> For the Javanese nothing is without meaning. The generation of meaning is a cultural pastime: visible or perceptible things are thought to be possible projections of more abstract or concealed meaning expressed in the word *surasa* (meaning, inner purpose). (Moertono 1968: 20–21)

Where people invent past events to give credence to present practice, *surasa* generates meaning where there was none before. Until recently most Javanese men, regardless of their background, delighted in the proliferation of names in their language, which results from language codes and word play, and call the resulting synonymy '*dasanama*' (ten names), found in the shadow play and other popular theatres.[15] The more features or identifications (*ciri*) an object, name or practice can generate, the better. Generating meaning through the play of sound and sense gives substance and weight. And knowing the codes and how to play with them has been an expression of belonging to and owning a culture, particularly in contexts of male interaction and discourses. Or, as Keeler writes, 'In interpreting such signs, a person seeks to control them, mastering and using – rather than falling subject to – their significance' (1987: 243). However, as in the shadow play, nationalistic rhetoric, pedagogy and numerology are used in an exegetical style to produce a moral code in a form that is easy to remember.

Weight also shapes the practice of naming in Java. Personal names 'match' (*jodoh*) their owner, but Javanese people change their name either because of persistent misfortune attributed to a mismatch between name and person, or because of a change in their rank (*mĕntereng*). A weightier rank requires a weightier (*abot*) name, with Sanskrit names being the most loaded (and dangerous). A young aristocrat and court musician recounted that when his grandfather was promoted to the rank of *riya* in the court, he changed his name to Brongtokoesoema ('flower of passion') and died

---

15. For Gonda, *dasanama* was the result of rank restrictions, taboos and poetic innovations to fit scansion patterns: 'No rigid line of demarcation can be drawn between the exigencies of magical danger, social tradition, poetical device, and the tendency which may be called mere playfulness or fun' (1952: 208). For Zurbuchen this proliferation may result from Java's exposure to many traditions: 'because ideas that come from a variety of cultural traditions are constantly being given new contexts, naming [*anganan* OJ] is done with abstractions as well as concrete entities' (1976: 20).

shortly after, the result of his name being 'too heavy'.[16] Names thus have a performative and instrumental power to shape the world, described as *mandi*, literally 'to transact, to sell'. In high and noble *adiluhung* culture names are thus often given for effect, not for meaning: the effect *is* their meaning. Significance lies in resonance and the potential to make connections, rather than what the individual elements necessarily mean. It is against this background that we need to understand the associative power of dance movement and the interpretive freight carried by *bĕdhaya* and other court practices.

The generation of meaning by *surasa* involves all kinds of rules and rationales. One approach is to play with extensions of a term through sound or sound and sense to produce false etymologies. The construction of etymologies is a favourite activity among Javanese intellectuals and aesthetes, and is also widespread in popular forms of word play that occur informally in joking as well as in songs and in all kinds of theatre, including *wayang wong*. Etymologies can be understood as miniature exercises in making history. The meanings generated feed back into wider cultural mythologies and ideologies, and some stick. This proliferation and surplus of meaning plays an important part in the rhetorical culture of Java and now Indonesia. So the discussion that follows is not a digression, but necessary for an understanding of the general tactics which inform the different interpretations which *bĕdhaya* carries and which contributes to its capacity to represent political power.

False or 'folk' etymology, *jarwa dhosok,* refers to the explication of (usually) Old Javanese and Sanskrit words, and is prevalent in the shadow play (Becker 1979: 236). *Kĕrata basa* is similar but less grandiose. During my fieldwork, Pak Barsana, an employee at the Sanabudaya Museum, performed *jarwa dhosok* on the court's name, 'Ngayogyakarta Hadiningrat'. This is how he arrived at the 'proper' interpretation: 1. *Ngayo* = *ngayu* (to beautify) = *ngarĕp-arĕp* (to desire) = 'want'. 2. *Gya* = *wilujĕng* (well-being) = *slamĕt* (ibid.) = 'well-being'. 3. *Karta* = *raharja* (prosperous) = *tĕntrĕm* (at peace) = 'at peace'. 4. *Hadi* = *linangkung* (most superior) = *edi* (beautiful) = 'beautiful'. 5. *Rat* = *nĕgara* (kingdom) = *praja* (government) = 'kingdom'. This produces the meaning: 'To want well-being and peace in a beautiful kingdom'.[17] These explications on the basis of a loose connection of sound and sense are common in Java to give weight to the mundane. For instance, Pak Mur, a court guide, revelled in this kind of interpretation, and told me that *sorjan*, the court jacket for men, is from *saroja* (lotus), thus giving extra value to the jacket by associating it with an important symbol from the Hindu-Java period (Pott 1966).

Dance sequence names are also given etymologies, though less than might be expected. One young dancer compared the arm position in *lampah atur-atur* used in *Golek Kĕnya Tinembe* at PBN to 'bringing offerings to the temple'. The other students

---

16. New names are not always used names: I nearly failed to meet the choreographer K.R.T. Wiradipradja who lived in my *kampung*, because everyone knew him as Pak Net, an abbreviation of his old name, Netya.

17. When Rama Sena was a court scribe, he had to *jarwa* old texts, polishing, refining – and sometimes censoring – metrics and imagery.

derided this, but her etymology was correct.[18] Dance names are subject to another common interpretive practice, which generates meanings through a loose association, to move from the specific to the general. As we know, hand positions are abstract. Comparisons are made to Indian gestures, but there are other, more idiosyncratic interpretations: *ngruji* is 'for Brahma' or 'avoiding evil'; *ngĕpel* is 'you must be strong, you can see when Bima uses it'; both *nyĕmpurit* and *ngithing* are *cakra*, the fearsome discus of Kresna.[19] It was significant that no one ventured an Indian origin for the only two named combined hand positions: *sĕmbah* and *tumpang tali* ('tugging on a rope'), in which the wrists are held against each other, left hand below in *ngruji*, right hand on top in *nyĕmpurit*, and then reversed. It was Pak Mur's gloss of *ngruji* which made me understand what people were doing when they interpreted movement: '*Ngruji* means Pancasila' – with each finger standing for one of the five principles of the Indonesian state philosophy. Dance movement is also subject to this kind of analysis. A group of musicians at a training session at PBN were discussing a dance movement in which the left hand turned and the right was held in *ngithing*; in answer to a question about the movement's meaning, the choreographer Rama Sas explained in Indonesian that it meant the desire to seek 'certainty and beauty'. This abstraction away from the material body to the immaterial one is a characteristic pattern in Javanese interpretation, as we will discover below.

It is against this background of using false etymologies to generate meanings and connections that we can now consider the associations which are brought to court *bĕdhaya* dances. The name of the form itself has been given a wide variety of false etymologies which exploit different spellings of the dance (*badhaya*, *bĕdaya*), even by dancers. Wisnu Wardhana argued for a *jarwa dhosok* link with Buddha (*budha*) (Wardhana 1981: 43), while Ben Suharto used *kĕrata basa* to break down the name into parts: *beda* meaning 'different' in Sanskrit, and '*ya*', the symbol for '9' in Javanese script, producing 'nine different'(17/10/83). Former Tamansiswa students linked it to a false etymology of the word for culture, *budhaya*, from '*budi*' (inner character) and '*daya*' (strength).[20] These etymologies can be understood as smaller-scale versions of the history-making strategies which trace *bĕdhaya* back to both the pre-Islamic and Islamic periods and shape the published account of *bĕdhaya*'s philosophical meaning

18. OJ *atĕr-atĕr* is 'bringing, lead' (Zoetmulder 1982). *Atur-atur* is also the name of a classical melody played by the Sĕkati *gamĕlans* at the Mauludan festival.
19. A Secondary School for the Arts teaching manual used in Yogyakarta interprets *ngĕpel* as *sikara* (peak), denoting 'love of God, no, above, below, ask' and *nyĕmpurit* as *hamsāsya* (goose), denoting 'light, pearl' (Supartha and Supardjan 1980: 4–5).
20. *Bedha* (war, rout), and *daya* (OJ power) invoke a link to the exertion of force in battle. Zoetmulder's OJ dictionary (1982) hints at other possibilities: *amadoni* ('to act [dance] a woman's part') or *badahi* = *padahi* (a kind of drum). Arabic etymologies may also be invoked: '*badhâh* (Ar. 'serving Him as a servant' then 'worship, cult') (Woodward 1989: 73), could means 'nine servants'. Or, *bidaya* (Ar. 'beginning: emanation') gives *ilbadaya* ('the one who begins'), which refers to women who participate in funerary lamentations (Elizabeth Wickett pers. comm. 1990). The simplest etymology is a metathesis of *hiyada*, 'female court servant who dances behind the king' (Horne 1974).

discussed below. Colonial traditions of Javanist scholarship were hostile to Islam (Steenbrink 1993) and focused on the influence and remaining forms of Hindu-Buddhism. Later attention was given to Islamic orientations (Johns 1964; Zoetmulder 1995). One scholar even argued that Javanese kingship in Yogya is based on a 'Sufi theocracy' (Woodward 1989: 164). As we will see, the official exegesis of *bĕdhaya* is a good example of how court culture combines ideas from different religions.

Bĕdhaya remains the best example of dance generating sense-making strategies which combine the visible and invisible, and the empirical and the imagined. Their power arises not from *one particular story* being the 'right' one but *because* it can carry so many stories. In the interpretation that follows, *bĕdhaya* emerges as an embodied representation which totalizes personal and social experience. This totalization is expressed through metaphors of self-realization, with the individual as a microcosmic version of the macrocosmic universe. These metaphors combine spiritual and secular power in a manner which is common to many forms of political symbolism, but here it is done in a particular Javanese style. The poetics of power performed in the *bĕdhaya* dance both as an instrument and as a property of royal power helps us to understand the Javano-Indonesian case of 'how it is that every people gets the politics it imagines' (Geertz 1972: 321).

The Yogyakartan Philosophy of Court *Bĕdhaya*

The only published interpretation of *bĕdhaya* philosophy in the court in Yogyakarta is by K.P.H. Brongtodiningrat. He interprets *bĕdhaya* as a metaphor for a mystical union and integration of the self in the densely allusive Javanese style of exegesis (*suraos*). His interpretation reveals connections which make up reality, understood as the visible and invisible. The principle is like that of allegorical interpretations in both mediaeval Europe and the Middle East, in which nature was a book of signs to be read as revealing God's purpose. Although this text might seem to present Javanese culture as something to be read in the context of the hermeneutic model of Javanese culture which developed in the nineteenth century, it can be understood in the wider context of allegorical interpretations which have arisen when different cultural traditions come together.

Every generation has had its leading dance expert or *ĕmpu*. It was in this capacity that Brongtodiningrat wrote scripts for dance dramas and papers about different aspects of court culture, including interpretations of the *bĕdhaya* and the court itself (Wibowo 1981: 216). Born in 1896, he became a court retainer in 1910, and in 1917 he married Hamĕngkubuwana VII's daughter by the secondary wife B.R.Ay. Pujorĕtno. Unusually, he became a royal son-in-law for a second time when he was widowed, and married his first wife's half-sister by the Sultan and another secondary Wife, B.R.Ay. Rĕtnapurnomo (Mandoyokusumo 1980). He served briefly as the Sultan's secretary until 1922 and became well known as a performer of female dances (*bĕdhaya, srimpi,* and *golek*) and his portrayal of small-bodied male characters, such as Janaka, the young Arjuna, in a *wayang wong* production of *Ciptoning* (Figure 5.5). He became a dance teacher in 1934 and was soon considered to be the leading teacher and choreographer. In Hamĕngkubuwana IX's reign (1940–88) he rose to the highest court rank (*tumĕnggung*), and is attributed with choreographing some of the embryonic *golek Menak* dance drama and *Bĕdhaya Sangaskara*, performed at the weddings of some royal children. His own daughter became the first of Hamĕngkubuwana IX's first four secondary wives, K.R.Ay. Ciptomurti.

These biographical data give some idea of the background of a twentieth- century Javanese court text-maker, and the way in which performance skills could lead to social status. It is unclear when Brongtodiningrat started to write his text on *bĕdhaya* and what its antecedents might have been. I first encountered it when his nephew, Gusti Suryobrongto, lent me a mimeographed copy dated 1971. I then acquired a slightly different version, also in Javanese, included in a collection of writings about Yogyakartan dance, edited and published by the Siswa Among Bĕksa dance association in 1981 as part of their efforts to transmit the values of Yogyakartan court dance to the next generation. Brongtodiningrat made this text available to preserve esoteric knowledge and restore power to court traditions, including *bĕdhaya*, at a time when it was losing its courtly significance due to diversification of its choreographies and performance contexts. By the 1980s, after his death, his writings were key references for Suryobrongto, who by then was the recognized authority on court dance.

We already know that dance movement in *bĕdhaya* is abstract. Reading Brongtodiningrat, it becomes evident that the 'meaning, intention and content' of *bĕdhaya* (and *srimpi*) are also abstract. Although *bĕdhaya* dances are accompanied by songs which may include storylines, Brongtodiningrat's exegesis refers to the staging, the formations, the sequence of choreographic floor patterns, the conflict between the two main dancers, Batak and Endhel Pajĕg, and the significance of the nine dancers. The two main themes of the exegesis are the path of the dance and the conflict between Leader and Follower. His account is obscure, even if one has extensive prior knowledge of the Hindu-Buddhist and Sufi traditions to which it alludes, so rather than simply summarizing his account, I will also provide a certain amount of clarification and contextualization; his own summary is in Appendix 3.

Figure 5.5 K.P.H. Brongtodiningrat dances Janaka (second left from centre) in *Ciptoning*. Reproduced with permission of the Ywandjono-Suryobrongto family.

The interpretation of the staging emphasizes the lack of difference between the dancers, who have identical costumes and make-up. Together the dancers, and some of the formations, represent the human body, and are identified as follows; the numbers refer to the position of each dancer in the key formations (Table 5.1 on page 130):

1   Batak (*Leader*) ('Head', etc.)
2   Endhel Pajĕg (Follower) ('Heart', etc.)
3   Jangga or Pĕnggulu (Neck)
4   Dhadha or Pĕndhadha (Chest)
5   Bunthil (Rear)
6   Apit Ngajĕng (Forward Flank)
7   Apit Wingking (Rear Flank)
8   Endhel Wĕdalan Ngajĕng (Front Follower)
9   Endhel Wĕdalan Wingking (Rear Follower)

As we will see, the Javanese idea of the *lair-batin* person means that Batak and Endhel do not just mean 'head' and 'heart'. The dancers are cast according to their different heights: Jangga, at the centre, should be the tallest dancer, and the two Apits and Endhel Wĕdalans are the shortest. They loosely represent the arms and legs of a body, and their position varies in different entrance marches.

The formations are interpreted to represent the processes of emanation and spiritual progress, activated by the conflict between Batak and Endhel Pajĕg. The account draws on the theory of emanations (*martabat*) first developed by the Sufi Ibn al-'Arabi (d.1240), and later expounded in Indonesia by the Sumatran mystic Shamsal-Din (d.1630).[21] This theory underlies this exegesis and associates *bĕdhaya* with mystical Islam. Brongtodiningrat interprets the first formation (Table 5.1a) as a representation of a Perfect Being (Insan Kamil), who is 'possessed' (*kapanjingan*) by five elements,

Figure 5.6 *Bĕdhaya Tunjunganom*, Court Festival, 1994

---

21.   Bruinessen (1994: 7). See also Gonda (1952: 155–66).

Table 5.1 Court Bĕdhaya formations in Yogyakarta[22]

a) Entrance and exit formation

```
        >     >
        6     8

  >     >     >     >     >
  2     1     3     4     5

        >     >
        7     9
```

b) Endhel Wĕdalans and Apits come out of line: 3 face east, 6 face west

```
     >                        <
     6                        8

        >        <   <   <   <
        2        1   3   4   5

     >                   <
     7                   9
```

c) Endhel Wĕdalans re-enter the formation: all dancers face west

```
                        <6

  <1   <3   <4   <2   <8   <5   <9

                        <7
```

d) *Rakit tiga,* the 'three-by-three' formation: all dancers face north

```
        2^   1^   8^

        6^   3^   5^

        7^   4^   9^
```

22   Formations in Table 5.1a, c, and d are from Brongtodiningrat (1971) but were not included in 1981. I have added b to clarify the discussion, and the directions as they occur at particular moments. The identification of the dancers was confirmed by Bu Yuda (26/7/92).

personality (*budi*), spirit (*roh*), light (*nur*), inner sense or feeling (*rahsa*) and desire (*napsu*), and four forces (water, fire, earth and air), and represents the last of the 'seven emanations'. In the first section of *bĕdhaya* the activating conflict is represented only by the Endhel Wĕdalans coming out of line (Table 5.1b). This choreographic moment is interpreted as the assertion of the will, which disrupts the unity of the Perfect Being formation. Brongtodiningrat does not comment on any ensuing asymmetrical formations but goes directly to the Endhel Wĕdalans' reintegration (Table 5.1c). He compares this to the Hindu trinity (Trimurti) of Brahma, Śiva, Wisnu, and to the manifestation of the subtle or spiritual body (*batin*), in which the 'three powers'(Tripusara), brain, heart and viscera are united; these powers are also compared to the three worlds (Triloka). Brongtodiningrat appears to confuse this formation when the Endhel Wĕdalans re-enter the line with a later formation called '*rakit tiga*' (Table 5.1d) which marks the close of each section in *bĕdhaya* dances. After the discussion of the formations Brongtodiningrat interprets the parts of the body. The four flanking dancers are reminders of the four central teachings of Islam which lead to perfect knowledge: *sarĕngat, tarekat, hakekat* and *makripat* (or Ar. *ma'rifat*). The number of dancers is significant because the human body has nine holes – the *male* body, that is.[23] Surprisingly, there is no mention here of the nine sages of Islam.

Gusti Suryobrongto interpreted the process of the dance as a balance between different human qualities in the microcosm and the macrocosm which are needed to secure the spiritual path (*sabil*) (annotations on the 1971 mimeographed version). The 'moral' of the dance is not a triumph of Batak over Endhel, but a meeting and unification of the two. Brongtodiningrat interprets this as a conflict between opposites, of which good and evil is one interpretation. This is expressed in metaphors of unity across a range of relationships, from the practical arrangement of a dagger in its sheath to the dyadic servant and master, at once personal and macrocosmic. The dualism of the conflict between Follower and Leader, and the potentially disruptive effect of Follower as impulse, will not be avoided by contemplation, but can be neutralized. This will prevent the Will, Endhel Pajĕg, represented by her Followers, from causing problems. It is necessary to overcome gut instincts and low desires, and to strive for the good in all things. Brongtodiningrat closes his argument by saying that it is very difficult to understand what this injunction means, but that it is also important not to turn back from the path to clarity and unity.

Metaphysics and Metaphors

Brongtodiningrat's interpretation of court *bĕdhaya* reveals *bĕdhaya* as capable of carrying a range of metaphorical meanings, which are revealed in order to generate identifications for those who are interested. The doctrines to which this analysis refers are by no means clear. This could be because Brongtodiningrat was protecting esoteric knowledge, or that he was demonstrating that court forms such as *bĕdhaya* are able to carry as many teachings as an expert cares to attribute to them.

---

23. It is often said in shadow theatre that it is desirable to clarify the thoughts by 'closing the nine holes' in meditation (*sĕmĕdhi*).

In representing *bědhaya* as the process of realizing one's nature as a Perfect Being (Insan Kamil), Brongtodiningrat juxtaposes terminologies from different mystical traditions associated with both Hinduism and Islam, in the manner associated with Javanese mystical poetry (*suluk*). A likely source is the well-known nineteenth-century poem by Ranggawarsita (1954), the *Sěrat Wirid Hidayat Jati* (Mysterious Teachings of God's True Guidance), 'a Hinduistic doctrine with a Muslim garment' (Hadiwijono 1967: 103–51).[24] His exegesis also has parallels with the well-known *wayang purwa* story, Dewa Ruci (or Bima Suci), adapted from the Mahābhārata. This tells how the one of the Pandhawa brothers, the strong and powerful Bima, embarks on a search for perfection and is tricked by his Brahman teacher, Durna, into seeking the elixir of life at the bottom of the ocean. After many adventures he here encounters the tiny deity, Dewa Ruci, who is a miniature version of himself. Dewa Ruci promises Bima he will find what he is looking for if he enters the tiny god's ear. Bima does this, and succeeds in finding his goal, which is his 'true self'. The moral of this story is that temptations (*sangka*) can eventually be overcome, and a person can achieve mystical union with the godhead that is their true self.[25] Both Dewa Ruci and *bědhaya* can be interpreted with reference to the philosophy origins, '*sangkan paraning dumadi*'. This can be translated as 'whence and whither', the cause and destiny of being. This process is, literally, about coming into existence and becoming embodied, but paradoxically it is also a process of metaphorization which produces disembodiment.[26] So Dewa Ruci and *bědhaya* can be understood either as an abstract embodiment of the path in which temptations of the soul are encountered and mastered so that the person becomes God, or as a process of realizing one's nature as a Perfect Being.[27]

It is significant that Brongtodiningrat draws on the same concepts and processes as his interpretation of *bědhaya* to interpret the physical structure of the court itself as a system of signs (*sasmita*). Unlike the *bědhaya* interpretation, this text has been translated from Javanese into both English (1975) and Indonesian (1978), and is sold to tourists at the court kiosk. In this text, the twenty sections of the court 'symbolize the 20 adherent characters of God, to strengthen our belief in Him and adoring him' (Brongtodiningrat 1975: 23). Brongtodiningrat analyses the court from south to

---

24. See also Zoetmulder's analysis of the relationship of the Islamic teachings to earlier Hindu-Buddhist ones (1995: 97–114)). The *Sěrat Wirid Hidayat Jati* elaborates the 'five elements' (*mudah*), the 'four forces' (*anasir*), Trimurti, and the four-stages of the Sufi path to *ma'rifat* or gnosis which are alluded to by Brongtodiningrat.

25. Brongtodiningrat omits the philosophy of *zat* (elements) but refers to Pramana, 'the life of and in the body' (Zoetmulder 1995: 191), and 'a means to acquiring a certain knowledge' (Gonda 1952: 159). When Bima gains self-knowledge, he also acquires a four-coloured checked *poleng* cloth. The black, white, red and yellow colours also represent the four aspects of fire symbolized by the four *srimpi* dancers in Brongtodiningrat's interpretation (Suryobrongto 13/4/1983).

26. This is the meaning of *dumadi* (OJ) (Zoetmulder 1982: 347)

27. Woodward overstates *Dewa Ruci's* exclusively Islamic character and the Sufi nature of service in the shadow play (1989:193–98); the story is also found in the Balinese shadow play and elsewhere.

north. Like the lack of differentiation between the *bĕdhaya* dancers, the southernmost part of the court represents the undifferentiated void. All life originates from God's word, which becomes embodied by Trimurti (water, fire and wind) and produces 'Potency' (Pramana). This settles in the heart, moves downwards in the embryo, and produces the Triloka (three potencies), Ngĕndraloka (spirits), Guruloka (gods) and Janaloka (men). These ideas are also used to explain formation 4c of the *bĕdhaya*. However, when he explains human conflict he also introduces an explicit Sufi dimension to the Triloka. The 'will' arises in the *betalmukaram* (in the head), and must be checked by connecting through contemplation to the *betalmakmur* (in the chest). This suggests a parallel between *betalmukaram* and Endhel and *betalmakmur* and Batak, although *bĕdhaya* interpretations tend not to embed these two roles too rigidly as 'head' and 'heart' (see below). The third element, *betalmukadas* (in the genitals) is expressed not in physical but metaphysical terms (Brongtodiningrat 1975: 11–15).

The northern part of the court, using the sultan's path in the court *garĕbĕg* ceremonies, is the path to perfection, the same narrative as that of the reconciliation between Batak and Endhel Pajĕg. In keeping with regional cosmologies that associate mountains with the divine, the idealized sultan sits in contemplation at the highest point of the palace, the Sitihinggil gazing towards the Tugu, an obelisk several miles north of the court. This symbolizes humanity meeting God (Brongtodiningrat 1975: 20).[28] In the Javanese idiom, it is the 'union of servant and lord' (*manunggaling* or *jumbuhing kawula lan gusti*), a formulation which applies to other symbols of the unification of the microcosm to the macrocosm (Moertono 1968: 22). Soekarno also partook of this symbolism when he was officially appointed first President of the Republic here in 1949 (Atmakusumah 1982: 284). Like the three-by-three formation in *bĕdhaya*, the overall metaphysics of the court produces an allegory of perfection and knowledge.

The court interpretation implicates *bĕdhaya* metaphorically in a unifying hierarchy that conflates the ruler's political control over his subjects with the self control (*mawas diri*) of the virtuous self over the wilful self, which produces a set of relations as follows:

in: out :: sultan: court :: *batin: lair* :: court: not court

These two interpretations represent court ritual and theatrical performances as embodied metaphors of perfection. They both endorse the actual power of the sultan and his court, which themselves reflect the universe and spiritual fulfilment.

Brongtodiningrat's account does not give *bĕdhaya* its meaning. Rather, it derives a meaning *from* it. We could say that his interpretation becomes a performance in its own right, a performance which acts instrumentally on issues of existential certainty and questions about what it is to be a human. Many Javanese philosophies specify the limits of knowledge and certainty, and advise caution in evaluating the relation of

---

28. See Woodward (1989: ch. 6), although his gloss of the sultan's return into the court (*jĕngkar dalĕm*) as 'a return to the eternal realm' (ibid.: 210–11) is incorrect.

language to experience.[29] This caution has a counterpart in Islamic doctrine, where *yakin* (certainty Ar.) is given different levels: '*ilm-ul-yaqin:* certainty by reasoning or inference; '*ain-ul-yaqin:* seeing is believing; and *haqqēul-yaqin:* the absolute truth, with no possibility of error of judgement. Sense operates as a veil, not as a revelation, and such veiling is given a spiritual significance. In Islamic thought, essence (*dhat*) is unknowable: only names and attributes can be known (Nicholson 1975: 83). Veiling becomes a poetic action which also points to a religious idea.

The power of *bĕdhaya* dances derives from the context of embodied performance and also from their capacity to carry different metaphorical associations, including Hindu-Buddhism and Sufi ones which form part of the legitimizing symbolism of the Central Javanese courts. In the final analysis, Brongtodiningrat's writings do not support a case for one religious influence over the other. His interpretation of the court has been used as evidence for its representing an Islamic cosmos (Woodward 1989: 200), but there is more than Sufism in both interpretations, and metaphors of unification override any particular or coherent adherence to a single doctrine.

Brongtodiningrat's models are not religious teachings as such. The imagery is a lesson in remembering (*eling*) which in Javanese metaphysics comes close to consciousness or to 'being aware of' (Sastrowardoyo 1991; also Keeler 1987: 219–25). These texts were produced by someone who had witnessed rapid social change, and are symptomatic of the nostalgic anxiety often expressed by survivors of his generation for whom the reign of Hamĕngkubuwana VIII marked the epitome of Javanese culture. The activation of meaning in the physical *bĕdhaya* formations or court architecture can be understood both as a form of memory theatre, and as a means of inscribing a text which will focus collective social memory for the future.[30] They make both *bĕdhaya* and court *good for remembering*: both are theatres of *potential* signs. So these interpretations provide mnemonic representations of a recurrent metaphysical theme, the cause and destiny of being, *sangkan paraning dumadi*.

Whenever this phrase comes up in conversation, it is also a sign that sense making will turn to talking about the One who is, by definition, beyond sense and language. Brongtodiningrat's approach is ultimately reductive: all signs, with their resonances and proliferating connections point to a final single truth. This approach has found favour with the powers promoting the court, and with those in charge of the content of dance training at Siswa Among Bĕksa. It could be argued that this is because the

---

29. 'From the objective non-personal world view, the key categories reality and certainty in the end have the sense of "exact knowledge of reality". These two categories are not much used in the world of Javanese experience … if the forces which confirm human life are not characterized objectively, but subjectively, for instance signs from spirits which have no exact characteristics, so they cannot be counted exactly – then there is no "objective reality" which can be known with certainty and relied upon. So "to seek certainty" in order to act "in accord with objective reality" in the Javanese view has an extremely limited meaning' (Magnis Suseno and Reksosusilo 1983: 95, translated from the Indonesian by the author).

30. Connerton (1989). Memory theatre was developed in classical Europe to remember speeches and narratives by organizing their elements in a physical space, usually a building (Yates 1966).

exegetical basis to Brongtodiningrat's analysis supports a trend in official Javanese culture, namely to give value to a rhetoric which maximizes connections. Remembering is about the future as well as the past, and is an aspect of Javanese historiography which, as already noted, writes the past from the present in a cyclical fashion. The more these connections are cited and reiterated in Javano-Indonesian culture, the more reality and real efficacy they are deemed to have. An emphasis on physical fluidity and the interconnectedness of meaning through word play allows diverse interpretations to coexist, and can undermine cultural constraints or attempts to package social practices as 'culture' as an agenda. Cultural politics imbues these systems with causational capacities. The more complex the connections, the richer the use of references, and the more determinate the form of identity and existence, the more powerful and *adiluhung* the art form or practice.

Interpretive Variations

These texts instead give an insight into postcolonial interpretive practices of the Yogyakartan court from the 1970s, showing what references have been mixed, and how they have become irreducible to their constituent parts: rather, it is the combination which is valued. An emphasis on balance and form, rather than content, characterizes this kind of exegetical approach. The abstruse style of reference used by Brongtodiningrat and the lack of dramatic differentiation in the dance suggests that it is of limited use to analyse *bĕdhaya* in semiotic terms (Hughes-Freeland 1991c). The references in this account are made in a piecemeal and opaque manner, with no detailing of connection or cause. These are not fixed signs in the classic Peircian sense of icons or indices, but possibilities and potentialities that can be fitted to different situations. The dance as embodied practice is distinct from its 'meanings', and this text is not an object of knowledge in itself. It has a very loose fit with *bĕdhaya* as performed. Nor does Brongtodiningrat's interpretation and comments on it do not vindicate the formal binary structuralism that is often used to explain classificatory systems in the region (Josselin de Jong 1977). The 'hidden meanings' may or may not coincide with elements of the performance; they certainly do not *explain* the performance. Nor is this interpretation necessary knowledge for the dancers and the audience; even if they have seen this text, they are probably unable to understand it. Like the dance it refers to, it provides a text-like reference which motivates a range of secondary interpretations, mostly among older people, and I often heard it referred to in conversations, but it was never taken as definitive in its complete form.

Because this was an authorized text, as it were, dance practitioners were reluctant to criticize Brongtodiningrat's discourse, but not everyone agreed with the tone or particular details of the analysis. The choreographer Bu Yuda's own explanations of *bĕdhaya* supported his general approach, but she had reservations about the Islamic content. She criticized Brongtodiningrat (1981) for not clarifying that the formations he describes all come from the first section of the dance, and not mentioning that *bĕdhaya* has two sections. She also said that he ignored the court convention that Endhel and the Apits should come out of line three times to produce asymmetrical formations (Table 5.1b). Most significantly, she explained the totalization of *bĕdhaya* in *physical*, not metaphysical, terms: 'Its rhythms are the rhythms of your own breathing.' Embodied rhythmic breathing is also a metaphor for perfection of selfhood, knowledge and identity.

It is significant that the recollections of Brongtodiningrat himself are marked by paradox. Bu Yuda remembered him as 'rather bowed in prayer', while Gusti Suryobrongto was more sceptical: 'Brongtodiningrat's philosophy is Islamic in the sense of being Javanese Islam [*Islam Kêjawen*], but it is very thin!' (15/6/93), and stressed his skill and enthusiasm for dancing with professional female dancers at *tayubans* (see below), hinting at interests in unions other than mystical ones. As I have explained, the court itself is interpreted using the same model as *bêdhaya*. The metaphors are multipurpose ones, dissolving the specific into the general, which itself becomes a motif of unification. Metaphysically, as in the aesthetics of physical dance movement, it is fluidity and continuity which are valued: unification is preferred to division. It was perfection and not victory in itself which emerged as the dominant motif of both oral and written interpretations *bêdhaya* up to the end of the twentieth century.

Interpretive variation is also evident in responses to Brongtodiningrat's treatment of the fight which normally occurs after 1950 *bêdhaya* dances. Military metaphors for erotic encounters are a distinctive feature of the Yogya court interpretive style. In *Bêdhaya Bêdhah Madiun* ('The Rout of Madiun'), the story tells how Panêmbahan Senapati, founder of the sixteenth-century kingdom of Mataram, wins the defeated regional ruler, Adipati Rangga Kêniten's daughter, Rêtnadumilah, by his magical prowess and chivalry. The singers sing of a fight, but the dance is a love dance (Bu Yuda 8/9/89). In Siswa Among Bêksa's production of *Bêdhaya Gandakusuma* in 1987, Janaka (the young Arjuna) wins the love of the nymph, Supraba, who has helped him defeat the disruptive demon king Niwatakawaca. Rama Sena interpreted the 'fight' through a play of words on the names of the protagonists: Janaka means '*jana*' (this world); Supraba means *praba*, which means *nur* (the light of the divine), 'So the *bêdhaya* represents Janaka gaining divine light' (in Hughes-Freeland 1988). The fight concludes not in winning and losing, but in momentary unification.

Two metaphors characterize the discussion of the fight. Firstly, there is the metaphor of unification. Many older people explained the alternation between Leader and Follower gaining the upper hand as an unending process of opposition and reconciliation, rather than the triumph of one over the other. Leader is not superior to Follower, and the fight must express a balance. 'Yogya's dances are all war dances, horizontally - because of war/conflict; vertically - between emotion and *rasa*' (Pak Pardjan 9/4/83; 20/9/94). In general, 'the fights show how life is'. What matters is the process, not the content: there must be a contrast, followed by unification, *loro-loro atunggaling*: 'although there are two they are united as one ... a symbol of purity' (Gusti Suryobrongto 1/6/83). This is illustrated by different interpretations of Batak and Endhel (Table 5.2). As Brongtodiningrat notes, virtue's role is to incorporate oppositions, but incorporation is never final. The conjunction of the themes of unending process and unification are also discussed by Prijotomo (1988: 85–87) in relation to Javanese architectural forms and ideas; he suggests that unending tension from confrontation is Hindu-Javanese, and the unification of dualities in a perfect balance as Sufi. The *bĕdhaya* appears to combine these two principles. What is stressed is that the two are in competition and alternate in gaining the upper hand, not that one triumphs over the other. Opposition and reconciliation alternate, but this occurs within a unity. What appears to be dualism is processed as monism.[31]

Table 5.2 Interpretations of Batak and Endhel Pajĕg

Batak	Endhel Pajĕg	Source
Head and five senses	First Will	Brongtodiningrat (1981)
Soul (*roh*)	Ratio(nality) (*akal*)	Suryobrongto (pers.comm.)
Head and mind or soul	Heart's desires	Soedarsono (1984: 80–1)

Secondly, there is a metaphorical transformation from sex, via war, to spiritual union. The metaphorical shifting from love to war to submission or marriage or as spiritual enlightenment is central to exegetical tactics in Java. The *bĕdhaya* dance has a number of formations that have been interpreted as representing the body undergoing a process of unification, either sexually or mystically. A similar process is evident in interpretations of the *golek* dance. The dancer is adorning herself to 'look for' (*nggoleki*) a man. She is then compared to the female *golek* puppet dance which closes the shadow play as a reminder for the audience to 'look for' the lesson of the night's play. The human *golek* performs physical self-adornment, which is a metaphor for the spirit's preparation to search for God and knowledge. So although *golek* is located closest to the boundaries between court decorum and sexual explicitness, it was nonetheless interpreted in such a way as to remove adornment from a mimetic, physical level to an abstract metaphysical one, thereby purifying *golek* of its sexual dimension.

These two metaphors both contribute to the representation of power in the court, and in turn feed back into its prestige. It is the accumulation of such identifications that gives performance practices such as *bĕdhaya* the status of *adiluhung*, the high and noble quality of being and action exemplified by court culture. The dance thus becomes a metaphor for embodied human experience and the life process that logically progresses to dissolution and death. It provides a theatre for the rehearsal of ideas, a metaphorical space that moves from the physical *lair* body to the invisible *batin* one. It is a dance that stretches the imagination.

The Power of Pervasiveness

We have discovered that metaphors drawing on pre-Islamic and Islamic interpretations reveal power strategies to gain legitimacy at the level of realpolitik, and truth at the level of personal spirituality. This does not rest on any essentialization or

---

31. A similar syncretism can be found in southern India historically (Bayly 1989: 13–14) and in its current martial arts practices (Zarrilli 1998: 150).

fundamentalism, but reduces a theme, image or number down to a basic truth, and then amplifies it to encompass all meaning that generates connections which might be very unfamiliar to their religious practitioners. A final example in this discussion of the *bědhaya*'s power to generate associations are the lyrics of the controversial *Bědhaya Sěmang*. Like mystical *suluk* poetry, where metaphors of musk and mirrors express transcendent inseparability and pervasiveness, these lyrics share with Brongtodiningrat's exegesis the allusive spirituality that converts metaphors of physical unification to ones of metaphysical union.

The value of pervasiveness became clear to me in a discussion about the names of the temporary court of the first Sultan, 'Ambarkětawang' (fragrant sky) and the court to which the seventh Sultan retired on his abdication in 1921, 'Ambarrukma', meaning 'aroma of gold', later incorporated into Yogya's formerly prestigious Ambarukmo Hotel to which it gave its name. *Ambar* in both names was described as being 'like scent, something coming from a flower, but also like petrol'. This pervasive, miasmic quality was compared to that of a ruler's energy (*sěkti*) and to the sweetness of honey (*madhu*) (Pak Pardjan 11/12/82).[32] In the *Bědhaya Sěmang* song lyrics, the boundless capacity of *ngambar* is epitomized in poetry by 'musk' (*kěsturi*): 'shimmer of musk floats to the heart gone a-roaming'.[33]

Like dance movement names, dance lyrics express two related qualities: expansion and concealment. They are redolent with imagery expressing a concern with boundaries and resonance, in a manner which may be sensual and spiritual. This opaque and allusive literary language, dense with archaisms, is also opaque performatively, sung in songs that are neither comprehensible nor audible, as the human voice in *gamělan* ensembles is treated like the two-string fiddle (*rěbab*), transforming text into texture. These lyrics neither communicate a theme to the audience nor provide verbal dimensions for the message in the dance movement in any clear and detailed way. It is helpful to discuss them because of what they indicate about aesthetics, interpretation and sense making in the Javanese court dance.

Like the songs in *Bědhaya Kětawang* (Florida 1992), the *Bědhaya Sěmang* songs also allude to the sovereign's prowess in war and love, and the beauty of his beloved, but are wrapped in metaphors and puns:

---

32. Compare this with the nineteenth-century poet Ranggawarsita's image: 'Like honey and its sweetness, you will certainly not find [it] if you separate [them]' (1954: 19).

33. This and the following are my translations from the *Sěmang* songs in *Sěrat Pěsindhen Candran Abdidalěm* (1836) from the reign of the fifth Sultan, and the oldest extant song text in the court. I read most of the many *Sěmang* manuscripts in the Widyabudaya library and the Kridha Mardawa archive. These texts consist of a scene-setting *lagon*, followed by the songs. Apart from the opening *kawin* songs, the songs for the two main sections of the dance are substantially the same in subsequent manuscripts. I worked on a translation into Indonesian with R.M. Soetanto. I subsequently reworked an English version extensively using Old Javanese meanings. I have recently refined my translation further after Garrett Kam provided me with his version of the text which uses even more Old Javanese, and which I have engaged with but not just replicated.

Swan-necked
Glowing in this 'war of milk'
'Parasols' meet thus in passion.
Lustful joy leads to love's honey.
As the splendour of song makes supple the maiden.[34]

The pun on '*songsong*', 'parasol' or holes', conjoins sex and status. So does another more common pun on *smara*, 'love', and *samara*, 'encounter, fight'. Military images both conceal and allude to sexual congress, which itself is a metaphor for kingly prowess. War is thus a metaphor for both eroticism and spirituality, and leads to elaborate word play and resonances. Praise and atmospheric evocation are generalized in the overall flow of dance movement, not denoted by specific gestures. The veiling of erotic motifs in language parallels the excision of any overt sensuality in accordance with *pathokan* for dance movement in the feminine mode. But it is probable that the meaning was never intended to be clear, for fear of losing a fragile beauty, as the lyrics suggest:

Florid songs like crushed flowers
Flowers of fame bloom everywhere
Their suppleness I read as a sign
Beauty among the maidens
Reaches the flower's opening
In abundance, look at me my darling, look at me, your love.

I was helped on manuscript transcriptions in the court by the chief librarian K.R.T. Widyakusuma, and the literary scholar R.M. Soetanto, who was often in the library working on another manuscript, and later helped me translate the *Sĕmang* songs into Indonesian. They explained that translation can only provide a 'flavour' of the lyrics because of the opacity of the allusions and word play, especially *wangsalans*, which use puns and coded rhymes in a question-answer form.[35] For example the elliptical line 'The green hawk flies to the northern world', was rejected as a literal reference to a bird because the line was a question in a *wangsalan*, with the 'answer' being '*alapana*', also a kind of hawk but more importantly a synonym for 'take': so the clue was 'green hawk' and the response, by means of 'hawk', was 'Come on, seize the

---

34. *Gĕndhing Ladrang* 17–40. In m.s. B/S 1B (1946) this *ladrang* is called *Sĕmang Nama Endhel*. The first seven lines refer euphemistically to a sexual encounter. In the first line '*rĕsmining*' means beautiful, glowing, but *sarĕsmi* in Old Javanese (*kawi*) means 'to have intercourse', which is probably why in B/S 1B the word has been changed to *rumakitrang*, 'beauty', instead. The remainder of this song is very compressed and includes a number of *kawi* words which produce ambiguous or incomprehensible meanings. A similar use of word play occurs in the equally opaque Balinese *kidung lelungid* (Zurbuchen 1987: 175–6).

35. This form is similar to *pantun*, song games using riddles found in Indonesia and the Malay peninsula (Pigeaud 1938: 297, 462–63).

veils of our beginning and our end'.[36] 'Seize the veils' reiterates the well-known message that it is dangerous to know too much before you are ready, so the hidden meaning of this imagery is also a form of protection for the uninitiated.[37] The meaning of the lines about the philosophy of 'whence and whither', discussed above, is so hidden and abstract that gestural rendition would be impossible. The lyrics hint at a quest for perfect love or for spiritual fulfilment, suggested in the line 'Choose your path so death leads not to sorrow'.

Apart from this metaphorical complexity, translating dance songs is further complicated by two practices. Firstly, some words function as cues (*sasmita*) to musicians. In the in the *kandha* from this text, 'Looking on honey [*madhu*], drowning together [*kěntharing*] in passion' was a cue for musicians to play the melody *Madhukěntar*.[38] Secondly, there is the coded and complicated calendrical system of chronograms (*candrasěngkala*), which provides a rich vocabulary and is extensively used in any Javanese text. For instance, *dahana*, meaning 'fire', stands for the number '3'; *gora* (bigger, mountain) stands for 7; *sonya* stands for 0, and also words for 'sky'. Thus, the *saka* year 337 becomes 'Three fearful things seen in the sky' (*Gora tri katoning tawang*) (Warsadiningrat 1987: 35). This imagery is similar to that at the close of the *Sěmang* songs accompanied by the *Kětawang* melody:

> The fine rain falls, the flowers fade, flashes of lightning
> Heavenly storms, wind of passion, wrestle and pull in total chaos
> Toppled the tree tops
> The gods are confused, so strong and swift the shaking 'storm'
> Look to the east, see the high-rising peak
> The sea, see too the sea stretched out
> Screaming, succumbing in difficulty, a terrifying tumult!

The song thus ends in images of devastation which remain a mystery. Do they refer to a cosmic holocaust? Or a volcanic eruption, of Mount Měrapi perhaps? Or might this be a sexual symbol, as storms are often metaphors for sexual encounters in

---

36. *Wulung wida měngaloring bana, Aya ta alapana alapana kěkudung sangkaning paran.* A completely different translation is also possible: 'Fragrant darkness ominously encircles northward regions' (Kam pers. comm. 2007).

37. The philosophy of 'whence and whither' can sometimes mean enlightenment which must be hidden from ordinary people. The *wali* Seh Siti Jěnar was famously punished precisely for breaking the rules of secrecy surrounding knowledge. Zoetmulder (1971) also discusses the theme of secrecy and the timing of the revelation of knowledge to protect the uninitiated in relation to the shadow play.

38. This signalling practice is widespread in the region, including in the shadow play. It takes a more improvisatory form in *tayubans*, where the dancers sing these codes to pass on requests for tunes to the drummer. When a dancer sings *aja lali*, 'don't forget' the drummer will play the tune *Eling-Eling*, 'Remember'; when she sings '*judu kěnaha*' this is a code for *pěrang kuku* 'all out war', so the drummer will play *Pangkur* (Field notes 1989).

the classical poetry of the region? No one could, or would, say.[39] As is the case with any highly allusive poetry whose context has been lost, we can only speculate and wonder.

The Vanishing Point of Being

This resonance and expansiveness of meaningfulness away from precise definition parallel the qualities that are appreciated in dance movements, which are themselves named after images of natural or expansive power. 'Waves of water', 'areca palm in the wind', 'looking in a mirror' all share a boundary breaking quality of expansive energy, expressed in the metaphor of fumes and refraction. They cannot be contained, nor necessarily understood.

'Looking in a mirror' (*ngilo*) is itself also a well-known metaphor for knowledge in Javanese literary traditions: the proverb 'Look at your own nape in the mirror' refers to self-knowledge – and its difficulty.[40] Looking in a mirror is the metaphor par excellence for the general process of dancing bringing together the physical body with the subtle body. Like fumes expanding beyond their source, sense spills out beyond signs, beyond material knowledge to spiritual bliss, transcendence, and the knowledge and perfection of *ma'rifat*, the final stage of the Sufi path. Although knowledge may be an attribute of status, its goal is not power but enlightenment. As with images of dispersing scent, the mirror metaphor goes beyond singularity and containment, and becomes an image of resonance and redundancy. It doubles what need only be single, just as *srimpi* dances, performed by two pairs of identically dressed dancers performing in unison and usually portraying a duel, reduplicate a single fight. This mirror analogy demonstrates the difficulty and inappropriateness of only limiting Javanese practices to their embodied form as well as to a particular context. What we are faced with is a demonstration of the metaphorical effect of extending sense from a particular set of actions at a particular time to a general interpretation. The sense that resonates from *bĕdhaya* (and to a lesser extent *srimpi*) is the relationship between *lair* and *batin*, and the search for human perfection.

So we find that a highly visible female physical presence first becomes a metaphor of a sexually productive human body, and at second remove a metaphor of human mortality. In the processes of power over performance, women's physical bodies disappear as their sexuality becomes euphemized. Physical embodiment and sexual energy become a symbol of unity of opposites, a process of conflict and resolution,

---

39. Brakel-Papenhuijzen compares the fire at the end to that after the orgiastic *ĕmprak* dance in *Sĕrat Cĕnthini* (vol. 8: 133ff.) and other purificatory fires, concluding that this song is typical of Islamic syncretism (1996: 163–64).

40. '*Ngilo githoke dhewe*' (Suryadi 1981: 209). The Sufi master al-Ghazzali often used the mirror analogy, hence its importance in Javanese *suluk* literature (Zoetmulder 1995: 269–74). In the seventeenth-century *Sĕrat Cabolek*, the mirror represents the body, and the person looking in it the spirit. 'Body and spirit go together; the spirit being the essential [vital] element of the body, it must be said that it mirrors itself in the body ...'. The mirror represents nondualism, the perfect unity of lord and servant (Drewes 1978: 49).

and finally a unification of the many into the one in death. *Bĕdhaya*, in short, is a metaphor for the meaning of life, but one in which gendered bodies become generalized into being and nothingness. This process of dematerialization can be illuminated with one final reference. The Indonesian writer Danarto concludes a collection of short stories inspired by Sufism with a tale of a *bĕdhaya* dance at a wedding. Scheduled to last for fifteen minutes, the dance continues for over two hours, when, still dancing, the dancers leave the stage and the hall:

> The seventeen dancers gradually disappeared. They reached the unreachable horizon. They seemed to be swallowed up by the skyline. Dissolved. The dancers disappeared to the South while their teacher, Mrs Soelistyami, flew northwards, under circumstances beyond belief.[41]

The initial alarm of the dancers' parents disappears as mysteriously as their daughters. They forget that there had ever been a dance, dancers or daughters, and leave the wedding with feelings of satisfaction.

In contrast to the socially dispersed power produced through dance education, the philosophical resonances and semiotic ambiguities of *bĕdhaya* still contribute to its exclusivity and its role as a symbol of natural and supernatural power. These dances continue to retain their association with the personal power and mystique of the sultan, and are the last of the ceremonial court forms to do so. I have argued that the Javanese court *bĕdhaya* dances are powerful because they resist being encompassed within a single text. Feminine dance movement itself is not a text which can be deciphered. Its general significance as a sign of social status is communicated semiotically or iconically, through the physical quality of movements. Its appreciation, though, is elaborately mediated through training, habit, and practice. When experts write that the meaning of dance gestures will become clear when one knows them, they do not mean that a lexicon will be revealed, but that foundations for appreciation will be established and sensitized. Although Javanese people have a reputation for making meaning out of anything, dance movement and lyrics *conceal*. The 'higher' a form is, the less self-evident its meaning. *Bĕdhaya* choreography is understood to represent the human body and is seen as a metaphor for different levels of conflict and resolution, expressed sexually, spiritually or morally. The interpretations of the dance form reflect on human experiences and the meaning of life and death. I have suggested that this is because of the abstract quality of the dance movement, their association with myths of political legitimacy, their capacity to accumulate semi-historical associations with a distant past, and their ability to generate metaphors about enduring metaphysical principles.

The Disappearing Feminine

As a final stage of this discussion of symbolism and power in *bĕdhaya* dances, I consider the process of disembodiment in relation to gender, and examine local ideas about the feminine as a source of danger that must be controlled.

---

41. Danarto (1982: 70), translated by the author.

Women generally play an important role as bearers of allegorical meanings (Warner 1996). I have explained that *bĕdhaya* makes women's bodies carry symbolic power by generating through dancing many meanings and indeterminacy, instead of functional 'natural' erotic power. The physical dance is transformed into a metaphor of metaphysical or mystical union. The bodies of the dancers are twice *disembodied*: first, choreographically, as ciphers in the dance formation; and, secondly, as a sign of the story of the path to perfection. Brongtodiningrat converted the *bĕdhaya* dance into a spiritual path, which assimilates but transcends the feminine. Despite allusions to pre-Islamic religious concepts, neither Brongtodiningrat nor other Yogyakartan discussants referred explicitly to tantric associations of *bĕdhaya* and royal power. The generative dimension and the gendered dualities have been desexualized and transformed into moral impulses; physical sexuality has been converted into metaphysical teachings. *Lair* has been lost from the *lair-batin* person.

Brongtodiningrat's interpretation specifically omits the association of *bĕdhaya* with the political myths of origin of the Central Javanese Mataram dynasty based on a sexual union between the Javanese sultans and Ratu Kidul, the mythological 'Queen of the South'. This explicitly sexual association is still recognized in court ritual, especially the *Bĕdhaya Kĕtawang* dance in the Kasunanan in Surakarta, considered to be a dance of placation, desire and power.[42] By contrast, in Yogyakarta's Kasultanan, the association is muted and treated with ambivalence. This ambivalence has to do with the mysterious cessation around 1914 of Yogya's 'heirloom' dance, *Bĕdhaya Sĕmang*, which I will suggest is linked to the former practice of males dancing *bĕdhaya*. As we will see, although women's court *bĕdhaya* presents an appearance of regulated femininity, the dance's context of associations and competing values has changed over the years. Women's dance retains the potential not only to represent contradictions, but also to tell different stories about gender itself. On the one hand, women are considered capable of being refined, in a region where women often seem to be excluded from spiritual virtue and, one might argue, from becoming Perfect Beings. On the other hand, the price of representing such perfection results in gender difference being refined out of existence in an ideology that neutralizes female capacities and, arguably, replaces complementarity between the sexes with a domination of the masculine. This raises questions about gender and performance in the nation state.

The subtle quality of feminine dance movement and the meanings given to *bĕdhaya* form part of the euphemization of sexuality which appears to have developed in the late colonial court (Hughes-Freeland 2006). The court excluded *tayubans*, which took place in princely residences until the 1920s. These events included the unusual interaction of men and women dancing together, although the women were paid professionals and not (usually) of the same social status as their male partners.

---

42. Brakel-Papenhuijzen argues that the *Kĕtawang* and *Sĕmang* songs do not allude to Ratu Kidul. The dance and offerings are for Ratu Kidul, but 'the sacred *bĕdhaya* songs serve basically as a spell to conjure up powerful spirits which in combination with other ritual actions should bring about the desired effect of peace and stability in the Javanese realm' (1996: 163–64).

They served drink, and provided an excuse for their partners to show off (Hughes-Freeland 1996). Brongtodiningrat reputedly said, 'In fact, what is called *tayub* is really a show of dance prowess' (Mbak Kadar 19/10/89), and enjoyed dancing at *tayuban*s in the evening, until the excesses of drinking made the situation become coarse (*wadeh, saru*).

After Indonesian independence there was a general move to abolish female performance that was not strictly controlled by men as 'culture' (Hughes-Freeland 1990). Contemporary *adiluhung* court culture as exemplary culture rested on a transcendental, nonmaterial ideology of honour as the basis for exchange, an ideology which is connected to the dissimulation or deflection of any physical expression of sexuality. By the 1980s, the formalization of the 'inside' (*jĕro*) coincided with the formalization of the feminine dance mode in the court as the only dance mode for women. The boundary between dancers who danced with men and plied them with drink and the court *bĕdhaya* and *srimpi* dancers is still emphasized, on both moral and aesthetic grounds. The resulting aesthetic – subtle and oblique – has rested on the absence of any signs of eroticism. *Bĕdhaya* dancers were often explained to me as being the opposite of *ledhek*. There is a structural relationship between the triumph of symbolic, exegetical power in 'high art', as opposed to sexual power in village *tayuban*s where *ledhek* move their hips and look at men (Figure 5.7).[43] This fits into

Figure 5.7 *Tayuban*, Gunung Kidul, 1989

43. This is demonstrated in Hughes-Freeland (1996); on *ledhek*s see also Choy (1984: 62–66); Sutton (1984: 121); Hughes-Freeland (1993a, 1997a).

a wider regional pattern of rulers controlling troupes of dancers which variously included or excluded wives, daughters and sisters, nieces, cousins: a general ethnography of ideologies of male control over women at the centres of power. We have a repression where we could have had continuity, as will become clear.

The Missing Figure: Ratu Kidul

As in many other Asian traditions, performance has established order in both the natural and social worlds, by making connections between the visible and invisible world. The *bĕdhaya* dances embody perfection, link royal control to self-control and control of women, and also serve as metaphors for the sultan's control over the natural and political environment, in a court situated strategically between the mountain to the north and the sea to the south. Since the earthquake and tsunami of 26 December 2004, it is perhaps easier for us to understand the cultural principle of the ruler mediating between the forces of nature and the human world. There are many Asian myths about pacts between rulers and sea spirits and deities (Mulyadi 1983: 32–34).

The authority of the ruler in Java has depended on ritual alliances with the invisible world, particularly the close relationship with a supernatural being, Ratu Kidul, Queen of the South (Sea).[44] The mythical contract between the house of Mataram and Ratu Kidul is honoured by the courts' annual *labuhan* offerings to her on the south coast (Bigeon 1982). Ratu Kidul is its patron, protector and champion, and one person even described as the guardian spirit (*dhanyang*) of the court (Pak Prapto pers.comm. 1989). Ratu Kidul has a genealogy drawing from Hindu-Buddhism and Islam. She plays a definitive role in a court myth about Agung's use of both religions to consolidate his authority. Her earliest appearance is in Kartasura court manuscripts in 1738 (Ricklefs 1998: 9). The Yogyakarta 'Court Chronicle' (1777–78) tells how Cĕmara Tunggal, a female hermit, helps the founder of the fourteenth-century kingdom of Majapahit and goes to live on the south coast (ibid.: 9–10). In *Babad Tanah Jawi*, the major Surakartan court history of Java, Sultan Agung's grandfather Panĕmbahan Senapati (r.1584–1601) made a contract with Ratu Kidul in the form of a sexual union. In a second version, Senapati's powerful meditation performed near the south sea caused so much heat that the water boiled, killed the fish, and threatened Ratu Kidul and her spirit court. In desperation she confronted the ruler and implored him to stop. Their confrontation

---

44. Ratu Kidul controls a horde of destructive spirits who bring famine or epidemics, and her desire to marry Mount Mĕrapi threatens to sever the kingdom (Resink 1982: 99). She shares these attributes with the Hindu goddess Durga, but also represents the fertility of the Javanese goddess, Dewi Sri (Pigeaud 1960–63, Vol. IV: 209–11; 300). In Yogyakartan mythology, there are up to three figures: Ratu Kidul, her two ministers, Nyai Lara Kidul and Nyai Kidul (Mandoyokusumo: n.d.). In popular folklore she has a daughter, Nyai Blorong, who gives wealth in exchange for souls and chases up defaulters in her true serpentine form. Both figures were the subject of a genre of Indonesian horror film in the 1980s. Among other stories of snakes in the *Sĕrat Kandaning Ringgit Purwa* ('shadow play stories', canto 165, L0r6379, Pigeaud 1967: 358 ff.) the mythical Aji Saka of Medang Kamulan has a snake-son, Naga Linglung, who marries Rĕtna Blorong. See also Poerbatjara (1962) and Jordaan (1984).

turned to love, and is commemorated in *Bĕdhaya Kĕtawang*. The third version describes how Sultan Agung goes to his second court in the southern ocean. She begs him to join her there as he only has two years to live but he refuses. She tells him to throw the dagger, Sangkĕlat, into the sea before he dies, and she will pass it on to his successor (Ricklefs 1998: 11–13).[45] This story is reminiscent of King Arthur's sword Excalibur being returned to the Lady in the Lake after his death. The Javanese stories are indeed mythological, but continue to have a presence in the court and in popular culture which the Arthurian legends have never had.

Ratu Kidul is still a force to be reckoned with. On 14 August 1994, friends took me to a beach at Glagah, a wild and unspoilt place in Yogya's Kulon Progo district, south of the Cĕmara Sewu mountains where the sea is even more tremendous and awesome than at Parangtritis. We were walking back to the car when a bus and mini-bus arrived, and some women wearing court dress and insignia got out. The party of about thirty from the Pakualaman court included a prince and the director and members of the Pakualaman's Yayasan Loro Jonggrang, which runs the Ramayana Ballet at Prambanan. They had come to make a *labuhan* offering to Ratu Kidul. Forty days earlier, Pak Suwita, a secondary school English teacher, had been dancing the monkey, Subali, in a Ramayana performance. When Rama shot Subali with his bow and arrow, the dancer fell to the ground. The audience had applauded because the death was so convincing. Normally a defeated or dead dancer goes down on one knee. But what the audience had seen was a real death. Pak Suwita had had a stroke. He was carried off, and the dance continued. The Pakualaman sends its annual *labuhan* from Glagah, and because of the exceptional circumstances of the death, the Yayasan's links with the Pakualaman, and the Pakualaman's link with Ratu Kidul, this ritual offering, which included the dance costumes of the monkeys Subali and Sugriwa, was considered appropriate. The expectation was that Ratu Kidul would prevent similar disasters from striking in the future.

Ethnographic Interlude 2: *Bĕdhaya Ketawang*, 1983

The alliance between Ratu Kidul and Sultan Agung is said to have produced the original *bĕdhaya* dance. The Kasunanan court in Surakarta still performs the fully ritualized heirloom *Bĕdhaya Kĕtawang* annually, to celebrate the *susuhunan*'s accession. It also holds equally ritualized monthly rehearsals. It is said to appease the destructive powers of Ratu Kidul, who is claimed to attend the dance and even possess the dancer representing Endhel. *Bĕdhaya Sĕmang*, Yogyakarta's heirloom equivalent of *Bĕdhaya Kĕtawang* (Surjodiningrat 1953:14), used to be performed for the birthdays of the sultan and of the crown prince, but has not taken place since the reign of Hamĕngkubuwana VII (1877–1921). Given the absence of an 'heirloom' *bĕdhaya* in

---

45. Other stories may be found in Warsaningrat (1987). Ricklefs reminds us that in the *Sĕrat Sakander* (The Book of Alexander) the Dutch were implicated in this mythology as the legitimate rulers of Pajajaran (1974). The V.O.C. representatives could watch *bĕdhaya* because they were Ratu Kidul's relatives (1998: 13). Hostetler suggests that the relationship between Sultan Agung and Ratu Kidul was transformed from a conjunction of opposites to a domination of the queen by the ruler (1982: 130–31).

Yogya, after lengthy negotiations and a suitable smart long-sleeved frock being made, I attended the Bĕdhaya Kĕtawang performance on 15 May 1983 to commemorate the thirty-eighth anniversary of Susuhunan Pakubuwana XII's accession.[46]

Tirtaamidjaja has described *Bĕdhaya Kĕtawang* performances as 'symbols of the highest authority in the kingdom, equal in rank to the sacred state regalia' (1967: 33). Nearly twenty years later, the atmosphere of the performance and its powers of association still gave the occasion a highly ritualistic quality. *Bĕdhaya Kĕtawang* took place in a larger social choreography. The process of the entire court seating itself according to status around the dance hall was a performance in itself. The Susuhunan sat on a raised throne to the west of the four central pillars, with honoured guests such as ambassadors, sons and brothers to his left and right. Behind him, lower down, sat his daughters and their companions. Facing him, level with the dancers, were the senior officials; below them were the lesser ranks, royal grandchildren and great-grandchildren. Guests have always been invited to the ceremony, and were seated to the north side. The recent controversial issuing of tickets to nonhonorary guests was the result of an agreement between K.R.T. Hardjanĕgara, at the time a high-ranking court official, responsible for the court's arts and culture administration, and also for Mitra Budaya (Companions of Culture), an elite cultural association based in Jakarta to which many of the guests, including artists and business people, belonged. There was ample opportunity during the two hours or so before the dance started for seeing, being seen and for gossip. The former chief of military police sitting next to me told me how he had refrained from using his noble title until he retired, and passed the time by pointing out the 'very important or very immoral!' rich and famous.

The event lasted four hours. First came the presentation of aristocratic ranks or 'stars' (orders of the realm) to deserving courtiers and others. Then, for nearly an hour and a half, nine dancers exquisitely costumed as brides moved languidly through elaborate asymmetrical formations. The repetitive undulation of the dance gestures hypnotically evoked the waves of the sea. The music was spare, punctuated by the chiming clarity of the *kĕmanak*, small curved split gongs made of bronze which are only used in *Bĕdhaya Kĕtawang* and *Sĕmang* and a few other dances (such as *Srimpi Ranggajanur* in Yogya), interwoven with the plaintive *mandaraka* singing (Kunst 1973).[47] The accompaniment, echoing eerily across from the Sasana Handrawina where the *gamĕlan* and singers were seated, sent shivers down my spine as I breathed in the heady scented smoke wafting from the incense burner. The dance seemed to communicate longing rather than eroticism, but the experience of being there made it easy to understand the reputation of the dance.

---

46. Despite claims by Warsadiningrat (1987), we can only know for sure that the dance has been performed at accessions since Susuhunan Pakubuwana X came to the throne on 30 March 1893 (Soeratman 1989: 151).

47. More like *kakawin* and *kidhung* singing in Bali than usual Javanese court performance, this is said to date from the Kediri kingdom of East Java (eleventh to thirteenth centuries). Singers used to be restricted to high-ranking court specialists, but by 1967 only three proficient singers in the style remained (Tirtaamidjaja 1967: 34–35).

The link between *Bĕdhaya Kĕtawang* and Ratu Kidul has produced a mythology which has been interpreted according to animist, Hindu, Tantric and Islamic ideas. Prince Hadiwidjojo of Surakarta (d.1980) has been the leading local voice in identifying *Bĕdhaya Kĕtawang* with Hinduism. He compares it to a ritual Hindu encirclement (*pradakṣiṇā*) around the Susuhunan, enthroned to the west of the centre of the building, by the nine *bĕdhaya* dancers, like stars around the sun, symbolizing the *yoni* encircling the Susuhunan as Śiva-liṅga (phallus). In this way *Bĕdhaya Kĕtawang* enacts the tantric conjunction of male and female powers.[48] Watching the dance, Hadiwidjojo's 'circle' was not literally 'round' the throne: the dancers entered from the Susuhunan's left, danced in front of his throne, and exited to his right. However, two of the formations (see Table 5.1b and c) may be compared to the moment before and the act of penetration, as represented in the famous carving of vulva and phallus at the fourteenth-century Sukuh temple on the slopes of Mount Lawu to the east of Surakarta.[49]

The tantric theme also extends further. The Susuhunan has had the right to pick one of the dancers afterwards for sexual intercourse, as a representative of Ratu Kidul herself. In 1963, five of the dancers were wives of Pakubuwana XII (r.1945–2004) (Anderson 1967: 70); he had taken six dancers over the three years following his accession to be his secondary wives (*garwa ampil*) and had thirty-six children by them. Apparently Ratu Kidul had informed Pakubuwana X that she would relate to him not as a lover but as a grandmother (Pak Yu 23/9/83), also the case with the ninth Sultan of Yogyakarta. This made it possible for princesses to perform, and by 1988 one of the Sunan's daughters and one granddaughter took part (Soeratman 1989). The present Sunan, however, has yet to use his royal privilege, and the taboo on his daughters performing the dance has been waived due to a shortage of hereditary dancers. Students from local dance academies were allowed to join in the rehearsals, and one has performed the most junior position, *buncit* (the posterior in the dance body).

Even without knowledge of the relationship of the Susuhunan to Ratu Kidul, the formality of the occasion, and the power of the performance, dominated by the thick clouds of incense and the resonating music and chanting, contributed to an effect of sacred spectacle. But this is more than theatre. For members of the court it is considered a revered ritual and living heirloom. The dance itself is hedged with ritual

---

48. Hadiwidjojo (1972: 121–24; 1981: 17). The most comprehensive Javanese 'histories' are by the court poet Ranggawarsita and the court musician K.R.T. Warsadiningrat (1987), which are discussed by Brakel-Papenhuijzen (1992). Stutterheim (1956) also made a case to link *Bĕdhaya Kĕtawang* to Tantric Buddhism. Becker has also interpreted the dance as a tantric representation of the *cakric* body (1991: 112–13) but in a rather general way; she later extended the *bĕdhaya* stories to include Brongtodiningrat's interpretation (1993).
49. Given ideas about royal potency, after seeing my diagrams for Table 5.1, Marlene Heins (pers. comm. Nov. 2005) reminded me about Sukuh, and also provided the first-hand information about the sunan's sexual rights over the dancers. This phallic imagery provides an alternative to religious reasons for why sultan Agung might have wanted two extra dancers for his own exclusive court *bĕdhaya*.

proscriptions whose breaching will lead to calamities such as the fire which ravaged the Kasunanan in 1985. Arriving with a *lampor,* the noise of hooves, a rushing wind, and maybe heavy rain, Ratu Kidul is said to attend the monthly dance rehearsals on Anggarakasih (Kliwon Tuesday), the final intensive week of rehearsal and the performance itself. These rehearsals are highly ritualized, require a minimum of seven dancers, and can only be cancelled for special reasons – as in August 1983, after the death of the Susuhunan mother. Dancers, singers and musicians must fast the night before the actual performance, and there is a taboo on taking photographs, although many people, including members of the royal family, snapped away, unawed. I had taken the prohibition literally and had left my camera behind, so was able to concentrate on watching and wondering about the green glow I saw on the forehead of one of the dancers. 'Seeing green' is reported as a sign of Ratu Kidul's presence, usually in the form of a possession of the dancer Endhel. To this day I am uncertain whether what I saw was a combination of expectation, sitting in the heat for four hours, and a camera flash on the paraffin wax used for the dancer's hairdo, or something less mundane.

The Mystery of *Bĕdhaya Semang*

After seeing *Bĕdhaya Kĕtawang,* I intensified my attempts to find out more about *Bĕdhaya Sĕmang*'s relationship to it. What had happened after the division of the kingdom and the founding of Yogyakarta in 1756? And although both dances have been described as 'sacred', is it more accurate to describe them as being imbued with the power of heirlooms, and more associated with dangerous forces than other *bĕdhaya* dances?[50] I also wanted to establish whether or not Ratu Kidul was supposed to have attended *Bĕdhaya Sĕmang,* and possessed one of the dancers as in *Bĕdhaya Kĕtawang.*

Warsaningrat's mythical history suggests that Sultan Agung's *Sĕmang* and *Rambu* melodies became the property of the court at Yogyakarta (1987: 91). *Cuplikan Sĕrat (Babad) Nitik* (1897), a manuscript which belonged to the first wife of Hamĕngkubuwana VI (r.1855–77), states that Agung's original dance was called *Sĕmang (Asmarandana* p. 25), but then describes a *srimpi* dance for *four,* not a court *bĕdhaya* for nine dancers.[51] Oral tradition in Yogyakarta claims that the *Sĕmang* and *Kĕtawang* dances have the same musical accompaniment, and that the existing *Kĕtawang* is only a section of the Yogyakartan dance. A related and also discredited view is that after

---

50. No nineteenth-century song texts and *kandha* give *Bĕdhaya Sĕmang* this status (Brakel-Papenhuijzen 1992: 274). Nonetheless, *bridal* costumes have always been worn in *Bĕdhaya Kĕtawang* and by *bĕdhaya* dancers in Yogya until the 1920s.

51. 'The Sultan [Agung] said in sweet and friendly tones: 'Daughter, my child, to your creation I give the name *Sĕmang;* let the full beauty of all dance movement be in that *Sĕmang,* and I ask also that it is arranged as well in a composition with four corners, and the number of dancers will be four and it will be called srimpi ...'. Drs Singgih Wibisono (letter 5 October 1985) provided an interpretation and Indonesian gloss of this extremely ambiguous passage. Soedarsono identifies the manuscript as *Sĕrat Nitik,* AD1897 (1984: 79).

Hamĕngkubuwana V's marriage to a Surakartan princess, her father Pakubuwana VIII sent a music expert to Yogyakarta to make the accompaniment for Sĕmang, and he used the Kĕtawang from Bĕdhaya Kĕtawang (K.R.T. Madukusuma, in Suharti 1972: 17–18). Scholars have suggested that Bĕdhaya Sĕmang was devised in the reign of Hamĕngkubuwana II (r.1792–1812).[52] Subsequent textual research has challenged this, and suggested that Yogya's heirloom bĕdhaya was Sumrĕg; confusingly, this became known as Sĕmang, although there was already another dance by this name.[53]

We do know from manuscripts that, with minor exceptions, the formations in Bĕdhaya Sĕmang, as other Yogyakartan court bĕdhaya dances, were very like those in Bĕdhaya Kĕtawang (Brakel-Papenhuijzen 1992: 219, 275). During the love dance in the second part, in keeping with Yogyakarta's militaristic spirit the dancer, Endhel, used to fire a pistol.[54] This was said to have been conventional during the reigns of the fifth and seventh Sultans; it ceased because the 'bang' frightened everyone and did not suit the rasa of the piece (R.M. Dinusatama 14/4/83). Bu Yuda told me that another dance, Bĕdhaya Tunjunganom, used pistol shots during the seventh Sultan's reign. When she revived this dance for the Court Festival in Yogyakarta (15 August 1994), all the dancers fired pistols in the first lajuran section; in the danced fight between the King of Banjaran and the Princess of the Spirits from Sagaluh, they used bows and arrows. Sagaluh is the mythic birthplace of Ratu Kidul, so it is possible that she might have been associated in this dance as well, but during the eight Sultan's reign, this dance was given another story (Bu Yuda 23/9/94).

It was very difficult to get a clear answer about the role of Bĕdhaya Sĕmang in the Yogya court and why it stopped being performed there. This was associated with extreme ambivalence both about Ratu Kidul and the possibility of possession. As usual, there was little consensus and much hearsay, but some common themes emerged. Bu Yuda said that some court people – 'I forget who' – claimed that Ratu Kidul attended Sĕmang performances. She had also heard that there used to be only eight bĕdhayas, and that Ratu Kidul joined in, making nine: 'if she attends, she dances Endhel' (13/9/83). Mbak Kadar remembered hearing that after three-and-a-half hours of performing, dancers often fainted, but the audience would still see nine performers – the implication being that Ratu Kidul manifested to make up the numbers (24/4/89). An aristocrat and local historian, Pak Yu, said that Bĕdhaya Sĕmang was about Senapati's love for Ratu Kidul, but that it was 'dangerous and not an appropriate theme for today'. Gusti Suryobrongto was irritated in general by

---

52. Soerjadiningrat (n.d.); Suharti (1972: 19, 24); Hostetler (1982: 139).
53. Brakel-Papenhuijzen has identified a Sĕmang text in the Kasunanan in Surakarta from 1772 (1992: 58). She claims that nineteenth-century song texts give not Bĕdhaya Sĕmang but Bĕdhaya Sumrĕg heirloom status, but these might have been indicated by the name Sĕmang in the court (1992: 274). The 'V' formation identified as Bĕdhaya Sĕmang in a photograph from Groneman (1888) and reproduced in Lelyveld (1922), correlates with Bĕdhaya Sumrĕg as notated in a court manuscript from the reign of the seventh Sultan (Brakel-Papenhuijzen 1992: 267–71).
54. This happened just before the start of the Kĕtawang melody, after gong 40 (m.s. D/6 1B Kridha Mardawa).

Hadiwidjojo's sexual interpretations of *Bĕdhaya Kĕtawang* described above: 'Solo has too much imagination. How *dare* Pangeran Hadiwidjojo make those claims?' (5/4/1983).

It is important to recognize one instance where Ratu Kidul is not taken literally in Surakarta, in the junior Mangkunagaran court. While discussing the 'meaning' of the fight between the nymph Suprabawati and Janaka in *Bĕdhaya Gandakusuma*, above, Rama Sena glossed *praba* as 'the light of the path to truth' (*sinar hakekat*). He than linked this to the interpretation of Ratu Kidul as *hakekat* in a discussion of her encounter with Sultan Agung's grandfather, Senapati, as described in the nineteenth-century philosophical poem, *Sĕrat Wĕdhatama*, written by Prince Mangkunagara IV. This poem interprets Senapati's encounter with Ratu Kidul as entering 'the path of truth' through 'mental discipline'. Ratu Kidul represents Senapati's progress along the spiritual path; she is a sign of *hakekat*, the stage before final knowledge. The metaphor of sexual congress has been stripped away to expose the idea of spiritual progress, for which sexual imagery is also a metaphor. However, rather than this poem being a strong Islamic statement against other geological layers in Javanese metaphysics, Senapati is an example for young men who obsessively emulate the Prophet without true understanding:

If you insist on imitation
The example of the Prophet,
Oh, my dear, you overreach yourself:
As a rule you will not hold out long.
Seeing that you are Javanese,
Just a little will be enough. (*Sinom*, Canto II, verse 10; Robson 1990: 31)

Not everyone in Yogya took my interest in Ratu Kidul too seriously. One day I was transcribing dance songs in the court library, when the assistant librarian, K.R.T. Wirodiprodjo, derided the notion that Ratu Kidul attends *Bĕdhaya Kĕtawang*. 'Those Surakartans have their heads in the clouds!' he said, punning on '*kĕtawang*' which means 'sky'. When I asked if Ratu Kidul was present at performances of *Bĕdhaya Sĕmang*, he was equally derisive: 'The heirloom *Bĕdhaya Sĕmang* – so what [*mbotĕn punapa-punapa*]?' (15/8/83). Encouraged by the levity and disrespectful mood – which had put an end to all thoughts of further transcribing – the chief librarian, K.R.T. Widyakusuma, launched into his version of the meeting of Ratu Kidul and Senapati:

Senapati had been given a sign that he would meet this legendary lady. So he's finished his battles, and he's walking along the beach, and he meets this woman – and of course, she's Ratu Kidul, and of course he goes off with her … !

Delivered in a swift and sarcastic *ngoko*, this anecdote rests on knowing that 'pilgrimages' to Parangtritis are mostly made to the many prostitutes who work there. It is also an important reminder that there is no single official version which is accepted by everyone, not even among high-status Javanese people.

It is difficult to tell whether ambivalence about Ratu Kidul caused *Bĕdhaya Sĕmang*'s mysterious cessation, or whether embarrassment about 'losing' the dance produced the views about Ratu Kidul. Dance teacher K.R.T. Dipuradanarta suggested that even during Hamĕngkubuwana VII's reign, the three-and-a-half-hour long dance was rarely performed, and then only as a dress rehearsal (18/7/1983). Court librarian K.R.T. Widyakusuma said it stopped half-way through Hamĕngkubuwana VII's reign (2/6/83). According to Gusti Suryobrongto, following the death of the Crown Prince in 1913, the seventh sultan lacked the spirit to arrange dance theatre, but *bĕdhaya*s were performed (20/4/83), apart from *Bĕdhaya Sĕmang*. Whether the cessation was deliberate, or a combination of this death, the outbreak of the First World War, and financial reasons, remains unclear. Court choreographer K.R.T. Wiradipradja said its disappearance was simply to do with people dying. Hostetler (1982) had suggested that the dance stopped because of Ratu Kidul's diminished significance in the court. If so, then why would a programme for *Bĕdhaya Genjong* on the celebration of the birthday of Sultan Hamĕngkubuwana VIII on Wednesday 4 July 1934, state that the number of dancers should never outnumber nine, and represent as many nymphs of Ratu Kidul? Was this just for the benefit of visitors to the court? If so, why was a new copy of the dance text (B/S 1B) made in the court in 1946?

In numerous explanations, feelings of fear about performing the dance were greater than about not performing it. For instance, one person said that the untimely death of the Crown Prince in 1913 had been caused by a mistake during the preparation and performance of the dance, angering Ratu Kidul who took the prince's life in revenge. A similar theme occurs in the story of the disaster that struck the home of the Dutch scholar, Resink:

> *Bĕdhaya Sĕmang* stopped in 1914. 1913 was only a practice (*latihan*). Resink wanted to document it, but while he was watching the rehearsal (by boys), his house – not his neighbours – was destroyed by wind. So all the dancers and musicians were too afraid to continue. In the years that followed, only usual *bĕdhaya* dances were performed. When they tried to revive it [in 1972], there was a short circuit in the Kĕsatriyan, and it might have burnt down – but it didn't. (R.M. Dinu 30/8/94).

The attempted revival in 1972 occurred when the court was developing itself as a centre of *adiluhung* heritage, sponsoring overseas tours of its dances, and about to introduce its Sunday dance rehearsals. In the 1980s, rationales about why the dance originally stopped appear to have been shaped by memories of this recent project, and support the view that *Bĕdhaya Sĕmang* ceased to be performed due to an excess of fear of Ratu Kidul, rather than a lack of respect. 'They were all afraid [*Sami ajrih*]', said B.Y.H. Sastrapustaka (10/8/83), the court musician who had initiated the revival.[55] Others spoke of a more practical fear of losing face, because the reconstruction was not going smoothly, and the dance movements were causing particular problems.

---

55. Suharti (1972: 20); see also Hostetler (1982).

Mbak Kadar pointed out that each gong cycle had sixty-four beats, and involved three '*ragam*' or dance motifs (24/4/1989), an apparent excess of movement which, by contemporary understandings of dance movement, would make *Sĕmang* come out very fast. This point was made independently by K.R.T. Dipuradanarta (18/7/1983), who added that musical reconstructions went well, except that the *kĕnong* notation was 'unreadable'; it seemed to be very very slow, so no one was able to figure it out. Bu Yuda (12/7/1994) also suggested that the music didn't work, because the musicians couldn't read the notes; she said the dancing was no problem, but they never got round to putting the dance to music. She later clarified that the revival had only reached the music, not the dance (26/8/99). She also said that although the songs are not about a royal encounter with Ratu Kidul, they are 'deep' so that their inner meanings frightened the female singers. The reason the dancing didn't progress was the problem of having nine girls not menstruating, for practices. This is why they often had male dancers for *Bĕdhaya Sĕmang*. She also suggested that the dance stopped because the offerings were too expensive. There were pilgrimages to Parangtritis and Imagiri to make offerings before the start of the project, and these were like those for a wedding, very costly. Mbak Kadar and others at the Kanwil Arts Unit (24/4/89) explained that offerings had to be made even for just typing up the music, and the typist had to wash her hair to purify herself (this is an Islamic requirement for a women who wants to pray after sexual intercourse has taken place). They also told how there was a flood in the court during the revival attempt, implying that this Ratu Kidul's work. When I later was lent tape recordings of the revived music, which turned out to be too damaged by the humidity to work with, my research assistant was very nervous and made offerings before listening to them.

One question is whether the rise of reformist Islam in Java, such as the newly founded modernist Muhammadiyah movement in Yogya, had anything to do with the disappearance of *Bĕdhaya Sĕmang*. In 1989 Hamĕngkubuwana X's brother, generally known as Gusti Joyokusumo, suggested to me (4/5/89) that plans to revive *Bĕdhaya Sĕmang* after 1972 had been shelved due to groups such as Muhammadiyah having problems with the Ratu Kidul mythology. This was despite Islamic interpretations of Sultan Agung's meeting with Ratu Kidul as a metaphor for being granted power by Allah. 'Javanese people tend to have *other* ideas', he said; it made sense that he had been the source of the story about Ratu Kidul riding in the coach with the Sultan after his accession. At this time no one else mentioned Islam or the modernist rationales of the burgeoning nationalist movement in connection with *Bĕdhaya Sĕmang*. Indeed, had they been significant, one might have expected *Bĕdhaya Kĕtawang* and female court dances to have been affected as well. These factors should not be discounted, and would merit further investigation.

Recent evidence suggests that a sufficiently influential individual in the court can change court practice.[56] When *Bĕdhaya Sĕmang* was finally revived in 2001 under the

---

56. This data comes from a conversation with Theresia Suharti (22/7/2006), who also told me about a number of supernatural occurrences during preparations for the last revival similar to those mentioned above. She is now writing a Ph.D. thesis about the dance.

leadership of Bu Yuda, the court performance in the Bangsal Kĕncana was cut to ninety minutes from a choreography that had originally lasted for four hours. The experience of participating in the revival process was technically and spiritually unique. After the performance, there were hopes of further performances, even one in France. But apparently Gusti Joyokusumo, now much more explicitly aligned with Muhammadiyah, had said that there would be no more performances, possibly due to the huge costs of the revival. Bu Yuda died rather unexpectedly soon after this was decided. Suharti added that the dance would lose something being let out of the court, but one has to wonder whether the successful completion of the revival has not been curtailed for similar reasons to the original cessation of the dance. In July 2006, I saw a rehearsal of *Bĕdhaya Sumrĕg*, which was being 'revived' for the celebrations of Yogya's 250th anniversary on 2 September. Despite manuscript evidence for its being the 'child of *Bĕdhaya Kĕtawang*', there was little evidence of costly offerings being made for rehearsals of this dance.

Male *Bĕdhaya* Dancers

I have been suggesting that in Yogyakartan court interpretations, the female body, which becomes a symbol of union with the divine in Hinduism, Tantric Buddhism and Sufism, is interpreted at a further remove, so that any notion of feminine saktic energy or sexuality, which may be represented by Ratu Kidul, is either silenced or turned into a different sort of energy. It is clear that Ratu Kidul remains present in the life-world of Yogyakarta, both inside and outside the court, but that many feel embarrassed by what they consider to be irrational superstitions. The difference in the performance ethos of Yogya and Surakarta already discussed extends to attitudes to Ratu Kidul. In the main court in Surakarta, *bĕdhaya* retains its link with Ratu Kidul, and is seen as an enduring Hindu-Buddhist Javanese tradition. In Yogyakarta, by contrast, Ratu Kidul is likely to be treated with scepticism, or identified with the spiritual path to perfection rather than with sexual encounters.

There is another factor which might explain why *Bĕdhaya Sĕmang* stopped being performed in Yogyakarta. As mentioned above, court *bĕdhaya* dances have not always been performed by women. In the Kartasura court there were several male *bĕdhaya* dancers dressed as women on 30 September 1737, but this did not become common as it did in the Yogya court, which also had a homosexual ethos.[57] Sultan Hamĕngkubuwana V is said to have introduced the practice of young men performing *bĕdhaya* and women's roles in dance theatre (Soedarsono 1984). The reasons are not explained, though it is likely that sexuality was one factor. During his reign, the *Sĕmang* melody was for male *bĕdhaya* dancers in drag, but women dancers also performed the shield dance (*jĕbeng*) dressed as males.[58] Cross-dressing in the

---

57. Ricklefs (1998: 206). Hamĕngkubuwana III's favourite was a *bĕdhaya* performer called Raden Suleman (Carey 1992: 156, 488). There were also male *badhaya* in the Mangkunagaran court (Kumar 1980: 23–24).

58. According to the *bathik* expert, Kawendrasusanta citing *Babad Ngayogyakarta* vol. 8, 118–20 (1981: 176).

Yogyakartan court was explained to me as resulting from the high status of women, who had to be protected from outside eyes. Statements by *abdidalěm* indicate that before Haměngkubuwana VII's reign, *bědhaya* were the daughters of court officials who lived in the female quarters, and a number became secondary wives of the sultan. They were subject to more stringent rules of purity and protection than the *srimpi* dancers, and so male dancers in female dress appeared in *bědhaya* dances performed for outside guests.

It should be emphasized that throughout the Malay Archipelago cross-dressing is very common in ritual and other performances. These often have a healing role, and are performed by women or by men in female dress or, less often, by women in male dress (Hughes-Freeland 1993a). Such roles gave women a status in the community which was severely undermined, but not totally eradicated, by the coming of Islam (Reid 1993: 161–63). There is historical evidence of cross-dressing in Javanese folk performance. In the compendious survey of Javanese performance, in parts of East Java *bědajan* referred to a performance by a man dressed as a woman (Pigeaud 1938: para. 330), whereas on the north coast *bědhaya* refers to a woman who sings and dances (ibid., para. 273–4). Court practices are less clear. Pigeaud's commentary (1960–63) on the translation of the fourteenth-century *Nāgarakṛtāgama* suggests that the *těkěs* actors were male, not female, but we do not know if they performed in drag. Robson (1995), however, thinks that the *těkěs* were female.

Despite these examples (and contemporary practice as well), there was an extremely sensitive mood about sexuality in court practices in the late twentieth century, as the past was supposed to provide examples for present practice. During my research it gradually became clear that the embarrassment about *Bědhaya Sěmang*, and its disappearance might be connected to the practice of having male *bědhaya* dancers, about which there was also considerable embarrassment. What remains of the *Bědhaya Sěmang* are manuscripts and memories.

In particular, a source from the reign of the eighth Sultan, the *Platen-Albums*, gives an impression of the role of *bědhaya* in the court before independence:[59]

> 'For his Highness's birthday and accession anniversary each year there will be a *sělamatan* and then a *bědhaya*, of which there are two kinds: for the royal birthday, the female *bědhayas* perform the '*lajuran*' [line] *bědhaya* with nine dancers … They all wear crowns with white feathers … and are dressed as brides, with green velvet tops … and *parang rusak gěndreh bathik* skirts, and carry daggers… Accompanied by female retainers of the right, they walk from the west side of Prabayěksa, and out from the centre of the Prabayěksa stage and then enter the Bangsal Kěncana, and stop in the middle of the central pillars (*saka guru*) as the music stops.[60]

---

59. The *Platen-Albums* are a series of illustrated books about court practices commissioned by the Dutch engineer Moens during the reign of Haměngkubuwana VIII.

60. *Platen-Album* 28, plate 7, blz 13–14 (Museum Nasional No. 952 Dj), Sana Budaya PBE 38, typescript p. 93.

For the accession anniversary there is a male *bĕdhaya* (*lĕlangĕn dalĕm bĕdhaya jaler*) .... They are dressed like the female *bĕdhaya*s, and if they want to appear, these male dancers have to conduct a night's vigil in the Tamanan ... Accompanied by the female retainers of the left [dressed like the females, but with blue tops], they walk from the Purwarĕtna building, led by the *abdidalĕm*s Lurah and Bĕkĕl Bĕdhaya, to the tune *Pandhĕlori*, leave the Purwarĕtna from the south and come out to the Plataran facing the Yellow Building; when they reach the north side of the Bangsal Kĕncana, they turn east and go to the centre of the stage of the Bangsal Kĕncana and stop.[61]

The *Platen-Albums* suggest that female *bĕdhaya* was for the Sultan's personal birthday (*tingalan dalĕm taunan*) at the centre of the cosmically powerful Bangsal Kĕncana. The male *bĕdhaya* was for the accession anniversary (*tingalan dalĕm jumĕnĕngan*). At an unspecified royal anniversary (*tingalan dalĕm*) there was a *srimpi*;[62] on another unspecified occasion, after a *bĕdhaya* performance, there was a male *srimpi* dance (*sarimpi jaler*).[63]

The problem with the *Platen-Albums* as evidence is that they do not necessarily specify dates or occasions. The above account does, however, support what Suryobrongto (5/4/83) told me about the male *Sĕmang* taking place on the stage of the Bangsal Kĕncana, with the dancers entering from the Purwarĕtna building, and would support the claim that *Bĕdhaya Sĕmang* was performed by male dancers for accession anniversaries. However, the account fits less well with, but is not precluded by, Bu Yuda's suggestion (9/3/83; 1/11/83) that there was a different division of function: the male *Bĕdhaya Sĕmang* was performed for Hamĕngkubuwana VIII's birthday when he was Crown Prince, while the female dance was performed for the Sultan's birthday. She said that, during the eighth Sultan's reign and after, unlike Surakarta the Yogya court did *not* have a special *bĕdhaya* for accessions and their anniversaries, but a new one was normally commissioned. In her view the demise of *Bĕdhaya Sĕmang* resulted from changes introduced by the eighth Sultan, when the restriction of the dance for nine to the court was lifted.

Another theory was that the female *Bĕdhaya Sĕmang* was performed until Hamĕngkubuwana VIII's reign to honour the Dutch Governor General and lasted for two hours; after this the Governor would be entertained with a normal *bĕdhaya* (Pak Yu 23/9/83). Pak Pardjan (20/9/94) also suggested that male *bĕdhaya*s provided secular performances in Yogyakarta, including for the Governor General. Bu Yuda also had photographic evidence that *Srimpi Rĕnggawati* was once performed for the Governor. There is a reference in *Platen-Album 29* to the *Pandhĕlori* melody being played, which suggests that on this particular occasion, *Bĕdhaya Pandhĕlori* was performed. So the *Platen-Album*s tell us that males performed at accession

---

61. *Platen-Album 29*, plates 37–43, blz 73 and 77, KG 37–39, Sana Budaya typescript pp. 27–29.

62. *Platen-Album 9*, pl. 11, blz 27G, TBG 71 blz 328 (Museum Nasional No. 934 Dj).

63. *Platen-Album 29*, blz 81–3, KG 42, Sana Budaya typescript pp. 30–31; the male *srimpi* portrayed a fight between Srikandhi and Larasati using bows and arrows.

commemorations in the heart of the court, and suggest that on the occasion mentioned the dance was not *Bĕdhaya Sĕmang*. However, as the albums were commissioned in the reign of the eighth Sultan, after the dance had ceased to be performed, oral history supports the argument that *Bĕdhaya Sĕmang* might have been performed for previous royal accession commemorations.

There is also evidence that the *Sĕmang* dance was only ever performed by males dressed as women. This idea was proposed by Rama Dinu (30/8/94), and is supported by dance song manuscripts. In the court manuscript *Sĕrat Kandha Bĕdhaya Srimpi* (1854), there are two versions for the opening *kakawin* songs for *Sĕmang*. There is some ambiguity in the gender attribution here. One version is for 'when male *bĕdhaya* wear women's clothes', and the second version is for 'when *Bĕdhaya Sĕmang* has male dancers'.[64] It is striking that in all the subsequent *Sĕmang* song texts I examined in the court manuscripts, *all* the *kawin* were the second version for 'when *Bĕdhaya Sĕmang* has male dancers'. This suggests that *Bĕdhaya Sĕmang* was *only* performed by male dancers. If so, it could be that the dance ceased to be performed in the reign of the seventh Sultan because the court's attitude to the gendering of certain *bĕdhaya* dances had changed. And an unvoiced reason for the fear which led to the end of *Sĕmang* performances might have been that Ratu Kidul was not pleased to have 'her' dance performed by male dancers, although through the 1920s and 1930s men continued to perform female roles in drag in *wayang wong* and the newly introduced *golek* dance.

Genre and Gender

The gendering of court dance has changed since male to female cross-dressing ceased in Yogyakarta. Since independence, women have had more options in court (and other) performance, and there has been more male-female interaction on stage. Despite these changes, professional village female dancing was still seen as the opposite to polite female court dance.[65] Elsewhere, female to male cross-dressing remains common. All the roles in the Mangkunagaran court's *Langĕndriyan* dance opera are played by women, and in commercial dance-theatre in Surakarta, a young woman dances the refined hero, Arjuna – a practice disapproved of in Yogyakarta. In rural Yogya, however, in the final years of the end of the twentieth century, village *tayuban* was being challenged by a new version of the folk *angguk* trance dance, which was performed by young women dressed as men, instead of the traditional male troupes. In so far as this represented an expansion of opportunities for young women, it is something to be desired. At the same time, however, it also increased the likelihood of their being the object of the male gaze – indeed, after the end of the period of this research, it was repressed by more extreme local Muslim leaders.

---

64. '*Bilih badhaya jaler pindha busana wanodhya*'; '*Bilih badhaya semang priyayi kakung*', before the *Sĕmang kawin* songs, m.s. B 24 (1854).

65. Despite Ben Suharto's attempt to sacralize *ledhek*s (1980), an interpretation which consigns (yet again) women to the role of either priestess (virgin) or whore opposition.

What was once a control of sexuality and rights over reproduction by the sultan has been transformed into an indirect control of female sexuality which is given generalized aesthetic exemplary value in the contemporary Javano-Indonesian culture. Court dancing represents the control by the sultan over female sexuality, a control which has become aestheticized in the *exclusion* of sexuality. One impact of the nationalistic and character-building agendas discussed earlier has been the introduction of the category of the 'housewife', and this has placed constraints on women's scope to manoeuvre (Brenner 1998: 243). In the world of court dance, women have extended their opportunities, both in the roles available to them and the opportunities to pursue high levels of education; this is in the context of the emergence of a respectability associated with modernity and the middle classes.

However, while *both* Yogyakarta and Surakarta are exemplary court centres associated with the 'Javanese values' which feed into Indonesian gender identities, there are differences which cut across any generalized notion of 'Javanese' culture. The differentiation between female dances outside the court has been expressed more extremely in Yogya than in Solo, and is reflected in the underplaying of Ratu Kidul, the gendering of the *bědhaya* dancers themselves, and the transformation of the sexual references of *bědhaya* in Surakarta to a metaphysical play of opposites. A senior official of the Kasunanan, K.R.T. Hardjanĕgara, suggested (23/11/89) that these divergences result from these different court ideologies of female performance which reflect the conditions under which the courts were founded. Whereas Surakarta is agrarian and maintains its links to rites of fertility, Yogyakarta celebrates its origins in rebellion and military prowess. The heirlooms of Surakarta are related to farming. A white buffalo, Kyai Slamĕt, leads the nocturnal perambulation on Javanese New Year's Eve; *Bědhaya Kĕtawang* is associated with the Pleiades because of their importance for timing the planting of the rice; both *Bědhaya Kĕtawang* and the Mangkunagaran court's *Bědhaya Anglir Mĕndung* are dedicated to Dewi Sri, goddess of rice, or her incarnation, Ratu Kidul. In the Surakartan traditions, performance is associated with fertility and thanksgiving, expressed in themes of marriage and sexual union, also expressed in plays and dances using Pañji and Damarwulan stories. Taking up Pigeaud's view that Nyai Loro Kidul is a version of Ratu Angin, a fecundity goddess, Holt (1967: 117) had suggested that all *bědhaya* dances are the remnants of fertility dances. However, in the Yogya court, by contrast, love and marriage only come into the story because they are part of abductions occurring in warfare (Bu Yuda, July 1992). Mahābhārata stories have been the most popular in the court, and by the late twentieth century, Pañji and Damarwulan romances were identified with 'folk performance' and excluded from the classical canon. The Surakartan feminine dance style was denigrated for being unseemly: its arm movements revealed the armpit, mostly concealed in Yogyakarta by both the costume and the lower elbow position, except in some arm gestures; the unlowered eyes were too coquettish, and altogether the dance was too lively (*linca*). The exposed shoulders of female dancers in the Surakarta court are regarded by Yogyakartans as wholly inappropriate. What has been 'purified' from the Yogyakartan court arguably remains in the Surakartan courts. The *gambyong* dance, performed by *ledheks* to open a *tayuban*, forms part of the court repertoire, and is referred to by Yogya diehards as the 'Surakartan palace *tayuban*'.[66]

At a period when the time-space continuum is being thought of more and more in imaginary or virtual terms, it is important to emphasize the power of specific embedded and embodied localized practices, and their contribution to people's sense of self, however ironic or play that may be in its performed presentation. The regional specificity of the way in which traditions have been used in relation to *bĕdhaya* provides a case for arguing, metaphorical disembodiment notwithstanding, that ultimately regional and local embodied communities are not easily subsumed to a general homogenous 'national' model. When 'Java' or 'Javanese' is used in the context of 'Indonesian' identity, the unity is not as absolute as is often suggested in day-to-day self-representations across the Javanese region. The detail of the different inflections of *bĕdhaya* in the Javanese heartland therefore is significant in contributing further evidence to the case for balancing the imagined community of the state with the particularities of local practices, which themselves include forms of imagining. What is important is the way in which previous associations and identifications of performance as well as its organization has changed, and the way in which this produces new versions of old ideas, and new roles within the community.

This relates to a broader issue in the analysis of gender and performance. Judith Butler has distinguished performativity, which constructs gender identity in a normative manner, from performance, which is personally selected and is a critique of performative normativity (1993: 234). This contrast works less well in relation to the gendering of dance in Java and cross-dressing in Java because, as we will see in the next chapter, male dance movement is classed on a continuum from feminine to robust.

One might also ask whether wearing a woman's or man's clothing transforms one's gender. Putting on drag for a performance is a matter of choice, as Butler would argue, but that choice exists within the broader social conventions which shape inversion into culturally acceptable forms. Despite subtle analyses of gender and performance in Java (Hatley 1995), it is difficult to make generalizations about gender relations in a society on the basis of performance practices, which of course invert as well as mirror – as famously demonstrated in Peacock's analysis of transvestites conveying messages of modernity in the East Javanese *ludruk* theatre (1968). There are cases of male cross-dressers offstage who may be economically successful but remain marginal, even while they are loved as celebrities. And is cross-dressing a transformation which can be compared to the change a person experiences during possession? Performance itself is always ambiguous. This is its point. In 'practised places' such as the Javanese court, it occupies an oblique relationship to the control of the sultan and of the state, and the representation of gendered identity is not a matter of individual expression or choice. In Java, as in comparable British traditions in pantomime, where an older man plays

---

66. *Gambyong* could be based on *Glondrong*, a dance performed by a female court singer, Mas Ajĕng Gambyong (Suharto 1980: 50). Pigeaud refers to a 1929 *gambyong* performance in the Kasunanan as a masked female dance accompanied by the *Ginonjing* melody (1938: para 39).

the Dame and a young woman plays the Prince, cross-dressing in performance is normative and conventional, a transformation which would not be classed in the same category as the dangerous trance transformations discussed in the next chapter. In general we need to be careful about transferring gender values from performance to the real world. The specifics of the ethnography would indicate that the possession of male and female attributes should therefore not be overly polarized in all cases, nor should they be essentialized across time, but that when there are attempts to polarize them, these should be recognized.

New Directions for *Bĕdhaya*

There have been changes in *bĕdhaya* aesthetics. In the court, despite the continuity in formations, innovations in *bĕdhaya* movement, perceptible only to experts, have always been encouraged. However, it seems that a dance characterized by nuance, subtlety and oblique deflection is being transformed by aesthetics which value more direct communication and more dramatic action. Gesture is becoming more denotational, with clear-cut information being given value.[67] During the reign of Hamĕngkubuwana IX, the abstractions of *bĕdhaya* were gradually replaced by a greater emphasis on the story in the second part of the dance, although the practice of naming a *bĕdhaya* for its melody continued. In 1983, though, Siswa Among Bĕksa's *Bĕdhaya Ngambararum* was also called *Bĕdhaya Pandu-Narasoma*, after its story of the conflict between the Pandhawa Pandu and his rival Narasoma for the hand of Kunthi, Princess of Mandura. The ninth Sultan had also encouraged having multiple fights in *bĕdhaya,* and these were developed by Rama Sas, first outside the court and then inside.[68] Bu Yuda told me (5/8/89) about the new *Bĕdhaya Hĕrjuna Wiwaha,* choreographed by Rama Sas for Mardawa Budaya's anniversary concert. Innovations included the main fight between Batak and Endhel being followed by a fight between three pairs of dancers, 'like an expanded *srimpî*'. The choreography omitted the final three-by-three formation, kneeling down, *nglayang* and *sĕmbah,* and went straight to the exit march. Bu Yuda thought the dance clever but too self-conscious, and the dancers were lacking in concentration.[69] Where there were ambiguous spaces there are now 'dramatic' aspects, and this brings *bĕdhaya* fights into the class of the more literal lower-status fights in *bĕksan* duels. The move from abstraction to mimesis also changes metaphorical resonances to more literal representations, with the relationship between song and movement becoming more denotative (even if the words remain inaudible). Thus, in the 'Accession Bĕdhaya', seven dancers represented the pillars of the building where the tenth Sultan had acceded.

---

67. This may be compared to changes in the symbolism of *sinulog* in the Philippines, which changed from the ritual dance to theatre and procession, and a shift from iconicity to indexicality (Ness 1992).
68. Siswa Among Bĕksa also performed a *bĕdhaya* (about Arya Pĕnangsang), with a fight for eight dancers, but Bu Yuda (9/3/83) couldn't remember when.
69. She also said that he hadn't asked the dancers to kick their pleats back in *gĕdhug* in the usual manner.

There has also been a general shortening. Since the early 1980s, *bĕdhaya* choreographers have been complaining about being asked to cut the abstract *lajuran* sections which need to be repeated three times to carry the philosophical message. For example, Bu Yuda was asked by the acting head of the court arts section to reduce the abstract formations of *Bĕdhaya Genjong* for a concert on 19 February 1983 to save time. Without Follower resisting Leader three times, the effect of an ongoing process of winning and losing is reduced to the appearance of a simple triumph of Leader over Follower. These abridgements and their glosses in programme notes undermine the Javanese interpretations about the conflict representing the unification of opposites. Commentaries in performance programmes aimed at English-speaking audiences also now tend to describe plots as the triumph of good over evil. [70] This shrinkage is not just in performances for outsiders – in fact *bĕdhaya* is rarely aimed at a uniquely tourist audience. The performance of *Bĕdhaya Gandakusuma*, which lasted for nearly one-and-a-half hours in 1987, was reduced to thirty minutes from start to finish at Siswa Among Bĕksa's annual graduation and anniversary concert in July1999 by combining the two main sections. Outside the court dance venues, *bĕdhaya* and the other forms have been shortened to as little as fifteen minutes.

Despite these compressions, *bĕdhaya* dances remain a powerful form in Javanese culture, and continue to capture the imagination of Indonesia-Javanese choreographers in different ways, both inside and outside the court. Outside the court, Bagong Kussudiardjo's *Bĕdhaya Edan-Edan*, performed in 1982/3, explored the Hindu-Javanese idea of times degenerating into madness (*zaman edan*). Dance students still train in *bĕdhaya* choreography and movement styles, which continues to provide a template for both new creation and *sendratari* compositions. Since the death of Bu Yuda in 2004, Mbak Kadar has taken on the mantle of chief female court choreographer, followed closely by Bu Tiyah, widow of Rama Sas, and Theresia Suharti, who maintains Bu Yuda's standards in ISI. Within the court not all new *bĕdhaya* are more dramatized. Rama Sas's 1990 *Bĕdhaya Amurwabumi* was deemed 'excellent' (*bagus*) by Mbak Kadar (1/1/91); the first part followed the usual *lajuran* formations, and she particularly liked the lovely new arm movement *lilingan konthen asta*, performed at the start of the very brief love dance (Anon 1990: 67). So this dance, like Bu Yuda's 'Accession Bĕdhaya', had no fights at all, but expressed unification through love. This indicates a return to the style of the recently revived nineteenth-century *Bĕdhaya Sĕmang* and *Bĕdhaya Sumrĕg*, which are completely abstract.

There is a final development in my story of the loss of the feminine and the muting of the relationship with Ratu Kidul in Yogyakarta. After the research visits to Java for this book, the choreographer Didik Hadiprayitno told me (21/2/2003) that he had revived the practice of males performing *bĕdhaya* in drag which had disappeared after independence. In 2001 he studied with the American Noh expert Rick Emmert in Japan, and with Bu Yuda's guidance choreographed *Bĕdhaya Hagoromo* for male dancers. The 45-minute-long experimental choreography was based on *Bĕdhaya Sinom*, and told the story of Hagoromo (The Heavenly Mantle),

---

70. On one occasion (8/8/89) Bu Yuda herself had recourse to the 'good versus evil' account.

the Japanese version of the Javanese Jaka Tarub who falls in love with a nymph and steals her wings – and a folk parallel to the court myths of Ratu Kidul. Endhel (performed by Didik himself) and Batak both wore kimonos, and all the dancers used fans and wore masks combining Noh and Javanese features (Figure 5.8). Rick Emmert and the composer Alex Dea sang songs which combined elements from Noh and *bĕdhaya*. Didik said that he wanted to make a wider statement about wider traditions of cross-dressing in Asia, and that the dance was specifically inspired by the Japanese *onagata* tradition of male to female cross-dressing. So this recent experiment in *bĕdhaya* returns us to the literal human body, and its ambiguous performance of gender.

This chapter has concentrated on movement and choreography in what has been a predominantly feminine dance form in the context of political and religious symbolism. Philosophically, women's court dance movement beautifies the world (*mĕmayuning jagad)* and being in the world. Culture consists of interpreting nature which is hidden – and nature is the interpretation of culture, achieved through texts. The latest of these texts is *Joged Mataram* (Pak Yu 27/4/83), a philosophical interpretation of dance which places the gendering of court dance in a broader aesthetic, moral and political context. This will involve us in an exploration of masculine dance movement modes and acting.

Figure 5.8 *Bĕdhaya Hagoromo*, premiered at Taman Budaya, Yogyakarta, 5 Nov 2001. Photo courtesy of Didik Hadiprayitno

Chapter 6

The Art of Dancing: Joged Mataram

> This wisdom only arises in the doing
> In actions controlled by discipline
> Which means discipline which strengthens
> Always doing right in the face of obstacles
> (*Sĕrat Wĕdhatama*)

I now explore the philosophy of Joged Mataram, 'the dance of Mataram'. Joged Mataram, the title of an influential text by Gusti Suryobrongto (1976) about the principles of Yogyakartan court dance, which are traced back to the seventeenth-century Javanese kingdom of Mataram. Joged Mataram represents the transformation of ritually resonanced performance into art with an aesthetic rather than a ritual instrumentality, but it has not eliminated the relationship between expression and spirituality which we have already encountered.

From one perspective, Joged Mataram is a product of the court, and inspired by the ethos of *wayang wong* (dance theatre) during the reign of Sultan Hamĕng-kubuwana VIII (1921–39). Although court dance has been modernized in the context of late capitalism, Joged Mataram is based on nationalist ideals from the earlier modern period. I explain its somewhat compressed explanations with conversations with Gusti Suryobrongto and others about their experiences as performers in court dance theatre (*wayang wong*), and the relationship of masculine dance modes to characterization. We also discussed what kind of a practice dance-acting is understood to be, and how it contrasts with other types of embodied physical practices outside the court. This involved us in deliberations about the relationship of dance as a moral code to religion, and the ongoing importance of a militaristic ethos to the spirit of Yogya, not only in dance but also as its regional identity.

From another perspective, then, Joged Mataram is a response to changes in the context of performance and its expanded audiences, and represents a secularization and rationalization of court dance. Despite its colonial ethos and its use of the court as a defining context, this text also marks the separation of court performance practices from the court. Significantly, Gusti Suryo was the first person to use the phrase 'classical Jogjanese dance' (1970), and this has become synonymous with

'Javanese classical dance in the Yogyakartan style' (Wibowo 1981: 25; Hughes-Freeland 1997b). His text has played an important part in formulating Javanese court dance as a category for consumption as Indonesian classical dance (*tari klasik* I). In the 1980s and 1990s, the answer to the question 'When is art?' (Goodman 1978: 59ff.) in relation to court dance in Yogyakarta would have been 'When it is Joged Mataram'. Whether it will be in the future is less certain, and I conclude this discussion with an example of Joged Mataram's manifestation outside the enclave of classical court dance.

Ethnographic Interlude: *Wayang Wong*

Over one thousand people are crowded in and around the Pagĕlaran, the northernmost building of the court. A large rectangular stage has been erected and decorated with red and white bunting and potted plants. Incense is burning. It is 9 o'clock at night on Saturday 19 February 1983, the close of a week celebrating Hamĕngkubuwana IX's 73rd birthday (*wiyosan dalĕm*), which has included a large offering to Ratu Kidul at Parangkusuma. This is my first experience of a full-scale court *wayang wong*.[1] In the best seats in front of the stage sit royal wives and children, local dignitaries and senior aristocrats; to the west are those with 'Special for Family' invitations: court retainers, court kin, and the usual sprinkling of researchers. In years to come there will be 'tickets' available to tourists for these birthday concerts. A huge standing crowd also spills out of the building. Before 8.00 pm Prince Mangkubumi, dressed in a contemporary Western-style outfit of jacket and trousers, makes a speech in Indonesian. The Sultan's ceremonial music is played and Hamĕngkubuwana IX's eldest wife, B.R.Ay. Pintakapurnama removes a red-and-white *cinde* cloth from his portrait. This remains at the front of the stage while a religious official from the court's *pĕmutihan* group performs an opening prayer, and is then placed behind the *gamĕlan* orchestra.

By now the audience has already seen *Bĕdhaya Genjong*. Prince Sulaksmana, two months into his role as acting head of the court Arts Section and anxious to prove himself in his first *wayang wong* production, gives the final instructions to the cast of eighty-six dancers. We wait for the play, 'The Birth of Gathotkaca', to begin.[2] It is common in Java for an individual to have a personal connection to a shadow puppet character, and most people here are aware of the identification of the ninth Sultan with Gathotkaca.

The plot (*lakon*) derives loosely from the Mahābhārata. In the first part the gods ask the Pandhawas for the baby Gathotkaca, son of Bima and his giantess wife Arimbi, to help them defend their kingdom, Suralaya, which is under attack by the giant king, Pracona. The first hour or so is taken up with extensive negotiations

---

1. The Sultan's annual birthday was one of the few occasions when *wayang wong* was performed inside the court during the reign of Hamĕngkubuwana IX; only Siswa Among Bĕksa regularly produced fragments outside the court.
2. The Javanese title, *Gathotkaca Jedhi*, is a pun on the word *jedhi*, which means both 'become' and 'crater'.

followed by the conventional 'upheaval' (*gara-gara*) clowning scene. The gods, Batara Guru (śhiva), Endra and Narada, then take Gathotkaca, represented by a plastic doll in a pink woolly hat, to the volcano, Candradimuka, where they 'bake' him in the crater to transform his body into that of a hero. The papier mâché volcano is the only scenery. The costume and dance movement provide the visual interest. Each of the eleven gods wears their own colour – black, red, pink, gold – and dances their own dance mode. The costumes and make-up mostly conceal the identity of the dancers, but I recognize Rama Sas in his usual role, Bathara Guru, resplendent in the characteristic twisting crown of the gods in gold and purple, a gold and purple *bathik* waistcloth and a purple velvet bodice (Figure 6.1). The giants wear red and black costumes and Surakarta-style *bathik*; the demons (*danawa*) wear horned masks and shaggy red wigs; little gauze wings stand up on their shoulders when they fly.

The baking is represented by special effects: flashing red lights and steam, produced by an *abdidalĕm* dropping water on hot charcoal. A small dancer then emerges from the crater, sporting Gathotkaca's characteristic moustache. His newly 'cooked' heroic body has 'muscles like wire, a skeleton like iron' and, most importantly, the power of flight. After this scene much of the audience leaves. The second half of the play shows the military training to develop Gathotkaca's heroic potential to defeat Pracona. We see the small Gathotkaca fight against the opposition's chief attendant, Sĕkipu, while the gods fight against masked demons. He exits fighting, and is replaced by an older boy, the teenaged Gathotkaca, who also fights and then exits. Finally, the adult Gathotkaca enters, and succeeds in defeating Sĕkipu. There follows a dizzying array of combats, as Gathotkaca and his Pandhawa uncles take on demons, giants and eagles. The play ends when Gathotkaca defeats Pracona

Figure 6.1 Rama Sas dances Bathara Guru in 'The Birth of Gathotkaca', 1983

and heaven's safety is assured. How Gathotkaca will win the mask to conceal the giant features inherited from his mother that make him such an embarrassment to his uncles is the subject of another story.

Joged Mataram

Joged Mataram is a philosophy (*falsafah*) and science (*ngelmu*, or *ilmu* I.) of acting-dancing. Gusti Suryobrongto (Suryo for short) was the spokesperson for court dance during the 1980s. The twenty-third son of Haměngkubuwana VIII by a secondary wife, B.R.Ay. Pujoningdyah, he performed in five of the eleven court *wayang wong* productions during his father's reign (between 1923 and 1939). He also taught dance in Kridha Běksa Wirama, the court, Běbadan Among Běksa, and ASTI (Wibowo 1981: 217), and has written widely on Yogya court dance. His formulation of Joged Mataram has become the authoritative account of the spirit of court dance, and his teachings are frequently cited, verbally and in print.

Most Wednesday mornings between March and June in 1983 during fieldwork, I had regular 'mini seminars' with Gusti Suryo and usually his life-long friend Rama Sena, to discuss court dance and the thinking behind his publications.[3] These meetings took place in his home, the *dalěm* Suryowijayan, situated in a *kampung* south of the court fortifications. Rama Sena came over from his home in the warren of alleys on the other side of the compound, and Gusti Suryo's wife also joined us when her busy schedule of community and domestic obligations allowed. We sat at one end of the partly-screened veranda in the family area at the back of the main building, behind the long high-ceilinged hall used for large family events and dance classes. The household servants would go about their business, and bring food to a large table nearby from a kitchen hidden away in the back, crossing the yard where turtle doves cooed in a small aviary and chickens pecked at the soil. This aristocratic home had grand spaces but few mod cons, and was typical of the princely residences where I studied, watched and discussed dance in the early 1980s. The family's wealth was in social status and relationships. Gusti Suryo told me that he had obligations to seven hundred people, in the *kampung* and outside it (18/5/83).

Intellectually and emotionally passionate about court dance, Gusti Suryo had strong opinions and expressed his pride in Yogyakarta belligerently. He was direct to the point of abruptness, in contrast to stereotypes of Javanese refinement and obliqueness. Such was his enthusiasm for the subject that when he became extremely ill during one conversation, he refused to let me take my leave. His wife eventually convinced him that he was having a stroke and needed urgent medical attention. This put an end to our conversations, and Gusti Suryo passed away in 1985.

Gusti Suryobrongto's account of Joged Mataram combines the values of the reign of the last colonial Sultan with the conflated heroism of the founding of both Yogyakarta and the Indonesian Republic. This is reflected in his language: he spoke Indonesian or Javanese but always used Dutch and Javanese terms. He attributed the low-level Javanese word for 'dance', *joged*, not normally used of court practices, to a

---

3.   Suryobrongto (1970; 1976: 22–23; 1981a: 14–15; 1981b: 92–93).

phrase used by Haměngkubuwana I.[4] He also distinguished between 'Yogya Dance' (*tari Yogya*) as 'container' or 'physical (*lahiriah*) technique', and 'Joged Mataram' as its 'content' and 'spirit' (*jiwa*) (1981: 88; 1981a: 14). In Chapter 4 we encountered how Gusti Suryo explained that dance movement embodies court etiquette, and how he described dance as education for *rasa* (23/3/83). Joged Mataram also rests on this principle, and explains how the dancer should achieve the correct *rasa* by identifying tensions and contradictions within the inner body of the person as well as between the inner and outer bodies. It is thus concerned with what has been described elsewhere in dance ethnography as 'inward focus' (Novack 1990), and explores the subtleties of human experience and expression, while resting on the injunction that spirit takes precedence over rules.

When Javanese people speak about *rasa* in relation to dancing, they use it in a more focused way than the general *priyayi* cultural version, so that it comes to mean embodied sensibility, the bodily expression of introspection, or consciousness. Joged Mataram stipulates four elements of *rasa* that are required to perfect the art of dancing.

1. *Sěwiji* (or *sawiji*), 'total concentration which does not strain the spirit (*jiwa*)'.
2. *Grěgět*, 'the dynamic, élan, spirit or fire which kindles in the spirit of a person … which compels a tenacity which permits a channelling of this energy in a proper direction … the dancer strengthens all his or her emotions to avoid unseemly uncivilized (*kasar*) behaviour'.
3. *Sěngguh*, 'self-confidence [sic], believing in oneself without becoming proud or arrogant'.
4. *Ora mingkuh*, 'do not be weak in spirit or fainthearted, nor be afraid to face obstacles or take full responsibility' (Suryobrongto 1976: 22).[5]

As we will discover, Gusti Suryo elucidated these somewhat gnomic statements mostly with reference to his memories of performing in the colonial court's *wayang wong* productions when men danced all the roles, but he applied the principles of Joged Mataram to *all* court performance.

Joged Mataram was claimed to be an oral tradition dating back to the first Sultan. *Sěngguh* and *grěgět* were first documented for use in the court dance school Kridha Běksa Wirama (Soerjadiningrat 1926: 8). They were criteria assessed in its examinations from the 1940s and in those of Běbadan Among Běksa from the 1950s.[6]

---

4. Suryobrongto (1976: 31; 1981b: 89–90), and the author's English translation (Freeland 1985). His source, *Babad Prayut*, ('Chronicle of Usurpation'), is probably from the section of the major court *babad* for 1757–68 (Ricklefs 1974: 138); elsewhere he cites 'the leading Dance Teacher, R.P. Rio Kertatmodjo [sic]' as his source (1981a: 14), from the reign of the seventh Sultan. Reports on a Taman Budaya seminar on Joged Mataram identify 'RR Kertoatmodjo' as source for Brongtodiningrat (*Bernas* 28/7/93; *Minggu Pagi* week 3 August 1993).
5. All translations are by the author from the Indonesian unless specified otherwise.
6. This was evident on examination papers which K.R.T. Měrtadipura kindly showed me (18/10/83).

So these two 'principles' were already featured being used to rationalize oral traditions early on in the nation state. Many discussions took place between educationalists and aristocrats at this time about the place of traditional Javanese performance in national culture, in order, for instance, to determine the curriculum of the first performing arts academies, KOKAR and KONRI. Joged Mataram was formulated by Brongto-diningrat, Suryobrongto, and two other court dance teachers, Atmanĕtya and Atmapinatapa, at a later stage of this process. Before leaving for a tour of Europe in 1971, they held weekly seminars over a period of three months for forty performers from the court troupe (Bĕbadan Among Bĕksa Kraton). Their aim was for everyone to give a consistent account of court dance to Western journalists and other interested outsiders.[7] So Joged Mataram translated the unbounded orality of court dance discourses into a bounded and manageable text, drawing on past practices to create a modern aesthetic. At the same time, its apparently regimented formulation presented a dynamic and paradoxical theory of acting (and action) which is now used to train dancers in contemporary Indonesia, but expressed in the idiom of colonial court practice.

Becoming a Puppet

Joged Mataram derives from the relationship between dance movement and expression in characterization (*wirama* and *wirasa*) in the distinctive court dance theatre *wayang wong*. A human version of the shadow play (*wayang purwa*), *wayang wong* takes place on a long rectangular stage that emulates the screen of the shadow play. The stage is occupied by gods, nymphs, kings, queens, officials, ambassadors, heroes, soldiers, attendants, monkeys, demons, giants and clowns, all modelled on puppet characters.[8]

A dancer is referred to as a puppet (*wayang, ringgit*) and portrays what appears to be a highly conventionalized character. In my first ever conversation with Gusti Suryobrongto he spoke about his experience when only men acted in *wayang wong*. He said that the dancer had to 'feel (himself) as the puppet' (23/3/83). The dancer not only had to look the part; to perform or 'sit in' (*lĕnggah*) a role, he had to 'become the puppet' (*menjelma* I.) (Suryobrongto 1981b: 88). The 'inner' aspect of characterization was considered to be complex: 'It takes 30 years to get the *wirasa*; *wirama* is easier' (Pak Barsono 17/12/82). Indeed, before independence a dancer specialized in one role for several years if not longer, a luxury today's state-trained professional dancers can no longer afford.

7. R.M. Muchas, K.R.T. Brongtodiningrat's son (26/7/92). Maybe there had been problems in the 1970 tour. Press reports on a Taman Budaya seminar on Joged Mataram give R.R. Kertoatmodjo as Brongtodiningat's source (*Bernas* 28/7/93; *Minggu Pagi* week 3 August 1993).

8. There is a huge literature on the shadow play. Of the sources in English, the most interesting overviews and relevant here are Clara van Groenendael (1985), Keeler (1987) and Sears (1996a); useful descriptions of characterization are in Mulyono (1977) and Soedarsono (1984).

How does one become a puppet? After studying the role, the dancer had to work on the embodiment of the puppet in his (and, nowadays, her) own dancing body, to achieve a balance between *rasa* and the physical body (*lair*) (Suryobrongto 30/3/83). Gusti Suryo danced Antarĕja (one of Bima's sons) for several years, and then became a celebrated Gathotkaca (Figure. 6.2). He had loved the character since childhood, and spent as much time as he could watching shadow plays featuring Gathotkaca and handling the puppet to internalize its character (*watak*): 'You have to adjust yourself to the character' (1/6/83). He also talked to a puppet maker about the meaning of the three different Gathotkaca puppets used for different aspects of the character (*wanda*): *wanda guntur*, with a very lowered black face and black body, used for talking in court scenes; *wanda pĕnglawung*, a lowered black face and gold body, used to represent his skill and flying powers; and *wanda thathit* ('lightning'), with a slightly raised black face and gold body, used to represent courage and resolution, and also flying (Suryobrongto 23/3/83; 1981b: 74). The connection between the puppet's form to represent behaviours in particular situations is significant as it rests on the important principle of fitting behaviour to place (*ĕmpan-papan*), discussed earlier.[9]

The first stage of becoming a puppet still involves developing a sense of the shadow puppet's form and character. The next is to bring the character to life by means of combined conventions of costume, make-up, speech (*antawacana*) and, most importantly for the purposes of this discussion, dance movement informed by Joged Mataram. *Wayang wong* is structured into a somewhat predictable alternation of static scenes of dialogue and action scenes, travelling or fighting, culminating in a series of fights, but the extension of distinctive puppet iconography into different costumes and dance modes produces a spectacular display of patterned contrasts. Gathotkaca, like his father, Bima, has strongly drawn make-up, and wears a black-and-white checked (*poleng*) loincloth. He dances the male mode called *kambĕng* ('encircling'), looking directly ahead, moving asymmetrically and dynamically, with distinctive energetic leg movements: he raises his leg ninety degrees to the torso, holds it, then pulls in the calf ninety degrees to the knee, again holds it, and finally plants the foot firmly on the ground. *Kambĕng* arm movements are very muscular, with the arms extended in fists and the sash is draped round the neck and fastened at the waist (Figure 6.3).

Gathotkaca's movement and characterization contrast with the slight figure of his uncle, Arjuna, who wears subtly patterned clothes and jewels, with his face, arms, torso and legs painted yellow. He and his mentor, Krĕsna, dance the *impur* ('crooked legs') mode, with eyes downcast, legs turned out, feet barely leaving the floor, holding out the sash handing from his waist or flicking it back to punctuate the protracted shift of weight from one leg to the other: he crosses space as uneconomically and slowly as possible in an asymmetrical relation to the general direction of the body (Figure 6.4). Sĕtyaki, a Pandhawa supporter, is a brawny character with exaggerated black eyebrows and a high facial colour who dances the *kalang-kinanthang* ('encircled

---

9.   A particular character may become popular due to the skill of a particular puppeteer in manipulating the puppet in question (Pak Pardjan pers. comm. 1983).

Figure 6.2 Gusti Suryobrongto dances Gathotkaca in *Pĕrgiwa-Pĕrgiwati*, 1939. Reproduced with permission of the Ywanjana-Suryobrongto family.

and embattled') mode, with arm and sash movements similar to *impur*, but with leg movements like *kambĕng* with more elaborate weight shifts. After not having seen *wayang wong* for a long time (July 1999), I confused *kalang-kinanthang* with *impur*, to the alarm of Pak Pardjan: '*Impur* is introspective, this is extrovert!' Wilful and proud characters like Prabu Pracona dance in *bapang* ('stretch arms out sideways'), using mostly asymmetrical movements and wide arm gestures without the sash, to convey a strength and tension. Bumbling and energetic demons wear masks and woollen gloves and socks and dance *bapang dhĕngklik kĕplok asta* ('stretch arms out sideways with body bounces and hand claps').

Figure 6.3 *Kambĕng* mode in *tayungan*, Bangsal Kĕsatriyan, 1989

I have described the style of dance movement (*bĕksa*) for different character types as 'dance modes'. Dance modes are structured along a classificatory continuum from *alus* (gentle, refined, reserved, introspective) to *gagah* (strong, muscular, brash, extrovert). There are four basic modes: *impur* (*alus*), *kambĕng* (*alus* and *gagah*), *kalang-kinanthang* (*gagah*) and *bapang* (*gagah* and *kasar*) (Suryobrongto 1976: 19; 1981b: 83). These modes may have originated from the need to match size and strength for fighting, for equally or unequally matched rivals, as in the lance dance (*Bĕksan Lawung*). During the 1920s they were developed and elaborated with close reference to shadow puppet characters. There is little actual relationship between

Figure 6.4 *Impur* mode danced by R.M. Dinusatama in *Suprabawati,* performed by Siswa Among Bĕksa, 1983

movement in the two theatres because most shadow puppets only have movable joints at the shoulder and elbow.[10] They have the flexibility of the wrists, waist, knees and neck that is so important for achieving 'flowing water' in the feminine and *impur* modes, and the strength of the raised legs in the other male modes. Table 6.1 shows the four basic male modes as a continuum of exemplifications with serial linkages, from *impur* at the *alus* end to *bapang* at the *gagah* end. *Alus* and *gagah* are not mutually exclusive: *kambĕng* represents both *alus* and *gagah* characteristics.[11] *Bapang* is described as *kasar* (rough), but it is also 'robust', so this is not simply a negative evaluation. These four modes have unequally distributed subvariants: *kambĕng* has two, *kalang-kinanthang* three, *impur* four and *bapang* five. 'Brushing moustache' (*usap rawis*), a sign of egotism, occurs in all but the *bapang* modes, which has three different versions of the sub-variant 'body bounces', where *kambĕng* and *kalang-kinanthang* only have one, and *impur* characters would never do body bounces.

The nuanced variations of character in the basic modes illustrate the importance of minute details in Javanese expressivity. A small semiotic differentiation has a powerful effect, but is not ultimately what determines value. Although a person's physical appearance and manners are often taken to be signs of character, and roughness is associated with untamed nature in contrast to civilized culture, Gathotkaca's half-giant character has not disqualified him from achieving high status and heroism. He has been a personal symbol for both the ninth and tenth Sultans, and President Soekarno identified the air force with Gathotkaca, and the navy with Antasena (Brandon 1974: 291–92). The characterization of Gathotkaca presents a challenge to the dancer because he is half arrogant, half *alus* (here 'reserved') – 'very difficult to do!' (Suryobrongto 30/3/83). The convergence of apparently paradoxical qualities is also evident in characters who dance the 'strong' *bapang* modes, such as demon kings, jinns, and the god Narada. With their huge ungainly bodies, large noses, round eyes, and red faces, they appear to be at the uncivilized (*kasar*) end of the behavioural (and epistemological) spectrum. But their dancing is more than a simple expression of uncouthness, and should reveal arrogance (*kongas*) as well. As Suryobrongto explained (pers. comm. 1983), for the demon king, Niwatakawaca,

---

10. An exception are the hand gestures *ngĕpel* and *nyĕmpurit*, which Soedarsono compares to *gĕgĕman* and *driji wanara* ('monkey fingers') in the shadow theatre (1984: 223–24). *Malangkĕrik*, from the feminine dance mode, where the right hand is curled at the waist in *ngĕpel*, is also found in the shadow theatre (Long 1982).

11. Soedarsono lists twenty-one modes, including the feminine mode, and provides Laban notation for each (1984: 225–29). To tabulate the modes and their variations, I have treated *kagok kinanthang usap rawis* as a variation of *impur*. In Kridha Bĕksa Wirama, *kagok kinanthang* is both proud and *alus* (Soedarsono 1984: 226), and one of eight basic modes (*joged pokok*), classed on an *alus-kasar* continuum: 1. the feminine mode, *ngĕncĕng ĕncot* or *nggrudha*; 2. *impur*; 3. *kagok kinanthang*; 4 *kambĕng*; 5 *kagok impur*, 6 *bapang*; 7. *lĕmbeyan kĕntrig*; 8 *mĕrak ngigĕl*. As a point of comparison, voices in the Balinese shadow play are classed as *alus*, *keras* (harsh) and *nangis* (tearful) (Hinzler 1981: 75). *Alusan* is often used of feminine and *impur* modes, but strictly speaking it refers to the shadow puppet characters who dance the *kalang kinanthang* mode.

Table 6.1 Male dance modes and character types *

Plain Modes	*IMPUR* humble and restrained: Arjuna	*KAMBĚNG* humble and robust: Gathotkaca	*KALANG-KINANTHANG* proud and robust: Sětyaki	*BAPANG* proud, robust and rough (*kasar*): Dursasana
Elaborations *ukěl asta* ('twisting hands')	humble and restrained gods: Wisnu			The robust and dynamic god Narada
ukěl asta ěncot ('twisting hands with flexing foot')	The humble and restrained god Bathara Guru (Śiva)			
kagok kinanthang or *kagok impur* or *kěntrog*	proud and restrained: Bhisma (*kagog kinanthang*)		humble and robust: Duryodana (*kagok impur*)	Bugis soldiers (*bapang kěntrog*)
usap rawis ('stroking moustache')	dynamic and restrained gods: Endra (+ *kagok kinanthang*)	robust and calm gods: Bayu	robust and dynamic gods: Brahma	
dhěnglik ('body bounces')		robust and humble monkeys: Hanoman	robust and proud monkeys: Sugriwa, Subali	
Three *Bapang* Variations on *dhěnglik* *sěkar suhun dhěnglik*				proud, robust and *kasar* kings: Niwatakawaca
dhěnglik kěplok asta ('hand claps')				proud, robust and *kasar* demons: Cakil
dhěnglik kěplok asta usap rawis ('hand claps'and 'stroking moustache')				proud, robust and *kasar* jinns and demons in general

As well as these eighteen modes there are five others: 19. *lembehan kěntrig* for apprentices, meditators and children; 20. *měrak ngigěl* ('dancing peacock') for servants, attendants and clowns; 21. *cantrik* for common people; 22. *joged manuk* for eagle; 23. *joged setanan* for comical ghosts, spirits and demons.

*This table draws on information from Suryobrongto (1981b) and Soedarsono, including his glosses of characteristics (1984: 226–29). The last three modes are from Koentjaraningrat (1959).

'there is just a "nuance" … he is wild but also noble (*anggung*), not just *kasar*: as a king he must have the dignity of a king'.[12]

Nuance becomes even more important in female characterization. There is only one feminine mode (*putri*) as opposed to twenty-three masculine modes, so it is more difficult to differentiate between female characters than male ones. The feminine mode uses variations of physical expression using the angle of the head, always an important index of character. The lowest angle represents gentle and obedient (*luruh*) characters; a more raised chin represents bold and aggressive ones (*branyak*); there is also in-between (*tumandak* or *tĕmantu*). In the shadow play, female roles are divided into *lanyap* and *luruh*, male into *branyak* and *luruh* (Long 1982). Srikandhi has three *wanda*, all *lanyap*, but for conversation she is *branyak*; for flirtation, *gambyong*, and for fighting *lincah* (Suryobrongto n.d. [m.s.]: 4). These three character types are identified with the three wives of Arjuna: Sĕmbadra is submissive and demure; Srikandhi is feisty, belligerent and lively; while Larasati, the first wife, is in-between.[13] As all female 'puppets' were played by young men in the Yogya court before independence, generalizing statements about gender attributes need caution. Nonetheless, people suggested that only one feminine mode was needed because women's bodies are more *alus* and flexible, in contrast to men whose bodies are more muscle-bound and inflexible (Hughes-Freeland 1995).

The imbalance of modes might be seen as a sign of imbalance in the social evaluation of women, but female characterization is dynamic, and varies over different genres and social situations over time (as discussed in the previous chapter). Character differentiation and the attribution of 'gentleness' is unpredictable. In *Bĕdhaya Bĕdah Madiun* (the Rout of Madiun), Batak dances Senapati (a male character) and is *luruh*, while Endhel dances the female role, Rĕtna Dumilah, and is *branyak* (Suryobrongto 6/4/83). Subtle differentiation in movement and expression is achieved by emphasizing different elements of Joged Mataram. In *bĕdhaya*, the two protagonists look the same and perform the same movements, but Batak should emphasize assurance (*sĕngguh*), and Endhel dynamism (*grĕgĕt*) (Bu Yuda pers. comm. 1983). Despite the tiny physical indices of character (angle of chin, arch of eyebrow), expression (*wirasa*) becomes much more important in feminine characterization. This is evident in what I was told about women's fights. When females fight, they should not show anger. Although these are the most stylized and abstract fights in the court repertoire, both protagonists should aim for the correct *rasa* ('energy' in this case) to fight with fire and vigour looking their opponent in the eye. Bu Yuda said how difficult it was to persuade dancers to do this, because they thought, wrongly, that by being delicate and evasive they would be *alus*. This was inappropriate to the

---

12. Niwatakawaca meets his end from Arjuna's arrow in *Arjunawiwaha* (Zoetmulder 1974: 234–37).

13. Soedarsono shows two different shapes for *luruh* and *branyak* eyebrow make-up in both *putri* and *alus* modes (1984: fig. 108). Srikandhi has a complex characterization. In the Indian Mahābhārata, Srikhandin (sic) has been reincarnated as a man to avenge herself on a wrong committed by the Korawa, Bhisma; in Balinese shadow theatre Srikandhi is regarded as a transvestite (*banci*).

circumstances. Even *bĕdhaya* fights require some naturalism. Although their spirit should be that of a warrior, their feeling (*rasa*) should be '*alus*'. And when 'strong' male characters fight, they should show anger, but this anger should come from a spirit which is controlled (*alus*) (Suryobrongto 5/4/83) (Figure 6.5).[14]

The philosophy of court dance emphasizes the impossibility of separating physical movement from inspiration or expression. Rama Sena explained this in an anecdote about his experience when he began training in the *impur* mode at the age of nineteen – 'rather a late start' – with Atmasastra, the well-known court dancer:

> When I began, he merely said to me: 'Try to stand with your own sense of inner gentleness. Do you understand or not? The most gentle feeling you have.' After three days he said: 'Now you can do it. Now walk.' I couldn't dance at all, so whatever I did, I was content. He said: 'Oh dear, it's broken. Now it's come back, now it's broken again.' After a week he said: 'Now it's holding up.' I didn't know what 'broken' or 'holding up' meant. But after a year or so, I'd worked it out. It was my gentleness (*kehalusan*) that was 'broken' or 'holding up'.[15]

Figure 6.5 Gusti Suryobrongto as Gathotkaca fighting a monkey. Reproduced with permission of the Ywanjana-Suryobrongto family.

---

14. This fighting spirit also has a historical reference: the second Sultan famously kept a female cavalry regiment, Langĕnkusuma, as his bodyguard. My suggestion that female dance hands might be influenced by a rider's hands holding reins did not meet with any enthusiasm, however.

15. Rama Sena, August 1987 (in Hughes Freeland 1988). This was the moment when I understood that '*alus*' could mean 'gentle', as I have translated it in this anecdote.

Rama Sena had to allow his physical movements to be suffused by feeling, 'to concentrate on compassion for mankind; then I had to dance and *rasa* that' (pers. comm. Sept. 1983). It is crucial that the physical dynamism of movement becomes second nature, and the character of the role is internalized: '[Acting] Arjuna is to feel it in your innermost being … That's *sĕngguh*' (ibid.). Self-confidence and concentration define the inner state. As the dancer concentrates (*nyawiji*), the movements move by themselves, and the dancer 'faces God', a meditative dimension which I will return to below.

The ideal balance between energy and inspiration as outlined in Joged Mataram was explained with reference to three aspects of facial expression: *pandĕngan*, the eyes or the gaze; *polatan*, facial appearance, and *pasĕmon*, expression (Suryobrongto 1981b: 60). The right expression is not achieved through muscles (*polatan*), but is *pasĕmon*, the reflection of the dancer's spirit.[16] When Bu Yuda spoke about *bĕdhaya* dances having a theme, she emphasized that 'It isn't play-acting, though! It's *pasĕmon*' (12/7/89). The three kinds of 'mimic' together produce '*mĕmanon*': 'the facial expression has to balance with the expression of the movements. Both have to be controlled by the spirit (*jiwa*) (Suryobrongto 1981a: 13). It is *mĕmanon*, the 'inspiration' (*penjiwaan* I.) of the dance, which produces a consistent performance: 'The ratio no longer functions, only instinct organizes and motivates' (Suryobrongto 1981b: 99). So the successful dancer in performance is no longer trying – the movements are right automatically, s/he is absorbed, and the face reflects this absorption in keeping with the character: *pasĕmon* for all *bĕdhaya* and *srimpi* dancers should be 'clear' (*padang*), and for 'strong' characters 'sharp' (*landhĕp*).

Gusti Suryo explained (1/6/83) that *pasĕmon* sums up the challenge at the heart of dancing: to overcome the paradox of showing and concealing in dance, of making the invisible person (*batin*) visible, but without the visible exertion of the visible body (*lair*):

> Yes, the 'transformation' is possession [*kĕpanjingan*] … that's 'acting', isn't it? There are muscles and there is appearance [*pasĕmon*]. You can use the muscles to make, for instance, a smile, but *you mustn't do this!* You have to be *alus*. Just *pasĕmon*, in your gaze and feelings. For instance, in *bĕdhaya*, you must have clarity of gaze and feeling. It comes from *inside*. Once you've grasped that, you've understood Joged Mataram.'

Casting *wayang wong* involves matching the 'face' (*wanda*) or 'build' (*dĕdĕg*) of the dancer to the iconography of the puppet. A slender man with delicate features will be cast as Arjuna; a large man with strong features as King Pracona. But more important than physical resemblance is the degree to which the dancer can *become* the puppet. Atmasastra (the dancer who trained Rama Sena) was rather small for the part

---

16. This concept is used in different forms of Javanese expression and symbolization which involve concealment or displacement of meaning and intention, and has been used to explain allegory in the shadow play (Sears 1996a: 7–11).

but he became known as the best Gathotkaca ever, due to his face, *grĕgĕt* and *sĕngguh*. He tried so hard to 'sharpen' his gaze, staring ferociously into the distance, that he nearly blinded himself. The Sultan paid for three operations, a reward for this exemplary fulfilment of dance duties and the demonstration of *ora mingkuh* (Suryobrongto 20/4/83).[17] It is significant here that the eye is the most important aspect of the *wanda* of shadow puppets themselves.[18]

Joged Mataram expresses the values of elite performances, and postcolonial *wayang wong* has been criticized for having 'the flavour of feudalism' (Soedarsono 1974: 7).[19] Princes and high-ranking officials tended to dance the main roles in *wayang wong* (Groneman 1899), but a good dancer of lower birth and rank could achieve such a role. So casting is not wholly determined by hierarchy. Status belonged to the domain of *lair*, but dancing allows the *batin* of a person to override circumstances of birth and destiny. This is a case of dance refracting social norms to become playful inversion. The same principle applies to female roles. A *bĕdhaya* dancer is cast according to height rather than looks, but she will become beautiful in performance if her spirit is good: 'You have to alter the Javanese saying, "ugly face, ugly heart" to "fine spirit, beautiful person"' (Rama Sena 24/7/83). As well as going against the collectivist physical determinism of hard-edged *alus-kasar* judgements, these examples show how personal determination could overcome both physical determinism and class hierarchy, and also how dance skill can produce social power.

Dancing from the outset requires a *balance* between the two parts of a person, the *lair* and *batin*; a more subtle understanding of the complexity of characterization then follows. Dancing does not simply unify the physical and spiritual bodies. It requires a separation of the elements in the spiritual which then need balancing. This is why Suryobrongto speaks of *balance*, rather than '*manukma*', the *fusion* of the physique and the *batin* (Wisnu Wardhana, pers. comm. Sept. 1983). These two views show two different understandings of human nature and the boundaries of a person, a point I will return to below. Expression is highly controlled, and acting is not simply the outward channelling of energy. To achieve the desirable effect (*alus*) concerns more than the intention of the performer. This helps to clarify the nature of the inward focus of contact improvisation derived from the classical Japanese martial arts form aikido, which has been contrasted with the presentational expression of ballet (Novack 1990). It is precisely the self-conscious intentionality of ballet that the dancer-as-puppet must avoid. Dance is also effort, but its object is to hide the effort, and transform it into beauty. It is not constraint, but restraint and discipline. It is an exercise in self-control.

---

17. On a Mangkunagaran tour in Cambridge, 1989, I saw the role of Rama performed by a rather short plump man with such exquisitely modulated feelings of tenderness that it seemed impossible that Rama could ever be danced by anyone else.

18. This was the reason that one puppet maker painted Sĕmar's eye (and also his tooth) in real gold (pers. comm. Sardjono, director of the Cahyo Tunggal Group, 24/7/2006).

19. In the Javanese context, 'feudalism' refers to social status based on age and rank (Hardjowirogo 1983: 11).

This is especially evident in *ora mingkuh*, the fourth element of Joged Mataram. This describes the tenacity, persistence, and stamina that make it possible to face up to the challenge of dancing, and to overcome fear and weakness: 'If you want to become a puppet properly, you have to reduce your human feelings of fear, and wanting to get a good name as a dancer and so on' (Suryobrongto 1/6/83). *Ora mingkuh* makes you keep on dancing, even as bees and wasps buzz round you, ants crawl up your nose, water rises around your knees, or marble tables fall on you – a real hazard when guests were served with food in the pavilion just *above* the dance stage adjoining it. Gusti Suryo's favourite story (20/4/83) concerned his younger brother, Pudjakusuma, when he played Angkawijaya, a leading role in *Pĕrgiwa-Pĕrgiwati*, the well-known story about Gathotkaca's search for a wife.[20] Suryobrongto persuaded Prince Pudjakusuma, who was shivering with malaria and unable to walk, to go to the court supported by his servants so he would be ready for his scene at 9.30 in the morning. After hearing the music and being made-up with warming yellow *boreh* (a fragrant skin powder based on turmeric), he went on stage to battle against the ferocious demon Cakil, and nine of his followers. Back in the small pavilion (*kothak*), he promptly fainted: 'It took a whole bottle of cologne to revive him! And as soon as he came round, he was ready to dance again. Three days later he was cured. Spirit overcomes sickness!'[21] This is the culmination of 'becoming a puppet': weaknesses are replaced by the heroic qualities of the character. Whereas the shadow puppet play transmits 'a description of the Javanese "ideal culture", the culture of the ancestors' (Bachtiar 1973: 100), *wayang wong* transmits the militarism which has been central to the Yogyakartan court's self-image, and the spirit of the heroic warrior expressed in the saying 'To value yourself you must be ready to die'.[22]

Becoming a puppet in *wayang wong* does not mean caricaturing shadow puppets by imitating their movements. Dancing a puppet is an expression of transformation. When a perceptive teacher recognizes a pupil's potential for *grĕgĕt* and *sĕngguh*, s/he trains the pupil to concentrate, to ensure that the aspiring dancer will manage these elements, which will subsequently be properly placed (*dipunmapanakĕn*). In performance, the music and declaimed introduction (*kandha*) help the dancer to

---

20. This probably happened in the play performed on 18–20 March 1939 to celebrate the '"*Sĕlapanan*" of seven bridal couples' (the 40th day after the closing of the wedding announcement *(huwelikssluiting)*' (*Tekstboek* 1939); *sĕlapanan* usually describes a commemorative ceremony thirty-five days after an auspicious event. The play text includes a photograph of Gusti Suryobrongto playing Gathotkaca as he spies on Pĕrgiwa from a tree (ibid., opposite p. 35).

21. Suryobrongto also spoke of his brother using opium on this occasion, and addicts or clowns used it regularly. Rama Sena, who disapproved of dancers drinking and smoking, remembered one addict playing Sĕmar who could not perform without opium (12/1/84). Crawfurd earlier had noted 'a universal passion for intoxicating drugs' in Java; 80,000 lbs of opium was consumed per year (1820, II: 268–70).

22. Although *satriya* derives from caste in Hinduism, it includes the ideal of the Sufi warrior, already influential in the Central Javanese court before Yogyakarta was founded (Ricklefs 1998: 123–4).

muster concentration and build up confidence, and allow the energies of the physical and spiritual bodies to become dance. The right balance of concentration, energy and self-confidence produces the correct *rasa* of feeling able (*sagah*) to perform, beauty (*kalĕrĕsan*), and, in the case of the gentle modes (*impur* and *putri*), the 'flowing water' quality of movement. Dancers have to make fine judgements in balancing arrogance in the character with self-confidence (*sĕngguh*), because too much self-confidence comes across as arrogance *in the dancer*, not the character. A 'bad' character can be redeemed through the skill of dancing, but conversely bad dancing can destroy a good one.

Alus and *Kasar*: Beyond Good and Evil?

To understand the spiritual and moral dimensions of Joged Mataram, and what this tells us about the boundaries between dance and everyday life, especially religion, it is helpful to consider the cosmological background of *wayang wong*. Like the shadow play on which it is modelled, *wayang wong* enacts Javanese philosophical and spiritual world-views. Characterization in Javanese shadow puppet theatre has been analysed as an expression of tolerance (Anderson 1965), epistemological diversity (Becker 1979), and as a metaphor of collectivization and conformity achieved by incorporating a wide range of characteristics (Hatley 1979: 16). Puppet theatre is removed from human experience, although interpreted symbolically to comment on the human condition, whereas human theatre *literally* is incorporative, because it requires the participation of the person. Nonetheless, Becker's challenge to determinism of *alus* in the production of monolithic culture is relevant to my discussion here. He proposes that epistemological differences represented by shadow puppet characters, and in *wayang wong* by the different dance modes, can be interpreted as representing the wide diversity of Javanese experience. This means that values are relative to context. Suryobrongto (pers. comm. 1983), for instance, described the Korawa in the Mahābhārata as bad, not essentially, but *because* they lose. What is significant is not the political expediency but an ethical consideration: the Korawa fail to fulfil the moral code of chivalry (*satriya*) and the requirements of orderly conduct (*tata-krama*). During the eighth Sultan's reign, Mahābhārata plots in *wayang wong* concluded with the restoration of the opposing side to its own place, not its annihilation. Or not until the ultimate destruction of both sides in the Great War, which teaches that any gains and losses are eventually subsumed by mortality, and the natural cycle of predestination and cosmic order. The interest of these stories lies in the processes which disrupt ordering structures, along with the paradoxes and ambiguities they reveal, and the way in which they offer hope of an escape from the vicissitudes of the social world.

An ordering structure which is disrupted by dramatic performance is the opposition between *alus* and *kasar*, even as it could be understood to define the conditions for that performance existing. However, the ultimate defeat of all participants in the Great War (*Bharata Yudha*) marks the defeat of established authority and is outside the social world. The logic of Joged Mataram and of court dance mode classifications do not identify *any* character as purely *kasar*. *There is no bĕksa which is kasar*. To dance properly is, by definition, not to be *kasar* and, tautologically, is also *alus because* it is not *kasar*. In this respect, court dance demonstrates how court values transcend the simple opposition of nature and culture, incorporating it into a cultured epistemological domain which can itself contain different sorts of ways of being in the world.

Mimesis is excluded, denied or dissimulated in the court aesthetic and in classical Yogyakartan-style dance today. This relates to the centrality of concealment and abstraction already discussed in relation to *bĕdhaya*. Suryobrongto described dancing as a kind of acting but he also *contrasted* dancing and acting in a discussion about animal characters in *wayang wong*. Performers wearing tiger suits and masks leap and roar in imitation of natural tiger movements. The famous tiger-player, Pragalba, a court soldier in the Nyutra regiment from which many dancers were drawn in colonial times, consulted a healer (*dhukun*) about how best to become a tiger. People who saw his performance swore that as a result of meditation and other ascetic practices, he had taken on the strength and ferocity of a tiger in his spirit, not just his limbs (Pak Barsana 17/12/82). Although no one mentioned it at the time, in Javanese villages there is often a special relationship between certain local spirits (*dhanyang*) and tigers. Gusti Suryo's view was that Pragalba was acting, not dancing, and coming dangerously close to possession, a point I will return to below.

Becoming a tiger differs from becoming a puppet because it is achieved by imitating nature, instead of transmuting nature into art as dance movement (*bĕksa*). Monkeys in *wayang wong*, however, do transcend imitation: they wear tails and monkey masks, are described as lively (*sigra*), but they *dance* as characters. Their *dhĕngklik* ('body bounces') dance elaboration has neck and shoulder movements and leaps which are not naturalistic but stylize monkey behaviour. Hanoman, who originates from the Rāmāyana but also appears in other plays, dances *kambĕng dhĕngklik* as befits a strong and humble character, while Subali and Sugriwa, being strong and proud, dance *kalang kinanthang dhĕngklik*. 'Monkeys here in Yogya are not *kasar* but *alus*' (Suryobrongto 20/4/83). They are dignified, humanized, and brought into the cultural domain.[23]

Joged Mataram denies that dance can be unmediated, natural and uncivilized (*kasar*). Dancing also redeems the most barbaric characters, as dancing belongs to the domain of civilization. The action of the shadow play arises when characters from different epistemological worlds come, *by coincidence*, into the same space at the same time (Becker 1979: 224). The *alus–kasar* relationship may be compared to the contrast between culture and nature, but both contrasts are situated in the social world and are produced by its mediations (Lévi-Strauss 1966). A popular scene in both puppet and human theatre is the fight between Arjuna, from the denatured, civilized world, dancing the *impur* mode, and the fanged demon, Cakil, more beast than man and from the natural world of the wild, dancing in *bapang dhĕngklik kĕplok*

---

23. Monkeys in Surakarta scratch and imitate monkeys in their own *kasar* mode, *laras bĕksa wanara*; demons and Buginese soldiers also have *kasar* modes (Soedarsono et al. 1978: 19; Prijono 1982: 70–72).

asta, the 'strong proud rough' mode modified with body bounces, an indicator of animal-like qualities, and distinctive arm movements. Neither dance mode is classed as *kasar*, but they reveal an opposition, with *kasar* action as the visible expenditure of energy confronting *alus* action – which appears as inaction, with no visible signs of energy or effort. Cakil waves his arms and leaps about, while Arjuna stands still, flicks his sash – and eventually wins.[24] *Alus* and *kasar* represent culture and nature in so far as *alus* types are found in courts and civilized spaces, while demons live in the forest. But civilized, well-behaved characters like Arjuna can only become so through lengthy meditating in the forest: nature is a precondition for civilization. And the wisdom acquired is not a matter of putting on airs and graces; quite the reverse, in fact. His dance may be *alus,* but 'refined' characters like Arjuna are usually described as *jatmika*, which means unaffected, having a plain manner. They gain something from outside the world dominated by social presentation and status. Also, as noted above, demon kings live in palaces, as befits kings, regardless of whether or not they are demonic. Status here trumps quality, or civilization (and hence culture) trumps nature.

This is not the case in the most dramatic embodiment of ambiguity in the shadow play and *wayang wong*. The hermaphrodite Sĕmar and 'his' three 'sons', Pĕtruk, Gareng and Bagong are the servant-clowns (*punakawan*) who always perform the *gara-gara* 'upheaval' which occurs at the crux of the shadow play and also in *wayang wong*. In some plays they accompany Arjuna, or whoever the young hero happens to be, on his quest. Grotesque in appearance, moving in the comical uncouth dance mode 'dancing peacock', the *punakawan* are everything that *alus* is not. Sĕmar combines divine and natural energies, transcends duality by a unification of contradictions, and is the true hero of Javanese cosmogony (Nakashima 1982). He is the ultimate 'King of Java'. Sĕmar and the *punakawan* undermine the semiotic force of *alus* and *kasar*, and subvert the empiricism of appearance representing reality and also the elite culture where 'manners maketh man'. The *punakawan* were used to comment allegorically on Javano-Dutch relations during the colonial period (Sears 1996a), and continued to so in the New Order. In *Dandang Seta*, a shadow puppet play performed for radio broadcast by the maverick puppeteer Ki Hadi Sugito in Yogya on 9 April 1983, Sĕmar took the form of a white bird and threw Bathara Guru, represented in this play as an authoritarian and dictatorial god, to the ground – to the delight of the audience, as everyone knew who he represented. As a mediator who never attains permanent worldly success, Sĕmar provides an escape from the determinism of politicians, and images both of historical circumstances and philosophical redemption, as a symbol of unification for many of Java's religious 'streams'.[25]

---

24. This minimal expenditure of energy is well-known in Indonesia and may be compared to 'subtle attack' in other martial arts (Zarrilli 1998: 193).

25. Sĕmar's energies have also played a crucial role in the millenarian ethos in New Order nation building (Stange 1989), a familiar example of a political regime attempting to subsume religion to its own ends.

So the opening of Anderson's statement, 'The ethics of halus-ness are at bottom the ethics of power' (1972: 43), might more appropriately be restated as, 'The ambiguities of kasar-ness ...' because the untamed forces of nature are the preconditions for virtuous action. This is certainly Suryobrongto's position when he stated that two sides are necessary for the good to become manifest. As we discovered with *bĕdhaya* interpretations, virtue arises from a process of dynamic opposition, which is why the idea of balance matters. Although less explicitly articulated in Java than in Bali, there is the sense that the person is a microcosm, and that everything that is in the world exists inside the individual as well. It is against these metaphysical ideas that action in Javanese theatrical spaces needs to be understood. And in the court spaces (if not all performance spaces, as will become clear), self-control in dance can redeem – albeit temporarily – the uncontrollable forces of nature and bring them safely into the world of cultured civilization.

Dancing is ranked above acting because it is inspired and moved by feelings and sensibilities (*rasa*), not by the imitation of appearances by an act of conscious will or muscle. Dancing includes a kind of acting, not in the Aristotelian sense of mimesis, but in a nonnaturalistic and highly formalized style. It creates the 'alienation effect' identified in Chinese opera where actors are seen to observe their own movements, and the audience's illusion of perceiving something happening 'out there' independently of their perceiving presence, is broken down (Brecht 1964: 139ff.). Rather than an objective theatre, Joged Mataram is an intersubjective model, in which the audience participates by implication. Although becoming a puppet requires the dancer to begin by looking at a puppet's form and movement style, and although characterization is differentiated by costumes and dance modes which look different, Joged Mataram emphasizes what is beyond the visible *lair* aspects of the person. Theatre director and theorist Richard Schechner has proposed an alternative to what he describes as 'the "theatron", the rationally ordered, analytically distanced panoptic' (2001: 29). Drawing on Nāṭyaśāstra, the Sanskrit text by Bharata-Muni already encountered in the discussion of *bharata natyam*, he proposes a 'rasaesthetics' based on 'snout-to-belly-to-bowel'. Joged Mataram of course also draws on *rasa*, but whereas Schechner stresses the feeding and tasting aspects of *rasa*, and addressed the literal materiality of 'guts' and innards, Joged Mataram emphasizes the other side of *rasa*, the invisible inner energies of the person.

This contrasts with the agency of Western acting as a conflation of motivation and intention (Hastrup 2004: 53–60). Many Javanese enjoyed telling me that Westerners are driven by their own desires, and are so busy thinking, consuming and producing that they leave themselves no space to cultivate *rasa* and awareness. A Western model of what it is good to express – emotions, passions, individuality – differs from Javanese ideals, which require these elements to be curbed or channelled in formal codes, not unleashed naturally on the world of others. Where 'Western' performance brings the emotions out, in court performance, the *rasa* goes in (Rama Sena in Hughes-Freeland 1988). This is also true of the audience's response. The experience of court dance is neither entertainment nor pleasure. A young English male tourist at the Sunday practice said he preferred female dancing because 'When you get bored you can watch the girls – they have such elegant shapes!' (not something most Javanese people would admit to). A Dutch woman in the audience burst into tears at the sight of *bĕdhaya* dancers' entrance march at a performance at The Hague in 1971, declaring that the dancers looked like 'angels ... No Javanese would dream of responding in such a way!' (Suryobrongto 20/4/83). And yet, although the dancer's *rasa* turns inwards, prompting the audience to do likewise, inwardness becomes shared: 'The audience sees not with its eyes, but with its *rasa*' (Rama Sena in Hughes-Freeland 1988). People spoke of feelings of yearning, nostalgia, homesickness (*nglangut*) and solemnity (*anggung*) when they heard a *gamĕlan* or saw a *bĕdhaya*.[26] So aesthetic pleasure is delayed, feelings are complex and bittersweet, and can be related to the negation of certain pleasure-giving actions in *kĕbatinan*'s ascetic practices, as well as to the social ethic of sharing. The aesthetics of Joged Mataram form part of a wider ethic which devalues personal gratification.

In some respects Joged Mataram's account of *rasa* may be compared to 'pre-expressivity' in 'Theatre Anthropology' and performance studies, the work done by actor-dancers to model 'the quality of their scenic existence' before intention comes into play (Barba 1995: 105). However, despite this similarity, different assumptions about acting and action are involved. At the risk of oversimplifying the diversity of Western acting methodologies, Joged Mataram draws a less defined boundary between theatre and everyday life than Western theatre in general. It concerns morality as much as pre-expressivity. It fuses aesthetics and ethics for a 'way of life'. The four basic elements mentioned before are also given a practical meaning for the conduct of everyday life:

1. *Sĕwiji*, whatever your aspirations, direct your concentration to your goal.
2. *Grĕgĕt*, direct your dynamism and energy to your goal through proper channels.
3. *Sĕngguh*, have complete confidence in your personal ability to achieve your goal.
4. *Ora mingkuh*, although you will encounter obstacles in your path, do not take even one step back. (Suryobrongto 1976: 22–23)

In this way Joged Mataram addresses the production of persons as well as dancers, which makes it a philosophy, not simply a Javanese form of 'Theatre Anthropology'.

Delimiting Dance and Religion

Human performance is the expression of the embodied introspection of the dancer-actor but, as the previous section shows, there is some ambivalence about the nature of the person who is doing the dancing. Suryobrongto described acting as '*kĕpanjingan*', possession: 'court dancers, by attending to their role, are in a kind of "trance" [sic]' (1976: 20). In a region noted for trance and possession in performances, including masked and unmasked dances which invite ancestral spirits

---

26. These feelings share in the aesthetic power of *langö*, the rapture described in a celebrated passage about aesthetic apprehension in old Javanese literature (Zoetmulder 1974: 173).

and supernatural forces into human space, it would be reasonable to expect that 'becoming a puppet' in *wayang wong* is a form of possession.[27] Joged Mataram does invoke the language of altered states, but the court repertoire and what people say about it show that a firm line is drawn between practices which take place in performances and other contexts outside the court in Java: masking, possession, spiritual techniques and the martial arts.

Masking and possession

Sĕwiji, the first element of Joged Mataram, means 'to be one with'. This word also describes Balinese dancers making their faces *like* the mask they will dance in; a monkey dancer will make a face like a monkey even though he will be wearing a mask (Nyoman Cahya, a well-known Balinese dancer, pers. comm. January 1991). Masks are powerful because they bridge the dangerous and ambiguous zone between cultured humanity and natural animality, and visible and invisible worlds.[28] They are gateways to the unknown, and attract ancestral and other spirits; these take possession of the wearer who enters in altered state, referred to as *ndadi* (*kesurupan* I.), and loses control.

Jathilan (horse dance) or *reyog* (tiger dance) in Javanese villages are highly dramatic forms associated with animist cults, and both include horse fights (Kartomi 1976). *Jathilan* consists of two teams of dancers dancing with woven bamboo hobby horses who first perform a choreographed fighting dance, and then free dancing under the influence of possessing spirits. The dance dramatizes the relationship between the spirit master (*pawang*) and the spirits, and is full of suspense and danger (Figure 6.6). Islamic influences have resulted in some dancers since the 1970s wearing sunglasses instead of masks in these forms in Central Javanese villages, but even just concealing the eyes with sunglasses is associated with a loss of self-control.[29] *Jathilan* performances are always full of suspense. Although the performers behave conventionally, eat glass and straw, and become very strong, no one can be absolutely sure how else the altered state might affect them. The tension is increased by the *pawang*, who sometimes presents as a menacing 'strong man' (*jago*) wearing a mask or frightening make-up. As a mediator he invites the spirits and attempts to control their dramatic manifestation in the visible world. He is also responsible for making sure that the violence of the possession causes no lasting harm either to the possessed or to the audience. A horse trance performer from the Sleman district of Yogyakarta explained (speaking Indonesian) the inner states and the expression of control in *jathilan*:

---

27. See discussions of cases in West Java (Foley 1992), East Java (Wessing 1999) and Bali (Suryani and Jensen 1993).
28. René Girard has written: 'There is no point in trying to determine the "nature" of masks, because it is their nature not to have a nature but to encompass all natures' (1977: 165).
29. In masked and possession dances, the performers can also be said to lose their voices. This contrasts with the crucial role of the voice by mediums in states of involuntary possession (*kĕpanjingan*) (Keeler 1987: 119–24).

Figure 6.6 *Jathilan*, Muntuk, 1999

If I'm in trance I'm not aware [*sadar*], I don't know what I've eaten – people will tell me after – but I just feel tired … No, it's not hard to come out of trance, the *pawang* tells the spirit [*roh alus*] to come out … Before a performance we have to fast for a day and night & sleep in the graveyard … I don't know which spirit enters me. The *pawang* invites our ancestors [*nenek lĕluhur*] to enter.[30] There are different spirits, different offerings [*sajen*]. One dancer is possessed by one spirit. Which spirits come depends on where we're performing. One spirit leader commands many 'soldiers', so the *pawang* has to ask the leader of the particular group for permission to invite the spirits. The *pawang* knows (has to know) which spirits are helpful, and which ones are destructive and dangerous. He invites the spirits in a manner according to his own beliefs. This is Javanese, Islam's just arrived. (Pak N. 23/8/99)

In Joged Mataram, *sĕwiji* means 'concentration', and distinguishes the state of 'puppet' court dancer from that of the possessed by the spirit of the mask. Yogyakartan court dance has been marked by an apparent absence of masked forms. Masks are only worn in *wayang wong* by some demons, monkeys and *garudha* birds. The masked dances now in the classical repertoire were not performed in the court, but outside in princely residences.[31] Kridha Bĕksa Wirama began to develop masked forms in the 1920s that were considered *kasar* by the court. State surveys classed masked dance as 'folk dance' (*tari rakyat* I.). In the 1980s the Suryakĕncana association started to revive and incorporate them into the classical repertoire. Evidence of this is the commissioning of a new set of masks via the Dinas office of the Ministry of Education and Culture by Gusti Darmakusuma for use in the Yogyakartan pavilion at Taman Mini in Jakarta (Mbak Kadar, pers. comm. 1994).

People explained the absence of masks in the Yogyarta court in different ways. Masks conceal the expression of balance of dynamism and self-confidence revealed through the 'inner' spirit in the dancer's eyes in *pasĕmon* (Rama Sena 22/9/83); they also muffle speech. This varies according to the masking technique employed. In Sunda actors hold the mask in place with their mouths and are silenced, as do actors in Balinese *wayang wong* Ramayana plays where the *dhalang*'s voice carries the story. Balinese *topeng*, however, uses whole masks for aristocratic and demonic characters and half-masks for characters whose speech is important for commenting on the action for the benefit of the audience. Soedarsono (1984)

---

30. In his group, the *pawang* dances a *barongan* (masked wild creature). The masks have their own spirits, and can make more than one person go into trance (*ndadi*) if the mask is passed on.
31. Soedarsono argues that in Yogyakarta *wayang wong* replaced masks, which were preserved in Surakarta; Susuhunan Pakubuwana II (r.1726–49) even danced the masked *klana* (1984: 14–15). When Mbak Kadar and I came across a red *klana* papier mâché mask with Gusti Suryobrongto's name on it, she said it was just part of his collection, and that he had never performed the dance. Bu Yuda mentioned that the Yogya court had a set of masks, but I never saw them displayed in the court.

suggests that the preference for unmasked Mahābhārata stories was the reason, but hybrid plays using parts of the Ramayana were produced in the eighth Sultan's reign (1921–39).

It is significant that no one referred to the Islamic censure of magical superstitions adhering to masks.[32] The differentiation between masked and unmasked performance was understood in relation to the dynamics of performance events and the state of the dancers, in relation to the court ethos and aspirations to modernity. Joged Mataram deliberately differentiates between the states and *rasa* of court performers and those of 'outside' dancers. The circumstances which caused masks to be removed from dancers not only allowed the dancer's self-confidence to be made visible; it also allowed the sultan to see, literally, who his friends were. Masked, trance and possession dancing goes against the personal spirit of *self-control*, itself a balance between control and surrender, which is central to court ethics and aesthetics, and also against the court as the orderly centre of a disorderly cosmos. To distinguish the transformation into a heroic 'puppet' from the wild cavorting of the entranced horse dancer, Suryobrongto used the term 'ecstasy' (1981a: 15). It is significant that this word was introduced by the Catholic Church precisely to distinguish legitimate extra-normal states in the sight of God from demonic possession by spirits (Rouget 1985: 8–11).

As Suryobrongto explained in our very first conversation (23/3/ 83), 'Mystical means unconscious. Dancing isn't mystical, it is still aware, it is between aware and not aware, what's the Javanese for that? Oh yes, *sĕmĕdhi* (meditation, contemplation)'.[33] He later explained (12/5/83) that this contemplative state is not emptiness (*kosongĕblong*): 'The dance is empty but full [*kosong nanging pĕpak*]'. This statement relates to a preoccupation in Java with awareness or remembering (*eling*).[34] Javanese people often express strong reservations about losing awareness, and say that the local tendency to avoid alcohol or hallucinogens is to avoid loss of control. An empty head or an absent mind attracts spirit possessions; people who had 'seen spirits' said it happened when they were 'not aware' – awake, conscious, but in a sort of daze where everything is excluded 'except for one thing'. 'Remembering' also protects you from being carried away physically (*kalap*) by supranatural agencies such as the Queen of the South, who accounts for numerous mysterious disappearances. These factors all contribute to possession in *bĕdhaya*, masks and trance becoming excluded from the Yogya court, a practised place that is controlled by the sultan's gaze as Allah's

---

32. *Kĕpanjingan* is used metaphorically in the emanation philosophy discussed in Chapter 5. Islam was given as the reason for the decline of possession in East Javanese *reyog* (Lono Simatupang pers. comm. July 2006).

33. This imported term, raised in Dutch in conversation, is a reminder that Javanese ideas about themselves are not impervious to other cultural systems (Hughes-Freeland 1997a).

34. Sastrowardoyo (1991); Pemberton (1994). *Eling* is sometimes spoken of as 'remembering one's own death', a kind of 'remembering ahead' that is also like the spiritual consciousness-raising involved in recurrent grave-visiting. It compresses time, and produces awareness of 'the whence and whither of all created things' discussed in relation to *bĕdhaya*.

representative.[35] In this view, the person is understood to be permeable, and susceptible to possession or removal by spirits, particularly in moments of absent-mindedness.

The dangerous engagement with the unbounded invisible world is associated with the powers of the natural world. Joged Mataram places dancing in between possession and acting, and dissociates it from religio-magical practices. Furthermore, by emphasizing the distinction between possession and concentration, it can be understood as a statement about modern identity. Rather than a sociocentric system subject to invasive interactions with invisible forces, a person is a unitary and bounded entity (Hughes-Freeland 1997b). In court dance there is an element of trance or forgetting only in so far as dancers lose their social inhibitions and are no longer constrained by rank; to this extent, they lose their personal selves. They are aware of their fellow dancers and the pillars in the building only in so far as they need to avoid colliding with them and to form a collective unity (in *bĕdhaya* and *srimpi*).

Spiritual techniques and the martial arts

Joged Mataram defines the aesthetic of court-originated Yogya-style classical dance as distinct from and in contrast to the ritual instrumentality of masked trance and possession performances outside the court. This might suggest that Joged Mataram represents a secularization of Yogya-style dance, although some have argued that it has been secularized and ceremonial since its foundation.

As well as having an ethical application, the principles of Joged Mataram also have a spiritual application, and are directed to divinity (*ketuhanan* I.):

1. *Sĕwiji*, always remember the Divinity.
2. *Grĕgĕt*, channel all activity and passion through the path of God.
3. *Sĕngguh*, feel proud of your destiny as a respected being.
5. *Ora mingkuh*, however many difficulties you encounter in your life, always believe in The Great Judge. (Suryobrongto 1976: 23)

This third level of interpretation, together with an inward focus, the emphasis on the powers of endurance, and tales of dancers practising at night alone as a form of meditation (Hughes-Freeland 1991b), suggests that dance had much in common with some practices used in *kĕbatinan.*

Many people in Java belong to *kĕbatinan* groups (*aliran*). Inspired by Vedanta, Confucianism, Christianity, Sufism and other philosophies, most *kĕbatinan* groups have a teacher, a belief system and spiritual techniques (*tirakat, tapabrata*). These include meditation ('closing the nine holes'), prayer, physical movement, and feats of endurance such as sleeping on hard rush mats, immersion in chilly, mosquito-ridden

---

35. In mystical systems, remembering is to be aware of the possibility of reaching 'total awareness', as in the Sufi practice of *dhikr*. These recitations induce trance, and are disapproved of by normative sectors of Islam (Woodward 1989), but not necessarily others (Rouget 1985; Zarrilli 1998:151).

rivers from midnight till dawn (*kungkum*), and fasting.[36] They cool desires and self-interest (*pamrih*) which disrupt how one 'sits' (*lĕnggah*) in the 'inner room' of one's self, and help the practitioner to 'become one with nature' (*menyatu dengan alam* I.) or achieve 'death in life' (*mati sajroning urip*) (Jong 1976: 27). In Subud *kĕbatinan*, movements constitute a meditative practice (*latihan*). So, like dance, *kĕbatinan* emphasizes the conjunction of *lair* and *batin*, and recognizes the spiritual person as embodied, not as residing in the cogito.[37]

One technique which may be used in *kĕbatinan* groups is *pĕncak-silat* (martial arts). We already know about the militarism of Yogya court dance. The centrality of fighting in most court dance forms invited frequent comparisons between dance and *silat*. *Silat* may be performed to music in the region, as in Sunda, or choreographed, as in the *pĕncak* dance in Banyumas in Cental Java (Kartomi 1973: 190ff.). Although it was not included in the court until Hamĕngkubuwana IX somewhat controversially included West Sumatran *silat* movements in his creation of *golek Menak*, it has influenced court dance. Rama Sena, an expert in both dance and *silat*, compared the rising and falling of dance hands in 'fixing earrings' to *silat* sequences which protect the face, and also compared the legwork in strong male modes to martial art kicks (see further de Grave 2001: 258–60). *Silat* has also inspired new choreographies – from Bagong Kussudiardjo's 'new creation' *silat* dance for six women, to the dance choreographed by one of Rama Sena's own martial arts students for his examination at ISI. The other similarities between dance and *silat* are in the quality of concentration, the use of inner resources rather than brute strength, the use of elaborate and contrived movements to build up to the brief but final combat and, most importantly, the emphasis on self-control. *Silat* is for *self*-defence; Rama Sena refused to take on students he considered 'too hot' to be entrusted with his deadly techniques because they would become a danger to themselves and to others.

Silat is usually associated with *kĕbatinan*. It may be taught in a *kĕbatinan* group as a technique to produce the knowledge or 'science' (*ngelmu, ilmu* I.) enabling the development of suprahuman feats such as flight, invulnerability, healing and other magical powers (Koentjaraningrat 1985: 398ff.). Advanced practitioners of *silat* often become notorious for their manipulation of an adversary by mental strength. Described as *ilmu kanoragan*, this gives strength for fighting. My research assistant's

---

36. One of my research assistants told me his father practised *pati gĕni*, an extreme kind of fasting in which one is buried in a hole in the ground for up to a week.
37. These groups are administered not by the Ministry of Religion but by the Ministry of Education and Culture under the category of 'beliefs' (*kepercayaan* I.). I often heard the view expressed that religion concerns the sphere of *lair*, with rules originating from outside one's own consciousness, whereas spirituality is a personal responsibility. This explains Suryobrongto baffling statement that 'dance affects the self more than religion because religion does not affect your behaviour' (pers. comm. 1983). Javanese philosophers might disagree with this, but would share the same pragmatism: 'the ultimate aim of religion is not correct belief, nor correct dogma, but correct behaviour' (Slamet 1977: 35; see also Hardjowirogo 1983: 17).

brothers gained different kinds of *ilmu* from their *silat* teachers. One acquired the ability to become possessed by *ilmu macan* (tiger, panther); another had 'monkey *ilmu*'; and two others had the *ilmu* to summon snakes, hold them, be bitten without harm, and also *sense* them. Their sister also had this ability; when I asked her what *kind of* consciousness (*rasa*) or sensation it was, she described it as 'being kissed by the senses' (*dicium indera* I.).

The main difference between dance and *silat* is that dancing does not develop powers of physical invulnerability and control over one's opponent nor does it affect others practically: it cannot – and is not intended to – kill or maim, unless a dancer is out of control and causes an accident. The more instrumentally driven *kĕbatinan* practices were described as the result of 'black magic' (*ngelmu klĕnik*), motivated by self-interest, in contrast to true magical power (*sĕkti*) which arises from disinterested spiritual intentions.

These details help us to understand how Joged Mataram relates dance to spirituality. 'Dance is a *kĕbatinan* art, not a *kĕbatinan* method for acquiring wisdom' said Suryobrongto (12/5/83; 1981a: 13). He explained that dance as a spiritual *art* was easy compared to some *kĕbatinan* and *silat* techniques. The dancing body is a subtle, spiritual, body (*batin*). Learning to dance is a lesson in humility, self restraint, and the overcoming of desire. As a spiritual art dance fosters the ability to restrain and discipline the inner forces and energies, to control, not to be controlled. It leads not to magical powers (*kĕsĕkten*), but to perfection (*kĕsempurnaan*).

Dance as a Spiritual Art

Javanese people use categories which Westerners might consider narrowly spiritual to explain psychology and philosophy. Different traditions yield theories that cannot be accounted for or subsumed to disciplines which arise from Western European traditions of enquiry alone. Dance represents an aesthetic which is ethical-spiritual, and yet which can be distinguished from the spiritual, in a similar vein to theories of *rasa* in India.[38] There is a blur between dance and religion only because of the separation of what might be more generally regarded as 'religious' attitudes from religious codes and practices. However, although court dance experts invoke the language of altered states and draw a firm line between practices which take place in performances and other contexts outside the court in Java, the aesthetic instrumentality of court dance philosophy has not completely eliminated the relationship between expression and spirituality.

Each principle of Joged Mataram has an implied opposition, which can be summarized as follows:

1. *Sĕwiji*: absorbed concentration but not possession or trance.
2. *Grĕgĕt*: dynamic energy but not imitation.
3. *Sĕngguh*: self-confidence but not arrogance.
4. *Ora mingkuh*: determination but not self-interest.

---

38. Deutsch makes some relevant points about Abhinavagupta's theory of *rasa* (1981, cited in Hughes-Freeland 1997b: 62).

As the first three aspects have already been explored, I will elaborate on how *ora mingkuh* is determination but not self-interest as further evidence for Joged Mataram being both a moral code and a theory of performance, and for what is meant by dance as a spiritual art.

Although dancers acquire social power, the achievement of grace on stage, like social grace, has the power to change a person's life – but such a result must be detached from desire. Self-interest (*pamrih*) damages the *rasa* of the dancer and the aesthetic impact of a performance which should be inspired by the correctly balanced condition of *batin* and *rasa*.[39] Gusti Suryo and other senior dancers criticized the dancers of the younger generations for their self-interest and lack of sincerity (*ikhlas*) in seeking fame and wealth, claiming that a dancer should never believe that s/he has succeeded, and always continue training to seek perfection. When I reported the findings of a fieldwork survey in which some dance students described their *rasa* during performance as feeling pleasure at being looked at, Suryobrongto gave a cry of dismay: the other dancers and the audience should not interfere with the dancer's concentration. Young dancers who try to please are operating in the world of form (*lair*) and passions. Joged Mataram is the moral counterpart to the concealment of eroticism in the aesthetics of female performance discussed previously, the principle being to watch the dance, not the dancer.

In our very first meeting Suryobrongto had described dancing to me as 'a pure duty to serve the dance' (23/3/83). The spiritual nature of the art of dancing developed in a context where financial incentives were submerged in a status system. Until recently these exchanges were conceptualized as traditions which are of value, noble, esteemed (*adiluhung*) and completely different from things that are exchanged as commodities (*barang*). Such 'honour' carried social status and material advancement, and social climbing by contact made in the training and production of court performance is still common, though never voiced as a reason for interest in court dance. To dance well would be its own reward within the context of the court community where remuneration, concealed and delayed, would occur. So material rewards came indirectly, not as the result of a direct transaction. This ideal, however, did not always strictly apply: in a conversation about the dancer's *rasa* in Joged Mataram, Bu Yuda said that *bĕdhaya* dancers have always tried to catch the eye of a potential partner, and used to twist their rings around so that the audience could see the jewels glittering in the *ngruji* hand position.

As a spiritual art, Joged Mataram represents dance as a court practice which excluded the uncontrollable and replaced it with a purposive act of service to the sultan. This endorsed an artistic distinction constituted by a series of oppositions between inside the court and outside. Possession, trance and mask dances eliminate the skilled mastery of gaze and voice, deemed essential to court values of *adiluhung*.

---

39. *Pamrih* has a negative meaning, and works in opposition to traditional 'Power' (Anderson 1972). Geertz's question, 'How is action possible, given compassion?' (1960: 272) could be rephrased, replacing 'compassion' with '*pamrih*'. Some intellectuals have seen a change in the evaluation of *pamrih* as a precondition for Indonesia to modernize (Takdir Alisjahbana cited in Jong 1976: 57).

The absence of masked forms in the court conflates the self-control implied in the aesthetic of Joged Mataram with political control. In other words, they are reinscribed with the seal of palace ownership and status. Just as the former *ledhek* could gain a new name and status as a *bědhaya* dancer, the fearsome mask, divorced from its link with the supranatural, in Yogya court traditions has become limited to animals who dance like humans, or to humorous demonic figures. It articulates a contrast between dance and instrumental practices. The ethos of Joged Mataram is that of the 'inside', constituted by the principle that *all* court dancing is *alus* and unmotivated by base interests and instincts (see Table 6.2).

Table 6.2 *Outside versus inside*

Outside (*jaba*)	Inside (*jěro*)
Underdetermined gesture: imitation	Overdetermined gesture: *běksa*
popular ritual conventions	purified conventions
violence, lack of self-control	heroism, self-control
material exchange	honour not cash
eroticism	grace
possession	concentration
masks	*pasěmon*

There is a relationship between disinterestedness and not dancing through an act of imitation based on the effort of will. As Suryobrongto put it, the manners of *wayang* become instinctive (1981b: 93). The dancer must lose self-consciousness, but not consciousness. A set of physical practices, as already noted, can become a means to transcend the body: when skilled dancers are dancing, they are not making physical gestures; these happen mechanically, and the dancer's self is beyond the weakness of the body, beyond human failings, heroic and also in contemplation of totalities. Joged Mataram does not describe the movement of emotional force into an artistic form; it teaches how the control of emotional movement defines the nature of the form. It is not muscle which dances, but consciousness. This most public of social actions, ceremonially presented at the heart of the kingdom, is the most personal of experiences, with the conscious self liberated from or transcending the awareness of physical control to an incommunicable inner space formed by the imagination. The internalization of balance and control to its extinction in the experience of the dancer is a move away from interaction and social relations. To dance is to go beyond the desires of the body.

So, we have a paradox. This most *public* of social actions, ceremonially presented at the heart of the traditional kingdom, is represented as the most *personal* of experiences. The conscious and concentrated self in dance movement is empowered by self-control, freed both from personal limitation and desire, and from both the rules and constraints of everyday life. At the same time, this most *private* of social events, exclusive to those invited to the court ceremony or the state reception, is the most social of actions. From the *lair* perspective, the dance represents harmonious interaction, with self-control the result of socialization, which is also an expression of political control. Also, while the inner self is imagined to be closed to possession by spirits, it is not simply a hermetic, egocentric, individual space. It is a microcosmic centre and is defined relationally to others, and as such it retains its sociocentric 'me' (*aku*). In this sense, dancing removes dancers from the principle of adjusting personal behaviour to place (*ĕmpan-papan*), and frees them to move in an ultra-social space, where they are in control, at least for the duration of the dance, but where they still share in the shared breath of the community.

Successful dance, like successful living, is evaluated in terms of timing and fitting behaviour to place, as we discovered previously. It is now possible to sum up the relationship between ethics and aesthetics. The appearance of ease which Joged Mataram strives for, both on stage and off it, is the ease which springs from the confidence of rank, whether by birth or achievement. Just as *kĕbatinan* is considered to be superior to sticking to the rigid rules of religion, so too Joged Mataram demands an internalized instinct for correct action, gracefully responding to the dynamic give-and-take of social interaction. The mature person understands his or her potential and limits and has a sense of certainty and resolution (*mantĕp*), of 'settled' confidence (*madĕp*). The pursuit of self-interest and ambition is the goal of the one who lacks rank and status. The action implied in the ideology of Joged Mataram correlates with status, with the positive and negative evaluations, that are generally classed as *alus* and *kasar* (Table 6.3). This describes the relationship between dance as fluid confidence and the hiding of base instincts through strategies of dissimulation and control, and acting, which is forcing action, imitating something one is not, and pursuing self-interest. Dance is alchemy of movement, through which the base metal of natural, animal energy is transmuted into the gold of *bĕksa*.

Table 6.3 Alus *and* kasar

Alus	Kasar
ease	lack of ease
dancing, being in place	effort, acting
humanity	animals
culture	nature

Conclusion

The ideas in Joged Mataram derive from the differences between dancing inside and outside the court, but are presented as a portable aesthetic, intended to apply beyond this situated 'inside-outside' opposition. As we have seen, Joged Mataram is a philosophy which is based on discriminations between practices defined as being of the court and those of the outside. It also represents the relationship between life and art in such a way as to transfer the values of court performance beyond the context in which it developed. On the one hand, Suryobrongto detaches Joged Mataram from the context from which it derives its values, that has partly been the reason for formulating it in the first place, and presents it as a form of pre-expressivity with a universal potential, giving it the status of a Javanese version of 'Theatre Anthropology'. But on the other hand, he gives it a spiritual purpose which differentiates it from the secular modernism of the spaces and theories of Western staged performance. Joged Mataram gives court dance practices a content which can survive away from the practised place which gave rise to them and become 'classical Yogya-style dance'. It has eliminated some of dance's instrumental power, bringing it into the domain of virtual power, but it retains resonances which are more than aesthetic, both in the way in which the dancer's *rasa* is explained, and in the moral and spiritual interpretations of the four principles.

It should be noted that the insights formulated as Joged Mataram are traditionally associated with wisdom and maturity. The prize-winning dancer Susindahati told me that she knew a dance philosophy existed, but laughingly said she didn't understand it: 'It's for older people!' Her own knowledge of dance lay in difficulties in the techniques of physical dancing, which she could explain very well (Hughes-Freeland 1988). So by making Joged Mataram a text for training, there is a further level of decontextualization, away from how knowledge used to be situated in relation to the gaining of experience over time, just as nowadays dancers in vocational training cannot afford to specialize in becoming one particular puppet character. In this sense then, Joged Mataram marks a break in the relationship to learning dance and the knowledge of it.

Joged Mataram is also more than a Javanese theory about performance practice and experience. It is a meta-cultural statement created out of the need to articulate between groups what need not be said within the group. That first target group was European journalists. Today, the groups are other Indonesian societies, within and without Java. So Joged Mataram expresses a dynamic transformability of a practice by the older generation to meet new challenges, and continue to provide an exemplar for a modern Indonesian identity, as well as constituting a form of Indonesian art. It has had a bridge-building role: to bring tacit, unspoken, embodied knowledge to people for whom such understandings are not tacit, bringing 'Javanese culture' to Others. The first others were foreigners; today 'others' include young Indonesians born in Yogyakarta and elsewhere.

However, there are two twists. Firstly, although Joged Mataram grows out of an ethos particular to the Sultan's court, and generates aesthetic boundaries which separate court dance as art, and makes it distinct from other ritual and spiritual techniques, Suryobrongto recognized that mimesis is of limited help in understanding dramatic representation, so he extended Joged Mataram to *all* performance. Despite the frequent disparagement of Surakartan court practices, he said that the same philosophy could be applied to Surakarta style performances – or, for that matter, any other kind of performance – 'Even Western ballet!' (pers. comm. 1983). What matters in all these performance worlds is to pursue perfection or purity of life (*urip sěmpurna*). Joged Mataram would appear to be advocating a reritualization of performance in the modern and secular world as well.

The second twist is this. Joged Mataram was formulated during the New Order regime, and defines dance in the 'high and noble' (*adiluhung*) traditional framework.

Its spiritual and ethical attitudes to self-interest have been transposed to the personality of the nation state: self-sacrifice serves modern political agendas. In a caustic critique of court performance traditions, the poet and dramatist W.S. Rendra warned that Javanese culture could easily become 'an old mattress for the people to sleep on', and invoked as inspiration to contemporary thespians the 'independent spirit of Ranggawarsita, Ken Arok, and Kartini', a pioneering Javanese feminist, instead of the 'coy [*kĕnĕs*] style of the nineteenth century' (1983: 6, 44). 'Coy' is of course the antithesis of the spirit of Yogya style performance, the very word Yogyakartan practitioners use to criticize Surakarta style court dance. In the early 1980s, the rhetoric of the Yogya style was antagonistic to its idealization in terms of 'refinement' and passivity, emphasizing its simple (*lugu*), disciplined and militaristic qualities. Rendra was suggesting that the national government's cooption of court dance was putting its spirit at risk.

Subsequent events indicate that Joged Mataram has not been subsumed by *adiluhung* as an 'old mattress', and that its rebellious spirit survives off the stages of the state. In 1994, the Pakualaman court hosted 'The Court Festival' in its prestigious *pĕndhapa*, including court *bĕdhaya* dances. Outside was a temporary stage housing 'The Festival of Traditional and Religious Art'. In the programme of 'folk' theatre and dance was a *ketoprak* play performed by members of Suryakĕncana, the dance association set up by Gusti Suryobrongto's son, R.M. Ywandjono who, together with his own sons, performed a number of very lively fights with the heroic spirit of Joged Mataram fully mustered (Figure. 6.7). Arguably the spirit of Joged Mataram was more evident outside the space of official 'high' culture in the performance taking place on a temporary wood and bamboo platform than the court performances

Figure 6.7 Suryakĕncana embody the spirit of Joged Mataram, 1994

enacted on the polished floors of the pavilion inside. Is it possible that the spirit of court dance is being squeezed out of the forms with which it has been associated? Or are the boundaries between court and folk culture being radically redrawn?

A number of questions arise from my discussion of Joged Mataram. Was this philosophy formalized just as it ceased to be credible, given the intensification of commercialization in the domain of performance, and that audiences for court dance are increasingly non-Javanese tourists? Or does the definition of dance as a spiritual art instead of a form of service make it possible for it to enter the commercial sphere? To answer these questions, I now turn to the conflict between art and commerce, and the challenges of commoditization to the principle of 'honourable' service which formed the economic basis to the ethics and aesthetics of Joged Mataram.

Chapter 7

Changing Styles of Patronage: Tourism and Commoditization

As we have discovered, the colonial dance repertoire of the Sultan's court in Yogyakarta has changed into a classical Indonesian dance form, but it retains references and identifications from Javanese world-views of the late colonial period. Joged Mataram in particular is a reformulation of court dance as classical Yogyakartan dance and aesthetics founded in an ethical and spiritual ethos from the reign of the eighth Sultan. Those values resonated with early postcolonial concerns, but have fitted less well with subsequent normalization. Joged Mataram framed dance as a resource to develop national character, but this 'educative capital' was already being challenged by 'cultural capital' (Bourdieu 1984). As well as representing the nation to its constituent communities, performance had also become implicated in policies to represent the nation to outsiders, and commercialization in the tourist sector became a new priority.

This chapter examines court dance as an art object facing commoditization in the commercial world of tourism against the background of the relationship and tension between national policies to develop and preserve traditions and to promote international and national tourism. I outline changes in the state administration of culture and tourism in the Special Region of Yogyakarta which continues to exhibit the bureaucratic fragmentation discussed in Chapter 3. This fragmentation also characterizes the patronage of court dance, which is now dispersed among state and private (*swasta*) interests, including the court itself, hotels, and dance associations. I conclude with a discussion about the feasibility of professionalism in a society where patron-client relationships and exchanges which belong to the sphere of gift giving continue to play an important role in the modern Indonesian economy.

Indonesia, Modernity, Tourism

As soon as dance became recontextualized as a 'spiritual art', a tension developed between art and commerce within the wider processes of retraditionalization and development. In postcolonial societies, the abstract concepts of independence and modernity are part of the construction of national identity and the transformation of local allegiances and identifications. Paradoxically, retraditionalization is inevitably found in the symbolic construction of national communities, especially after changes brought about by armed struggle, and provides a sense of continuity and predictability.[1]

Retraditionalization has also been implicated in the global economics of tourism. During the 1980s, the tourist industry was targeted as Indonesia's main generator of income.[2] By this time, classical Yogyakarta-style dancing was being performed in state ceremonial, educational displays and competitions, commercial hotel shows and concerts or dinner-dances given by local associations for the local and international tourist markets, and latterly as a form of corporate entertainment.[3]

In Java ancestrally ascribed 'high and noble' traditions are described as '*kagungan adiluhung*', and include exemplary and uncommercial practices which may be artistic, such as dancing, or customary, such as traditional Javanese wedding ceremonies (Hughes-Freeland 1997a). The court elite was competing among itself and forming alliances with other interest groups to determine how the past would shape the future and whether *all* the things handed down would survive. People still used the word *adiluhung* to describe high-status practices, but they did so with an added awareness that these things that had been passed down would not necessarily endure without extra attention. There were debates about how to accommodate the values of *adiluhung* to those of culture and art as defined by the Indonesian state, which themselves were coming under pressure to be sold in the market, particularly the tourist market. After being criticized for 'prostituting the arts' in his work with tourist projects, the head of Yogyakarta's Arts Council invoked caste distinctions to explain the lack of commerce in the court, which had a 'warrior' (*satriya*) ethos of not handling money in contrast to the mercantile castes, and reckoned that *adiluhung* should be reinterpreted to include financial exchange (Bakdi Soemanto 3/3/89).

The conflict between the values of art and of the market was further complicated by the equation of noncommoditization with authenticity in the context of tourism (MacCannell 1976: 176 in Desmond 1999: xvii). The relationship between power and culture has been reconfigured through the processes of patronage that are part of a wider and unpredictable social dynamic. The material resources for nation building become implicated in the construction of symbolic self-images which feed back into

---

1. Anderson has referred to the 'archaizing iconography' of New Order Indonesia (Anderson 1983: 146).
2. Between 1989 and 1999 my research in Yogyakarta included tourism as a patron. Dahles' (2001) study of tourism in Yogyakarta up to 1995 includes detailed ethnographic data that demonstrate the limits of state effectiveness, but nevertheless tends to see Yogyakarta from Jakarta's point of view. My findings differ because I consider tourism in relation to cultural and educational polities over a long period and from different points of view in Yogyakarta, so I do not see Yogyakarta as an economic and political backwater, as she does.
3. For comparable analyses in Southeast Asia, see Hough (1992) on Bali, Rutnin (1993) on Thai performance, Tan (1993) on commercial Malay *bangsawan* theatre, and Lindsay (1995) on cultural production across the region.

social interactions. In this way Urry's (1990) tourist 'gaze' has been implicated in representations of personal and national self-definition.

Take the case of Bali, now Indonesia's main tourist region. Bali has been a tourist destination since the 1920s, and its self-images have long been constituted in response to the gaze of outsiders, with the Balinese becoming who they are seen to be (Vickers 1996: 27; Picard 1999). By the late 1970s, Balinese performances were classified to differentiate secular (*bali-balihan*), semi-sacred (*bebali*) and sacred (*wali*) performances according to their orientations to the sacred mountain and profane sea, within the temple precincts, to delimit what could and could not be sold in the tourist market. Although this strategy failed (Picard 1990: 74 in Wood 1993: 67), the categories were used as descriptors of Balinese performance culture (Bandem and deBoer 1995). In his work on tourist performances in Java, Soedarsono (1989/1990) similarly set up a typology of dance forms, to recognize the impact of tourism.[4] He proposed that special tourist dances should be developed along Balinese lines, but argued that in Yogya, unlike Bali, contemporary local practices threaten performance standards, rather than tourism.

Authenticity, like tradition, plays a part in both personal and national politics of identity construction, and is highlighted when we consider tourism and performance. As Desmond (1999) has shown, the visibility of dance makes it an excellent medium for spreading and standardizing culture as *appearances*, and for reproducing stereotypes. These in turn become references to orientate cultural identity, and an example of self-citation (De Certeau 1984). By saying it over and over, it becomes true. Tourism has added another rationale to the state's interest in dance as a form of iteration which presents an appearance of culture to the outside world. However, although court dancing has been implicated in the tourist market, it cannot be explained as simply 'tourist art' (Graburn 1976). This is because it has connections with power, and it is also personal.

Authenticity needs to be treated with caution. Writing about tourist performances, Daniel has also argued that one should include the 'experiential authenticity' of the dancer, as well as the tourists' desire for authenticity (1996: 783). But when has performance ever been free of the wish to impress outsiders with a display? What differentiates a tourist from a nontourist audience? It could be argued that these differences are not essential. They are historical and circumstantial, and depend on the extent of shared identity of interests and knowledge. Desmond (1999) has criticized the emphasis on the gaze. Consumption in the analysis of tourism has neglected the body, even though tourism reifies the visible body in a process of 'physical foundationalism', and reproduces stereotypes embodied in skin colour and sexual characteristics or race and gender (1999: xxiv–xxv). Her theoretical and practical solution is to emphasize 'the participatory aspect of the kinaesthetic dimension of tourism' (ibid.: 252).

---

4. Soedarsono classes court dance as 'pseudo-ritual' and distinguishes tourist dances from commercial ones. However, the only example of a commercial form is the monthly radio broadcast of the shadow play (Soedarsono 1989/1990); see also Hughes-Freeland (1993: 146–47).

Participation became an important policy word in Indonesian tourism in 1999, but only time will tell whether or not intercultural understandings can be dislodged from the determinism and primacy of the visual image as Desmond proposes. State policies in Indonesia have relied on local enthusiasm to sustain interest in the targets of particular projects. However, tourism, not art, has provided a rationalization for the diversification of patronage of both *adiluhung* and popular performance, and also for maintaining practices which are repackaged as 'traditions'. From the mid-1980s, tourist interests became increasingly important as a factor in the competition between groups for cultural control and the definition of standards, even though government projects might put tourism last in a list of objectives for local development priorities (Hughes-Freeland 1993b: 149–50). In the meantime, it is no simple matter to differentiate cultural policy from tourist policy in Indonesia, and it is important not to reduce the first to the second. What is clear is that audiences of tourists from other parts of Java, Indonesia and overseas understand neither Javanese language, *rasa* and Joged Mataram, nor the literary, philosophical and aesthetic references embodied in court dances. The question facing performers and producers is what to do about this gap between court codes and the changing knowledge bases of the different potential audiences, and how to maintain a patronage base.

Authenticity is also problematic as an aesthetic criterion for judging 'live' cultural products because it ignores cultural dynamism, social change and processes of interaction and strategizing by social actors. This has been argued in the context of tourism: 'we must increasingly see people as active and strategic users of culture, participating in contexts where no single set of cultural interpretations has an inherent claim to truth and authenticity' (Wood 1993: 66).[5] The diversity of local responses to the challenges and opportunities offered by tourism has prompted changes in analytical perspectives. It is now recognized that local people are neither powerless nor passive in their response to tourism, which occurs in a context made up of state structure and policies, an existing field of ethnic relations, and other features of the industry (Wood 1997:15).

This change in analysis reflects my own emphasis on the importance of dynamic process. As we will discover, both national development and the challenges of the tourist industry put pressure on people to make decisions about things that have been passed down to them. These decisions often produce practices that may be at odds with the rationales and rhetorical validation for what those cultural objects are. It is also the case that the material expectations produced of tourism by hosts do not match the outcomes. Thus, previous reservations about tourism being a panacea for the ills of underdevelopment remain an issue, but within the framework of a more dynamic approach.

---

5. Wood himself has changed his approach here. Previously he had argued that 'Tourism involves many of the basic attributes of underdevelopment ... international tourism is a poor candidate for "national" industry' (1979: 282–83).

Changes in the Administration of Culture and Tourism

In late 1998 the first 'Reform Order Government', led by President A.J. Habibie, restructured the two ministries involved with culture and tourism, the Department of Education and Culture (Depdikbud) and the Department of Tourism, Post and Telecommunications (Parpostel). As explained earlier, these were administered at provincial level by 'level 1' or regional offices of the central government (Kanwil), and 'level 2' provincial offices (Dinas), and there were lines of fracture between the level 1 and 2 offices for Education and Culture and for Tourism.[6] The restructuring separated Tourism from Post and Telecommunications, and combined it with Arts and Culture to form a new Department of Tourism, Arts and Culture (Deparsenibud), but the existing Department of Education and Culture remained.[7] Cultural policy was thus divided between culture-as-education and culture-for-tourism.

The restructuring increased tourism's significance as a mark of modernity and rationalization, and its importance in shaping the role of culture in national development. Even during the late 1980s, international tourism to Indonesia has been the lowest in ASEAN (Association of South East Asian Nations) apart from the Philippines (Walton 1993: 226), and yet tourism was targeted to be the third largest earner by the end of the fifth Development Programme (1989/90–1993/94). The most popular destination was Bali, and Yogyakarta was promoted as a second cultural centre.[8] The then Minister of Tourism, Soesilo Soedarman, attempted to resolve these problems by integrating cultural development and tourism. He designated 1989 as 'Tourism Awareness Year' (*Tahun Sadar Wisata*), in preparation for 'Visit Indonesia Year' 1990, which then expanded into 'Visit Indonesia Decade 1991–2000'.[9]

One effect of his policy was the introduction of festivals. Festivals had the added advantage of being *regular* events that could be included in a calendar of events for marketing them as tourist attractions. They would also overlap with the state competitions conducted to improve local interest in cultural traditions. Soesilo Soedarman introduced the Court Festival, which was intended to rotate around the

6. In Yogyakarta's tourist offices, Kanwil handles hotels, travel bureaux, national objects, routine subsidies and private tour operator licences; Dinas handles restaurants, local objects and project subsidies (Pak Maryatmo, head of Kanwil Parpostel 29/4/89)

7. In 1999 the Minister of Education and Culture was Juwono Sudharso and the Minister of Tourism, Arts and Culture was Marzuki Usman.

8. Between 1989 and 1993 the number of one- to five- star hotels rose from eleven to twenty-one, a growth of 108 per cent (*Laporan Tahunan 1993/4*, 1994: 3).

9. Born in Banyumas, Central Java, he had studied at Tamansiswa in Yogya and maintained close links with his alma mater, in common with many other public figures, including President Suharto's half-brother, Pak Probosutedjo, and the then head of the armed forces, General Wiranto. Tamansiswa continues to influence nationalism and its networks, but the Javanism it promotes is synthetic and detached from agrarian practices, a modern *priyayi* style of culture, influenced by Western educational values and systems as well as colonial bureaucracy, producing a new bourgeoisie made up of a postcolonial urban middle class.

major court cities. This joined the Yogyakarta Arts Festival, which had started in 1989.[10] By 1994, after Joop Avé had taken over as Minister of Tourism (and Soesilo Soedarman was Minister for Coordinating Politics and Security), the festivals policy was making its mark.[11] Court festivals had taken place in 1991 and 1993, organized and funded by the Department of Tourism, but with the Sultan as the executive, and the head of the Kanwil Arts Unit, R.M. Dinusatama, as coordinator.

In 1994 the Court Festival was hosted in Yogyakarta by the junior Pakualaman court. There were performances by the senior and junior courts of Yogyakarta and Surakarta and, for the first time, the three courts of Cirebon (Kasepuhan, Kanoman and Kacirebonan).[12] On 15 August, there was a one-hour 'court' *Bĕdhaya Tunjunganom* performed by Siswa Among Bĕksa; a 'Little Lawung' dance from the Pakualaman court; and a fashion show of ceremonial court dress (Hughes-Freeland 1997a: 490). At the same time, the Kanwil Parpostel was running the 'Festival Competition of Traditional and Religious Art and Folk Music of the Special Region of Yogyakarta' just outside the Pakualaman gates on the kind of temporary stage normally associated with performances by itinerant *ketoprak* troupes.[13] Programme notes provided were in Javanese or Indonesian, suggesting that this was aimed at local and domestic audiences.[14] It included popular forms of dance theatre normally held in villages for special religious or national holidays and also, significantly, as one of three representatives of Yogya Municipality, the Suryakĕncana association, normally involved in court dance production, which performed a fragment of *ketoprak* folk-theatre. Bagong Kussudiardjo's military-sponsored 'Sapta Mandala Kodam IV Diponegoro' troupe closed the event with a 'Performance of Folk Theatre' ('PERTUNRA', *Pertunjukkan Rakyat*, a new name – for *ketoprak*). Festivals, like the administrative statistics discussed earlier, were altering the ways in which performance

10. This festival took place in both Yogya and Solo; it also provided court inputs to the 1990–91 cultural mission, 'Indonesian Arts in the United States' (KIAS).

11. In my field notes for my first week back in Yogya for five years I noted that 'There's an *intensification* or *proliferation* of festivals. It seems "chaotic" – is there a replication which may be fractal?'(3/8/94). The aim of the 1994/5 in the Fifth Development Programme (Repelita V) was to priorize the development of the Court Festival and 'tourism week' for 1994–95, increase the average length of stay in Yogya from 1.9 days to 3; the number of overseas tourists from 250,000 to 305,000 (and 399,000 domestic tourists), and the occupancy target from 60 per cent to 70 per cent of 1,100 rooms (Pak Maryatmo, head of Kanwil Parpostel, 29/4/89; *Laporan Tahunan 1993/4*, 1993: 36).

12. The Kacirebonan sent *Bĕdhaya Mĕnjangan Wulung* (or *Sonyaragen*) and *Tari Pĕnyĕnggrama Agung*, both of which had been revived and developed (*Kedaulatan Rakyat* 15/8/94).

13. In March 1989, a Festival of Traditional and Religious Art had also taken place as a project of the Dinas Depdikbud; this had happened since 1970 on the *alun-alun*, but this year was presented as a carnival along Jalan Malioboro, to attract tourists (*Kedaulatan Rakyat* 20/3/89).

14. I am grateful to Mbak Esti Windayani, head of Marketing Analysis in the Kanwil Parpostel office, for providing me with the documentation for this festival, and also to Pak Titaley, head of marketing.

practices were being classified. In the process the spirit of Joged Mataram was being divided between the domains of the noble sublime and popular theatre.

Tourist policies were successful in as far as the target for overseas tourists for the end of 1994–95 was reached and there was a steady increase in tourist numbers (Table 7.1). Nonetheless there was a decline in the growth of foreign tourists to Yogya from 60 per cent to 6.5 per cent between 1989 and 1995 (*Kanwil Deparpostel DIY 1996* in Dahles 2001: 80). Also, the length of stay for overseas tourists fell from 1.84 days in 1989 to 1.60 in 1993, and for domestic tourists from 1.73 to 1.63. Between 1997 and 1998 the total number of tourists visiting Yogyakarta's 'star' and 'jasmine' hotels dropped to nearly one-third. This was largely due to the number of domestic visitors going down by 50 per cent as a result of the economic crisis. After dropping from 344,265 in 1995 to 27,847 in 1997, the number of overseas tourists had nearly trebled during 1998. So overseas tourism started to recover more swiftly after the ecological and economic disruptions of 1997 than domestic tourism, which in 1998 was less than half of 1997.

Table 7.1 Tourist visits to Yogyakarta, 1986–98[15]

year	total	overseas	domestic
1986	436,791	n/a	n/a
1987	547,527	n/a	n/a
1988	570,444	145,883	424,561
1989	664,416	188,549	483,520
1990	587,185	188,549	398,636
1991	708,097	216,051	492,046
1992	819,114	260,392	558,772
1993	910, 251	299,433	610,251
1994	963,995	323,194	640,801
1995	1,818,530	344,265	873,265
1996	1,253,117	351,542	901,575
1997	916,399	27,847	638,552
1998	387,928	78,833	309,095

When I returned to Yogyakarta in July 1999 for the final fieldwork for this study, economic and political developments had overtaken policy and planning, and morale was low. The monetary crisis of 1997, smoke from forest fires in Kalimantan, and political unrest and outbreaks of violence in 1998 had drastically reduced the numbers of tourists visiting Indonesia. Between August 1997 and March 1998, there

---

15. Yogyakarta statistics only calculate stays at 'star' and 'jasmine' ranked hotels. Data are from the following sources: 1986-88: *Statistik Kapariwisataan DIY 1988*, 1988; 1989–93: *Rencana Pembangungan Lima Tahun Keenam 1994/1995–1998/1999*, 1994: 96; 1994: *Statistic Parpostel 1993*, 1994: 36; 1995–98: *Statistik Parsenibud 1998*, 1999:1–2. The number of local and overseas tourists using travel agents: this declined from 211,217 in 1994 to 12,492 1998 (*Statistic Parsenibud 1998*, 1999: /1). *Statistic Parpostel 1993* (1994: 2) has slightly higher figures for 1988: 664,416; 180,896; 483,520.

had been an 11.9 per cent decrease in overseas visitors to Indonesia compared to the same period in 1996–97, with a 2.6 per cent decrease in foreign exchange earnings (*Indonesian Handbook* 1999: 175).[16] This decline was compounded by an 80 per cent decrease in the value of the Rupiah which was worth only Rp18,000 to the US$ and Rp10,000 to the £ in August and September 1999. A taxi driver explained what this meant: 'You used to eat for Rp1,000; now you need Rp3,000.'

The government's response to the decline in tourism was to invest US$10 million in a 'Let's Go Indonesia' campaign. A 'Happy Day' on 30 July 1998 attracted an estimated 15,000 foreign visitors with offers of free hotel rooms, meals and tours, and August 1998 was designated 'Magic Month' (*Indonesia 1999*: 177) – a case of gift giving from the poor to the rich, arguably contributing further to the shared poverty of Indonesian citizens. People in Yogya remarked on the sharp decline of overseas tourists since the summer of 1997 and the continued presence of Indonesian visitors.[17] Inflation had hit domestic tourism, while the political disruption had affected overseas ones, although the weakness of the Rupiah was attracting visitors back by mid-1999.[18] Furthermore, during the final years of President Suharto's New Order government, Yogyakarta was being sidelined.[19] By 1994 local artists noticed that Taman Budaya in Surakarta was getting more funding and more press prioritization at national level. The local airport at Surakarta was revamped to give it international status, and opened in 1996 to flights to and from Singapore. The effect of this on Yogya 'was not yet felt', nor had talk five years before of bringing overseas charters to its own airport come to anything.[20] Only one of five

---

16. The national target for Repelita VI (1994/5–1998/9) was 6.5 million overseas tourists spending US$9 billion, an annual increase of 18.6 per cent, and 84.2 million domestic tourists, spending Rp9 trillion, generating 900,000 new jobs (*Indonesia* 1999: 66, 174). For the first six months of 1998, there were only 1.4 million overseas visitors when the annual target was 4.6 million (ibid.: 176).

17. The rate of growth had fallen from 2.11 per cent in 1996 to minus 71.63 per cent in 1998 (*Statistik Parsenibud 1998*, 1999: 2). Total income from tourism had dropped from Rp32,776,277,900 in 1996 to Rp22,696,380,121 in 1997 to Rp13,108,957,798 in 1998 (ibid.: 80). Ironically, by 1999, the provision of star accommodation in the Province for conference and convention tourism, which had been targeted as a growth area in 1994, had risen from twenty-two hotels in 1994 to thirty-eight in 1998, from a capacity of 2,264 rooms to one of 3,783 (ibid.: 23).

18. This seemed to be improving again during August 1999, although this is high season and also includes independence celebrations, although this year Yogya's city and provincial governments did not provide the usual 'happy stages' (*panggung gembira*) for public entertainment on 17 August.

19. Dahles suggests that Yogyakarta was the being developed as a 'regional "peak" culture' (2001: 86-87) although elsewhere she says that Central Java was (2001: 220).

20. In 1993 visitors from Taiwan had been the most numerous (nearly 60,000, a massive increase since 8,088 visitors in 1989) due to new air links, closely followed by Japan (42,084) and the Netherlands (39,904) (*Statistik Parpostel 1993*: 5). In 1998 the Dutch (12,520) headed the list of overseas visitors, a deviation of minus 63.56 per cent (*Statistik Parsenibud 1998*, 1999: 3). Following a failure of the Taiwan market in 1994 the Chinese market was being developed (Pak Slamet Sukardjo 19/9/94). By 2006, international flights from Singapore were landing at Yogyakarta.

Indonesian airlines which merged Garuda and Merpati had survived the economic crisis. Indeed, domestic air traffic at Yogya had dropped drastically, partly due to the new daytime 'Argo-Wilis' train which ran daily between Bandung and Surabaya, complete with airline-style meals, video screenings and armed security guards.

By mid-1999, government officials in Yogya were getting to grips with the impacts of the administrative restructuring of culture and tourism. Close collaborations between all the offices handling culture was expected. For instance, Tourism, Arts and Culture had recently organized three horse dance (*jathilan*) festivals, and Education and Culture had selected the groups. At the Dinas office of Education and Culture (Depdikbud), the new 'Custom and Art' (Adat dan Kesenian) section, headed by Pak Pangarsobroto, was for 'basic development'.[21] In the newly structured Department of Tourism, Arts and Culture, the 'Tourism' section was to promote agrarian, industrial and nature or eco-tourism, and to maintain convention tourism, while 'Arts and Culture' was *to sell* arts and culture to tourists with the support of outside organizations such as the Arts Council, as well as helping artists make a living and assisting the process of professionalization:

> We're trying to help performers so they can keep going – for example we help with the musicians' clothes, at Pudjokusuman and Sonobudaya [an arts venue]. We've helped *ketoprak* PS Bayu with new costumes, to give them a fighting spirit.[22]

This central 'Tourism' section was supposed to work with the regional Tourism office to promote Yogyakarta elsewhere in Indonesia and overseas:

> In June (1999) we promoted Yogya at the Bali Travel Mart – I can't remember with what … small groups have gone to Taiwan, Hong Kong, Bangkok, Germany, Holland, Spain. But there are no current plans to go overseas because of the economic crisis (*krismon*).

Apart from the proliferation of cultural policy administrators, the previous fractures between central- and provincial- level offices also continued to produce confusion and reduplication in the administration of tourism. Interviews with managers in the new central Department of Tourism, Arts and Culture revealed that lines of fracture were producing divergence between policy and practice. Their office was situated away from the other offices outside the city on the road towards the airport, so collaboration was no simple matter. In the meantime, nobody had anything positive to say about the new arrangements. This office had produced a very

---

21. The two other new sections of Dinas Depdikbud were 'Museums', responsible for documentation and conservation, including a project from 1998 to conserve a number of court buildings (Sĕkar Kĕdhaton, Gĕdhong Jĕne and Srimanganti), and 'Administration and Support' (Pak Priyo Mustika, head of 'Museums', 23/8/99).
22. Interviews with Pak Supriyanto (Tourism) and Pak Djadjusman (Publications) (5/8/99), and Pak M. Lakoni (Arts and Culture) (11/8/99), *Kanwil Deparsenibud DIY*.

professional glossy brochure with a 3-D map of Yogya and extensive tourism information in reasonable English. The regional office had also produced a brochure, with notes in Indonesian on local attractions, but without a map. I admired both brochures, but as I did so, complaints were voiced about the regional office going ahead and organizing things without coordinating with the central sector. One manager said that he was hoping to overcome this sort of problem by developing the use of the internet, although longer-established technological innovations, such as the telephone, had not done much to improve communications.

Private Patrons: the Court

Apart from state institutions, Yogyakarta's tourist industry incorporates all sectors of society, from the Sultan down to the smallest *kampung* entrepreneur.[23] They work for their own interests, but also cooperate with state administrators on committees created for particular policies and events.

The Sultan controls a traditional client base, but the court is a client of the state, which is itself also administered by many who are court kin. This court network has been more active in the Department of Education and Culture than in the Department of Tourism. A number of the Sultan's brothers were involved in private tourism enterprises and sat on committees, but the Sultan's kin were less involved in this state sector, which was more the domain of the Pakualaman family.[24] The move of culture into the new Department of Tourism and Culture is likely to have some effect on this overlap in the future, and will increase the role of tourism as a patron of culture. The overlap between state and court in organizing cultural events in Yogyakarta does not preclude a conflict of interests, as is evident from the tenth Sultan's view of the state's patronage of the court.

As we know, court dancing belongs to the domain of *adiluhung*, a high and noble activity which ideally is above commerce and cannot be exchanged for money. This ideal ignores the reality of the close connection between court performance and tourism during the ninth Sultan's reign. The court tourist office had been established in 1969, and in 1973 Hamĕngkubuwana IX had revived court performance to attract local and international tourists to the court. When he sent court dancers to tour Europe in 1975, the Jakarta-based car company PT Astra provided some of the finance (Hadi 1988: 90). In 1987 the court sold tickets to tourists for court performances for Hamĕngkubuwana IX's birthday. And in 1988, Happy Suryajaya, the wife of Astra's Chinese-Indonesian director, who studied Surakarta style dance in Jakarta and claimed to be driven by the spirit of Ratu Kidul to protect Javanese dance,

---

23. Dahles uses an analytical contrast between 'official' street-side tourist enterprises and 'unofficial' *kampung* business (2001: 94), despite being 'artificial boundaries' cross-cut by social ties that are stronger than government regulations (2001: 25). The princely residences hosting tourist performances are mostly in *kampung*s, as, it could be argued, is the court.

24. In 1989 Sri (Paduka) Pakualam XI, then Governor of Yogyakarta, was still in charge of Yayasan Lara Jonggrang which ran the Ramayana Ballet at Prambanan, assisted by his daughter Rĕtno Diwayani, whose husband was head of the Natour travel bureau at the Garuda Hotel; his son, Prince Gondokusumo, worked in the regional Tourism office.

was a leading patron of a cultural mission, also funded by two hundred Japanese business sponsors, which took dancers, musicians and singers from all four Central Javanese courts on a concert tour to Tokyo.[25]

The commercial dimension of court activities of the previous thirty years was largely ignored until the eldest son of the ninth Sultan, K.G.P.H. Mangkubumi, became Sultan Hamĕngkubuwana X on 7 March 1989. The financial sponsorship for the accession provided by about thirty corporations, including PT Astra, BMW, Coca-Cola and Mitsubishi, was alleged to be Rp300 million. Many spoke of a Jakarta take-over, and accused the court of selling out.[26] Nonetheless, Prince Mangkubumi was transformed from an Indonesian businessman and *haji* into a Javanese sultan, the first ever to have made the pilgrimage to Mecca, with the legitimacy to maintain the heirlooms of his father's dynasty. He moved into the court with his wife and five daughters, dissipating scepticism about his fittingness to follow his father among many of Yogya's elite and media: as one aristocratic legal professional said, 'Yogya's culture is now fully restored' (Pak Maharto 8/3/89).[27] Others, however, insisted that the sultanate had only been sustained 'because the tourists like it if Yogya has a king'. Indeed, the court (like the other Central Javanese courts) was reputedly receiving a regular annual subsidy of up to Rp1 million in its capacity as 'a site of culture' (*cagar budaya* I.), and the government had also subsidized extensive renovations of sections of the court open to tourists, as well as the Widyakusuman library (completed in 1996 except for air-conditioning) and the 'western court', home to the new Sultan.[28] The accession of the new Sultan brought into the open the issue of how to maintain court practice as *adiluhung,* above the commercial sphere, and its relationship to the state. There were signs that the court was keen to control tourism as it had once controlled excellence and ideas of superior skill, but when a money changer said that

---

25. The late film director, Ami Priyono, who documented the tenth Sultan's accession (20/2/89), described Mrs Suryajaya as 'an Irish among Sicilians': the self-styled inclusivity of the Javanese courts has not extended to Chinese settlers, with a few notable exceptions. During the tour Happy danced the role of Trijatha in the Ramayana and one of the leads in *Bĕdhaya Durodasih*. This collaboration combined court styles along gender lines; in the Ramayana fragment men danced in Yogyakarta style, women in Surakarta style (Pak Pardjan pers.comm. 1999). This controversial experiment originated with Sulistyo, a leading Jakarta dancer with ties to the Kasunanan and the Ministry of Tourism (and also to Mrs Suryajaya as her teacher), and has (so far) been a one-off. Happy Suryajaya died not long after the tour (M. Heins, pers. comm. Nov. 2005).

26. See further Hughes-Freeland (1991a: 144–46). The organizers of the accession planners were probably anxious to avoid the commercialization of the accession of K.G.P.H. Mangkunagara IX in 1988, where Rp10,000 bought the media the right to film or photograph (Pak Narno, filmmaker, pers. comm. March 1989).

27. He cited the 1945 Ordinance, Article 18, which states the ninth Sultan and his descendents should govern the Province, so any alteration would be a breach of the Indonesian constitution. The ninth Sultan apparently said that his successor as governor could be decided later (Atmaksumah 1982: 66, 123).

28. This was reported as Rp1,256,351,000, another two sums of Rp35,537,000 and Rp47,675.000 would be contributed to the accession (*Kedaulatan Rakyat* 24/2/89).

the court was 'going with modernity, going with the state' (*ikut modern, ikut pemerintah*), I began to wonder whether the institution would become a brand, despite the continuing kinship structures associated with the court, or whether it would maintain itself as a counter-space (in De Certeau's sense) to the marketplace. These issues dominated previous concerns about the relevance of Javanese style classical dance for the younger generations from the early 1980s, although these were still discussed.

Haměngkubuwana X has attempted to deal with these challenges to the legacy of his father in several ways. His speech writer, an East Javanese businessman married to a daughter of a court dance dynasty, invoked one of Joged Mataram's guiding principles of 'not turning back' (*ora mingkuh*) and the title of a book celebrating the ninth Sultan's seventieth birthday, 'A Throne for the People' (*Tahta untuk Rakyat* I.), a platform which the new Sultan set out in his accession speech:

> I promise faithfully to secure *the throne for the people* for the preservation and well-being of the sociocultural life of the people. With such a resolution, the aspiration to make the court a centre of cultural events and development in the harmonious spirit of *adiluhung* tradition with the support of every faction will hopefully be achieved. As a member of the succeeding generation, I will *not turn back* from the implementation of the revolutionary ethos of the founder of the court, Prince Mangkubumi.[29]

As well as the controversy about commercial sponsorship in general, there had been criticisms of the stylistic details of the accession, particularly of the Sultan producing his speech out of his pocket instead of having taking it from a tray presented to him by a kneeling retainer, but overall it was a successful initiation. It was less straightforward for the tenth Sultan to put into practice his father's legacy during the months to come.

The opening of the first court Sĕkaten exhibition (29/9/89) since the death of Haměngkubuwana IX was rather subdued. A Pagĕlaran employee said that people had liked the ninth Sultan, 'And now he's dead'. A man selling toy windmills said: 'Only the roots are left; the authentic ones have all died' – a metaphor which illustrates the importance of regeneration in Javanese thinking. This opening turned out to have been quiet because people were waiting for the 'new dates' when salaries are paid, so that they could afford the entrance fees of Rp500 and to buy treats from the many stalls. Invitations to the court's performance to open Sĕkaten were limited to about fifty of the Sultan and Governor's close family members. They watched *bĕksan golek Menak* and a *wayang wong* Ramayana fragment, but no *bĕdhaya*. By contrast, the close of the week of Sĕkati *gamĕlans* playing at the Great Mosque (11/9/89) was quite different from before, because the Sultan himself threw the traditional *udhik-udhik* offerings, consisting of grains of yellow rice and Rp50 and Rp100 coins, over the *gamĕlans* on his way to the mosque. I caught a glimpse of him leaving the mosque

---

29. *Kedaulatan Rakyat (Bonus)*, 8 March 1989, p. 1, translated from the Indonesian by the author.

after the religious teachings (*pengajian*) under his golden parasol, before the *gamĕlan*s were packed up to be taken back to the court and the public was scrabbling around to collect the coins.

Several months later, on the Sultan's forty-third birthday (*wiyosan dalĕm*) on 2 December 1989, there were two dances. *Bĕdhaya Hĕrjuna Wiwaha* had a new 'traditional' staging: a procession with a lamp, the text (*kandha*), and the choreographer, Rama Sas, under a parasol, followed by the *bĕdhaya*s escorted by a group of armed women retainers (*kĕparak*). I had never seen anything like this in the early 1980s. The dance itself included more fights than usual, with three simultaneous duels at one point. It lasted about 75 minutes, rather than the usual 90, but was longer than many *bĕdhaya* dances. The *Bĕksan Lawung Agĕng/Gagah* dance, which included 'veteran' performers like Pak Pardjan, was particularly spirited (Figure 7.1). It held the audience's attention and, unusually, received enthusiastic applause. Although the atmosphere at the start had been rather stiff and official, this event seemed to reassure those present that there could be continuity without a sell-out, despite the change of sultan.

The Sultan quickly set to work to preserve court culture and promote tourism, as his father had done. His ambassadorial responsibilities at home and overseas led to in an increase of dance performances in the court to entertain guests, such as their Royal Highnesses Prince Charles and Princess Diana, who were received in November 1989 in the Srimanganti pavilion in the court. Guests were normally treated to the *Lawung* dance and a *Bĕksan* duel between two women mounted on eagles in the *golek Menak* style. The only grand performances of *golek Menak* after 1989 were fragments performed at Court Festivals; the form relied on developments by members of

Figure 7.1 *Bĕksan Lawung*, Pagĕlaran, 1989

Mardawa Budaya and Siswa Among Bĕksa. The Sultan also played his part in cultural politics overseas, and was looking forward to taking a group of sixty-two 'court dancers' to the USA for the Indonesian-American Cooperation (KIAS), a commercial promotion of Indonesia in 1990–91. This project was part of Soesilo Soedarman's tourist policies, which included the court's participation in the Court Festival and other schemes to increase the number of fixed features in the calendar of events for tourists.

In 1989 the Sultan upgraded the Sunday morning practices into concerts to make dancing in the court more attractive to both tourists and performers. There were no plans in the court to provide luncheons with performances, as recently introduced by the Kasunanan in Surakarta, and which lasted for a few years. From 3 December 1989, a new 'rota' in the court's Bangsal Kĕsatriyan was initiated. Siswa Among Bĕksa performed a Ramayana *wayang wong* fragment with full costume and make-up, for which the association was paid Rp150,000, apparently out of the Sultan's own pocket.[30] Before the dance performance there was a ceremony, attended by key cultural players, although the chairs reserved for the Sultan and his wife remained empty.[31] Local practice still took precedence over commercial tourist-pleasing. Gusti Yudhaningrat, head of the court Arts Section as well working as a civil servant, made a speech structured into sections announced as 'a', 'b', 'c' etc. His uncle, G.B.P.H. Puger, then spoke about the need to increase Yogya-style dance and its appreciation. These orations prompted several Dutch tourists to leave, complaining vociferously about 'all the men talking'. After the speeches came the *sĕlamatan*, or ritual sharing of rice. After a religious court official (*mutihan*) had recited the *Al-Fatiyah* sura from the Qur'an, R.M Dinusatama (head of Siswa Among Bĕksa) gave a knife to G.B.P.H. Puger who cut the *tumpĕng* (rice cone) on a table at the centre of the *pĕndhapa*. Everyone applauded, gratefully. Siswa Among Bĕksa performed their normal Ramayana, which lasted till one o'clock, despite the new one-hour rule.

There had always been problems with performances in the Bangsal Kĕsatriyaan. There was no clearly designated space for the audience, and tourists usually blocked the entrance and exits of the dancers. By December 1990, these concerts had been moved to the Bangsal Srimanganti, a larger hall which allowed an area to be defined for the audience. I saw part of Mardawa Budaya's performance here, on 11 September 1994. There was a *srimpi*, *klana*, and two other dances scheduled. The show lasted for 60 minutes, which allowed only 15 minutes for each dance. I watched for a while, but went on to the Bangsal Kĕsatriyan, and nostalgically watched *Bĕksan Lawung Agĕng*, which was being rehearsed for a court banquet in honour of a group of parachutists.

---

30. Mbak Kadar (3/12/89). The other participants were Suryakĕncana, Mardawa Budaya, Kridha Mardawa (shadow play), and SMKI.
31. Sitting at tables on the north side of the pavilion were Hamĕngkubuwana IX's wives, the head of Depdikbud, Princes Puger, Yudhaningrat and Prabukusumo, Prof. Dr. R.M. Soedarsono, B.R.Ay. Prabuningrat, Bu Yuda and other senior women aristocrats; behind them were the younger women aristocrats and dance teachers from participating groups, including Mbak Kadar and Mbak Tiyah (wife of Rama Sas).

These old-style training sessions continued to run parallel to the tourist concerts, and a daily *gamělan* practice had also been introduced.[32]

By 1999 the number of regular performance events in the court had increased. Performance groups from across the Province were being invited to perform in the court, a policy that was maintained despite the fall in tourist numbers. In August 1999 the 'Court Daily Program' was as follows:

Sun	11–12	Dance rehearsal in Kěsatriyan /Javanese dance in Srimanganti
Mon	10–12	Javanese music
Tues	10–12	ditto
Weds	9–12	*Wayang golek* ('wooden puppet')
Thurs	10–12	Javanese music and dance [= Sunday rota, new since 1994]
Fri	10–11.30	*Macapat* (singing)
Sat	9–1	*Wayang kulit*

The number of visitors was consistently high with seasonal fluctuations between overseas and domestic tourists (Table 7.2 and 7.5). In 1989 there were seventy full-time guides and three helpers paid on a daily basis; *abdidalěm*s also received their monthly honorarium. The entrance fee was Rp250 for Indonesians and Rp500 for foreigners. By 1994 there were eighty full-time guides. Overseas tourists paid Rp1,500 and domestic ones Rp500. By 1999 overseas tourists paid Rp3,000 and Rp500 for a photo permit – and court guides were wearing new sateen shirts in a deep gold shade. It has been claimed that Indonesian tourists prefer 'Disneyfied' attractions, and that the Indonesian government has failed to recognize the postmodern breakdown between high and low culture (Dhales 2001: 224, 227). Nonetheless, during the 1990s, the court remained Yogyakarta's top attraction for overseas tourists after Borobudur and Prambanan temples, and sixth favourite for domestic tourists after Parangtritis, Prambanan, the zoo, beaches in Gunung Kidul, and the Yogya Kembali monument (Tables 7.3 and 7.4).[33]

---

32. New to the rota were troupes from the Teachers Training College, Gadjah Mada University, and the Institute of Indonesian Arts (ISI), but only Siswa Among Běksa performed *běhaya* dances, choreographed to last one hour (R.M. Dinusatama 30/8/94).

33. *Statistik Pariwisata, Seni dan Budaya* (henceforth *Parsenibud*) 1998, 1999: 66-67; these figures exclude Borobudur in Central Java. Over one million domestic tourists visited Parangtritis beach annually from 1989 to 1997, down to 921,163 in 1998 (*Statistik Parpostel 1993*, 1994: table 17; *Statistik Parsenibud 1998*, 1999: 67); over one million visitors, mostly domestic, went in 1990 and 1991 to the recently opened Yogya Kembali monument and (1990–92) to Borobudur (*Statistik Parpostel 1993*, 1994: 61, 65). Within the DIY, Prambanan was the top overseas destination; visits of domestic and overseas tourists from 1990 to 1992 ranged from 606,534 to 922,500 (*Statistik Parpostel 1993*, 1994: 66). Annual visits 1994–97 to Yogya Kembali, Borobudur and Prambanan had risen to over 500,000, 2 million and 1 million, but fell in 1998 to 1,388,396, 290,434 and 646,396 respectively (*Statistik Parsenibud 1998*, 1999: 50, 54, 55)

Table 7.2 *Visitors to the Sultan's Court, 1989–99**

Year	Overseas	Domestic	Total
1988	101,556	287,629	389,178
1989	120,126	280,887	401,013
1990	153,713	332,004	485,717
1991	167,132	276,785	443,917
1992	204,929	266,434	471,363
1993	205,619	297,357	502,976
1994	230,842	282,592	513,416
1995	211,590	347,922	559,512
1996	196,559	342,412	538,971
1997	158,288	311,084	469,372
1998	54,191	211,716	265,907
1999	51,149	261,729	312,878

* The sources are as follows: 1988, 1989, 1998 and 1999: monthly Court Tourist Office statistical records; 1990–93: *Statistik Pariwisata, Pos dan Telekomunikasi 1993*: 61; 1994–97: *Statistik Pariwisata Seni dan Budaya 1998*: 50.

Table 7.3 *Visitors to the Purawisata, 1994–98*[34]

Year	Overseas	Domestic	Total
1994	33,459	183,949	217,408
1995	38,207	170,163	208,370
1996	43,187	179,829	223,016
1997	38,505	201,202	239,707
1998	22,698	144,803	167,501

Table 7.4 *Visitors to the Ramayana Ballet, 1994–98*[35]

Year	Overseas	Domestic	Total
1994	28,488	3,790	32,278
1995	47,915	5,626	53,541
1996	31,141	5,869	37,010
1997	32,440	4,631	37,071
1998	8,160	3,489	11,649

Although the Sultan was living in the court, more buildings were being turned into museums:

> The old tea house (*Patehan*) has been turned into a porcelain and tea-making museum, but behind there is a big kettle for use in a new court event, the

---

34. *Statistik Pariwisata Seni dan Budaya 1998*, 1999: 62.
35. *Statistik Pariwisata Seni dan Budaya 1998*, 1999: 63.

Table 7.5 Court tourist visits by the month (Overseas/Domestic)

Month	1988		1989		1994		1999	
Jan	6820	9216	7283	18475	13789	24579	2415	13,450
Feb	7894	16855	9284	24712	23523	16565	2884	16,400
March	6808	10566	8746	16181	17560	3837	3241	26,817‡
April	7229	11078	7864	11547	14214	11952	3809	15,223
May	6866	11415	9645	20748	22754	17393	2800	18,700
June	6675	35916	8795	70998	20207	65342	3095	16,405
July	13255	21771	11713	13345	25464	15781	7032	38,656
Aug	14142	8181	16692	8603	28174	14247	8896	22,215
Sept	10036	17542	13354	12186	n/a	n/a	7463	16424
Oct	6076	11724	2369	15760	n/a	n/a	4056	43,549
Nov	7773	10073	9932	12843	n/a	n/a	2583	24,395
Dec	7982	133,319*	9297	57089†	n/a	n/a	2875	9,495
Total	101556	287629	120,126	280,887	230,824	282,592	51,149	261,729
Grand Total	**389178**		**401,013**		**513,416**		**312,878**	

* The death of the ninth Sultan had caused a dramatic increase in domestic tourists in the December 1988 holidays.

† The 1989 figures for December and the totals are from *Satistik Pariwisata, Pos dan Telekomunikasi DIY 1993*. The totals for 1994 are from *Satistik Pariwisata, Seni dan Budaya Propinsi Daerah Istimewa Yogyakarta 1998*: 50. Court statistics for Sept-Dec 1994 were not available.

‡ Domestic visits in 1999 increased as the school holidays coincided with the religious festivals Idul Adha in March, and Mauludan in July.

'sacred' tea ceremony, which has been done every day at 11.00 for two years. There are also the bat-occupied museum, the genealogy museum w/ paintings, the old museum with all the foreign gifts, the photo museum, and the sparkling new HB IX museum. This is next to the Widyabudaya library, an air-conditioned glass *pĕndhapa*-type structure. The glass is engraved with HB IX's insignia, and the roof is elaborately carved and painted in red and gold (rather coarsely compared to the other court *wulu*). It houses a number of carved statements and key documents about HB IX and Indonesia, and a historic round table. Other rooms display the remnants of HB IX's life: photos, gloves, boots, cameras, his photographs (in a 1950s USA photojournalism style), an impressive array of national and overseas medals and awards, scouting, football, and of course, guerrilla fighter trophies, and all kinds of dress: coronation, military, court, scouting uniform, circumcision costume, western formal dress, etc. Socks are sometimes draped in front of photos. There are photos of him with his mother and first wife, and of dances he 'created', but none with his father or his own children, an interesting lacuna, though there are Javanese versions of rag books from which his father gave him *bathik* identification lessons. The photos are captioned in Indonesian, but unfortunately few are dated. The golden throne and replicas of the royal attributes have been moved here from the old museum. The guide told me the museum cost around £570,000 (Rp2 billion). Surprisingly there are no *kĕris* displayed here either – these presumably have all been handed down to children, brothers, followers and friends – or remain in the Prabayĕksa with the other heirlooms. The number of court buildings turned into museums reduces the lived-in quality: now it feels more like the Kasunanan at Solo. Since the death of Hamĕngkubuwana IX's first three Yogya wives the *kĕputren* which used to house the sultan's wives and children has been empty;[36] there are no sons to live in the *kĕsatriyan*; in ten years, I wonder who'll still be living in the 'western court'? (Field notes 11/9/94)

The new Hamĕngkubuwana IX museum had been funded by the central government. It seemed that by accepting such funding, the Sultan would remain a client of the state and a curator rather than a creative force for change. He was in an invidious position, holding a position of power in his own region, but dependent on both on the Governor and Jakarta for his policies. This was summed up by his cousin, who then headed the Kanwil Arts Unit:

The future of the court would be fine as long as it adapts to the government's plans; there's a conflict over what kind of culture the court should represent. A private organization can work with overseas groups, but it has to go through government channels. The court is still a *Javanese* centre. The problem with the court is to make it a 'source of heirlooms' [*sumber pustaka*

---

36. I later discovered that a wife of Hamĕngkubuwana VIII was still living there at the time.

I.]. There's a shortage of knowledgeable staff, so the court needs to recruit people who are expert in culture. It's not a financial problem, but the court won't ask. All it needs is a letter from Haměngkubuwana X to do this – people would do it out of respect for the court'. (R.M. Dinusatama 30/8/94)

The state had defined the Sultan's role as 'cultural', not political. However, as he developed the court's appeal as a tourist object, in accord with government policy, and ruled over an exemplary centre of the Indonesian cultural project, the tenth Sultan had his own dream.[37] From the outset he consistently aimed to develop the court not just as a centre of *Javanese* culture and excellence but also of international art and culture, a resource to educate and inform the people of Yogyakarta. This was not the museum of Javanese heritage desired by Jakarta. When I raised this issue with the Sultan in 1994, he replied to my question about outside opposition as follows:

> No – but there are some people against – there's an argument: talking about Javanese culture, we have to distinguish between skin and content … whether I wear a jacket or a *kain* [court dress], that's just the skin, the content is important, it has universal dimensions that won't change, such as doing good and evil … Times are indeed changing, the important thing for us is to manage the changes well … . If the court is to become a cultural inheritance [*peninggalan kebudayaan* I.], I have the obligation to develop it, but for me this would be fatal as it would be the end of the court functioning as it should, and would not be valued by the public.

The Sultan's policies can be understood as his struggle for more political power within the nation state, but they would separate the notion of Javanese cultural excellence from court cultural traditions as they had become known since Indonesian independence (Hughes-Freeland 1993a: 102). In 1989 he was already extending the court's patronage to the international sphere, and spoke of bringing *into* the court overseas artists such as the symphony orchestra from Cologne which had played in the court's Srimanganti pavilion for invited guests the previous week. He was less interested in art forms than in developing opportunities for cosmopolitan patronage, such as his proposal to Australia for an Australian institute in Yogyakarta. While sharing the government's view of culture, he wanted to be an agent of change: a political actor, not a cipher or symbol. For nine years he struggled with Jakarta and the Provincial Governor, Sri Pakualam, to make this a reality, not always successfully. His plans to set up a cultural connection with the Japanese city of Kyoto and cultural links with Australia ran into difficulties in 1994 partly, it was

---

37. This analysis is based on three private interviews with H.R.H. Sultan Haměngkubuwana X in the western court (8/12/89 and 13/9/94), and in the governor's office at the Kěpatihan (26/8/99).

alleged, by Jakarta's strategic blockage of visas.[38] In 1994 he also continued to assert that court patronage of the performing arts should be for the people (*rakyat*) of Yogyakarta, not for domestic and international tourists. He wanted to help them appreciate overseas culture, open up their horizons, and to lead to innovations; for instance, in October an origami artist from Japan was coming to help kindergarten teachers. He still spoke of inviting ' Japanese, French (ballet), German (chamber music), Czech (opera), and Australian (music) artists' to the court, and since 1990 had been planning a new institution (*lembaga* I.) outside the court to liaise with PPPG,[39] and also to change the court into an institution. He anticipated major changes in the court during the next ten to twenty years.

The Sultan still patronized traditional court performances. When President Suharto conferred the posthumous title of National Hero on the ninth Sultan in 1990, the court produced its own event and text to celebrate this and also Haměngkubuwana X's birthday. The booklet included writings about the life of the ninth Sultan and the philosophical content, music and choreography (by Rama Sas) of *Bĕdhaya Sang Amurwabumi*, created in his memory. Haměngkubuwana X was attributed with deriving an appropriate philosophical concept of unification, and the booklet included a photograph of him in formal court dress and spectacles peering at a typewriter, ostensibly writing the story (Anon 1990: 70). This comes from the mediaeval *Pararaton* chronicle in which the adulterous Queen Ken Dedes (Prajnaparamita) achieves 'unification' with the murderer of her husband, her lover, Ken Angrok (Amurwabumi) who becomes king; these acts result in the prophesied destruction of the family of the man who made the murderous dagger (Zoetmulder 1974: 364). In the 1990 version, the marriage of Prajnaparamita and Amurwabumi symbolized the spirit of patriotism and the philosophy of leadership – a case of the ends justifying the means. The Sultan had also personally advised on the costumes, and attended performances to check on progress. In the first performance the dancers

---

38. Yogyakarta's Regional Government and Central Arts Unit give permission for overseas tours, but Jakarta can override these decisions. The government also interfered with the programme for the Surakartan Mangkunagaran court's concerts on their UK tour in 1989 (Hughes-Freeland 1989).

39. This prestigious Educational Training Centre (Pusat Pengembangan Penataran Guru) which was developed from the centre through Kanwil with the help of a British consultant in theatre design to train school teachers through Indonesia, opened on the slopes of mount Merapi in 1987. Courses take place monthly and end with a concert. Officials of Dinas Depdikbud claimed (5/9/89) it was 'the best of its kind in ASEAN'. Its activities include annual dance training sessions in which three representatives from each district learn a dance. In 1989 the dance was a 'new creation' by Ngatini from Bagong Kussudiardjo's Padepokan Dance Studio, 'The Cat' (*Si Meong*), which had won a dance competition in 1988. The representatives then hold sessions in their own district for primary school teachers, who then teach a dance to children. The children at different levels perform it during the arts week the following year, to show what they can do; there are prizes, but it is not a competition as such. In 1994 the head of PPPG was Pak Pardjan; when he retired, R.M. Dinusatama took over.

wore bridal outfits (*dhodhot* and *paes agung*), a return to the custom under Hamĕngkubuwana VII; the Sultan had also asked for the earpieces (*sumping*) to be made of cassava leaves instead of gilded leather. The dancers also had false eyelashes 'to make their eyes show up more', explained Mbak Kadar. This went against the former practice of not making court *bĕdhaya* dancers look attractive. Previously, the yellow *boreh* foundation and *jaitan* eye make-up aimed to make them all look alike, with inner beauty being reflected in the facial radiance (*pasĕmon*). The new make-up was evidence of a change in the representation of female beauty to a more visible one relying on modern make-up. It moved *bĕdhaya* into the domain of show, addressing the eye of the audience, rather than their inner selves (*batin*).

Bĕdhaya Amurwabumi was chosen to represent the court in a live broadcast to celebrate Indonesian Television's 37th birthday, 'A Present from the Regional Stations' (*Bingkisan (Kado) Setasiun Daerah*), on 10 August 1999. The broadcast was significant because although court performances are routinely videoed, it was unprecedented for the court itself to go to the television studio.[40] Formalized studio productions of various kinds of theatre and dance broadcast on the Balinese station of state television have been valued as exemplars of the performing arts (Hughes-Freeland 1998), but the *adiluhung* aspirations of court performance in Yogya had hitherto prevented it from being transformed into a regular media event as a means of ensuring its cultural survival.

The content of this broadcast reveals something of how the Yogya media chose to represent itself to the nation. After observing the preparations at the studio (Figure 7.2), I was able to get home from the television studio in time to watch the live

Figure 7.2 Dancers prepare for the television broadcast of *Bĕdhaya Amurwabumi*, 1999

40. As far as I am aware, the same dance had been announced for TVRI's 1990–91 New Year's Eve programme, but did not appear to be included.

broadcast with my family. Yogya's input was three dances: the first, *Gema Nusantara* by senior Yogyakarta choreographer Bagong Kussudiardjo (half-brother to Rama Sena and with family ties to the court), was performed by couples dressed in costumes from different provinces (Bali, East Indonesia, Kalimantan and Jakarta), followed by a long interview with Bagong; *Bĕdhaya Amurwabumi*, cut to 14 minutes; and a new choreography, 'The Unity in Diversity Dance' (*Tari Bhinneka Tunggal Eka*) performed by the Garis Sembilan ('Nine Lines') group, with many movements involving men and women putting their arms around each other's shoulders, quite against traditional norms: 'like rhythm exercises' declared a fellow viewer; 'This isn't Javanese anymore', retorted her mother. Back at the television station, Bu Yuda had referred scathingly to the 'shrunken' *bĕdhaya*, while G.B.P.H. Yudhaningrat, the prince in charge, had said 'Why bother? You can't even begin to feel it when it's so short.' The 'feeling' was not helped by a prerecorded speech by the sultan appearing in a small oval insert in the right-hand corner of the screen and talking about the ten Javanese principles of leadership. Others had described the trend to shrink and compress as 'a sign of the times' (Pak Pangarsobroto, as above). Cultural politics, not aesthetic appreciation, seemed to be the game, but with one of the most budding choreographers of the court style working in the training centre for multimedia, this appears to be the start of a new trend. Increased television viewing was explained to me as a way of saving money, and a factor shaping taste in musical styles. It also appeared to be producing a more intense attention span but with a need for greater stimulus. However, Didik Hadiprayitno (pers. comm. August 1999) made a case against a monopoly of influence, because television ends up boring people, and produces a reaction against it.

The relationship of the court to the state was to change, as were the Sultan's powers of negotiation within that relationship. In 1998, nearly ten years after becoming Sultan, he finally achieved his father's national role, and became Governor of the Special Region of Yogyakarta after the death of the previous incumbent, Prince Pakualam. This happened just before President Suharto resigned in May 1998, throwing Indonesian modernity into a new kind of identity crisis. Becoming Governor helped the Sultan to implement some of his plans for restructuring of the organization of court administration and the management of its 1,400 employees. In 1998 he doubled the salaries of court servants to a monthly wage of between Rp3,600 and Rp24,000, to bring these into line with the 'modern economy'. He was fulfilling both symbolic and executive roles in the political arena, and negotiating his traditional role in relation to his national one. His rhetoric insistently and consistently centred on how to keep the court alive to serve the people of Yogya, as it had long before the decentralizing policies of the two Presidents who succeeded Suharto, Habibie and Abdurrahman Wahid. So the Sultan was not simply strategizing in the context of suggestions that he might make a suitable presidential candidate in the 1999 elections.[41]

In my final interview with the Sultan in 1999, I asked him about his vision of the future role of the court, and the place of Javanese culture in Indonesia. Shortly before,

---

41. Hughes-Freeland (2007b). After this interview I asked a senior aide about the Sultan's presidential promise. 'Let him be Governor first', he replied.

at the opening of the Tamansiswa Cultural Seminar II, attended by powerful people from Jakarta including General Wiranto, the then head of the armed forces (ABRI), he had been reported as saying that the Javanese dominance which had kept Indonesia's cultural pluralism hidden for thirty years (referring to Suharto's New Order regime) was a factor which increased risk of social conflict, along with the economic situation, and political and religious divisions and conflicts.[42] He explained that the numerical dominance of Javanese people in Indonesia is generating conflict, and that there needs to be a cultural counterbalance. One way of doing this is to use the court as a cultural centre, rather than just a museum of Javanese culture; to maintain traditions but to develop an appreciation of art beyond the classical:

> I want the court to be a living asset, not just an inheritance. There are still dance rehearsals, and also Yogya style dances by Bagong. The court subsidizes the different groups, and more come in from the *kecamatan* (sub-districts) now. People feel proud to have performed in the court. This is the 'format' [sic] we're using to look after the court ... In the court I've done *ketoprak* ... wedding clothes and make-up from all over Indonesia at the Pagělaran ... In 1996, I put on a 'people's cultural show' [*gelar budaya Rakyat*] with *ketoprak*, music, rock, drama on the *alun-alun*.[43] I think that in the court we shouldn't just see *tari klasik*, but the court has to patronize other kinds of contemporary art activities and so on. Why? Because these are produced by the people, no way can the court produce those things. But it can provide facilities and patronize [*mendukung*] and support them. Because of globalization, the Yogya public needs to know classical, music, drama, ethnic, and it also needs to appreciate things from outside Indonesia ...

In addition to extending patronage to international performance, the Sultan had been including other forms of local art. The most dramatic example of this was his commission to Bagong Kussudiardjo to choreograph a dance drama for his birthday in September 1996, instead of a *bědhaya* and *wayang wong* which had normally been performed on such occasions since the reign of the eighth Sultan. The result was *Sang Aji* ('The King'), costing Rp20 million.[44] Bagong's '*kreasi baru*' had once stood for incomprehensibility and a threat to tradition; now his work was 'Yogya style dance'. Several months later, on 13–14 December 1996, a 'Festival of *Wayang Wong* in the Yogya Court Style' was held at the Kěpatihan under the same combined patronage of Dinas PDK, local government and Kridha Mardawa that had produced the *golek Menak* project in 1989. Performances were by Suryakěncana, the Teacher's Training College, Siswa Among Běksa, Mardawa Budaya and the Secondary School of Indonesian Arts (*Bernas* 10/12/96), but not the Indonesian Institute of Arts (ISI). This suggested a new balance, with 'traditional' court culture being patronized in conjunction with the local government offices, and new choreographies being patronized by the court. As an

---

42. *Kedaulatan Rakyat* 20/7/99, editorial p. 6.
43. This was for his first eight years (*sěwindu*) of rule (Hatley 2004. 83).
44. *Bernas* 27/9/96; *Kompas* 30/9/96.

indication of this trend, on 20 May 1998, as the national political crisis was coming to a head, the Sultan sponsored a huge performance that included modern theatre by local actors, mime artists and so forth, at the request of local artists, attracting an audience of one million people (Didik Hadiprayitno 12/8/99).

The extension of court patronage to a wider range of performance has broken down the distinction between court dance, contenders for classical status, popular and folk performance, and beyond. These innovations included the practice of hosting events that displayed 'traditional' wedding make-up and costumes, in collaboration with Martha Tilaar's cosmetic company, Sari Ayu ('Essence of Beauty'), exemplified by the fifth meeting (*Rakemas* V) of the Association for Indonesian Bridal Make-up (Himpunan Rias Pengantin Indonesia, rejoicing in the acronym 'HARPI'). It had included a procession of horse-drawn carriages bearing eighteen bridal couples to the court and a ten-minute *golek Menak* 'bird' dance for the participants of a 'Seminar on Bridal Make-up' (*Kedaulatan Rakyat* 4/8/99, 5/8/99). In his opening speech the Sultan referred to the court as 'a cultural centre that grows and is grown from and by the people to open up the secrets of an *adiluhung* [high and noble] cultural inheritance, namely the art of make-up [*seni paes*]' (*Kedaulatan Rakyat* 8/8/05: 8).

Writing about the inclusion of fashion in the 1994 Court Festival (Hughes-Freeland 1997a), I had suggested that *adiluhung* and 'art' do not mean the same thing. By bringing the ethos of business and corporations into the court as explicitly as these activities do, the cultural values represented by the notion of *adiluhung* risk becoming cosmetic in more than a literal sense. Given his characterization of bridal make-up as *adiluhung*, I was surprised to hear the Sultan's response when I asked if *adiluhung* was still a relevant concept:

> I think it is relative. The word is only used to criticize or to tie, wherever people are, to value their own culture. *Adiluhung* is only self-arrogance … But there's no use for it if there's the appreciation I've just described … In the interaction between generations, there must be changes, in information and technology. What matters is the way the changes are connected.

This response links to his repeated statement of the need for 'transformation and transparency'. The latter had been a New Order slogan, but there seemed to be more at issue now.

The Sultan was critical of bureaucrats who don't understand the arts or the needs of artists, and had his own ideas for developing facilities appropriate for encouraging appreciation, such as taking festivals like the Sendratari Festival, normally held at the Kěpatihan, to the *pěndhapa*s and *alun-alun* of the subdistricts (*kecamatan*):

> This will encourage the artists to be creative. It's been an elite setting for fifteen years, and the audience has been made up of family members of the dancers, not the public. But it's important for the public to get a chance to appreciate the creativity of artists, and to learn to discriminate between a good and bad dancer, a good and bad painting. Otherwise we won't be able to appraise creativity.

Display and the spectacular have long been part of something more complex and numinous in court practices. One wonders whether the 'auratic', in Walter Benjamin's sense, can survive the modernization of the court necessary to keep it alive. The Sultan was managing to balance the charismatic aspects of his role with the demands of bureaucracy and post-Suharto politics. Whether this would be feasible as he implemented his vision for the new role of the court as patron of the arts remained to be seen.

Other Private Patrons of Court Dance

As the court extended its patronage to non-court performance, the patronage of court dance as 'classical performance' continued outside the court. Since the dance performances for paying audiences started at Prambanan in the 1960s, hotels in Yogyakarta have been producing classical dance shows, mostly *sendrataris* enacting scenes from the Ramayana. These were usually performed not in Yogya style but Surakarta style, for practical reasons, as managers in hotels and travel bureaux explained:

> Mostly we have Solo [Surakarta] style – I get the impression from tour leaders that people like it better than Yogya. In Yogya style we have *Marmaya-Marmadi* [a *golek Menak* duet], *Golek Sulandayung*, and sometimes Ramayana ... A *big* problem with Yogya is the cost of the costume. The Yogya style crown for Lesmana [in the Ramayana] costs Rp55,000, while the Solo one is Rp15,000.'[45]

The Tri Murti 'covered' theatre at Prambanan, subsidized by the Ministry of Tourism, produced one Yogya-style performance, by Siswa Among Běksa or Suryakěncana, for every six Surakarta style ones (Figure 7.3). This was allegedly due to the problem of persuading dancers to come from Yogya and the lack of travel expenses. After 1999 a minibus was provided, but there were still more Surakarta style performances. The theatre's director also criticized Yogya dancers performing in Surakarta style for their tendency to slip back into Yogya style in fights. Between 1989 and 1994 the situation had improved because more dancers were available from the Indonesian Institute of Arts (ISI), but there was still competition from the hotels; this was a good reason to encourage hotels to diversify and reduce the number of Ramayana performances.[46]

Within metropolitan Yogya during the 1980s, only MB/PBN at the Pudjokusuman and the court gave regular performances of Yogya style *court* dance for tourists. This provided further impetus for entrepreneurship among other Yogyakarta style dance associations. The activities of the Suryakěncana and Siswa Among Běksa are indicative of the changes in court dance patronage outside the court itself.

Suryakěncana had performed in a number of hotels as early as 1983, and continued to accept sporadic commissions. In 1989 the association agreed a one-year

---

45. Pak Cuk Sutoyo, PR Manager in charge of dancing, Ambarukmo Palace Hotel (2/12/89).
46. Pak L. Guntur Purnomo Adi (November 1989 and January 1994).

contract with Prince Joyokusumo, to provide 'pure Yogya style' performances for dinner dance packages (*andrawina*) in his traditional residence close to the court. These packages were highly priced and aimed at luxury small-group tours.[47] The highly trained and experienced dancers performed a series of abbreviated dances from the court repertoire: the *golek* dance, and *wayang wong* or *golek Menak* fighting dances. Suryakĕncana's directors, Mbak Kadar and Mas Ywandjono, kept me informed of developments and often invited me to watch the show from backstage, so I was able to observe how the tourist audience shaped the way dance was performed. During a performance of the *golek Menak* dance 'Adaninggar and Rĕngganis Rĕtna Dewaningsih', I noticed Mas Ywan wincing. He explained that the dialogue was coming out backwards. The foreign audience was, of course, oblivious to this. However, within a month the troupe had decided to cut all dialogue from these fighting dances. This is one example of a form being adapted to its audience, a process driven by the relationship of production to reception, not by government directives. Indeed, the court dance network perceived state interference at the level of tourist marketing, not control of the forms. After the changes, the aesthetic result was the dance-only model exemplified by Javanese-style *sendratari*.

Figure 7.3 Surakarta style Ramayana, Tri Murti Arts Hall, Prambanan, 1994

---

47. Sources varied on the cost per head, from US$6.50 (for 'lunch') to Rp4,000, with the tour agency taking 10 per cent.

Siswa Among Bĕksa had a different experience of engaging with tourism. The association was kept busy through R.M. Dinusatama's government job as head of the central Arts Unit. It also had the patronage of Pak Probosutejo, half-brother of President Suharto and a hugely wealthy (and somewhat notorious) businessman from Jakarta, who had bought and restored the Ngabean residence in 1983. The Yogya elite tended not to close ranks against such arrivistes because of the welcome financial patronage. For instance, it was rumoured that the Rp4.5 million expense of replacing the association's two *garudha* birds, their plumage depleted by years of staged battles, had been met by an unidentified general, and that Pak Probosutejo had given them Rp5 million. His aide began to attend Siswa Among Bĕksa rehearsals and video-taped performances. The association then started to run a course at the newly restored Ngabean as well as rehearsing twice weekly at their usual charming, if slightly shabby, venue down the road at the Purwadiningratan residence. They also performed for him on special occasions, such as the inauguration in 1987 of his private university, situated in a residence to the west of the south square.

Siswa Among Bĕksa's first brush with tourism was in 1984 when a group of travel bureaux organized themselves under the name of the 'Yogyakarta Visitors' Bureau' (Grehadika Yogyakarta Pariwisata, or GYP) to arrange performances for tourists (see further Kam 1986). The association had a one-year contract to provide two performances a week, one each at the Purwadiningratan and Ngabean. This arrangement stopped after a year: 'we were broke, materially and non-materially … The tourist offices think too much of themselves and not enough of art' (R.M. Dinusatama 27/11/89). GYP's ongoing arrangement with the Pudjokusuman had also ended by 1994. By 1989 Siswa Among Bĕksa was performing at commercial dinner- dance packages at the Ngabean, charging the travel bureau Rp325,000 or Rp800,000 for a special package.[48]

During the 1990s Probosutejo's patronage of Siswa Among Bĕksa continued. The association had training and rehearsals twice a week in the Kanĕman (the new name for the Purwadiningratan), and weekly courses at the patron's house, as well as its regular slot in the court's Sunday rota. It also participated in the 1990 Court Festival, and in the following month gave twenty-four performances. By the end of 1991, Rama Dinu's government role led to it performing two-hour-long Ramayanas three times a week at the Arts Unit's *pĕndhapa* at Notoprajan. In 1992, in collaboration with G. K.R.Ayu Anom in the Kanĕman, Siswa Among Bĕksa started dinner-dance packages for chartered tours aimed at overseas tourists. I attended one of these.

Two groups from Holland and Singapore arrived on a tour bus ('Van Ginkel'). At 7.30 there was a 12 minute-long *Golek Pamularsih*, while the guests ate snacks. Dinner was served in the *paringgitan*, while a Ramayana (lasting 45 minutes) was performed in the *pĕndhapa* opposite. There were 11 dancers, 17 musicians, 2 male and 2 female singers: 33 people, with the *golek* dancer. The package cost US$12 per person excluding alcohol, with a minimum of 15 people, max not limited. Janto [my research assistant] and I

---

48. Pak Hereman, Musi holidays, Garuda Hotel (2/11/89).

sat behind, in front of the dressing rooms, with Rama Dinu and the other SAB veterans; there was no question of watching – unusually for SAB, it felt rather awkward, that special quality of Javanese awkwardness … But we were able to interrupt their chat for some conversation. They do other fighting dances, including the bird dance, and Lawung. Earlier that day Rama Dinu had said that dancers were always from SAB, the wage was Rp3,000 a person, and the profit went to the travel bureau: 'Yes, artists are exploited'. SAB also cater for tours at the Ngabean, and gets a flat fee of Rp1 million, or Rp15,000 a person [the dancers said Rp5,000]; the 1989 charge per head was US$10. The association maintained its patronage of *bĕdhaya*, and were the only troupe to perform it in the court, for a full one hour. They had performed *Bĕdhaya Tunjunganom* in 1992 at their 40th anniversary concert, and again at the 1994 Court Festival, but at their anniversary in 1994 [unusually], they had produced a night-long shadow play. The Min-On group sponsored a tour of Japan in 1995, and they had other activities planned in USA and Germany. Meanwhile male numbers are still low for the courses, and they try to get them to do competitions as an incentive. (Field notes, edited, 30/9/94)

Meanwhile, the Suryakĕncana association had been performing regularly at the Joyokusuman for nearly two years. They had also started to perform for local government guests hosted by Pak Probosutejo at the Ngabean. I noted Mbak Kadar's answer to my question whether Suryakĕncana planned to start their own dinner-dance packages at the Suryadiningratan:

There's a plan, but we'd have to do it as a family. We need capital. Travel bureaux don't help with that … the Kanĕman cost a lot to restore, but the house was ok so they could start performances and cover costs as they went. Here, the *pĕndhapa*'s too old, it would need replacing. If we did dinner, we wouldn't change things – except the bathroom. But the *pĕndhapa* floor would need doing.' Mbak Kadar and Mas Ywan who just arrived told me they were working with the Dinas Tourism office, and twice a year had been doing performances for promotions in Bali. They didn't answer my question about pay, but Mbak Kadar said that in 1993 they had had a contract for twenty people over five days, and did Ramayana, the Janaka-Cakil dance, and *klana topeng*. (Field notes, edited, 24/9/94)[49]

These developments show that dance associations, which had competed in the 1980s to be the custodian of *adiluhung* tradition, were by 1999 routinely contracting and transacting court dances. These were not new dances made for tourists, but

---

49. Suryakĕncana had previously collaborated in a promotion in Bali in December 1988, when they gave five performances (at Rp10,000 a time) at the airport for stopover passengers; their members had also been on a long European tour arranged by a European impresario.

transformations within existing genres. They were neither the court forms passed down from the ninth Sultan, nor were they new inventions in *sendratari* style. However, the trend to eliminate elements such as dialogue and prioritize dance movement, as in the case of the *golek Menak* duet performed at the Joyokusuman tourist packages, and the shortening of *wayang wong* Ramanyanas was a sign of the *sendratari* aesthetic encroaching on the aesthetic of court performance.

Restagings such as these bring us back to questions about authenticity. In the 'ramified performances' of the Los Angeles Festival in 1990, where the Yogya court performed as part of the Indonesian–American Cooperation (KIAS), the location of authenticity shifted from the object to 'the moment of aesthetic reception' (Kirshenblatt-Gimblett 1995: 251), and provided a new context for evaluation. National and international festivals often replace defunct contexts for performances. Restagings of court forms can either be understood as dynamic adaptations to new circumstances of reception, or as the end of the life of these forms to embody memories and resonances of identifications previously limited to the court context. But we should not forget that audiences for court performances are not only made up of paying and/or tourist members. As well as restaging existing 'court' classicism, dance associations also continue to revive nineteenth- and twentieth-century dances created in princely houses outside the court, and perform them for local audiences as part of other occasions. For example, Siswa Among Běksa revived *Golek Gambyong*, described in Chapter 3. In 1989 they performed it for a local audience at the close of a leave-taking of seventeen performers from Yogyakarta selected in a central government office project directed by R.M. Dinusatama, before they left for the Poetry Reading Festival and National Literature Show in Jakarta. By 1994 they had performed it twice for tourist audiences too (R.M. Dinusatama, 30/8/94).

These examples show that the changes of patronage and context for performance of Yogya-style classical dance have in some cases led literally to 'airport' art, but in most other cases they result in equivocally positioned restagings. Some of these replicate forms as 'authentic' continuations of previous practice for nontraditional paying audiences. Others produce 'shrunk' versions for mixed traditional and nontraditional audiences, either live, or mediated by technology, as in the case of the television broadcast. Whether these revivals sustain court standards or become contenders for compression remains to be seen. A contributing factor to the outcome is the impact of tourism and market forces on performers.

The Viability of Performance as a Profession

The production of specialized professional artists in Indonesia, as elsewhere, has produced a problem of rationalizing their place in the society's market systems.

For Indonesia's dance professionals the questions is not 'What or who is this performance for?' but 'How do I live from it?' The transformation of dance training from a controlled court sphere to that of the state had produced many qualified dancers. An excess of university graduates in the field of performing arts resulted in the promotion of the vocational stream for secondary-level pupils from 1984. This stream included the secondary dance academy in Yogyakarta, but its director was doubtful about his pupils' future, and anticipated that good dancers would have to work as pedicab drivers or noodle-sellers. By the end of the 1980s, there were more academic dancers with higher degrees, but ISI could not absorb any more graduates into its staff. These dance graduates had expectations that the system of court prestige would be replaced by the modern prestige of middle-class professionalism, but instead, some of them find themselves working as parking attendants.

The relationship of Javanese court dancing to the Indonesian state and the creation of Indonesian culture produces a paradox. The formalization of court dance training and its subsequent classicization raised expectations of a largely 'amateur' activity combining serious play and socialization becoming transformed into a professional one, but the current commercialization of court dance and revenues from performances for tourism do not support a professional status (Hughes-Freeland 1993b). This is connected to a contradiction between the roles of the artist and the professional also found in long-industrialized societies. As Bourdieu (1993) has shown, in Europe the art market freed artists from dependence on patrons but hardened the demarcation between artistry and commerce. Normally the 'profession' of writer or artist is one of the least professionalized there is, and artists usually require a 'secondary occupation which provides their main income' (or another wage-earner in the household). Western ballet dancers earn low wages, have insecure working conditions, and strive for a more 'professional' status (Wulff 1998b).

Despite globalization and capitalization, the relevance and practical appropriateness of professionalization varies according to social and situational context. Modern Indonesian aspirations invoke the establishment of expert classes based on a model of the professional, although the alternative 'reflective practitioner' based on mutual negotiations is closer to existing pattern of patron-client relationships in the region (Schön 1982 in Hughes-Freeland 2001b: 217). It is also the case that the role of the artist is still emerging. Government offices in Yogya have tended to emulate court values in relation to the domain of capital exchange and professionalization. The concept of *adiluhung*, honourable and not commercial, also manifested itself in the modern honorarium economy, based on the rhetoric of self-sacrifice for the national good, rather than service to the sovereign. This has created resistance to the development of institutions which many performers and low-level administrators consider necessary to improve the working conditions and protect the interests of professional and semi-professional performers. For instance, in the adjacent Province of Central Java, the local government issued 'artists' identity cards to help performers of different kinds move around the region and to gain professional legitimacy. Aristocratic government officials in Yogyakarta considered this to be pretentious. They claimed that everyone is an artist, or that there are simply gifted amateurs. Yet rural performers in the Special Region of Yogya envied their Central Javanese counterparts who take pride in this proof of occupational identity, a basic 'professionalism' and protector of their reputation as they travel to the next performance venue, in contrast to itinerant 'vagabonds or whores'. By 1990 the government's position in Yogya was already inconsistent. Since 1981 the regional office of Education and Culture had been making ten 'Appreciation of Artistic

Contribution' (*Penghargaan Seni* I.) awards annually, giving validation to the category of 'artist'. The lack of recognition on identity cards continued to present problems for aspiring professionals.

Noncommercial values associated with the court have also prevailed in state practices of gift giving, even for tourist events. Tickets for the 1994 Court Festival were distributed free of charge, an action described by a tourism official as 'a present from the government to the people', even if the recipients were mostly overseas tourists. This conforms to an expectation, explained by an aristocratic entrepreneur who early on set up the Agastya institute which produced shadow plays for overseas tourists:

> Traditional arts cannot be commercialized because there is a tradition of not paying for performance, *sĕdĕkah*: it's to bring pleasure and to entertain as part of ritual work. People will pay to see a film, but they feel it isn't right [*cocog*] to pay to see the shadow play, for instance. One old man said he loves *wayang* but wouldn't pay to see it even though he could afford to.[50]

The gift economy also extends to state publications of texts such as government publications in the fields of literature, history and philosophy which are 'not for sale'. Rather than becoming commodities which may be traded for profit, these objects gain value through scarcity, and are exchanged within certain spheres – they are *not* subject to commercial transactions. The court libraries receive these texts as gifts, and anyone wishing to read them has to go through the proper court channels. The effect is an ongoing limitation on the circulation of written knowledge, which is associated with traditional cultural and political ideas about access to power. Selling culture for cash, let alone profit, is still contrary to local ideas about exchange and obligation.

Running parallel to bureaucratic fragmentation in the state sector is a multiplex economic system. It is not only artists who need a 'day job'. Village work in Java is often less an occupation than a set of multiplex occasional roles (Jay 1969). Performers who work in the tourist sector often slide down to the fragile niche of the urban-dwelling landless labourer, who makes do by subverting the norms of capitalism and modernity. In this way they transport the self-exploitative rationality of precapitalist modes of production into that most capitalist of spheres, the tourist industry. What appears to be a capitalist commercialization of performance is really, as the examples from Yogyakarta court-classical dancing have made clear, a transformation of dancing for honour-not-cash into dancing for an honorarium. This illuminates a more widespread characteristic of the Indonesian labour market. Civil servants, including teachers and lecturers in state institutions, are also paid an honorarium. One university lecturer at the prestigious ITB

---

50. Pak Slamet Sukardjo, Nitour Branch Manager, chairman ASITA (Association of Indonesian Tour and Travel Agencies) (1/11/89). He developed Agastya to stimulate local interest: 'Young people aren't interested because they weren't brought up with it. To appreciate *wayang kulit* you have to know a lot – and if you start young.' Five years on, he told me that ASITA's membership had risen from 30 travel bureaux in 1989 to 59 in 1994 (19/9/94).

at Bandung described her job as 'social work', and said that her real earning was done outside the government sector. Self-exploitation in the name of national development was a key feature of the late twentieth-century Indonesian economic system.[51] This disjunction is of the same order as the gap between the rhetoric applied to the objectives of cultural development projects and the practicability and relevance of implementing them. Or to put it another way, the contemporary production of performers and modern rationales is out of sync with prevailing structures and expectations.

It is difficult to extract clear financial data from Javanese people, but regular questioning over ten years as well as the use of local research assistants (in 1994 and 1999) allowed a more reliable set of figures to emerge than might have been possible. In 1989, dancers were lucky to earn Rp60,000 a month, even if they danced every night (Pak Pardjan 2/4/89).[52] The going rate for a dancer at a tourist performance at both the Joyokusuman and Pudjokusuman residences was Rp2,000. In the Joyokusuman, the association reputedly received Rp90,000, and after paying twenty-five performers who get Rp2,000 each, would gain a profit of Rp40,000, but this had to cover costs, including costumes maintenance and replacement.

By 1994 the Pudjokusuman had lost GYP's patronage, and dancers' earnings depended on audience numbers. If there were under thirty visitors they earned Rp2,000, and if over thirty, Rp3,000. Elsewhere there had been a slight rise, with reports of Rp5,000 from Suryakĕncana performances. At Probosutejo's Ngabean venue, dancers could get Rp5,000 (and musicians Rp3,500). This was the same as at Prambanan, which later rose to Rp6,500 basic with Rp8,500–10,000 for the choreographer and directors of music and costume. An IKIP dance student who performed at the Pudjokusuman said he couldn't save, and used his monthly dance earnings of Rp20,000 maximum to pay his fees. He could earn as much as Rp30,000 a performance at productions by the choreographer Didik Nini Thowok (see below) but these performances were less frequent (SW, 4 and 7/8/94). A dancer I knew for many years who had been to Europe with Suryakĕncana in 1988 reported that per performance she earned Rp2,000 with Siswa Among Bĕksa (not Rp3,000 as reported elsewhere), Rp2,000 rising to Rp2,500 at Suryakĕncana at Joyokusuman, but could get Rp60,000 performing at Bagong Kussudiardjo's Padepokan venue. In 1990 she went to Bali for a tourist promotion and was paid Rp25,000 plus pocket money, a total of Rp50,000 (Anggara 18/9/94). There were occasionally discrepancies:

> Here performance happens every day, so it's Rp2,500 minimum a perfor-mance, or Rp3,000 or Rp5,000; elsewhere you can get Rp10,000–15,000, but only four gigs a month. I do Surakarta style because there's Yogya style at Pudjokusuman, Kanĕman and Notoprajan. The entrance fee is Rp10,000

---

51. Ethnographies of work in both rural (Wolf 1992) and urban sectors (Brenner 1998) show the unevenness of modernity in Java.

52. The value of the Rupiah to the £ in 1989 averaged Rp3,000, in 1994 Rp3,500 and in 1999 Rp10,000, when a kilo of rice cost Rp3,000, the cost of a meal from a food stall (previously Rp1,000).

for overseas and Rp5,000 for domestic; guides get a 20% tip. (Azwar, manager of Purawisata 25/8/94)

However, a graduate of the Teachers' Training College who performed at Purawisata said she was receiving Rp1,000, and was now up to nearly Rp2,000; for Ramayana she earned Rp70,000 – to nearly Rp80,000 a month (S. 16/9/94). The Hotel Santika charged US$17.50 per head for a dinner-dance and paid Rp250,000 for a concert of twenty dancers, and each dancer received Rp8,000. Hotel Aquila paid Rp275,000 (Accounts employee, 30/8/94). Garuda Hotel charged US$6 for dance, $18 for dinner-dance and paid Rp100,000 a show, paying a dancer Rp5,000 and a musician Rp3,500 (Y., dancer and organizer of Kusuma Aji, 30/8/94). The Prambanan covered theatre charged Rp15,000, Rp12,500, or Rp9,000 per ticket.

It is clear that little of what the tourists paid went to the dancers. By 1999 dancers who relied on tourist patronage were suffering the most as a result of the economic crisis. The only regular tourist performances were in the court, Mardawa Budaya (at the Pudjokusuman), and the two venues at Prambanan. Private sponsorship was also down, and all performers were affected by the high rate of inflation following the 1997 economic crisis. To make matters worse, at elite weddings, instead of hiring dancers to entertain guests as they were served food in their seats, there was a new mobile system in which guests queued to see the enthroned couple and then moved on to an assembly of self-service food stalls. In August 1999, normal earnings in the Sultan's palace were in the range of Rp2,500 to Rp12,000. Less qualified dancers with a secondary school qualification reported on fees in other venues in the town of Rp2,000–3,000. Of these one reported a fee of Rp10,000 at one of Yogyakarta's newest four-star hotels. Another reported earning Rp15,000 performing Ramayana at the outdoor stage at Prambanan.

Even these low earnings were more than what the performer takes home. Dancers spoke of the increasing problems of middlemen who take up to 60 per cent of the fee. Classically trained performers who had adapted their skills for simulacra of classical traditions in television and film projects reported being cheated by the producers and middlemen. In a survey of seventeen performers, four married women aged between twenty-three and thirty nine, all with children, admitted that financial problems had caused them to turn to prostitution as a means to supplement their performance income. In this older profession, they can earn almost ten times as much for an hour's work as they would dancing (Rp50,000 instead of Rp6,000). This supplementary activity has long been imputed to rural professional women performers such as *ledhek* (Hughes-Freeland 1993a), but has not been associated with court dancers in the modern era. Other respondents said that they supplement their income by teaching privately, or working as a parking attendant (male), as a laundress (female) and so forth. Those who were fortunate enough to gain positions as teachers in the state academy could earn a monthly wage of up to Rp450,000, but most said that private patronage brought in the best earnings.

There appear to be two options open to Indonesia's aspiring professional dance artists trained in 'classical' dance. The first, as for many Western artists, is to 'get a day job'. In Java it has been normal for performers to be semi-professional or sporadically professional, inside and outside the court. Older performers inside the court are still gifted amateurs, ranging from aristocrats who work in government offices to low-status farmers, such as 59–year-old Pak Sugĕng Subarjo, often seen performing in court training sessions and *lawung* dances in the 1980s and 1990s (see Figure 6.3 above). When asked the question 'Is the payment you receive for performing enough to live on?' he answered:

> I've never had any expectations of dancing as a means of earning a living. To dance in the court of Yogyakarta is to be a 'court servant' ... I've never thought about how much or how big the honorarium is that I am given (pers.comm. 1999).

In the court he earned Rp5,000 for a performance; at a performance outside Yogya, this rose to between Rp25,000 and Rp50,000. The senior dance teacher K.R.T. Dipuradanarta and his daughter both described dancing in general as community service (*gotong royong*), and in classical circles for prestige and honour (11/4/89). But out of the seventeen performers surveyed, only Pak Sugĕng described court dancing as a sphere of activity specifically removed from earning power.

Indeed, by 1999, Siswa Among Bĕksa was the only dance organization in Yogya which attracted performers who were not training as professionals. Most of these 'amateurs' were court kin. Recruitment of new dancers was in decline, especially among boys. In 1989, the ratio for registration at Siswa Among Bĕksa was in the region of five girls to one boy. In 1999, twenty-three girls and six boys graduated. For boys and girls, academic pressures have reduced the time available for dancing as a hobby, and young men especially are being drawn to a wider range of sporting and cultural activities. The amateur option appeared to be at severe risk from the competing demands of modern education and increased options for leisure.

Even a diversification of dancing skills might not be the answer. Nowadays tertiary-level students also learn folk dances such as *tayuban* and *jathilan*, the horse dance, the favourite 'folk' form in 1999, superseding previous favourites *tayuban* and *angguk*.[53] Although these performances are part of formal education, and have had government projects to process them like other *adiluhung* objects, they still remain the province of labourers and farmers. As Sugiyono, a 46-year-old farmer who runs a *jathilan* troupe, explained: 'You can't earn a living: it's too little, and too uncertain ... We can earn Rp500,000 performing from 8.00 am to 12 pm; each person gets about Rp5,000 and tips, food, drinks etc' (pers. comm.1999). Government cultural policies introduced in 1999 to bring dance to the people and promote *jathilan* may assist groups like this, but help had only been in the form of money to buy new costumes,

---

53. See further Hughes-Freeland (1997a). Contrary to expectations in 1994, state-trained *tayuban* performers have not yet dislodged the traditionally-trained village women, who continue to maintain their earning power as performers alongside work in the household and in agriculture.

and have certainly not solved the problems of formally trained dancers aspiring to become professionals.

The second option is to take control of modernity's symbolic resources and ideologies, and to combine art and entertainment, making something both new and familiar. The one successful example of this in Yogyakarta is the choreographer, dancer, comedian and make-up artist Didik Hadiprayitno, who performs as Didik Nini Thowok. Multiply marginal, Didik is half-Chinese, Protestant, and a cross- dresser. He can earn up to Rp5 million for a performance in Bali or Jakarta, but will as often perform in the street (*ngamen*) to raise money for charity. He works from a traditional foundation in whatever genre he draws on, but also he produces new choreographies to cater for the occasion (Hughes-Freeland 2007a). He also rides the tide of trends, and in 1999 appeared regularly in the newest popular genre in Indonesia, 'humorous ketoprak', the newest version of Javanese historical drama developed in the 1920s, which uses plots and costumes from different regional genres and Indonesian as its core language, with some Javanese interventions. In the spirit of the New Order, he claimed that his work is not political, but his choreography in which he changed his shirt on stage, 'The Nation Changes Its Shirt Dance' (*Tari Negeri Berganti Baju*), was performed in June 1998 in Jakarta, and in July in Yogya, to mark the change of national leader, as well as making a comment about opportunism, his own, perhaps, included. His clowning conforms to the common use of humour as a way of dissimulating criticism, but his economic success is highly unusual.

Didik sees his responsibilities as aimed not only at entertainment but at education and human development. He has taken an ethical approach to profit management and has set up a trust for elderly performers. His dream is to open a dance centre, Taman Mini Tari, in Yogyakarta; this would be a private venture, using extensive networks (Didik Hadiprayitno 12/8/99).[54] When I had lunch at his house in 1999, it had not changed in ten years. The profits are reinvested in the business, and not spent on the conspicuous consumption of Indonesia's new rich (Hughes-Freeland 2001: 223–25). He also confirmed the reason why so many dancers had expressed a preference for private patronage:

> Supposing a full performance costs Rp10 million. The middleman [*calo*] asks 10%, so I build that into the budget. But sometimes the *calo* may offer 10 million, but gets 20 million! So I prefer to make a contract with the sponsor. If you don't look out for yourself, you'll be exploited. There's too much fatalism [*pasrah*] and acceptance [*nrimo*]. You need to recognize the context [*ĕmpan-papan*]. (Didik Hadiprayitno 9/8/99)

This allusion to the core Javanese concept, *ĕmpan-papan*, the need for responsive adaptability, rather than a passive acceptance, is significant here. It supports my earlier arguments in Chapter 4 about tactical manoeuvring as a form of agency and social

---

54. Miniaturization has been seen as a sign of the New Order's cultural vacuity, but I would not wish to belittle Didik's dream with this kind of association.

power in everyday Javanese interaction. While most dancers cannot command Rp10 million, the principle of taking responsibility for drawing up one's own contract in direct negotiation did seem a practical step in responding to the realities of the business world.

Meanwhile, the reluctance at government level to formalize artists in a professional sense results in a lack of protection for wages as dancers undercut each other, and also become the victims of middlemen. There are no professional associations, and no minimum wage.[55] In August 1999, when I suggested to the Sultan in his capacity as Governor of the Province that performers needed unions or a minimum wage, he responded with the alarming proposal that performers should form groups of ten people, and share their profits. This would mean that successful performers like Didik would be subsidizing his less fortunate fellow performers – while the state gives the freebies mentioned above as incentives to overseas tourists. This was a surprising (and worrying) suggestion of a communal system by a modernising sultan, reminiscent of controversial involution models from the 1960s based on the premise that agriculture can assimilate labour without increasing investment or productivity if poverty is shared. There is a long way to go before Indonesians find a way of living from their art, a problem they share with many performers and artists in an increasingly commoditized and profit-driven world.

Conclusion

Court dance traditions have survived independence and a change of context which completed a transition in their status from court ceremonial to art. This survival was assured because although the different forms of patronage were diversified away from the court, these diversifications nonetheless gained legitimacy from continuing court support by the Sultan and court kin, some of whom combined the role of state and of private patronage in one person. The training of dance outside the court that started in 1918 is now dispersed around state academies where dance graduates continue to present a full-scale traditional dance in their final examinations. The hard line between 'inside' and 'outside' the court has also become blurred due to dance training and performance being entrusted to royal relatives and situated in their houses rather than in the inner court precincts. Patronage of court performed by the state as one form of 'classical' dance was well established by the start of the tenth Sultan's reign. Since his accession, Sultan Hamĕngkubuwana X has strategically promoted a new egalitarianism of manners, although the hierarchies of the court survive in Indonesian civil service and military status systems. The values of *adiluhung* were still being invoked in 1999, but there were signs that the Sultan himself was no longer committed to it as a relevant value, and that the cultural landscape and signs of distinction were about to change.

---

55. The New Order opposed attempts by workers to organize themselves (Aspinall 1999), though in Bali performers have tried to set up a minimum wage. This has been instituted more widely with the implementation of Regional Autonomy after the completion of this study.

Although classical dance has long been sold in hotels and theatres, the various dance organizations which competed during the 1980s to produce 'authentic' forms did not engage wholeheartedly with commercial tourist enterprise until the late 1980s when they adapted forms to sell them to tourists in exclusive dinner-dance packages. Before this, the apparent fracture of *adiluhung*, championed by Siswa Among Běksa, versus artistry, championed by MB and PBN at the Pudjokusuman, was not as it seemed. Siswa Among Běksa was already venturing into the commercial domain by the mid-1980s, and the closely related Suryakěncana had done so even earlier. A senior woman dancer (who will remain anonymous here) had warned me early on not to take Gusti Suryo's ideals too literally: 'Look at his kids, all commercial!' (18/12/83). In 1989 Siswa Among Běksa was referred to as 'more traditional' by teachers at the Pudjokusuman (MB and PBN), but there had already been a convergence between the two even as they competed; for instance in 1989, each produced its own special *bědhaya* dance to celebrate the accession of the tenth Sultan. The court's patronage was still providing the incentive to choreograph the traditional repertoire, with a dynamic development within the conventions.

What is clear is that the distinguishing characteristic of court dance as a purely amateur activity (however skilled the performer), is likely to be lost, and its performance praxis will be incorporated into practices which are classed as artistic or cultural. Dancers now are graduates of the secondary and tertiary training institutions, and whether they are talented outsiders or aristocrats, they have professional expectations that during the course of this study remained unsatisfied by the economic structures. As noted, this has also been the case in more comprehensively 'rational' economies. The venues available for dancing have expanded, and the practice of performing on a proscenium arch stage initiated on a massive scale at Prambanan in the 1960s has become more commonplace, although the newest theatre at Prambanan is in the round. The demand for court dance increases from tourist audiences and as a prestige entertainment within Indonesia and overseas. In 1999 high-cost court performance productions were increasingly limited to high-status events sponsored either by hotels for prestige events, or under the patronage of the Arts Council or academies for the purposes of video documentation. During my last six weeks of research in 1999 my impression was that court dance had declined in popularity among local audiences since 1994 for reasons other than political and economic crises. The changed format of wedding ceremonies was one factor. However, the interest from outside, as well as the value placed on past practices in postcolonial states and elsewhere in global nostalgic 'heritage' culture, means that it is likely to survive as a live embodied practice, and not become a memory or visual document, in the form of films and videos, recorded by dance scholars and various heritage documentation projects. It is possible that there will be the same kind of enthusiasm that one finds in historical reenactment societies in Britain, for example. So it is unlikely that court dance will die out completely, but it will become a different kind of social activity, and will probably lose its powers to produce persons as well as performances.

Meanwhile, the players in the cultural landscape had changed. In 1992 the directorship of Yogyakarta's Institute of Indonesian Arts (ISI), academic flagship of Yogyakarta tradition, passed from Prof. Dr R.M. Soedarsono, the Javanese dancer and historian, to Prof. Dr I Made Bandem, the Balinese dancer and academic who had already built up ASTI at Denpasar. A number of definitive figures had also vanished. Rama Sas had had a stroke during a performance in August 1994 and died in April 1996. R.M. Ben Suharto, star classical dancer and lecturer in the 1970s and 1980s at ASTI (later ISI), who attempted to bridge tradition and modernity and East and West with shamanistic new age dances, died in December 1997. And finally, on 26 August 1999, Yogya also lost G.B.P.H. Puger, youngest of the Sultan's uncles, and former Director General of Culture.[56] It is possible that his death will come to be seen as marking the completion of the transformation from court culture to Indonesian classicism, and the beginning of a new aesthetic for Indonesia. By this point, the New Order had also become history, and everyone was eager to speak about politics without having to conceal it in cultural metaphors.

---

56. Many others have died since 1999, including my dance teacher, Bu Yuda (d.2004) and the choreographer Bagong Kussudiardjo (d.2004).

Chapter 8

Conclusion: Embodied Communities in the Nation State

> The body may be the fundamental way that we belong to each other, but it is also the way that we are uniquely individuated. To encounter another human body is thus to encounter, indissociably, both sameness and difference. The body of the other is at once strange and familiar. It is exactly the fact that we can relate to it which highlights its otherness. Other things in the world are not strange to us in the same sense at all.
>
> Terry Eagleton, *After Theory*, p.161

This account of Javanese court dance has raised a number of questions about what the anthropology of dance can contribute to the theorization of culture, society and the body as it moves into the city and the global village. An anthropology of dance is distinctive for including a cultural account of embodied movement elicited primarily, though not exclusively, through local and emergent categories used against backgrounds of nationalism and postcolonialism. It has an important part to play in explaining how bodies and performance are understood and conceptualized culturally, and in reminding ourselves that modernity is not uniform.

The epigram for this chapter states that our bodies always make us separate from each other. We can never become 'the other', even in the community (or communities) in which we ourselves have been socialized and learnt our first (and second, etc.) languages. But as well as opening ourselves up to other languages and other cultures, we can also attempt to learn other forms of embodiment in particular societies and situations, as I have done in the research for this book. The exercise is methodological, because one brings to the research site a culturally constituted self, to learn anew in the field, or fields – even participant-observation research is rarely single-sited in the sense of occurring in one location – but it also requires that what one has learned be written in such a way that it can be understood by those who remain outside that experience, as well as by those from within it. A close-grained analysis of what people say and do in dance worlds in the context of a longitudinal study allows patterns of change to be identified. Over time, one's responses in the field become tempered by other texts. A number of other studies located in a large-scale modern setting, with a colonial historical background have helped me frame my data, but I have also emphasized the importance of starting from particular local frameworks and concepts, wherever they have come from, to elucidate a number of more general points, as follows.

Dance helps us understand the relationship between embodied and imagined communities, and between social control and conformity and personal freedom and self-realization. It is because it is embodied that dance is a powerful political symbol. Combining a political analysis of dance with attention to embodied dance movement, intrinsic and extrinsic approaches, gives insight into the cultural significance of dance movement and the social context in which it is produced and also produces, in this case the real and imagined communities of the nation state. To understand the politics of dance, it is necessary to take account of the perspectives of dancing as embodied and as representational, in terms of visual witnessing and imaginative stories and metaphors. I have analysed dance as 'being', as 'being seen', and as 'being interpreted'. Dance movement generates stories and comes to represent what those stories have imagined. Nationalist histories seek to locate dance in an ancient 'other', to give temporal depth to a shallow political community. If we examine these three aspects, we can move away from a purely ritual analysis of performance as event. Instead dance has significance as a cultural resource in the banalities of everyday life. An analysis therefore needs to demonstrate the forms of availability, their transformation, and the ways in which individuals deploy them in the context of their different social roles and interests.

As an embodied phenomenon, dance itself resists being explained simply as direct communication. It is a form of action, a practice that has personal existential significance. I have drawn on theories that situate duality in everyday life, such as De Certeau's idea of tactics, to evoke how people manoeuvre the increasingly controlled spaces of social life, but restored the flesh to his textual analysis. The dancing body has instrumentality which can produce imagined national belonging, but only as part of smaller-scale communities. It also produces persons who themselves are active producers. The dancing body is an embodied maker of worlds, which in turn makes more dancing bodies. Dance is more than an emblem, even when it is incorporated into the symbolism of the nation state. Dancing is embodied action which begins in the physical material body but does not end there. It goes beyond the material and the visible, to the domains of energies and forces, of language, and of imagination. It is neither a version of linguistics, nor is it visual anthropology only. It is crucial that dance is seen, but that is only part of it. I have shown how that process occurred, and how the transmission of dance from one generation to the next changed by gaining a textual dimension. However, despite these changes, it is ultimately the inherently nontextual, embodied aspects of dancing which themselves resist the more logocentric or vision-centric models. In principle, dance is what it is because of its inherent capacity to elude entextualization when performed by human beings. Despite the ubiquitous notion of 'spectacle' as the now reduced version of human performance, I have argued that dance is more than spectacle, and part of the serious business of life, and that it creates worlds. I have used the terms 'references' and 'identifications' to describe the process in which dance can make worlds. And these worlds are multiple, simultaneous, and capable of maintaining contradictions.

Dance analysis in general reveals the importance of paradox in social and cultural analysis, and goes to the heart of the encounter between the self and the social. Dance embodies and dramatizes theoretical issues, which is why, like performance in general, it is often used to produce metaphors. It is public culture and personal experience. It is visible and concealing. It is the result of socialization, but produces an inner space for personal freedom and expression. It is the result of a response which is both controlled and creative. It is motivated by noble disinterest and self-interest. This paradox can also be applied to the imagined community of the nation, which is produced by the embodied agency of active individuals in geographically specific locations, without which there could be no transcending unity. For this reason, dance is never *only* emblematic, even if in some circumstances it might appear to have become so, momentarily.

The analytical framework has been shaped by local categories of the person and local interpretations of dance forms and movement. Categories used to explain embodiment, dance, dance movement, and social and aesthetic values were used by people I worked with in Yogyakarta for over twenty years. The Javanese concept of embodiment (*lair-batin*) comprises physical materiality and *rasa* which perceives the world and makes sense of it. While Java is not a post-Cartesian culture, this dual understanding of the Javanese person is a useful reminder that accounts of social conduct and action need to include the material and visible aspects of the person, and the complexities of these, in their presentation, in Goffman's sense, and in their social construction, from Mauss to Bourdieu. An anthropologist is more likely than a sociologist to recognize that tradition, dance, art, artist, are categories that need to be explained, and not to assume that they are being used in the same way as we might expect, despite working in a modern urban location. My argument also considers modernities in the plural, not of modernity as a uniform condition. I would argue that a processual analysis of dance as embodied movement and its place in the construction of community such as I have offered here are also relevant to the sociology of dance. But this assumption needs to be questioned 'at home', if home is the Western city. Ideas of embodiment here are not uniformly and predictably shaped by post-Enlightenment formulations. Despite sociological statements to the contrary, we do not live in a post-god society. So the questions that an anthropologist brings to dance in an overseas location are ones which are appropriate in closer communities, and recognize the possibility of differences within the same nation.

Re-embodying the Person in the Nation

Re-embodying the person within the nation requires a reappraisal of recognized theoretical models. Although I have referred to a western conceptual apparatus to discuss the theorization of the body, and also to scholarly debates about dance and other matters in Java, my analysis has been largely based on ethnographic data. Any imported concepts, such as tactics and dissimulation, are ones that I have selected because they fit with the data – they are *cocog*, as they say in Java. This has been especially relevant in the political dimensions of my analysis. Secrecy and concealment were politically obligatory during the New Order. The nation became depoliticized, and culture replaced politics. Politics was something that was not spoken about. Framing the relationship of dance to society outside the terms of reference of Indonesian cultural politics has therefore required a meta-theoretical framework.

In attempting to deal with this problem, Pemberton (1994) has argued that Javanese culture has been a long form of the ritual process (Turner 1969). The ritual process is based on the opposition of social structure and communitas, or the idea of an expressive liberation from the constraints of everyday life, in a special time and place defined as liminal, a concept that Turner (1982) later developed into 'liminoid', to describe modern spaces of play and escape, including dance and theatrical performances, and later media. I have found both the ethos and three-part structure of Turner's analysis unhelpful for thinking about Javanese dance (among other things) as the ritual process is structured as single plot narratives which cannot accommodate the social and experiential complexity of cultural and political contexts. Instead I recognize the diverse aspects of human social existence in a more fluid sense, in relation to both the physical and the discursive aspects of experience, including memory and the imagination.

This is why I have theorized dancing in the context of everyday life, and as an aspect of prestigious events within public culture. Dance is excellent for spreading and standardizing culture as appearances, and court dance has become an example of self-citation because of its visibility. But appearance is only part of the story, just as the physical, visible body is only part of the *lair-batin* person. Dancing is a skill which is empowering. It contributes to behaviour which is persuasive in dealing with powerful patrons. Javanese people make explicit connections between dance movement and court conduct, and extend that connection to argue that dance is a more general form of socialization. Dance movements, especially the restrained dance modes for men and women, embody the principle of dissimulation which is a vital part of using politeness tactically in social interaction, a politeness which in the context of patron-client relationships manoeuvres the higher-status person into a position of obligation. Even at the technical level of learning dance, it soon becomes clear that, rhythmically, the movement is not driven by the music, but works in dialogue with it, moving beyond the beat, slightly off-beat, late-but-not-late: the perfect Javanese paradox. Dancing is more than the simple constraining conventionalization of the body. The person who performs Javanese dance is not danced *by it* and regimented into obedience. Court dancing may be a rigorous training akin to militaristic drilling productive of conformity, but it is not only understood by its practitioners simply as a matter of social control or as self-expression. The quality of movement and the sensibilities of the body required by this dance are quite different from those needed to march up and down in the street for Indonesian Independence Day.

So this dance is not 'liberating' in an exuberant cathartic sense which would belong to the liminality or liminoid spheres of the ritual process, but it does provide room for manoeuvre. It is in the domain of the tactical while being located in a panoptic place, even if this places is itself in the purview of the state. There are, if you will, nesting panopticons, hierarchies of surveillance, and a fragmentation which, like the formation of bureaucracy itself, works against the unifying principles of the modern nation-state.

Court dance has also provided the movement styles for the celebration of the status quo in prestigious concerts that can be understood as symbols of power and legitimacy. In contrast to socially dispersed dance power in everyday life, the *bĕdhaya* dances continue to retain their association with the personal power of the sultan, and are the last of the ceremonial court forms to have a mystique. The abstract quality of their dance movement, their association with myths of political legitimacy, their capacity to accumulate semi-historical associations with a distant past, and their ability to generate metaphors about enduring metaphysical principles have made them particularly useful in a religiously plural society which is undergoing radical change and which has also been strongly censorious of open criticism.

Dancing has also played an important part in the processes of Indonesian cultural politics. Local government projects such as competitions lead to the circulation of skills and ideas around the Province, and their recentring in the Provincial capital. I have suggested that this circulation cannot entirely be explained as a manifestation of top-down policy. Individual interests influence what happens or not, and the form it takes. While situated in the period of late modernity, Indonesian politics is also marked by the networks of kin and patronage that work alongside bureaucracy, and undermine its monolithic impact. This process is partly due to the proximity of Yogya and its court to powerful networks in the Indonesian capital, which means that there is more scope for manipulation than there might be in marginal areas that are more intensively targeted for national development. Javanese people use available references in different ways. Even within the Yogya elite, there is a heterogeneous set of attitudes, and people draw on different dance histories and styles of practice to justify what they claim to be the correct standard. I have also suggested that this process applies to the politics of tourist development, and have shown that in thinking about tourist performance, it is important to examine who is producing the tourist spectacles, and what their interests are. The Javanese case suggests a discrepancy between professional expectations and cultural attitudes to performance as something that should not be paid for, but provided through the gift of patronage. Ideas such as these are critical for understanding the wider processes of tourism within the community, and the significance it comes to have in the lives of those who are involved in it and the way it influences local ways of doing and being. Instead of a rational capital economy, precapitalist forms of exchange continued to shape expectations about performance being part of a gift of hospitality, a responsibility from a patron to his or her clients. Modernity has not eliminated economic 'irrationality'.

There is an emergent and contingent relationship between movement, politics and culture that appears inevitable, until we examine the process by which that relationship develops. Court dance discourses have situated central moral and intellectual issues in the body. The discipline and self-control associated with perfecting dance skills are good not only for producing what to people outside the shared circle of *rasa* might see as gorgeous and over-long spectacle. The discipline not only produces skill that gives the individual person power to perform socially, but it also empowers the dancing body. It also allows the person to engage with the extra-social, the transcendental. The view that the transcendental is simply a version of material inequalities is not culturally relevant in the Indonesian context. Even when court dance is promoted by cultural politicians, there is an ultimately personal agency which allows the dancers to slip between the rules, to find another kind of place. It is this sense of option, however tiny and fleeting, which has made De Certeau's concept of tactics appropriate for framing this ethnographic material, in the hope of generating future comparison. 'Tactics' as an analytical device is ethnographically appropriate because of Javanese tendencies to avoid conflict by being evasive and by dissimulating one's feelings. In dance studies, resistance has often been discussed in relation to marginal and minority groups, but I have shown that an elite also has its moments of resistance, as it engages with communicative indirection and dissimulation and produces a place for resistance, against appearances of elaborate cultural disciplining of the body. De Certeau's model breaks down the body into text, which creates a problem for where agentive tactics can be grounded. This process of disembodiment interestingly is one that emerged in Javanese exegeses, but where flesh becomes text in De Certeau, in Javanese interpretations flesh becomes spirit. There is, however, an intriguing parallel between textuality and metaphors of disembodiment and spirituality. This is less surprising if we think of poststructural theorization like De Certeau's, which is itself as a form of evasion tactics from the constraints of the empirical world. Deferred mysticism has long been recognized as a characteristic of such theory. Although the political context differs from Java's colonial and postcolonial one, the process of theory and interpretation in both contexts has a similar form. Both move towards disembodiment, something that can be understood even as a remembrance of the death that is everyone's future.

Court dance has been an expression of ceremony and prestige, an instrumental means of beautifying the world, a leisure activity for pleasure, and lastly, a way of earning money. In this particular example, the aesthetic and performative qualities of dance movement resist regimentation and require a reflexive, responsive relationship with the musical rhythms. The aesthetic of 'flowing water' requires the agency of the dancer to be engaged, not only at the physical level, but also with the inner aspect of the self. The Javanese word *rasa* reminds us of what words cannot contain, and how they act as starting points for sense which goes beyond meaning and returns us to the whole sensorium. The idealized state of the dancer, according to the court dance philosophy Joged Mataram, is 'empty but full'. This philosophy itself represents a paradox as well. This local performance theory was set down in the 1970s to represent court dance to outsiders. As the philosophy consolidated court dance's separation from its context, it simultaneously consolidated a code which could be separated from the specific forms of embodiment which made up the court repertoire.

And yet this philosophy builds on a spirit of martial fervour and the spirit of revolution used to characterize the ethos of Yogya as founded under its first Sultan. However, this ethos is cast through memories of early Indonesian nationalism. While the state supports the image of martial heroism, it has discouraged its citizens from any acts of heroism or political engagement. So although Joged Mataram was formulated as a text, it was not simply complicit with dance as spectacle as political symbolism because it included notions of transformation and transcendence of the rules governing everyday life and social interaction. However, although it was not included in published texts, the spirit of Joged Mataram was explained verbally as being transferable to forms other than Yogyakarta court dance.

Embodiment is an important element of modernity, 'a story that people tell themselves about themselves in relation to "others". It is a powerful story because nation-states organize the body politic around it' (Rofel 1997, cited in Hughes-Freeland and Crain 1998: 4). It is a mistake, however, to think of modernity as a condition which results in the past being left behind, but it is also a mistake to ignore how the relationship with the past is devoured by modernity, as my analysis of court dance in Java has demonstrated. One of the issues of modern personhood in Java that was vexing philosophers at this time was the question of the motivating powers of self-interest, and the problems of dissimulating it. However, during the period covered by this book, in Javanese experience, the social could not be accounted for by the collectivism of state rhetoric on identity or individualistically as the sum of motivations shaped by unitary self-interest. In court dance, the experienced performer 'becomes a puppet' by losing human weaknesses and transforming into a heroic character. Just as court dance models exemplary behaviour, Joged Mataram extends the four principles for performing Yogya style court dance as a model for good living. Possession by heroism chimes with the national agenda of creating heroic exemplars, but in Joged Mataram, heroism is deeply personal. Although in Java there is an ideology of shared personhood, a communality which ideally takes precedent over individual interests, it would be wrong to deny the individual style implied by Joged Mataram.

The idiom of possession is significant in the context of social transformation and debates about what modernity should be. Taussig (1997) has compared the circulation of the dead to the circulation of money, and in that parallel has identified the 'magic of the state'. This circulatory mimesis is a sign of the penetration of the state into the innermost irrational and imaginary domains of person and society. But while we can find a comparable irrational instrumentality in Java, I do not see this as evidence of the pervasive force of the state. Rather it is an expression of longstanding local attitudes to nature as animated, and a recognition of the limits of control, expressed by the constant presence of visible and invisible forces. My arguments draw on other evidence that the Southeast Asian state is fragmentary and nonpanoptic, and also on critiques of the illusion of national unity in the face of the fragmentary nature of rational bureaucracy. These arguments indicate that the state is not the be-all and end-all of magical modernity.

Rasa has been presented as a short-circuiting word that cuts off questions which might lead to places where there are no answers. If this is the case, then arguably an aesthetic of *rasa* in Java has been a sort of stalling tactic, a putting on hold, a provisionality. The celebrated writer and political critic Pramoedya Ananta Toer used his fiction of colonial Java as an allegory for the surveillance of the New Order, which resulted in him being imprisoned for twenty years and his works being banned. In a dialogue in 'The House of Glass' (Toer 1992), a metaphor for the surveyed nation, a Javanese character is berated for his opportunism. The role of *rasa* in Javanese aesthetics and Indonesian selfhood could in these terms be thought of as an expression of a longstanding survival tactic, in the uncertain world described by Toer where force prevailed over justice. It is possible now that the time is ripe for the long postcolonial transition to mature.

Future Worlds, Future Aesthetics

The political aspects of dance, and the relationship of embodied communities to the imagined nation state, demonstrate that the state and its manifestations at ground level are both emergent. In postcolonial states, attempting to come to terms with the relationship between the past and the future is of a different order for similar concerns in former colonising nations, and the period of transition appears to be open-ended. In a postcolonial society, the growing distance from the time of struggle distinguishes the generations from one another. If a generation is twenty-five years, then in the postcolonial situation, the crunch comes with the third generation who forget (about fifty years down the line). The second generation still hears about the colonial past directly from parents and grandparents. As those generations die, the memories and the values associated with the dance become diluted, and rely on different kinds of mediation: texts, videos, notations and so forth.

The process of transition I have described also applies elsewhere. Points of comparison with *bharata natyam* dance in India made at the start of this book show that what has happened through Javanese court dance is not unique, although the particulars are. In Java, the period of transition has extended the social capital of dance from family to education to market, by a process of accretion, not loss. In other cases this process may take a different path with different consequences. It will be interesting to see if the transition process results in a theoretically 'modern' bureaucracy, or if the state and its artistic practices will retain their family networks.

Dance changes worlds and is changed by them. A crucial moment for the future of court dance was the founding of the dance school Kridha Běksa Wirama, in 1918. This initiated practices that would shape court dance and allow it to survive as classical dance after independence, including standardizing and writing down movement sequences, classifying dance modes, shortening the duration of performances, allowing women to perform in more forms, reworking forms from outside the court, from princely houses and villages, and introducing mimetic movements into some dances. As these developments were taking place, court dance was also being adopted into the new nationalist Tamansiswa schools. Its educative significance had been identified before independence as having an important function in socialization, and this sustained a passionate amateur interest that continued after independence. From 1945, the ninth Sultan became absorbed by national governmental responsibilities, and delegated court dancing to the court branch, Bĕbadan Among Bĕksa, based in a princely house. There was a proliferation of dance training associations run by teachers and pupils of Kridha Bĕksa Wirama as well as court dancers teaching court dance in different styles. From the mid-1950s, dance training began in educational institutes: first in the dance conservatory, which became part of the secondary tier of education, and then at ASTI, at tertiary level. In the early 1960s a large-scale dance performance of the Ramayana, synthesizing the styles of all four courts in Yogya and Surakarta, was performed on the open stage beside the temple at Prambanan, the first attempt to perform dance as a commercial spectacle.

The consolidation of court dance as Indonesian art in the classical tradition coincides with the appearance of conditions that are opposed to art, the commercial tourist market. It was only in 1973, after the establishment of the New Order, that dance returned to the court precincts in the form of weekly training sessions as part of a project to build up a sense of the nation's past and to attract tourists. Mardawa Budaya had already started tourist concerts in 1971 and, over the next fifteen years, other associations which had been inspired by passionate amateurism and a nostalgic moralism would also cater to the tourist market. Hotels and commercial theatres would also imitate smaller-scale versions of the Ramayana Ballet, and *sendratari*, a dance form which emphasized gestural narrative, would come to challenge the more complex court forms by appealing to audiences without particular linguistic skills. Although court dance had become classical and moved into the tourist market by the end of the ninth Sultan's reign (1988), it retained some of its previous characteristics. Amateur enthusiasts of court dancing continued for pleasure, and then rationalized it with reference to 'culture' or 'tourism' as an afterthought. Pragmatic responses to diversified dance audiences resulted in dances being customized, being made shorter and losing any dialogue sections.

The relationship between Javanese embodiment and national identity is in transition. As the late eminent Javanese sociologist and novelist Umar Kayam wrote in a feature about Hamĕngkubuwana X's accession, 'Yogya's tempo is still Javanese. But Java is no longer Java, and Indonesia isn't quite there yet' – '*Belum jadi*' (*Tempo* 18 March 1989: 57). Court dancing is a social practice which provides a site for the exploration of control and selfhood, and the dynamics of variously situated codes of value, from the local to the national. The institutional basis for the performance and customs formerly associated with the Javanese court had receded further, and the concept of responsive adaptability to circumstances, *ĕmpan-papan*, can no longer be understood with reference to memories of court life. Those who had danced before the end of the colonial period with memories derived from personal experience were dying; their descendants were constructing memories at several removes from direct experience, building up representations of the tradition in a manner that merged myth and history (Hughes-Freeland 2006). The notion of 'remembering', *eling* has been important in postcolonial Javanese mysticism and New Order philosophy. Forgetting has arguably been even more important: forgetting President Soekarno, forgetting the events which allowed Suharto to seize power. Memory and forgetting are always intertwined. Court dance has had a function as political symbolism for the Indonesian state, but for those who perform it and embody it, the dancing carries so many historical, mythological and philosophical references that it eludes simple message-bearing, and resists becoming mere propaganda or a clear enactment of a disappearing past.

The interpretive community for court dancing has changed, as has the idea of what the tradition is. The inner spaces of the court had been imagined ideological ones, but between 1980 and 2000, the recognized boundaries of the embodied communities became more in keeping with actual dance practices, Court dance belonged to a family and territory based society, with *kampung* as neighbourhoods and kin networks as foundation of embodiment. Court dance not only took place in princely houses, but as a classical form was also incorporating dance forms which previously were not of the court itself. The spatial and metaphorical boundary of inner and outer was finally ruptured by the extended network of close and distant kin that have always constituted the world of the Javanese court. During the 1970s, court traditions were already being described as 'classical Yogya style dance' by aristocrats considered to be the most traditional in outlook. During the 1980s there was a concern with authenticity and purity, but dance associations that stood for these values were already embarking on entrepreneurial activities which developed into a more commercial attitude to court dance as classical dance during the 1990s. Surveys of performance groups show that classifications have changed from distinguishing classical from folk to distinguishing traditional (*tradisi)* from 'choreographed' (*garapan)* and from 'nontraditional' (*non tradisi).*

Court dance in Yogya has also changed considerably in relation to the court since the accession of the tenth Sultan. The embodied politeness of court dance is becoming distanced from that of everyday life: the handshake has replaced the *sĕmbah;* Indonesian is the main language in education. The relevance of court behaviour for everyday politeness and its spiritual and moral concepts are being challenged. Joged Mataram might well have outlined the theory of performance which transformed court dance into a classical Indonesian practice, but it did so on the foundation of the aesthetic intersubjectivity of the *rasa,* its shared assumptions. The Sultan himself now regards the court as a living resource that would benefit from rationalization and modernization, and to that end he has already expanded the range of performances that are welcomed into the court. Since his accession, the Indonesian-speaking Sultan Hamĕngkubuwana X has questioned the state's definition of the court's institutional identity, and has attempted to shape its future role as a centre of excellence for the local community, and a means of educating them in cultures beyond those of Java and other Indonesian regions. The survival of *bĕdhaya* and other court forms and their future transformations will depend on the Sultan's patronage and how the court develops as a cultural foundation.

The question facing dance practitioners now is whether or not the *rasa* of Javanese court-as-classical dance can still construct worlds, or whether a new aesthetic is needed. If the 'spirit' of dance comes from a particular world-view, will it survive as a perennial philosophy, or be transformed by history? This issue has been discussed in relation to *bharata natyam,* where style has been linked to lineage (Gaston 1996; O'Shea 1998), and there has been disagreement about the sustainability of these communities and the dance itself. Despite its diasporic expansion, *bharata natyam* does not necessarily thrive at home, and decreases in quality as a result of linguistic proficiency and a shortened time scale influenced by audience expectations that have been shaped by Bollywood (Pillai 2002). More than changes in the dance style, it is changes in the audience, which is now cosmopolitan, heterogeneous, and with mixed levels of awareness, that challenge the foundation in intersubjective experience between spectator and artist of Abhinavagupta's theory of *rasa* which shaped Rukmini Devi's *bharata natyam*. Spectators are no longer co-creators, and *rasa* now inheres in the performer's own subjectivity and mental concentration, and a 'post-colonial aesthetic, a theory that can describe and evaluate the secular realities of dance in all its marvellous multiplicity' (ibid.: 20) is needed. Others have argued that *bharata natyam* has been able to ride the waves of change, and performances by immigrants to Delhi from the south continue to bring into the world the same spirit of auspiciousness created by the *devadasi*s (Ram 2000: 272). The context may have changed, but the dance is still instrumental.

Although Javanese court dance is older than *bharata natyam*, it lacks its claim to be founded in classical antiquity. Joged Mataram is the result of modern interactions and audience needs for meaning and context, although there are parallels with Old Javanese *rasa* philosophy. Joged Mataram concentrates on the inner *rasa* of the dancer, rather than the intersubjective *rasa* of the relationship between the dance and the audience. It does not represent the secular rationale of performance as one might have expected, but presents court dance as a spiritual art, building on the aesthetic principle of *rasa* which is part of the *lair-batin* person. Despite sharing some common ground, dance as spiritual art differs from trance and possession dances outside the court, and from spiritual techniques in *kĕbatinan,* which have overtly instrumental ends. In considering the aesthetics of *rasa* and changing audiences, we need to beware of assuming that the aesthetic has to be popular, a mistake made in Java in the 1980s. Other kinds of dance can fulfil the demands of a different audience. Nor should we not overlook the importance of dance connoisseurs, a group equivalent to the *rasika* in India (Gaston 1996: 268). In Java a keen, educated, artistic elite has been emerging from the aristocratic one. Arguably, as long as there are local enthusiasts for difficult forms, there will be an audience and patronage for them. Popularity is not necessarily the measure for survival.

Indonesian modernity is on the move. I have been describing dance as a practice, not as an object, except when that characterization becomes part of what people do to and with dance. By 1999 the tight-knit, face-to-face nature of the residential and visually defined community in Yogya was changing fast. Now members of those groups with an interest in practising dance have new options for employment, leisure and marriage partners. At least two female stars of court dance from the 1980s married Indonesian men from outside Java, and moved away from Yogyakarta. There are now more Jakarta connections, and rapidly changing demographies and geographies. Despite these changes, there has been no clear division between tradition and modernity, and there is also a complex intertwining of Indonesian and Javanese interests, which defy neat categorizations.[1]

---

1.   There are, of course, intercultural encounters which I do not address here for reasons of space and emphasis.

Multiplex ties produce ambiguity in classifying allegiances and interests as Indonesian or Javanese. When I returned to Yogya in 1999 after an absence of five years, I discovered that the long-planned ring road had been completed, and now encircled an expanded city which was creeping north towards the village of Kaliurang on the slopes of Mount Merapi and south towards the coast. Children of old friends had grown up and moved to new *kampungs* adjacent to or far beyond the ring road. Marianto (1997) has written about the different lifestyles in the seven kilometres between Yogya's main street (Jalan Malioboro) and the southern ring road. He contrasts the 'organic' lifestyle beyond the ring road with 'a kind of cultural stuttering and stammering' approach to modern technology, evident in how people wear their helmets undone when riding their motor cycle, making them similar to ritual offerings to the local spirit (1997: 92, 96).[2] In my experience, the life style near to the northern section of the road was no longer 'organic'. Previous styles of interaction, especially the common habit of dropping in on the off-chance of finding someone at home, were becoming impractical. The increased density of traffic and the greater distances meant that it took much longer to reach family and friends on the other side of town. Although businesses and some middle-class families had telephones before, it was only now that they were really starting to use them. To my surprise (and relief), I was phoned by the Governor's office to reschedule my interview with the Sultan – this would have been unthinkable five years before.[3] Like Jakarta, which has long ceased to be a pedestrian or trishaw city, time and space in Yogyakarta have been forced into modernity by town planning and demography. As the geography of community has altered, so have the expressions of status: when I visited the director of ISI, I found that he was living in a brand-new gated community to the north of the city, with its own security guard and checkpoint protecting the wealthy inhabitants from the masses. This is tangible evidence, perhaps, of the break-down in the patron-client relationship, with its checks and balances against exploitation.

The aesthetic and moral dilemma can be summed up by an anecdote. After a seminar I gave about *tayuban*,[4] the poet Linus Suryadi (d.1999) proposed a reason for apparent hypocrisy in the fuss about the sexual display of women at *tayuban* (visible to Javanese people if not Western viewers) in the light of the much more overt pelvic rotations and knicker-flashing exhibitions of female singers at nightly *dangdut* concerts in town. The different standards arise because *ledheks* are identified with a community, a named village, whereas *dangdut* singers are '*moderen*' and anonymous. This view accords with more general ideas about the purity of 'tradition' as a repository of value. Indonesian modernity, by contrast, permits a public show of sexuality which is linked to social anonymity and a removal from social obligations. The question in Java and elsewhere is how locality and modernity will accommodate each other.

2. These helmets were first required in the mid-1980s, and are the subject of visual joke weaving through my film about dance (Hughes-Freeland 1988).
3. In 1999 very few people I knew in Yogya had cell phones; by 2006 it was rare to find someone who did not.
4. At Gadjah Mada University 'Centre of Cultural Research and Study' (Pusat Penelitian dan Studi Kebudayaan), 16/12/89 (see Hughes-Freeland 1990).

Epilogue: From Cultural Peaks to Mixed Essences?

Court dance has provided a physical expression of social memory: real memories of colonial court practices, and ideological memories of resistance and rebellion. Court performances have made sense to Yogyakartans by providing both real and imagined continuity, and also the futures it allows groups to imagine. During most of the research period, these imaginings formed part of a millenarian utopianism, which lurked amidst the militarism of the New Order. The limitations or even failure of so-called state homogenization in the case of particular performance cultures had been common well before President Suharto stepped down. However, during the New Order, the creative anarchy that might have been appropriate to finding a living and heterogeneous Indonesian culture had been contained by military control and a culture of caution and sometimes fear. When I returned to Yogya in 1999, I discovered that after over thirty years of political silence, there was a febrile excitement. The only thing anyone wanted to talk about was politics – despite one person's jaded observation that 'It's all performance now!' The new openness was a huge relief to the older generation, who had always talked politics in private with people they could trust not to report them to the authorities. But for the post-1945 generation, and those born into the New Order, it was a source of anxiety; 1998 was the first big political change since 1966. Many had learnt to accept what the government said as the truth, and not to question it. For them New Order ideology provided certainty. Now they had to accept that the 'regime of truth' had changed the stories, and that history might be different from what those in authority had said. These were interesting times. After having had only two presidents in over fifty years, Indonesia has seen three presidents come and go since 1998, and a fourth is now in place. There have been a number of post 9/11 acts of terror in Jakarta and Bali, and the independence movement in Aceh was 'resolved' after the tsunami of 2004.

In May 1998 the future had become the present when President Suharto's regime ended with his resignation and with it the New Order regime's policy to control and define court tradition as art. President Habibie's speech on state television, 26 July 1999, announcing the legitimacy of the election before results were later ratified at midnight, made the important point that instead of monopolistic top-down policies, it was time for a diversity of patronage. Beyond political developments in the field of actual performance I noticed changes in policies for tourist performances, in the content of what could be performed, and the extent of the popularity of new hybrid forms.

In the domain of tourism, by 1999 there were signs that performance was moving off the stages of the state back on to the streets and squares. Hotel managers, tourist brokers and officials, and dancers were expressing dissatisfaction with the ubiquitous classical Ramayana packages, and turning to the many kinds of local folk performance. As one tourism official said, we need to bring dance to the people:

> We also aim to get the public involved, so they know about things. We've used an open space at Sostrowijayan [one of Yogya's two 'alternative' *kampung* tourist areas] for performances. Our mission is to make art live

among the people, not just on stage. Traditional forms like *tayuban* would be interesting for tourists – it's communicative, aggressive, and above all there's audience participation. Last month at ISI there was a Cultural Festival of National Folk Performance (Budaya Nusantara Pertunjukkan Rakyat), with fifteen folk dances (*tari rakyat*). In July we also staged *tayuban*, two from each district and from ISI. Promoting folk dance is one way to develop the performing arts; if we can sell it, then we'll get it into the hotels. (M. Lakoni 11/8/99)

The policy to alter the balance from sightseeing to action holidays had been on the cards for ten years, but participation was being taken more seriously, no doubt because of the change of regime:

There should be participation for tourist interest, not just these staged choreographies. There's to be a 'Display of Yogya Wedding Customs' on Jl Parangtritis km 17 in August with westerners dressed in Javanese clothes [!] to promote village tourism. (Ibid.)

This kind of participation has been advocated as a way of combating stereotypes fostered by tourists watching performance (Desmond 1999). It will be interesting to see if the new political order extends participation to dancing and, unlike previous attempts in the 1950s with *Tari Lenso*, produces social dancing in Java.[5]

The use of political allegory and symbolism, of course, predates New Order censorship, and allusiveness and dissimulation are unlikely to disappear as a result of the 'reform' era. In the last chapter I mentioned Didik Nini Thowok's 'The Nation Changes Its Shirt Dance' as an example of this. When I visited the painter Djoko Pekik, a former category C 'communist' who had spent eight years in prison, he showed me a big puppet of a boar that he'd made for a shadow play to celebrate the forthcoming independence celebrations. The play, 'Sarapadha Captures the Boar', would represent ex-President Suharto and his family, and would refer to political events in its usual oblique manner, although Suharto's recent departure was causing more outspoken statements. Djoko Pekik had also just completed a large painting of boar in front of a mass of people and the Jakarta skyscape beyond. 'Indonesia in 1998 Hunting the Boar' shows the boar slung from a pole, with performers from folk dances in front: *jathilan, reyog, ledhek* (Figure 8.1). His next painting was a response to Suharto's recent hospitalization entitled, (prematurely, as it turned out), 'Without Telegrams and Flowers of Condolence'. Djoko Pekik was due to hold an exhibition in Australia, supported by the Sultan and the Wollongong local government. He had already been waiting for a passport for four months. We speculated as to whether or not there would be obstructions to his leaving Indonesia, even though the writer

---

5. As I finalize this book, fear of military terror in Indonesia is being replaced by fear of religious terror, and current trends are unlikely to be conducive to increased participation in performance, especially where men and women come together in the same space. *Bedhaya jilbab* (veiled) is now a possibility.

Pramoedya Ananta Toer, another famous ex-political prisoner, had been allowed to travel overseas. Djoko Pekik finally obtained a passport after Abdurrahman Wachid became President later in 1999. He has visited other countries, but has 'not yet had the chance' to go to Wollongong (pers.comm. Nin Soebakdi March 2008).

Old habits die hard, and it will no doubt take time for 'vertically structured patron-client relationships' to disappear, even though they may become 'less tightly integrated and more vulnerable to political contestation than they have been' (Robison 1998: 203). But after 1998, one could expect a decline of censorship, more overt and literal narrative, more denotative mimetic gesture, and also more demos and agit-prop. During fieldwork in 1999, because of the lack of security and political tension, like many people I often stayed in after dark and watched television. In July the household was watching a music programme on the state television channel TVRI when my 'mother', a well-known senior academic, exclaimed 'This isn't allowed!'. She explained that the song, by Tono & Yani of the *campursari* group C.S. Bondo Ati, was *Turi-Turi Putih* ('White Sesbanias' – a small ornamental shrub). 'It's a Communist Party song!' We were all astonished to realize that songs banned under the New Order were not only being performed by *campursari* music groups, but were even being shown on the state-run television station.

I also watched the very popular 'humorous ketoprak', broadcast on RCTI, a privately owned channel, every Saturday night at 8.30 pm. On 7/8/99, the performers were mostly from the *gamělan* programme at ISI, and Didik Hadiprayitno played one of the leads. The story, set design and costumes were Balinese. The basic language was Indonesian, and a number of Javanese phrases (not all) were subtitled in Indonesian.

Figure 8.1 Djoko Pěkik in front of his painting *Boar Hunt, Indonesia 1998*, symbolizing the end of the New Order, 1999

The songs were Javanese. There was much sexual innuendo, and when Javanese was used, the tempo speeded up. The juxtaposition of Balinese set and clothes with Javanese banter was bizarre. This broadcast contrasts with that of the shrunken *bĕdhaya*, described in the previous chapter. It was not at all *adiluhung*, and also showed a mixing of regional and generic performance which ten years earlier would have been inconceivable. Was this, I wondered, the future of Indonesian culture?

During the previous twenty years, embodied communities were often conservative and critical about experimental innovations, as was the case with the court's last dance theatre, *golek Menak*, and more extreme innovations. So community can provide confidence for the performer who feels at home, or it can be repressive, limiting options and the scope for innovation. There are two kinds of creativity: getting it right (like court dance); or making it new – either very visibly (Didik Hadiprayitno's work), or behind the appearance of an existing form, such as Rama Sas's innovations in 'court' dance (Hughes-Freeland 2007a). What was clear was that the mood was for mixing it up. Different kinds of traditional performance were being combined in the folk domain, such as horse dancing and *tayuban*, or horse dancing and Ramayana. These combinations were described generically as *campursari* ('mixed elements'), a name first applied to mixing traditional *gamĕlan* instruments (drums, gongs and other percussion instruments) with modern instruments, such as electronic keyboards, small guitars, and untraditional percussion instruments, such as maracas, tambourines and side drums. The music comes across as an odd mix of *karawitan* and Portuguese-influenced *keroncong*, with *dangdut*-style openings, and is somewhat dissonant due to mixing pentatonic and diatonic scales; a number of academic musicians have made their dislike public. Pak Manthous, a musician from Wonosari in the Province of Yogyakarta, developed this new eclectic style around 1995 and it has since become ubiquitous, at live performances at weddings, circumcisions and state celebrations, and on television and radio. Even the Sultan knew the going rates for these events, and explained that people hire *campursari* for weddings instead of *wayang kulit*, which costs Rp5million, because it normally costs Rp1–2 million, although Pak Manthous's group charges Rp10 million. *Campursari* has taken off in an unexpected way.

Of course hybridization is not new. In the Yogya court, side drums have been used for *bĕdhaya* marches, since before Walter Spies was director of (Western) music there in the 1920s. In 1989 at a 'Tayuban Festival' in Surakarta, produced by four journalists with support from the Minister of Culture, I saw a performance by a troupe from Sragen who presented as *Ta-La-Dut*, consisting of a choreographed *tayuban*, Javanese rock and roll songs (*lagu*), and a comedian (*badut*). It closed with young men from the audience dancing with the female dancers – a *tayuban* which ended up being more like a disco.

By 1999, innovative mixes were taking place within the local community for their own pleasure, even if they were produced with one eye on attracting outside interest. Although *campursari* started in the final years of the New Order, its overtly hybridized aesthetic can be understood as a response and expression of resistance to the purist cultural policies of the New Order. Its popularity and extension to dance and dance theatre performance could also be understood to be an expression of reform in the spheres of art and culture which parallels the excitement about the possibility of creative political reform anticipated in the 'Reform' period (Young 1998). During my last interview with the Sultan I tried out my theory about hybridization as a new aesthetic. He said:

> Yes indeed, it's bound to happen everywhere. Now, what's important this is how classical lately grows into *campursari*, which comes from the guidance by the people. But the important thing is for the people to be able to see classical dance or gamelan that are pure and authentic, they can value them. So we need a change of attitude, transparency and transformation. Without that, it won't happen. (Sultan Haměngkubuwana X, 26/8/99)

The signs are that the unofficial culture that has continued, surreptitiously and sporadically, is now able to emerge, dynamically, creatively, chaotically in what may either be a transitional anarchy, or the start of a more protean cultural landscape. For all the government's attempts to manipulate performance, it is what the performers want to do, and their success in finding an audience which is ultimately what matters: instead of a structural top-down effect, we find a grassroots dynamic, which in some cases may conform with cultural policy, but not necessarily. Only time will tell whether the 'reform' generation will sustain this momentum, or whether old habits will die too hard and 'Reform' turn into the 'New New Order' (Orbaba). Will amateur enthusiasm continue to transmit the spirit of court dance, as transforming embodied practices which respond, subtly and supply (or otherwise) to changing circumstances, even on the temporary stages of folk festivals? Or will it become archival dancing, as traces in recordings and photographs, as texts for the future, and as disembodied culture? These are questions that will be able to be answered in the future.

Reigns of the Sultans of Yogyakarta[1]

Hamĕngkubuwana I	1749–92 (son of Amangkurat IV, deposed)
Hamĕngkubuwana II	1792–1810 (son); 1810–11 as regent; 1811–12
Hamĕngkubuwana III	1812–14 (son)
Hamĕngkubuwana IV	1814–22 (son)
Hamĕngkubuwana V	1823–26 (son)
Hamĕngkubuwana II	1826–28 (great-grandfather, restored)
Hamĕngkubuwana V	1828–55 (great-grandson, restored)
Hamĕngkubuwana VI	1855–77 (brother)
Hamĕngkubuwana VII	1877–21 (son)
Hamĕngkubuwana VIII	1921–39 (son)
Hamĕngkubuwana IX	1940–88 (son)
Hamĕngkubuwana X	1989– (son)

---

1.   Mandoyokusumo (1980); Ricklefs (1974).

Appendix II

Illustrating 'Flowing Water' (Chapter 4)

'Flowing water' can be illustrated by *ngěndherek*, one of the simplest movement sequences from the *Saritunggal* dance. The dance lasts about thirty minutes and is accompanied by the musical form *kětawang*, which has a gong cycle of sixteen beats, marked by the large gong (*gong agěng*), every eighth beat being marked by the *kěnong* (set of vertically hung gongs), and every other beat alternatively by *kěthuk* and *kěmpul* (small horizontally hung gongs). The dancer fits her movements to the music by attending to these instruments, notated below as *gong, nong, thuk* and *pul*. For the dancer these sixteen beats are counted as eight, as shown in the following example (in Javanese; some teachers use Indonesian); the numbers represent how the sequence is counted out in dance training, both before and after music being used:

> *si-ji, lo-ro, ti-ga, pa-pat, li-ma, e-nem, pi-tu, wo-LU.*

In contrast to Western accents which fall on the first note of a bar, *gamělan* accents fall on the gong, which is called *ulian*, so 'LU' marks the accent of the big gong on the sixteenth beat.[2]

The sequence is performed three times, with the gong falling on the first and third repeats. The dashes indicate the places filled by basic and elaborating instruments and the rhythm-directing drum (*kěndhang*):

1	2	3	4	5	6	7	8
–	[thuk]	–	pul	–	thuk	–	nong
1	2	3	4	5	6	7	8 'LU'
–	thuk	–	pul	–	thuk	–	nong/gong

1. Knee bend, look right, left hand *ngruji*, flick back right sash
2. Tap left foot (the '*thuk*' is not sounded on this beat of the cycle).
3. Up on toes (*jinjit*), body weight slightly forward.
4. Knee bend, left foot back a little, right sash held, body leans left, look left.
5. Prepare to
6. Tap right foot, flex left wrist.
7. Lean right.
8. Flick back right sash and look right, left hand unchanged.

---

2. Beats are normally grouped in eights, with stresses on the eighth, sixteenth, twenty-fourth, thirty-second, etc. beat, depending on composition structure and rhythmic style (see Kunst 1973; Sutton 1991; Brinner 1995).

Summary from Brongtodiningrat's Interpretation of Court *Bĕdhaya* (Chapter 5)[3]

This exegesis can be summarized as follows. The 'line' (*lajuran*) part of *bĕdhaya* carries a philosophy; in the court the *bĕdhaya* is often known as '*lajuran*'. Follower and Flank symbolize the thoughts of mankind (desires) and are constantly trying to attract Leader (the spirit), but Leader has control of the human soul and has already chosen the straight path which is connected through the whole body. After Follower fails to influence Leader, she surrenders by ensconcing herself in Leader's line (Table 5.1c).

However, Follower does not give in and become a follower of Leader. She frees herself from Leader's influence and again interrupts her, but Leader will not be swayed. In the end Follower surrenders and becomes one with Leader, symbolizing the unity of Servant and Lord, and the *bĕdhaya* takes the shape of the three-by-three formation (Table 5.1d). This means that perfection has been achieved and the unification of 'Trimurti' (birth-life-death), or, in other words, the completion of a human in this world.

The second part tells a story in which Leader always fights with Follower and ends in perfection. The dancers take up the opening formation which symbolizes that life goes on: birth-life-death-birth again etc.

The costumes in *bĕdhaya* show that there is neither beauty not ugliness, everything is empty. The audience will not be attracted by the dancers' faces but should focus towards the dance. This is a sign that a person's value is not in her appearance but that behaviour is the most important.

All the dancers are armed with daggers that show that everyone has a weapon with which to defeat evil influences from outside. Good or bad comes to everyone because of the influence of others or the situation.

Because the 'line' section of *bĕdhaya* dancing has a basic philosophy, the pattern of the dance is always the same, although in the second part the pattern is not fixed, but depends on the development of the story.

---

3. I have translated this summary from the Indonesian which was provided after the Javanese text in the unpublished mimeographed version (Brongtodiningrat 1971).

Glossary

Javanese words are sometime used in Indonesian; specifically Indonesian words are marked (I.)

abdidalĕm	court servant or official
adiluhung	noble and refined
alam	world, environment
alus	refined, restrained, gentle
Arjuna, Janaka	third-born Pandhawa
atma	spirit or soul
babad	chronicle
bagongan	court language
bangsal	hall
Batak	lead dancer in *bĕdhaya*
Bathara Guru	Śiva, one of the Hindu trinity
bathik	cloth painted with wax and then dyed
becak	trishaw bicycle
bĕdhaya	dance for (usually) nine females
beteng	fort
bĕksa	dance movement, dance
bĕksan	collection of dance movements, fighting choreography
Bima	second-born Pandhawa
budaya, kabudayaan	culture, civilization
cara jawi	Javanese language; the Javanese way
dalĕm	house
dĕdĕg	physique, presence
dhalang	puppeteer; narrator
eling	remembrance, awareness, consciousness
ĕmpan-papan	'knowing one's place', impression management
ĕmpu	expert
Endhel	lead dancer in *bĕdhaya*
gamĕlan	ensemble of instruments, the sound they make
garĕbĕg	processional court ceremony
garudha	mythical bird
garwa ampeyan	secondary wife
Gathotkaca	son of Bima, second-born Pandhawa

gĕndhing	melodies played on *gamĕlan* etc.
golek	round wooden rod puppet, dance for one female
golek Menak	dance theatre using Menak stories of Amir Hamzah
grĕgĕt	dynamism, passion, drive: third element of Joged Mataram
gunungan	rice mountain
hawa nafsu	passions, desires
jaba	outside
jagad	sphere, world, universe, cosmos
jarwa dhosok	forced etymology
jawa, jawi	Javanese (culture)
jĕro	inside
jiwa	'spirit'
joged	'dance'
Joged Mataram	dance philosophy
kagungan dalĕm	prerogative of the sultan
kampung	urban neighbourhood, rural community
kandha	chanted introduction to a performance
kasar	harsh, undesirable, natural in a derogatory sense
Kasultanan	Sultan's palace, Yogyakarta
Kasunanan	Susuhunan's palace, Surakarta
kawula-gusti	unification of servant and lord
kĕbatinan	Javanese spiritual group, 'mysticism'
kebudayaan (I.)	culture, civilization
kĕpanjingan	possession, in trance
kesenian (I.)	art
kĕtawang	musical form
Kĕtawang, Bĕdhaya	protypical *bĕdhaya* of the Kasununan
ketoprak	popular human theatre enacting historical plays
klana	dance for one male
Korawa	antagonists in the Mahābhārata epic
krama (k.)	polite language code
kraton	palace, court
labuhan	offering on water
lagon	short song
lair-batin	visible and invisible parts of the person and the world
lajuran	first part and formations of *bĕdhaya*
lakon	action, plot
lawung	spear, male dance
Langĕndriya	dance opera
ledhek	female professional village dancer
loka	sphere, world
luwĕs	pleasing, beautiful, fluent
magang	apprentice, initiate
mapan	in place

Mataram	kingdom(s) in Central Java
Maulud(an)	(celebrations for) the Prophet's birthday
naluri	things passed down, 'tradition(s)'
nĕgara	state
ngoko (ng.)	familiar language code
ora mingku	do not turn back: fourth element of Joged Mataram
pamrih	self-interest, expectations, motives
pancadriya	five senses
Pancasila (I.)	Indonesian state philosophy based on five principles
Pandhawa	five brothers and their allies in the Mahābhārata
pasaran	five-day market week
pasĕmon	facial expression, allusion
pathokan	preconditions, standards, constraints
patrap	arrangement, disposition
pĕncak silat	martial arts
pĕndhapa	open-sided pavilion
pĕrang	fight, conflict
pĕsindhen	female singer
pocapan	dialogue in dance theatre and duets
priyayi	colonial bureaucrat, white-collar worker
punakawan	'attendant'; 'clown' in shadow play
pusaka	heirloom
putra-dalĕm	prince
putri	feminine dance mode
putri-dalĕm	princess
rame	lively
rasa	embodied sense, sensibility, consciousness
Ratu Kidul	Queen of the South, spirit spouse of Javanese sultans
ringgit	puppet; performer in *wayang wong*
ronggeng	female dancer from outside the palace
rukun	harmonious appearances
sajen	offerings
sandiwara (I.)	Western-style theatre
santri	orthodox Muslim
Saritunggal	training dance in the feminine mode
sasmita	cue for musicians, pun, message
satriya	knight, warrior, gentleman
sĕkti	special energy, 'power'
sĕlamatan	communal ritual meal
sĕlir	concubine
Sĕmang, Bĕdhaya	lost heirloom *bĕdhaya* of the Kasultanan
Sĕmar	senior 'clown' in shadow theatre and *wayang wong*
sĕmĕdhi	contemplation
sendratari (I.)	dance ballet

sĕngguh	confidence: second element of Joged Mataram
sĕntana-dalĕm	palace kin
sĕrat	writing, book, letter
sĕwiji	concentration, first element of Joged Mataram
Srikandhi	second wife of Arjuna, third-born Pandhawa
srimpi	dance for four (usually) females
surasa	interpretation, exegesis
Tamansiswa	Javanist educational system founded in Yogyakarta
tari (I.)	dance
tari klasik (I.)	classical dance
tata-krama	knowing and doing things according to *cara jawi*
tayuban	dancing party with professional female dancers
Tayungan	basic male dance training
topeng	mask, masked dance
toya mili	'flowing water'
trah	ancestor group
tumpĕng	small rice cone offering
udhĕt	dance sash
upacara	regalia; ceremony (I.)
wangsalan	elaborate pun
watak	'character'
wayah dalĕm	grandchild of a sultan
wayang wong	dance theatre

Bibliography

Manuscripts

Brongtodiningrat, K.P.H. 1971. '*Surahosipun Lĕlangen Bĕdoyo serta Srimpi*'. Unpublished mimeograph, collection of G.B.P.H. Suryobrongto.

Cuplikan Sĕrat (Babad) Nitik. 1897 (1827 A.J.). Yogyakarta: mimeographed transcript from the collection of G.B.P.H. Suryobrongto.

Noeradyo, R.M. Wibatsu. 1983. '*Peringatan 2 tahun pendidikan tari Yayasan Siswa Among Bĕksa Yogyakarta 6 Agustus* 1983' [Commemoration of two years of dance education]. Mimeograph, 7 pages. Yogyakarta: Siswa Among Bĕksa.

*Platen-Album*s (The Albums of Ir. J.L. Moens). 1933–37. Vols 1–30. cat. nos. 925–955 Dj. Jakarta: Museum Nasional. Latinized transcripts of the original Javanese text. PBB 32–35, PBE 2, PBE 37–38, Sanabudaya museum, Yogyakarta.

Sĕrat Kandha Bĕdhaya Srimpi. 1854 (1782 A.J.). B 24, Widyabudaya Library, Karaton Ngayogakarta Hadiningrat.

Sĕrat Pasindhen Candhran Abdidalĕm. 1836 (1764 A.J.) B 23, Widyabudaya library, Kraton Ngayogyakarta Hadiningrat.

Sĕrat Pasindhen Sarta Bĕksa Bĕdhaya Sĕmang. 1946 (1877 A.J.). B/S 1B, K.H.P. Krida Mardawa archive, Kraton Ngayogyakarta Hadiningrat.

Suryobrongto, G.B.P.H. n.d. '*Wayang-wong gaya Ngayogyakarta*'. Unpublished mimeograph, collection of G.B.P.H. Suryobrongto.

Government Reports (Published in Yogyakarta unless Otherwise Indicated)

1999. *Indonesia 1999: An Official Handbook*. Department of Information: Jakarta.

1994. *Laporan Tahunan 1993/4*. Kantor Wilayah VIII Parpostel DIY.

1977. Proyek Penelitian dan Pencatatan Kebudayaan Daerah. ENSI Musik/Tari Daerah DIY. Departemen Pendidikan dan Kebudayaan.

1994. *Rencana Pembangunan Lima Tahun Keenam 1994/1995–1998/1999, Buku I*. Pemerintah Propinsi DIY.

1988. *Statistik Indonesia 1988*. Statistics Bureau, DIY.

1988. *Statistik Kaparawisataan DIY 1988*. Statistics Bureau, DIY.

1998. *Statistik Kesejahteraan Rakyat*, Welfare Statistics 1997. National Socio-Economic Survey, Jakarta.

1994. *Statistik Parawisata, Pos dan Telekomunikasi DIY 1993*. Kantor Wilayah VIII Departemen Pariwisata, Pos dan Telekomunikasi, DIY.

1999. *Statistik Pariwisata, Seni dan Budaya[Parsenibud] Propinsi Daerah Istimewa Yogyakarta 1998*. Kawil Departemen Parsenibud: DIY.

1999. *Statistik Penduduk DIY 1998*. Statistics Bureau, DIY.

Monographs, Edited Books, Journal Articles, Films and Doctoral Theses

Acciaioli, Greg. 1985. 'Culture as Art: from Practice to Spectacle in Indonesia', *Canberra Anthropology* 8(1–2): 148–72.

Allen, Matthew Harp. 1997. 'Rewriting the Script for Southern Indian Dance', *Drama Review* 41(3): 63–100.

Amit, Vered (ed.). 2002. *Realizing Community: Concepts, Social Relationships and Sentiments.* London and New York: Routledge.

Anderson, Benedict O'Gorman. 1965. *Mythology and the Tolerance of the Javanese.* Modern Indonesia Project Monograph Series. Ithaca: Cornell University Press.

———. 1967. 'Diachronic Field-Notes on the Coronation Anniversary at the Kraton Surakarta Held on Dec 18 1963', *Indonesia* 1 (Apr): 63–71.

———. 1972. 'The Idea of Power in Javanese Culture', in C. Holt (ed.), *Culture and Politics in Indonesia.* London: Cornell University Press.

———. 1983. *Imagined Communities: Reflections on the Origin and Spread of Nationalism.* London: Verso.

Anon. 1990. *Syukuran Anugerah Pahlawan Nasional Bagi Swargi Sri Sultan Haměnku Buwono IX. Ahad Kliwon, 18 Nopember 1990.* Yogyakarta: Karaton Ngayogyakarta Hadiningrat.

Archer, Margaret. 1995. *Realist Social Theory: The Morphogenetic Approach.* Cambridge: Cambridge University Press.

Arjo, Irawati Durban. 1989. 'Women's Dance among the Sundanese of West Java, Indonesia', *Asia Theater Journal* 6(2) (Fall): 168–78.

Aspinall, Ed. 1999. 'Democratisation of the Working Class and the Indonesian Transition', *Review of Indonesian and Malay Affairs* 33(2): 1–32.

Atmakusumah (ed.). 1982. *Tahta untuk Rakyat* [A Throne for the People]. Jakarta: PT Jakarta.

Bachtiar, Harsja W. 1973. 'The Religion of Java: a Commentary', *Sastra Indonesia* V, 1: 85–117.

Bandem, Made I and Frederik deBoer. 1995. *Balinese Dance in Transition: Kaja and Kelod,* 2nd edn. Oxford, Singapore, New York: Oxford University Press.

Barba, Eugenio. 1995. *The Paper Canoe: a Guide to Theatre Anthropology.* London: Routledge.

Barba, Eugenio and Nicola Savese. 1991. *A Dictionary of Theatre Anthropology. The Secret Art of the Performer.* London: Routledge.

Barber, Karin. 1991. *I Would Speak until Tomorrow: Oriki, Women and the Past in a Yoruba Town.* Edinburgh: Edinburgh University Press for the International African Institute.

Bayly, Susan. 1989. *Saints, Goddesses and Kings: Muslims and Christians in South Indian Society.* Cambridge: Cambridge University Press.

Becker, Alton L. 1979. 'Text-Building, Epistemology and Aesthetics in Javanese Shadow Theatre', in A. Becker (ed.), *The Imagination of Reality: Essays in South East Asia Coherence Systems.* New York: Ablex Publishing Corporation.

Becker, Judith. 1991. 'The Javanese Court Bedhaya Dance as a Tantric Analogy', in J.C. Kassler (ed.), *Metaphor: A Musical Dimension.* Sydney: Currency Press.

———. 1993. *Gamelan Stories: Tantrism, Islam and Aesthetics in Central Java.* Monographs in Southeast Asian Studies. Arizona: Arizona State University.

Bell, Catherine. 1992. *Ritual Theory, Ritual Practice.* Oxford: Oxford University Press.

Berg, Cornelis C. 1965. 'The Javanese Picture of the Past', in Soedjatmoko (ed.), *An Introduction to Indonesian Historiography.* New York: Cornell University Press.

Best, David. 1978. *Philosophy and Human Movement.* London: Allen and Unwin.

Bigeon, Cécile. 1982. 'Labuhan: Rite Royal du Kraton de Yogyakarta Célébré sur la Plage de Parangtritis', *Archipel* 24: 117–26.

Black, Max. 1979. 'More about Metaphors', in A. Ortony (ed.), *Metaphor and Thought*. Cambridge: Cambridge University Press.

Blacking, John. 1977. 'Towards an Anthropology of the Body', in J. Blacking (ed.), *The Anthropology of the Body*. ASA Monographs 15. London: Academic Press.

——— 1985. 'Movement, Dance, Music and the Venda Girls' Initiation Cycle', in P. Spencer (ed.), *Society and the Dance*. Cambridge: Cambridge University Press.

Bonneff, Marcel. 1974. 'Le Renouveaument d'un Rituel Royal: les Garebegs à Yogyakarta', *Archipel* 8: 119–46.

——— (ed. and trans.) 1986. *Pérégrinations Javanaises. Les Voyages de R.M.A. Purwa Lelana: Une Vision de Java au XIX Siècle (c.1860–1875)*. Etudes insulindiennes, *Archipel* 7. Paris: Editions de la Maison des Sciences de l'Homme.

Bourchier, David. 1997. 'Totalitarianism and the "National Personality": Recent Controversy about the Philosophical Basis of the Indonesian State', in J. Schiller and B. Martin-Schiller (eds), *Imagining Indonesia: Cultural Politics and Political Culture*. Athens: Ohio University Center for International Studies. Monographs in International Studies Southeast Asia Series No. 97.

Bourdieu, Pierre.1977. *Outline of a Theory of Practice*, trans. R. Nice. Cambridge: Cambridge University Press.

——— 1984. *Distinction: A Social Critique of the Judgement of Taste*. London: Routledge and Kegan Paul.

——— 1993. 'The Market of Symbolic Goods', in P. Bourdieu, *The Field of Cultural Production*. Oxford: Polity Press.

Brakel, Clara. 1976. 'The Court Dances of Central Java and Their Relationship to Classical Indian Dance', *Archipel* 11: 155–66.

Brakel-Papenhuijzen, Clara. 1992. *The Bedhaya Court Dances of Central Java*. Leiden: E.J. Brill.

——— 1996. 'Reflections on the Meaning of a Sacred Songtext', in S. Headley (ed.), *Towards an Anthropology of Prayer: Javanese Ethnolinguistic Studies*. CNRS. Aix-en-Provence: University of Provence.

Brandon, James. 1974 [1967]. *Theatre in South East Asia*. Cambridge, MA.: Harvard University Press.

Brecht, Bertold. 1964. *Brecht on Theatre*, ed. and trans. J. Willett. London: Eyre Methuen.

Brenner, Suzanna A. 1998. *The Domestification of Desire: Women, Wealth and Modernity in Java*. Princeton, NJ: Princeton University Press.

Brinner, Benjamin. 1995. *Knowing Music, Making Music*. Chicago: University of Chicago Press.

Brongtodiningrat, K.P.H. 1975. *The Royal Palace (Karaton) of Yogyakarta: Its Architecture and its Meaning*, trans. R. Murdani Hadiatmaja. Yogyakarta: Kraton Museum.

——— 1978. *Arti Kraton Yogyakarta*, trans. R. Murdani Hadiatmaja. Yogyakarta: Kraton Museum.

——— 1981. '*Falsafah Běksa Bědhaya sarta Běksa Srimpi ing Ngayogyakarta*' [The Philosophy and *Bědhaya* and *Srimpi* dances in Yogyakarta]', in Dewan Ahli Yayasan Siswa Among Běksa (eds), *Kawruh Joged- Mataram*. Yogyakarta: Yayasan Siswa Among Běksa.

Browning, Barbara. 1996. *Samba: Resistance in Motion*. Bloomington: Indiana University Press.

Bruinessen, Martin van, 1994, 'The Origins and Development of Sufi Orders (*Tarekat*) in South East Asia', *Studia Islamika* 1(1): 1–23.

Bruner, Edward M. and Judith Becker. 1979. *Art, Ritual and Society in Indonesia.* South East Asia Studies No.55. Ohio: Ohio University Press.

Buckland, Theresa J. 1999a. 'All Dances are Ethnic – but Some are More Ethnic than Others: Some Observations on Recent Scholarship in Dance and Anthropology', *Dance Research* XVII(1): 3–21.

———— 1999b. 'Introduction: Reflecting on Dance Ethnography', in T.J. Buckland (ed.), *Dance in the Field: Theory, Methods and Issues in Dance Ethnography.* Basingstoke: Macmillan Press.

———— (ed.) 2006. *Dancing the Past in the Present: Nation, Culture, Identities.* Studies in Dance History, Series of the Society for Dance History Scholars. Wisconsin: University of Wisconsin Press.

Bull, Cynthia. 1997. 'Sense, Meaning and Perception in Three Dance Cultures', in J. Desmond (ed.), *Meaning in Motion: New Cultural Studies of Dance.* Durham and London: Duke University Press.

Butler, Judith. 1993. *Bodies that Matter: On the Discursive Limits of Sex.* London: Routledge.

Carey, Peter B.R. 1974. 'The Cultural Ecology of Early Nineteenth Century Java: Pangeran Dipanegara, a Case Study'. Occasional Paper No. 24. Singapore: Institute of Southeast Asian Studies.

———— (ed. and trans). 1981. *Babad Dipanagara: An Account of the Outbreak of the Java War (1825–30).* Kuala Lumpur: Malaysian Branch of the Royal Asiatic Society.

———— 1984. 'Jalan Maliabara ("Garland Bearing Street"): the Etymology and Historical Origins of a Much Misunderstood Yogyakarta Street Name', *Archipel* 27: 51–62.

———— (ed. and trans). 1992. *The British in Java 1811–1816: A Javanese Account.* British Academy Oriental Documents X. Oxford: Oxford University Press.

———— 1993. 'Dance Drama (Wayang Wong) and Politics at the Court of Sultan Hamengkubuwana III (1812–14) of Yogyakarta', in B. Arps (ed.), *Performance in Java and Bali.* London: School of Oriental and African Studies.

Carey, Peter B.R. and Vincent Houben. 1987. 'Spirited Srikandhis and Sly Sumbadras: the Social, Political and Economic Role of Women at the Central Javanese Courts in the 18th and Early 19th centuries', in E. Locher-Scholten and A. Niehof (eds), *Indonesian Women in Focus.* Dordrecht: Foris.

Carter, Alexandra. 1998. *Rethinking Dance History.* Routledge: London and New York.

Chakravorty, Pallabi. 2001. 'From Interculturalism to Historicism: Reflections on Classical Indian Dance', *Dance Research Journal* 32(2), Winter 2000–1: 108–19.

———— 2004. 'Agency in Tradition: Gendered Subjectivity through the Practice of Kathak' in P. Chakravorty (ed.), *Dance in South Asia: New Approaches, Politics and Aesthetics.* Proceedings March 3 2002. Swarthmore College, USA.

Choy, Peggy. 1984. 'Texts through Time: the Golèk Dance of Java', in S. Morgan and L.J. Sears (eds), *Aesthetic Tradition and Cultural Transition in Java and Bali.* Centre for Southeast Studies Monograph 2. Wisconsin: University of Wisconsin.

Clara van Groenendael, Victoria M. 1985. *The Dalang behind the Wayang: the Role of the Surakarta and the Yogyakarta Dalang in Indonesian-Javanese Society.* V.K.I. 114. Dordrecht: Foris.

Coedès, Georges. 1944. *Histoire Ancienne des Etats Hindouisés d'Extrême-Orient.* Hanoi: Imprimerie d'Extrême Orient.

Cohen, Abner. 1977. 'Symbolic Action and the Structure of the Self', in I.M. Lewis (ed.), *Symbols and Sentiments: Cross-cutting Studies in Symbolism.* London: Academic Press.

_____ 1993. *Masquerade Politics: Explorations in the Structure of Urban and Cultural Movements.* Oxford: Berg.

Collingwood, Robin G. 1979 [1938]. *The Principles of Art.* Oxford: Oxford University Press.

Connerton, Paul. 1989. *How Societies Remember.* Cambridge: Cambridge University Press.

Crawfurd, John. 1820. *History of the Indian Archipelago,* 3 vols. Edinburgh: Archibald, Constable and Co.

Crossley, Nick. 1995. 'Body Techniques, Agency and Intercorporeality: on Goffman's Relations in Public', *Sociology* 29(1): 133–49.

_____ 1996. 'Body-Subject/Body-Power: Agency, Inscription and Control in Foucault and Merleau-Ponty', *Body and Society* 2(2): 99–116.

Csordas, Thomas J. 1994. *Embodiment and Experience: The Existential Ground of Culture and Self.* Cambridge: Cambridge University Press.

Cuisinier, Jeanne. 1951. *La Danse Sacrée.* Paris: Presses Universitaires de France.

Dahles, Heidi. 2001. *Tourism, Heritage and National Culture in Java: Dilemmas of a Local Community.* Richmond: Curzon/IIAS.

d'Almeida, W. Barrington. 1864. *Life in Java: with Sketches of the Javanese,* 2 vols. London: Hurst and Blackett.

Danaan, Lly de. 1986. 'The Blosson Falling: Movement and Allusion in Malay Dance', *Asian Theatre Journal* III(1): 110–17.

Danarto. 1982. '*Bedoyo Robot Membelot*' [Bedoyo Betrayal Blast-off] in *Adam Ma'rifat.* Jakarta: Balai Pustaka.

Daniel, Yvonne Payne. 1996. 'Tourism Dance Performances: Authenticity and Creativity', *Annals of Tourism Research* 23(4): 780–97.

Day, Tony. 2004. *Fluid Iron: State Formation in Southeast Asia.* Honolulu: University of Hawai'i Press.

deBoer, Frederic. 1989. '"Balinese Sendratari", a Modern Dramatic Dance Genre', *Asian Theatre Journal* 6(2): 179–93.

De Certeau, Michel. 1984. *The Practice of Everyday Life,* trans. S. Rendall. Berkeley: University of California Press.

De Grave, Jean-Marc. 2001. *Initiation Rituelle et Arts Martiaux.* Paris: L'Harmattan.

Desmond, Jane C. (ed.). 1997. *Meaning in Motion: New Cultural Studies of Dance.* Durham and London: Duke University Press.

_____ 1999. *Staging Tourism. Bodies on Display from Waikiki to Sea World.* Chicago: University of Chicago Press.

Dewan Ahli Yayasan Siswa Among Běksa (eds). 1981. *Kawruh Joged-Mataram.* Yogyakarta: Yayasan Siswa Among Běksa.

Dewey, Alice. 1978. 'Deference Behaviour in Java: Duty or Privilege?', in S. Udin (ed.), *Essays Presented to Sutan Takdir Alisjahbana on His Seventieth Birthday.* Jakarta: Dian Rakyat.

Djoharnurani, Sri. 1991. 'Beksa Lawung Kraton Yogyakarta sebagai Media Transmisi Makna', *SENI* 1/02, July: 89–101.

Drewes, Gerardus W.J. (ed.). 1978. *An Early Javanese Code of Muslim Ethics.* Bibliotheca Indonesica K.I.T.L.V. 18. The Hague: Martinus Nijhofff.

Dumarçay, Jaques. 1991. *The Palaces of South-East Asia: Architecture and Customs,* ed. and trans. M. Smithies. Singapore: Oxford University Press.

Eagleton, Terry. 2003. *After Theory.* London: Penguin.

Echols, John M. and Hassan Shadily. 1990. *Kamus Indonesia-Inggris. An Indonesian-English Dictionary,* 3rd edn. Jakarta: Penerbit PT Gramedia.

Errington, J. Joseph. 1988. *Structure and Style in Javanese: A Semiotic View of Linguistic Etiquette*. Philadelphia: University of Pennsylvanian Press.

Evans, Grant. 1998. *The Politics of Ritual and Remembrance: Laos since 1975*. Honolulu: Hawai'i University Press.

Evans-Pritchard, Edward E. 1928. 'The Dance', *Africa* 1: 446–62.

Farnell, Brenda (ed.). 1995. *Human Action Signs in Cultural Context: the Visible and Invisible in Dance*. Metuchen, NJ: Scarecrow Press.

Felföldi, László. 1999. 'Folk Dance Research in Hungary: Relations among Theory, Fieldwork and the Archive', in T.J. Buckland (ed.), *Dance in the Field: Theory, Methods and Issues in Dance Ethnography*. Basingstoke: Macmillan Press.

Finnegan, Ruth. 2002. *Communicating: The Multiple Modes of Human Interconnection*. London: Routledge.

Florida, Nancy. 1992. 'The Badhaya Katawang: a Translation of the Song of Kangjeng Ratu Kidul.' *Indonesia* 53: 21–32.

—— 1995. *Writing the Past, Incribing the Future: History as Prophecy in Colonial Java*. Durham and London: Duke University Press.

Foley, Kathy. 1992. 'The Medium and the Message: Sintren, Trance Performance of Cirebon', in K. Foley (ed.), *Essays on Southeast Asian Performing Arts: Local Manifestations and Cross-cultural Implications*. Berkeley: University of California.

Foster, Susan Leigh (ed.). 1996. Introduction, *Corporealities: Dancing Knowledge, Culture and Power*. London: Routledge.

—— 1998. 'Dancing the Body Politic: Manners and Mimesis in Eighteenth Century Ballet', in S.E. Melzer and K. Norberg (eds), *From the Royal to the Republican Body*. Berkeley, CA: University of California Press.

Freeland, Felicia H. 1985. 'Revivalism as a Defining Stand in Yogyakartan Court Dance', *Indonesia Circle* 37: 35–43.

Gaston, Anne-Marie. 1996. *Bharata Natyam: From Temple to Theatre*. Delhi: Manohar.

Geertz, Clifford. 1960. *The Religion of Java*. New York: Free Press.

—— 1972. 'Afterword', in C. Holt (ed.), *Culture and Politics in Indonesia*. London: Cornell University Press.

—— 1973. *The Interpretation of Culture*. New York: Basic Books.

—— 1980. *Negara: The Theatre State in Nineteenth Century Bali*. Princeton: Princeton University Press.

Geertz, Hildred. 1961. *The Javanese Family: A Study of Kinship and Socialisation*. New York: Free Press.

Girard, René. 1977. *Violence and the Sacred*. London: Johns Hopkins University Press.

Goffman, Erving. 1956. *The Presentation of Self in Everyday Life*. Monograph No. 2. Edinburgh: University of Edinburgh Social Sciences Research Centre.

Gonda, Jan. 1948. 'The Javanese Vocabulary of Courtesy', *Lingua* 1(3): 333–76.

—— 1952. *Sanskrit in Indonesia*. Nagpur: International Academy of Indian Culture.

Goodman, Nelson. 1976. *The Languages of Art*, 2nd edn. Indianapolis: Hackett Publishing Co. Inc.

—— 1978. *Ways of Worldmaking*. Sussex: Harvester Press.

Graburn, Nelson. 1976. *Ethnic and Tourist Arts*. Berkeley: University of California Press.

Grau, Andrée. 2005. 'When the Landscape Becomes Flesh: An Investigation into Body Boundaries with Special Reference to Tiwi Dance and western Classical Ballet', *Body and Society* 11(4): 141–63.

Groneman, Isaac. 1888. *In de Kedaton te Jogjakarta: Oepatjara, Ampilan en Tooneeldansen.* Leiden: Brill.

—— 1895. *De Garĕbĕgs te Ngayogyakarta.* K.I.T.V.L.. The Hague: Martinus Nijhoff.

—— 1899. *De Wayang Orang Prĕgiwa in de Karaton te Jogjakarta in Juni 1899.* Semarang: Van Dorp.

Guinness, Patrick. 1986. *Harmony and Hierarchy in a Javanese Kampung.* A.S.A.A. Singapore: Oxford University Press.

Hadi, Y. Sumandio. 1988. 'Seni Tari di Keraton Yogyakarta Pembentikan dan Perkembangannya dalam Masa Pemerintahan Sultan Hamengku Buwana IX (1940–1987)'. Unpublished Pasca Sardjana thesis, Gadjah Mada University, Yogyakarta.

Hadiwidjojo, K.G.P.H. 1921. *De Bĕdhaya Ketawang.* Java-Institut. De handelingen van het eerste congress voor de Taal- Land- en Volkenkunde van Java, Solo 25–26 December. Weltevreden: Albrecht and Co.

—— 1972. 'Danse Sacrée à Surakarta: la Signification du Bedojo Ketawang', *Archipel* 3: 117–30.

—— 1981. *Bedhaya Ketawang: Tarian Sakral di Candi-Candi.* Jakarta: Balai Pustaka.

Hadiwijono, Harun. 1967. *Man in the Present Javanese Mysticism.* Baarn: Bosch and Keuning.

Hamera, Judith. 2002. 'An Answerability of Memory: "Saving" Khmer Classical Dance'. *The Drama Review* 46(4): 65–85.

Handler, Richard. 1988. *Nationalism and the Politics of Culture in Quebec.* Madison: University of Wisconsin Press.

Hanna, Judith L. 1979. 'Movements towards Understanding Humans through the Anthropological Study of Dance', *Current Anthropology* 20(2): 313–38.

Hardjowirogo, Marbangun. 1983. *Manusia Jawa.* Jakarta: Yayasan Idayu.

Hastrup, Kirsten. 2004. *Action. Anthropology in the Company of Shakespeare.* Copenhagen: Museum Tusculanum Press, University of Copenhagen.

Hatley, Barbara. 1979. 'Ketoprak Theatre and the Wayang Tradition'. Centre of South-East Asian Studies Working Paper 19. Monash: Melbourne University.

—— 1995. 'Women in Contemporary Indonesian Theatre', *B.K.I* 151 (IV): 570–601

—— 2004. 'Global Influence, National Politics and Local Identity in Central Javanese Theatre', *Review of Indonesian and Malaysian Affairs* 38(2): 63–100.

Heine-Geldern, Robert von. 1942. 'Conceptions of State and Kingship in South East Asia', *Far East Asian Quarterly* 2 (Nov): 15–30.

Hellman, Jörgen. 1999. 'Longser Antar Pulau: Indonesian Cultural Politics and the Revitalisation of Traditional Theatre.' Unpublished doctoral thesis, Department of Anthropology, University of Göteborg.

Helsdingen-Schoevers, Beata van. 1912. *Het Srimpi Boek.* Jakarta: Volkslectuur.

Henry, Rosita, Fiona MacGowan, and David Murray. 2000. 'Introduction' to 'The Politics of Dance', *The Australian Journal of Anthropology* 11(3): 253–60.

Hinzler, Heidi I.R. 1981. *Bima Swarga in Balinese Wayang.* K.I.T.L.V. Verhandelingen 90. The Hague: Martinus Nijhoff.

Hobsbawm, Eric and Terence Ranger (eds). 1983. *The Invention of Tradition.* Cambridge: Cambridge University Press.

Holt, Claire. 1937. 'The Dance in Java', *Asia* 37 (Dec): 843–46.

—— 1967. *Art in Indonesia: Continuities and Change.* Ithaca: Cornell University Press.

Hopkins, Jeffrey (ed. and trans.). 1977. *Tantra in Tibet: The Great Exposition of the Secret Mantra by Tsong-Ka-Pa.* London: Allen and Unwin.

Horne, Elinor. C. 1974. *Javanese-English Dictionary.* New Haven: Yale University Press.

Hostetler, Jan. 1982. 'Bedhaya Semang: the Sacred Dance of Yogyakarta', *Archipel* 24: 127–42.

Hough, Brian. 1992. 'Contemporary Balinese Dance Spectacles as National Drama'. Working Paper 74, Claydon (Victoria): Centre of Southeast Asian Studies, Monash University.

Hughes-Freeland, Felicia. 1988. *The Dancer and the Dance* (16mm film and DVD). London: The Royal Anthropological Institute.

———— 1989. 'Indonesian Image Enhancement', *Anthropology Today* 5(6): 3–5.

———— 1990. 'Tayuban: Culture on the Edge', *Indonesia Circle* 52: 36–44.

———— 1991a. 'A Throne for the People: Observations on the Jumenengan of Sultan Hamengku Buwono X'. *Indonesia* 51: 129–52.

———— 1991b. 'Javanese Visual Performance and the Indian Mystique', in L. Chandra (ed.), *The Art and Culture of South-East Asia*. Delhi: Aditya Prakashan.

———— 1991c. 'Classification and Communication in Palace Performance', *Visual Anthropology* 4(3/4): 345–66.

———— 1993a. 'Golek Menak and Tayuban: Patronage and Professionalism in Two Spheres of Central Javanese Culture', in B. Arps (ed.), *Performance in Java and Bali*. London: School of Oriental and African Studies.

———— 1993b 'Packaging Dreams: Javanese Perceptions of Tourism and Performance', in M. Hitchcock, V.T. King and M.J.G. Parnwell (eds), *Tourism in South-East Asia: Theory and Practice*. London: Routledge.

———— 1995. 'Dance and Gender in a Javanese Palace Tradition', in W. J. Karim (ed.), *'Male' and 'Female' in Developing South East Asia*. Oxford: Berg.

———— 1996. *Tayuban: Dancing the Spirit in Java* (hi-8 video and DVD). London: The Royal Anthropological Institute.

———— 1997a. 'Art and Politics: from Javanese Court Dance to Indonesian Art', *Journal of the Royal Anthropological Institute*. 3(3): 473–95.

———— 1997b. 'Consciousness in Performance: a Javanese Theory', *Social Anthropology* 5(21): 55–68.

———— 1998. 'From Temple to Television: the Balinese Case', in F. Hughes-Freeland and M.M. Crain (eds), *Recasting Ritual*. E.A.S.A. Series. London: Routledge.

———— 2001a. 'Dance, Dissimulation and Identity', in J. Hendry and C.W. Watson (eds), *An Anthropology of Indirect Communication*. ASA Monographs 37. London: Routledge.

———— 2001b. 'Performers and Professionalization in Java: between Leisure and Livelihood', *South-East Asia Research* 9(2): 213–33.

———— 2005. 'Visual Takes on Dance in Java', *Oral Tradition* 20(1): 58–79, with *eCompanion at http://www.oraltradition.org.

———— 2006. 'Constructing a Classical Tradition: Women's Dance in Java', in T.J. Buckland (ed.), *Dancing the Past in the Present: Nation, Culture, Identities*. Studies in Dance History, Series of the Society for Dance History Scholars. Wisconsin, University of Wisconsin Press.

———— 2007a. 'Tradition and the Individual Talent: T.S. Eliot for Anthropologists', in E. Hallam and T. Ingold (eds), *Creativity and Cultural Improvisation*. ASA Monographs 44. Oxford: Berg.

———— 2007b. 'Charisma and Celebrity in Indonesian Politics', *Anthropological Theory*, 7(2): 177–200.

———— and Mary M. Crain (eds). 1998. 'Introduction' in F. Hughes-Freeland and M.M. Crain (eds), *Recasting Ritual*. E.A.S.A. series. London: Routledge.

James, Wendy. 2003. *The Ceremonial Animal: A New Portrait of Anthropology*. Oxford: Oxford University Press.

Jay, Robert. 1969. *Javanese Villagers: Social Relations in Rural Modjokuto*. London: M.I.T. Press.

Johns, Anthony H. 1964. *The Gift Addressed to the Spirit of the Prophet*. Oriental Monograph Series, Centre of Oriental Studies. Canberra: Australian National University.

Jong, S. de. 1976. *Salah Satu Sikap Hidup Orang Jawa*. Yogyakarta: Yayasan Kanisius.

Jordaan, Roy E. 1984. 'The Mystery of Nyai Lara Kidul, Goddess of the Southern Ocean', *Archipel* 28: 99–116.

Josselin de Jong, P.E. de (ed.). 1977. *Structural Anthropology in the Netherlands*. K.I.T.L.V. Translations Series 17. The Hague: Martinus Nijhoff.

Juynboll, Hendrik H. 1906. 'Tooneel', in *Encyclopaedie Nederlandische-Indië*. The Hague: Martinus Nijhoff.

_____ 1915. *Het Javaansche Tooneel*. Weltevreden: Commissie voor de Volkslectuur.

Kaeppler, Adrienne L. 1971. 'Aesthetics in Tongan Dance', *Ethnomusicology* 15(2): 175–85.

_____ 1978. 'Dance in Anthropological Perspective', *Annual Review of Anthropology* 7: 31–49.

_____ 1985. 'Structured Movement Systems in Tonga', in P. Spencer (ed.), *Society and the Dance*. Cambridge: Cambridge University Press.

Kam, Garrett. 1986. 'Javanese Court Dance and Tourism: Behind the Scene Dynamic in a Modern Performing Group', *U.C.L.A. Journal of Dance Ethnology* 1: 39–47.

_____ 1987. 'Wayang Wong in the Court of Yogyakarta: the Enduring Significance of Javanese Dance Drama', *Asian Theatre Journal* 4(1): 23–51.

_____ n.d. 'The Symbolic Ship of State: Maritime Imagery in the Bedhaya Dances of Central Java'. Unpublished paper first presented to 'The State of the Art', an international seminar on Southeast Asian performing arts at the Universiti Sains Malaysia, Penang, 10–13 August 1992.

Kapferer, Bruce. 1991. *A Celebration of Demons: Exorcism and the Aesthetics of Healing in Sri Lanka*. Smithsonian University Press: Berg.

Kartodirdjo, Sartono. 1973. *Protest Movements in Rural Java*. Singapore: Oxford University Press.

Kartomi, Margaret J. 1973. 'Music and Trance in Central Java', *Ethnomusicology* 17: 163–200.

_____ 1976. 'Performance, Music and Meaning of Reyog Ponorogo', *Indonesia* 22: 85–130.

Kats, J. 1923. *Programma van de Wajang-Wong-Opvoering in den Kraton te Jogjakarta op 3,4,5 en 6 September 1923*. Weltevreden: G. Kolff and Co.

Kawendrasusanta, Kuswadji. 1981. 'Tata Rias dan Busana Tari Gaya Yogyakarta', in F. Wibowo (ed.), *Mengenal Tari Klasik Gaya Yogyakarta*. Yogyakarta: Dewan Kesenian Propinsi DIY.

Keeler, Ward. 1987. *Javanese Shadow Plays, Javanese Selves*. Princeton: Princeton University Press.

Kenji, Tsuchiya. 1987. *Democracy and Leadership: The Rise of the Taman Siswa Movement in Indonesia*. Monographs of the Centre for Southeast Asian Studies, Kyoto University 18. Honolulu: University of Hawai'i Press.

Kersenboom, Saskia. 1995. *Word, Sound, Image. The Life of the Tamil Text*. Oxford: Berg Publishers.

Kertzer, David I. 1988. *Ritual, Politics and Power*. New Haven and London: Yale University Press.

Kirshenblatt-Gimblett, Barbara. 1995. 'Confusing Pleasures', in G.E. Marcus and F.R. Myers (eds), *The Traffic in Culture: Refiguring Art and Anthropology*. Berkeley: University of California Press.

Kleen, Tyra de and P. de Kat Angelino. 1923. *Mudras auf Bali: Handhaltungen der Priester.* Folkwang-verlag G.M.B.H. Hagen i.w. under Darms. Hagen: Druck van Bald & Kruger.

Koentjaraningrat, R.M. (ed.).1959. *Tari dan Kesusasteran. Buku Peringatan Ulang Tahun ke-VIII Indonesian Tunggal Irama.* Yogyakarta: Pertjetakan Taman Siswa.

—— 1980. 'Javanese Terms for God and Supernatural Beings and the Idea of Power', in R. Schefold et al. (eds), *Man, Meaning and History: Essays in Honour of H.G. Schulte-Nordholt.* K.I.T.L.V. Verhandelingen 89. The Hague: Nijhoff.

—— 1985. *Javanese Culture.* Singapore: Oxford University Press in Asia.

Kumar, Ann. 1980. 'Javanese Court Society and Politics in the Late Eighteenth Century: the Record of a Lady Soldier', *Indonesia* 29 (Apr): 1–46.

Kunst, Jap. 1973. *Music in Java,* trans. E. L. Heins. The Hague: Martinus Nijhoff.

Kurath, Gertrude P. 1960. 'Panorama of Dance Ethnology', *Current Anthropology* 1: 233–54.

Lakoff, George and Mark Johnson. 1980. *Metaphors We Live By.* London: Chicago University Press.

Langer, Suzanne. 1959. *Form and Feeling: A Theory of Art Developed in 'Philosophy in a New Key'.* London: Routledge and Kegan Paul.

Lelyveld, Theodore B. van. 1922. *De Javaansche Danskunst.* Den Hague: Hadi Poestaka.

—— 1931. *La Danse dans le Théatre Javanais.* Paris: Librairie Floury.

Lévi-Strauss, Claude. 1966 [1962]. *The Savage Mind.* London: Weidenfeld and Nicolson.

Lewis, John L. 1992. *Ring of Liberation: Deceptive Discourse in Brazilian Capoeira.* London and Chicago: University of Chicago Press.

Lim, V. King. 1995. 'Setting Modern Traditions: a Look at Sendratari, a Contemporary Performance Genre in Indonesia', *Review of Indonesian and Malaysian Affairs* 29(1&2): 107–18.

Lindsay, Jennifer. 1985. 'Klasik, Kitsch or Contemporary: a Study of the Javanese Performing Arts'. Unpublished doctoral thesis, Sydney University.

Lindsay, Jennifer, R.M. Soetanto, and A. Feinstein. 1994. *Preliminary Descriptive Catalogue of the Manuscripts of the Kraton Yogyakarta, Indonesia.* Jakarta: Yayasan Obor Indonesia.

—— 1995. 'Cultural Policy and the Performing Arts in Southeast Asia', *B.K.I.* 151 IV: 656–71.

Lombard, Denys. 1990. *Le Carrefour Javanais: Essai d'Histoire Globale,* 3 vols. Paris: Editions de l'Ecole des Hautes Etudes en Sciences Sociales.

Long, Roger. 1982. *Javanese Shadow Theatre: Movement System and Characterization in Ngayogyakarta.* Ann Arbor: University of Michigan Research Press.

Magnis Suseno, Franz and S. Reksosusilo. 1983. *Etika Jawa dalam Tantangan.* Yogyakarta: Yayasan Kanisius.

Mandoyokusumo (ed.). 1980. *Sĕrat Raja Putra.* Yogyakarta: Museum Kraton.

—— n. d. *Sejarah Pasareyan Pajimatan Imogiri Ngayogyakarta.* Yogyakarta: Museum Kraton.

Marianto, M. Dwi. 1997. 'Teks-Teks Sepanjang Jalan dari Malioboro Mall hingga Ring Road Yogya, *Jawa,* I: 92–103.

Marglin, Frédérique A. 1985. *Wives of the God-King: The Ritual of the Devadasis of Puri.* Delhi: Oxford University Press.

Mauss, Marcel. 1973 [1935]. 'Techniques of the Body', *Economy and Society* 2(1): 70–88.

Mayer, Leendert. Th. 1897. *Een Blik in het Javaansche Volksleven,* 2 vols. Leiden: E. J. Brill.

McClary, Susan. 1998. 'Unruly Passions and Courtly Dances: Technologies of the Body in Baroque Music', in S.E. Melzer and K. Norberg (eds), *From the Royal to the Republican Body.* Berkeley, CA: University of California Press.

McVey, Ruth. 1967. 'Taman Siswa and the Indonesian National Awakening', *Indonesia*, 4 (Oct): 128–49.

Meduri, Avanti. 1988. 'Bharata Natyam – What are You?', *Asian Theatre Journal* 5(1): 1–22.

Melzer, Sara E. and Katherine Norberg (eds). 1998. *From the Royal to the Republican Body*. Berkeley, CA: University of California Press.

Merleau-Ponty, Maurice. 1962. *Phenomenology of Perception*, trans. C. Smith. London and Henley: Routledge and Kegan Paul.

Mitchell, J.Clyde. 1956. *The Kalela Dance: Aspects of Social Relationships among Urban Africans in Northern Rhodesia*. Rhodes Livingstone Paper 27. Manchester: University of Manchester Press.

Moedjanto, G. 1986. *The Concept of Power in Javanese Culture*. Yogyakarta: Gadjah Mada University Press.

Moerdowo. 1963. *Reflections on Indonesian Arts and Culture*, 2nd edn. Surabaya: Permata.

Moertono, Soemarsaid. 1968. *State and Statecraft in Java: A Study of the Later Mataram Period, 16th–19th centuries*. Modern Indonesia Project Monograph Series. Ithaca: Cornell University Press.

Morris, Gay (ed.). 1996. *Moving Words: Rewriting Dance*. London: Routledge.

Morrison, Miriam J. 1977. 'Women's Dance and Tradition in Jogjakarta', in A. Kaeppler, J. van Zile, and C. Wolz (eds), *Asian and Pacific Dance: Selected Papers from the 1974 CORD-SEM Conference Dance Research Annual VIII*. New York: CORD.

Mulyadi, Sri Wulan Rujiati (ed.). 1983. *Hikayat Indraputra: A Malay Romance*. Bibliotheca Indonesica 23. Leiden: K.I.T.L.V. Press.

Mulyono, Sri. 1977. *Human Character in the Wayang*. Jakarta: Pustaka Wayang.

Nakamura, Mitsuo. 1983. *The Crescent Arises over the Banyan Tree*. Yogyakarta: Gadjah Mada University Press.

Nakashima, Narihisa. 1982. 'Classification, Symbol and Metaphor in the Figure of Semar, a Clown of Wayang Purwa', *Journal of Asian and African Studies (Ajra Afurika Geno Buoka Kenhyu)* 23: 73–75 Vol 23: 73–5 (pp 75–90 Japanese text).

Ness, Sally Ann. 1992. *Body Movement and Culture: Kinesthetic and Visual Symbolism in a Philippine Community*. Philadelphia: University of Pennsylvania Press.

———— 2004. 'Being a Body in a Cultural Way: Understanding the Cultural in the Embodiment of Dance', in H. Thomas and J. Ahmed (eds), *Cultural Bodies: Ethnography and Theory*. Oxford: Blackwell.

Nicholson, Reynold A. 1975. *The Mystics of Islam*. London: Routledge and Kegan Paul.

Nietzsche, Friedrich. 1956. *The Birth of Tragedy and the Genealogy of Morals*, trans. F. Golffing. New York: Doubleday Anchor Books.

Nor, Mohd Anis MD. 1993. *Zapin. Folk Dance of the Malay World*. Singapore: Oxford University Press.

Novack, Cynthia J. 1990. *Sharing the Dance. Contact Improvisation and American Culture*. Wisconsin: University of Wisconsin Press.

Onghokham. 1983. *Rakyat dan Negara*. Jakarta: Sinar Harapan LPES.

O'Shea, Janet. 1998. '"Traditional" Indian Dance and the Making of Interpretive Communities', *Asian Theatre Journal* 15(1): 45–63.

Peacock, James L. 1968. *Rites of Modernization*. Chicago: Chicago University Press.

Pemberton, John. 1994. *On the Subject of 'Java'*. Ithaca: Cornell University Press.

Picard, Michel. 1999. 'The Discourses of Kebalian: Transcultural Constructions of Balinese Identity', in L.H. Connor and R. Rubinstein (eds), *Staying Local in the Global Village: Bali in the Twentieth Century*. Honolulu: University of Hawai'i Press.

Pigeaud, Theodore G. Th. 1938. *Javaanse Volksvertoningen: Bijdrage tot de Beschrijving van Land en Volk*. Batavia: Volkslectuur.

—— (ed. and trans.). 1960–63. *Java in the Fourteenth Century: A Study in Cultural History. The Nāgarakṛtāgama by Rakawi Prapañca of Majapahit 1365 A.D.*, 5 vols. K.I.T.L.V. Translation Series 41. The Hague: Martinus Nijhofff.

—— 1967. *Literature of Java*, 3 vols. Leiden: University Press.

Pigeaud, Theodore G. Th. and Hermanus J. de Graaf. 1976. *Islamic States in Java*. Verhandelingen van het K.I.T.L.V. 70. The Hague: Martinus Nijhoff.

Pillai, Shanti. 2002. 'Rethinking Global Indian Dance through Local Eyes: the Contemporary Bharatanatyam Scene in Chennai', *Dance Research Journal* 34(2): 14–29.

Poerbatjaraka, R.M. 1962. 'Njai Lara Kidul', *Penelitian Sedjara* III (5): 20–4; III(6): 17–23.

Poerwadarminta, W.J.S. 1939. *Bausastra Jawa*. Batavia: J.B. Wolters.

Porter, Roy. 2003. *Flesh in the Age of Reason*. London: Penguin.

Pott, Peter H. 1966. *Yoga and Yantra: Their Interrelation and their Significance for Indian Archaeology*, trans. R. Needham. The Hague: Martinus Nijhofff.

Prijono. 1982. *Indonesia Menari; Indonesian Dances*. Jakarta: Balai Pustaka.

Prijotomo, Josef. 1988. *Ideas and Forms of Javanese Architecture*. Yogyakarta: Gadjah Mada University Press.

Pringgobroto, Sudharso. 1959. 'Perkembangan Methode Mengajar Seni Tari Jawa', in R.M. Koentjaraningrat (ed.), *Tari dan Kesusasteran. Buku Peringatan Ulang Tahun ke-VIII Indonesian Tunggal Irama*. Yogyakarta: Pertjetakan Taman Siswa.

Programma van de Wajang-Orang-Voorstelling 1932–38. Yogyakarta: Kraton.

Pudjasworo, Bambang. 1982. 'Studi Analisa Konsep Estetis-Koreografis Tari Bedhaya Lambangsari'. Unpublished *Seniman Tari* thesis, ASTI, Yogyakarta.

Raffles, Thomas Stamford. 1978 [1817]. *The History of Java*. Kuala Lumpur: Oxford University Press.

Ram, Kalpana. 2000. 'Dancing the Past into Life: the *Rasa, Nṛtta* and *Rāga* of Immigrant Existence', *AJA* 11(3): 261–73.

Ranger, Terence O. 1975. *Dance and Society in East Africa: The Beni Ngoma*. London: Heinemann.

Ranggawarsita, R.Ng. 1954. *Wirid Hidajat-Jati*, ed. R. Tanojo. Surabaya: Trimurti.

Reed, Susan A. 1998. 'The Politics and Poetics of Dance', *Annual Review of Anthropology* 27(1): 503–32.

Reid, Anthony. 1988. *Southeast Asia in the Age of Commerce 1450–1680*. Vol I: *The Land below the Winds*. New Haven and London: Yale University Press.

—— 1993. *Southeast Asia in the Age of Commerce 1450–1680*. Vol II: *Expansion and Crisis*. New Haven and London: Yale University Press.

Rendra, W.S. 1983. *Mempertimbankan Tradisi: Kumpulan Karangan*, ed. Eneste Pamusuk. Jakarta: PT Gramedia.

Resink, G.J. 1982. '*Mers Javanaises*', trans. C. Pelras, *Archipel* 24: 97–100.

Resink-Wilkens, A.J. 1924. 'De Klana-Dans', *Djawa* 4(2): 99–105.

Ricklefs, Merle C. 1974. *Jogjakarta under Sultan Mangkubumi 1749–1792: A History of the Division of Java*. London: Oxford University Press.

—— 1981. *A History of Modern Indonesia c.1300 to the Present*. London: Macmillan.

—— 1993. *War, Culture and Economy in Java 1677–1726*. A.S.A.A. Southeast Asia Publications Series. London: Allen and Unwin.

—— 1998. *The Seen and Unseen Worlds in Java 1726–1749. History, Literature and Islam in the Court of Pakubuwana II.* A.S.A.A. Southeast Asia Publications Series. London and Honolulu: Allen and Unwin and University of Hawai'i Press.

Robison, Richard. 1998. 'Indonesia after Soeharto: More of the Same, Descent into Chaos or a Shift to Reform' in G. Forrester and R.J. May (eds), *The Fall of Soeharto.* Bathhurst, NSW: Crawford House Publishing.

Robson, Stuart O. 1990. *The Wědhatama: An English Translation.* K.I.T.L.V. Working Papers 4. Leiden: K.I.T.L.V. Press.

—— (trans.) 1995. *Deśawarṇana (Nāgarakṛtāgama) by Mpu Prapañca.* Verhandelingen van het K.I.T.L.V. 169. Leiden: KITLV Press.

Rouget, Gilbert. 1985. *Music and Trance: A Theory of Relations between Music and Possession,* trans. and revised B. Biebuyck. Chicago: Chicago University Press.

Rutnin, Mattani Modjara. 1993. *Drance, Drama and Theatre in Thailand: The Process of Development and Modernization.* Centre for East Asian Cultural Studies for Unesco. Tokyo: The Toyo Bunko.

Sairin, Sjafri. 1982. *Javanese Trah: Kin-Based Social Organisation.* Yogyakarta: Gadjah Mada University Press.

Sastrapustaka, B.Y.H. 1984. '*Wedha Pradangga Kawedhar.* Knowledge of Gamelan Revealed', trans. A. Sutton, in J. Becker and A. Feinstein (eds), *Karawitan: Source Readings in Javanese Gamelan and Vocal Music,* Vol I. Michigan: Center for South and Southeast Asian Studies.

Sastrowardoyo, Subagio 1991. '*Eling, Sikap Batin Jawa yang Paling Inti*', in Sulastin Sutrisno, Darusuprapta and Sudaryanto (eds), *Bahasa – Sastra – Budaya: Ratna Manikam Untaian Persembhana kepada Prof. Dr P.J. Zoetmulder.* Yogyakarta: Gadjah Mada University Press.

Sastrowiyono. 1981. *Rambangan Langěn Mandra Wanara.* Yogyakarta: Sekolah Menengah Karawitan Indonesia.

Savigliano, Martha E. 1995. *Tango and the Political Economy of Passion.* Boulder, Col: Westview Press.

Schechner, Richard. 2001. 'Rasaethetics', *The Drama Review* 45(3): 27–50.

Schieffelin, Edward. L. 1998. 'Problematizing Performance', in F. Hughes-Freeland (ed.), *Ritual, Performance, Media.* ASA Monographs 35. London: Routledge.

Scott, James C. 1975. *The Moral Economy of the Peasant.* New Haven: Yale University Press.

—— 1985. *Weapons of the Weak: Everyday Forms of Peasant Resistance.* New Haven and London: Yale University Press.

—— 1998. *Seeing Like a State: How Certain Schemes to Improve the Human Condition have Failed.* New Haven and London: Yale University Press.

Sears, Laurie J. 1996a. *Shadows of Empire: Colonial Discourse and Javanese Tales.* Durham, NC: Duke University Press.

—— (ed.). 1996b. *Fantasizing the Feminine in Indonesia.* Durham and London: Duke University Press.

Selosoemardjan. 1962. *Social Change in Yogyakarta.* New York: Cornell University Press.

—— 1978. 'The Kraton in the Javanese Social System', in Haryati Soebadio and Carinne A. du Marchie Sarvaas (eds), *Dynamics of Indonesian History.* Amsterdam: NY Holland Publications.

Shapiro, Toni. 1995. 'The Dancer in Cambodia', *Asian Art Culture* 8(1): 8–23.

Sheets Johnstone, Maxine. 1984. 'Phenomenology as a Way of Illuminating Dance', in M. Sheets Johnstone (ed.), *Illuminating Dance.* Cranbury, NJ: Associated University Press.

Shennan, Jennifer. 1991. 'Maori Dance Terminology', *Dance Studies* 15: 68–99.

Slamet, Ina E. 1982. *Cultural Strategies for Survival:The Plight of the Javanese.* Comparative Asian Studies Programme. Rotterdam: Erasmus University.

Slamet, Muhammed. 1977. 'Priyayi Value Conflict', in M. Slamet, B. Anderson and M. Nakamura (eds), *Religion and Social Ethos in Indonesia.* Monash: Centre of Southeast Asian Studies.

Soebardi, S. 1975. *The Book of Cabolèk.* Bibliotheca Indonesica 10. The Hague: Martinus Nijhoff.

Soedarsono, R.M. 1974. *Dances in Indonesia.* Jakarta: Gunung Agung.

――― et al. 1978. *Kamus Istilah Tari dan Karawitan Jawa.* Jakarta: Proyek Penelitihan Bahasa dan Sastra Indonesia dan Daerah (mimeog.).

――― 1984. *Wayang Wong, the State Ritual Dance Drama in the Court of Yogyakarta.* Yogyakarta: Gadjah Mada University Press.

――― 1989/1990. *Seni Pertunjukan Jawa Tradisional dan Pariwisata di Daerah Istimewa Yogyakarta.* Yogyakarta: Departemen Pendidikan dan Kebudayaan.

―――, Darusuprapta, and Harjana Hardjawijana. 1989. *Sultan Hamengkubuwono IX, Pengembang dan Pembaharu Tari Jawa Gaya Yogyakarta.* Yogyakarta: Pemerintah Propinsi DIY.

Soemargono, Farida. 1979. *Le 'Groupe de Yogya' 1945–1960. Les Voies Javanaises d'une Littérature Indonésienne.* Cahiers d'Archipel 9. Paris: Association Archipel.

Soeratman, Darsiti. 1989. *Kehidupan Dunia Kraton Surakarta 1830–1939.* Yogyakarta: Penerbit Tamansiswa.

Soerjadiningrat, B.P.A. 1923. 'De Javaansche Dans', *Djawa* 3(2): 41–44; 3(3): 96–97.

――― 1926. 'Een beschouwing over Jaavansche danskunst', *Oudaya* III(15): 176–78.

――― n.d. *Babad lan Mekaring Djogèd Djawi.* Yogyakarta: Kolf-Buning.

Spencer, Paul (ed.). 1985. *Society and the Dance.* Cambridge: Cambridge University Press.

Sperber, Dan and Deirdre Wilson. 1988. *Relevance: Communication and Cognition.* Cambridge, MA: Harvard University Press.

Stange, Paul. 1984. 'The Logic of *Rasa* in Java', *Indonesia* 38 (Oct): 113–34.

――― 1989. 'Interpreting Javanist Millenial Imagery', in P. Alexander (ed.), *Creating Indonesian Cultures.* Oceania Ethnographies 3. Sydney: Oceania Publications.

Steenbrink, Karel. 1993. *Dutch Colonialism and Indonesian Islam: Contacts and Conflicts 1596–1950.* Amsterdam: Rodopi.

Strauss, Gloria. 1975. 'The Art of the Sleeve in Chinese Dance', *Dance Perspectives* 16(63) 1–47.

Stuart-Fox, Martin. 1986. *Laos: Politics, Economics and Society.* London and Boulder, CO: Pinter and Rienner.

Stutterheim, Willem F. 1956. 'A One Thousand Year Old Profession on Java', in W. F. Stutterheim (ed.), *Studies in Indonesian Archaeology.* The Hague: Martinus Nijhofff.

Suharti, Theresia. 1972. 'Bědhaya Sěmang'. Unpublished Bachelor's thesis, Yogyakarta, ASTI.

――― 1989. 'Kridha Beksa Wirama: Sebuah Nostalgia?', *Citra Yogya* 10(11): 5–12.

Suharto, Benedictus. 1980. 'Tayub: Pengamatan dari Segi Tari Pergaulan serta Kaintannya dengan Unsur Upacara Kesuburan'. Unpublished research report. Yogyakarta: ASTI.

――― 1981. 'Perkembangan Tari Klasik Gaya Yogya', in F. Wibowo (ed.), *Mengenal Tari Klasik Gaya Yogyakarta.* Yogyakarta: Dewan Kesenian Propinsi DIY.

Sullivan, John. 1980. 'Back Alley Neighbourhood: Kampung as Urban Community in Yogyakarta'. Centre of Southeast Asian Studies Working Paper 18. Monash: Melbourne University.

Supardjan, N. 1975. 'Hubungan antara Tari dan Kerawitan Gaya Mataraman di Yogyakarta'. Unpublished Masters Dissertation, Japp Kunst Centre, Amsterdam.

Supartha, I Gusti Agung Ngurah, and N. Supardjan. 1980. *Pengantar Pengetahuan Tari I.* Yogyakarta: SMKI-KONRI.

Surjodiningrat, B.P.H. 1981. 'Tamansiswa dan Kesenian', in Soeratman et al. (eds), *Tamansiswa 30 Tahun 1922–1952.* Yogyakarta: Tamansiswa.

Surjodiningrat, Wasisto. 1953. 'Tari Bedaja', *Budaya* 1(1): 11–19.

——— 1970. *Gamelan, Tari dan Wajang di Jogjakarta.* Yogyakarta: Gadjah Mada University Press.

Suryadi AG, Linus. 1981. *Pengakuan Pariyem.* Jakarta: Penerbit Sinar Harapan.

Suryani, Luh Ketut and Gordon D. Jensen. 1993. *Trance and Possession in Bali.* Kuala Lumpur: Oxford University Press.

Suryobrongto [Surjobrongto], G.B.P.H. 1970. *The Classical Yogyanese Dance.* Yogyakarta: Lembaga Bahasa Nasional Tjabang II.

——— 1976. *Tari Klasik Gaya Yogya.* Yogyakarta: Museum Kraton (dan PDK).

——— 1978. 'The Classical Yoganese Dance', *Kalakshetra Quarterly* 1/3 Oct–Dec: 9–16.

——— 1981a. '*Tari Klasik Gaya Yogyakarta*', in Dewan Ahli Yayasan Siswa Among Běksa (eds), *Kawruh Joged-Mataram.* Yogyakarta: Yayasan Siswa Among Běksa.

——— 1981b. Eight short chapters, in F. Wibowo (ed.), *Mengenal Tari Klasik Gaya Yogyakarta.* Yogyakarta: Dewan Kesenian Propinsi DIY.

Sutton, Richard Anderson. 1984. ' "Who is the Pesindhèn"? Notes on the Female Singing Tradition in Java'. *Indonesia* 37: 119-33.

——— 1991. *Traditions of Gamelan Music in Java: Musical Pluralism and Regional Identity.* Cambridge: Cambridge University Press.

Tambiah, Stanley J. 1985. 'A Performative Approach to Ritual', in *Culture, Thought and Social Action: An Anthropological Perspective.* Cambridge, MA: Harvard University Press.

Tan Sooi Beng. 1993. *Bangsawan: A Social and Stylistic History of Popular Malay Opera.* Singapore: Oxford University Press.

Taussig, Michael. 1997. *The Magic of the State.* London and New York: Routledge.

Tedjokoesoemo. 1981. 'Joged Sari-Tunggal', in Soeratman et al. (eds), *Tamansiswa 30 Tahun 1922–1952.* Yogyakarta: Tamansiswa.

Tekstboek van de Wajang-Wong-Voostelling Pregiwa-Pregiwati te Houden in de Kraton te Jogjakarta op 18, 19 en 20 Maart 1939. Yogyakarta: Kraton.

Thomas, Helen. 1995. *Dance, Modernity and Culture: Explorations in the Sociology of Dance.* London: Routledge.

——— 2003. *The Body, Dance and Cultural Theory.* London: Palgrave Macmillan.

Thomas, Helen and Jamila Ahmed (eds). 2004. *Cultural Bodies: Ethnography and Theory.* Oxford: Blackwell Publishing.

Tirtaamidjaja. 1967. 'A *Bedaja Ketawang* Dance Performance at the Court of Surakarta', *Indonesia* 3: 31–61.

Toer, Pramoedya Ananta. 1992. *House of Glass.* Harmondsworth: Penguin.

Turner, Victor W. 1969. *The Ritual Process.* London: Routledge and Kegan Paul.

——— 1982. *From Ritual to Theatre: The Human Seriousness of Play.* New York: Performing Arts Journal Publications.

Uhlenbeck, Eugenius M. 1978. 'The Words Morphologically Related with Javanese *Rasa*', in *Studies in Javanese Morphology.* The Hague: Martinus Nijhoff.

Urry, John. 1990. *The Tourist Gaze: Leisure and Travel in Contemporary Societies.* London: Sage.

Varela, Charles. 1995. 'Cartesianism Revisited: the Ghost in the Moving Machine or the Lived Body', in B. Farnell (ed.), *Human Action Signs in Cultural Context:The Visible and Invisible in Dance*. Metuchen NJ: Scarecrow Press.

Vatsyayan, Kapila. 1980. *Traditional Indian Theatre: Multiple Streams*. New Delhi: National Book Trust.

Vickers, Adrian. 1996. 'Introduction', in A. Vickers (ed.), *Being Modern in Bali: Image and Change*. Monograph 43. New Haven: Yale University Southeast Asia Studies.

Wainwright, Steven P. and Bryan S. Turner. 2004. 'Narratives of Embodiment: Body, Aging and Career in Royal Ballet Dancers', in H. Thomas and J. Ahmed (eds), *Cultural Bodies: Ethnography and Theory*. Blackwell: Oxford.

Walton, John. 1993. 'Tourism and Economic Development in ASEAN', in M. Hitchcock, V.T. King and M.J.G. Parnwell (eds), *Tourism in South-East Asia*. London: Routledge.

Wardhana, Wisnu. 1958. 'Konfrontasi Seni Tari di Indonesia dan Barat', *Budaya* 7(5–6): 191–208.

―――― 1981. 'G.P.H. Tejokusumo', in F. Wibowo (ed.), *Mengenal Tari Klasik Gaya Yogyakarta*. Yogyakarta: Dewan Kesenian Propinsi DIY.

Warner, Marina. 1996. *Monuments and Maidens: The Allegory of the Female Form*. London: Vintage.

Warsadiningrat, R.T. 1987. *Wédha Pradangga* (Sacred Knowledge about Gamelan Music), trans. S. Pratt Walton, in J. Becker with A. H. Feinstein et al. (eds), *Karawitan: Source Readings in Javanese Gamelan and Vocal Music*, Vol 2. No. 30, Michigan Papers on South and Southeast Asia, Center for South and Southeast Asian Studies. Ann Arbor: University of Michigan.

Watson, Conrad W. 1987. 'State and Society in Indonesia: Three Papers'. Centre of South-East Asian Studies Occasional Paper 8. Canterbury: University of Kent.

Wessing, Robert. 1999. 'A Dance of Life: the Seblang of Banyuwangi, Indonesia', *B.K.I.* 155(4): 644–82.

Wibowo, Fred (ed.). 1981. *Mengenal Tari Klasik Gaya Yogyakarta*. Yogyakarta: Dewan Kesenian Propinsi DIY.

Widodo, Amrih. 1995. 'The Stages of the State: Arts of the People and Rites of Hegemonization', *Review of Indonesian and Malaysian Affairs* 29(1 & 2): 1–36.

Wieringa, Saskia E. 2002. *Sexual Politics in Indonesia*. Houndsmill: Palgrave Macmillan.

Williams, Drid. 1991. *Ten Lectures on Theories of Dance*. Metuchen, N.J.: Scarecow.

Wisseman Christie, Jan. 1986. 'Rāja and Rāma: the Classical State in Early Java', in L. Gesick (ed.), *Centers, Symbols, and Hierarchies: Essays on the Classical States of Southeast Asia*. Monograph Series No. 26. Yale: Yale University Southeast Asia Studies.

Wolf, Diana L. 1992. *Factory Daughters:Gender, Household Dynamics, and Rural Industrialization in Java*. Berkeley and Oxford: University of California Press.

Wolff, Janet. 1995. 'Dance Criticism: Feminism, Theory and Choreography', in *Resident Alien: Feminist Cultural Criticism*. Cambridge: Polity Press.

Wolff, John U. and Soepomo Poedjosoedarmo. 1982. *Communicative Codes in Central Java*. Ithaca: Linguistic Series VIII, Data Paper No. 116, Southeast Asia Program, Dept of Asia Studies.

Wood, Robert. 1979. 'Tourism and Underdevelopment in Southeast Asia', *Journal of Contemporary Asia* 9: 274–87.

―――― 1993. 'Tourism, Culture, and the Sociology of Development', in Michael Hitchcock, Victor T. King and Michael G. Parnwell (eds), *Tourism in South-East Asia*. London: Routledge.

—— 1997. 'Tourism and the State: Ethnic Options and the Construction of Otherness', in M. Picard and R. Wood (eds), *Tourism, Ethnicity and the State in Asian and Pacific Societies*. Honolulu: University of Hawai'i Press.

Woodward, Mark R. 1989. *Islam in Java: Normative Piety and Mysticism in the Sultanate of Yogyakarta*. The Association for Asian Studies Monograph XLV. Tucson: University of Arizona Press.

Woodward, Stephanie. 1976. 'Evidence for a Grammatical Structure in Javanese Dance: Examination of a Passage from Golek Lambangsari', *Dance Research Journal* 8(2): 10–17.

Wulff, Helena. 1998a. 'Perspectives toward Ballet Performance: Exploring, Repairing, and Maintaining the Frames', in F. Hughes-Freeland (ed.), *Ritual, Performance, Media*. ASA Monographs 35. London: Routledge.

—— 1998b. *Ballet across Borders*. Oxford and New York: Berg.

Yampolsky, Philip. 1995. 'Forces for Change in the Regional Performing Arts of Indonesia', *B.K.I.* 151(IV): 700–25.

Yates, Frances A. 1966. *The Art of Memory*. London: Routledge and Kegan Paul.

Young, Ken. 1998. 'The Crisis: Contexts and Prospects', in G. Forrester and R.J. May (eds), *The Fall of Soeharto*. Bathhurst, NSW: Crawford House Publishing.

Zarrilli, Phillip B. 1998. *When the Body Becomes All Eyes: Paradigms, Discourse and Practices of Power in Kalarippayattu, a South Indian Martial Art*. Delhi: Oxford University Press.

Zoetmulder, Petrus J. 1971. 'The Wajang as a Philosophical Theme', *Indonesia* 12: 85–96.

—— 1974. *Kalangwang: A Study of Old Javanese Literature*. The Hague: Martinus Nijhoff.

—— 1995. *Pantheism and Monism in Javanese Suluk Literature: Islamic and Indian Mysticism in an Indonesian Setting*, ed. and trans. M.C. Ricklefs. K.I.T.L.V. Translation Series 24. Leiden: K.I.T.L.V. Press.

—— with Stuart O. Robson. 1982. *Old Javanese–English Dictionary*, 2 vols. The Hague: Martinus Nijhoff.

Zurbuchen, Mary. 1976. *Introduction to Old Javanese Language and Linguistics*. Michigan Paper in South and Southeast Asia Language and Linguistics 3. Ann Arbor: Michigan University Press.

—— 1987. *The Language of Balinese Shadow Theatre*. Princeton, NJ: Princeton University Press.

Indonesian Newspapers and Magazines

Bernas
Kedaulatan Rakyat
Kompas
Minggu Pagi
Tempo

Index

www.ingramcontent.com/pod-product-compliance
Lightning Source LLC
Chambersburg PA
CBHW072054020426
42334CB00017B/1509